The Mortal Messiah
From Bethlehem to Calvary
Book II

The Mortal Messiah

From Bethlehem to Calvary
Book II

Bruce R. McConkie

Deseret Book Company
Salt Lake City, Utah
1980

THE MESSIANIC TRILOGY

The forerunner of this work is *The Promised Messiah: The First Coming of Christ*, which deals with the Messianic Prophecies. This work, *The Mortal Messiah: From Bethlehem to Calvary*, is a Life of Christ published in four books. This is Book II.

᛫ BOOK II

Section IV   Jesus Begins the Great Galilean Ministry
Section V   The Twelve, The Sermon on the Mount, and
          Rising Pharisaic Opposition
Section VI   The Continuing Galilean Ministry

The other books on the Life of Christ are published separately as follows:

BOOK I

Section I   A Root Out of Dry Ground
Section II   Jesus' Years of Preparation
Section III   Jesus' Early Judean Ministry

BOOK III

Section VII   The Galilean Ministry Reaches Its Peak
Section VIII   The Later Judean Ministry
Section IX   The Perean Ministry
Section X   From the Anointing to the Royal Reign

BOOK IV

Section XI   The Paschal Feast, The Private Prayers and
          Sermons, and Gethsemane
Section XII   The Trials, The Cross, and The Tomb
Section XIII   He Riseth; He Ministereth; He Ascendeth

The concluding work in this whole series will be *The Millennial Messiah: The Second Coming of the Son of Man.*

©1980 Deseret Book Company
All rights reserved
Printed in the United States of America

No part of this book may be reproduced in any
form or by any means without permission in writing
from the publisher, Deseret Book Company,
P.O. Box 30178, Salt Lake City, Utah 84130.

First printing February 1980
Second printing November 1982
Third printing October 1983
Fourth printing March 1986
Fifth printing July 1987
Sixth printing July 1988

Library of Congress Cataloging-in-Publication Data (Revised)

McConkie, Bruce R.
    The mortal Messiah

    Includes indexes.
    1. Jesus Christ—Biography. 2. Christian
biography—Palestine. 3. Judaism—History—Post-
exilic period, 586 B.C.-210 A.D. I. Title.
BT301.2.M16   232.9'01   79-19606
ISBN 0-87747-803-1 (v. 2)

ABBREVIATIONS

Scriptural references are abbreviated in a standard and self-identifying way. Other books are cited by author and title except for the following:

Commentary I   Bruce R. McConkie, *Doctrinal New Testament Commentary.* Vol. 1, *The Gospels.* Bookcraft, 1965.

Edersheim   Alfred Edersheim, *The Life and Times of Jesus the Messiah.* 1883.

Farrar   F. W. Farrar, *The Life of Christ.* London: Cassell & Co., Ltd., 1874.

Geikie   Cunningham Geikie, *The Life and Words of Christ.* 1886.

Hymns   *Hymns, The Church of Jesus Christ of Latter-day Saints.* 1948.

JST   Joseph Smith Translation (Inspired Version) of the Bible.

Mormon Doctrine   Bruce R. McConkie, *Mormon Doctrine,* 2nd ed. Bookcraft, 1966.

Sketches   Alfred Edersheim, *Sketches of Jewish Social Life in the Days of Christ.* 1876.

Talmage   James E. Talmage, *Jesus the Christ.* 1915.

Teachings   Joseph Fielding Smith, comp., *Teachings of the Prophet Joseph Smith.* 1938.

Temple   Alfred Edersheim, *The Temple: Its Ministry and Services As They Were at the Time of Jesus Christ.*

CONTENTS

Chapter 41

Chapter 42

Chapter 43

Chapter 44

Chapter 45

Chapter 59

SECTION IV

JESUS BEGINS THE GREAT GALILEAN MINISTRY

JESUS BEGINS THE GREAT GALILEAN MINISTRY

We believe that through the
Atonement of Christ, all mankind may be saved,
by obedience to the laws and ordinances
of the Gospel. (Article of Faith 3.)

Jesus—a Preacher of Righteousness, a Mighty Minister, a Man of God—now goes forth into Galilee, where, on their streets and in their synagogues, he preaches the gospel of the kingdom: that salvation comes by him and is gained by those who believe and obey.

He brings forth a new gospel dispensation; calls sinners to repentance; applies the Messianic prophecies to himself; and calls Peter, Andrew, James, John, and Matthew to follow him.

He heals a nobleman's son; casts an evil spirit out of a demoniac; cleanses a leper; forgives sins; heals a paralytic, and an impotent man, and one with a withered hand.

Above all—while at the Passover in Jerusalem—he proclaims his divine Sonship; makes himself "equal with God"; promises to take the gospel to the dead; announces that men are resurrected, judged, and assigned their glory, by the Son; and expounds the divine law of witnesses.

He is rejected by his own in Nazareth, and because he says God is his Father, and because he violates the rabbinical sabbath rules, the Pharisees spy upon him and join with the Herodians to plot his death.

Our Lord's ministry is now well under way, and the proceedings of the present are a precursor of the future. The Son of God ministers among men, and the sons of Lucifer seek to destroy him.

3

Chapter 33

JESUS PREACHES THE GOSPEL IN GALILEE

This is the gospel which I have given
unto you—
that I came into the world
to do the will of my Father,
because my Father sent me.
And my Father sent me
that I might be lifted up
upon the cross; and after that
I had been lifted up upon the cross,
that I might draw all men unto me. . . .
Now this is the commandment: Repent,
all ye ends of the earth,
and come unto me and be baptized
in my name,
that ye may be sanctified
by the reception of the Holy Ghost,
that ye may stand spotless before me
at the last day.
Verily, verily, I say unto you,
this is my gospel.
(3 Ne. 27:13-14, 20-21.)

"Repent Ye, and Believe the Gospel"
(Mark 1:14-15; Matthew 4:17; Luke 4:14-15; JST, Luke 4:15, John 4:43-45)

We come now to the three verses in the Synoptic Gospels that set the tone for everything that came from the pens of the synoptic authors: Matthew, Mark, and Luke. The message they contain applies also to all that is recorded in the gospel of the Beloved John.

We were with Jesus at Bethabara when he was baptized by John. We saw the heavens open and the Holy Spirit of God descend in bodily form to rest upon him. We went with him into the wilderness when he fasted and communed with his Father for forty days, and then overcame the wiles of the archtempter. We saw angels minister to him; heard John identify him as the Lamb of God, which taketh away the sin of the world; and heard him call Andrew and Simon, Philip and Nathanael, and John to follow him.

We attended the wedding celebration in Cana, drank the sweet wine that once was water, and then went with him to the Feast of the Passover in the Holy City. There, in thunderous yet righteous indignation, wielding a whip made of small cords, he drove the moneychangers from the Court of the Gentiles, overturned their tables of greed, and freed the animals and fowls that desecrated his Father's House.

We sat in reverent awe as he taught Nicodemus about spiritual rebirth and the salvation that results therefrom, and heard him say with his own lips that he was the Only Begotten of the Father and that whosoever believeth in him should not perish but have everlasting life.

Then we traveled and tarried with him for about nine months, through all the cities and villages of Judea, as he proclaimed his own divine Sonship and poured words of eternal life into the ears of his Jewish hearers. We are aware of John the Baptist's great pronouncement, made at Aenon near Salim, that all who believe in the Son shall have everlasting life; and we know that our Lord's Forerunner is now languishing in a vile and evil dungeon in a fortress near a palace where Herod Antipas revels in lustful splendor.

Only a few days ago we arose early to walk with him through rugged hill country, from northern Judea to Sychar in Samaria, where Jacob's Well is found. There, at the well and in the city, we continued to hear the words of wisdom and truth that none but he have ever spoken, and then we traveled on with him into his own Galilee.

Except for the accounts of his baptism and the temptation that followed, all that we have seen and heard and felt has come to us from John's Gospel. In all of it John was either present in person or received firsthand accounts from others, including the Lord Jesus himself. But now, after nearly a year of his active ministry, and with only about three months left before his Second Passover, we are turning also to the synoptic accounts to learn of him of whom we are already so much in awe.

And for the first time we find recorded, in plain and clear language, exactly what Jesus is doing as he goes forth to do the will of him whose servant he is. We come to the three verses that set the tone and give meaning and perspective to all that is written in all of the Gospels.

Jesus is going back to his homeland, to the land of his childhood and youth and maturing years, to the place of which he himself "testified, that a prophet hath no honour in his own country." But he is going back "in the power of the Spirit" to a people who "received him, having seen all the things that he did at Jerusalem at the feast: for they also went unto the feast." This time "a fame of him" will spread "through all the regions round about"; and as he teaches in their synagogues, he will be "glorified of all who believed on his name." Whereas he was once without honor in his own country, now, for a season at least, many will flock to him, and all will know of the wonderful works he is doing.

In the three verses of which we speak, Matthew says: "From that time Jesus began to preach, and to say, Repent: for the kingdom of heaven is at hand"; and Mark says: "Jesus came into Galilee, preaching the gospel of the

7

kingdom of God, And saying, The time is fulfilled, and the kingdom of God is at hand: repent ye, and believe the gospel."

In these verses we find the key that opens the door to an understanding of all of Jesus' teachings. In Galilee—and elsewhere and everywhere—he invited men to believe and repent; to believe in him as the Son of God and to repent of their sins; to accept the gospel that he preached and to become members of his earthly kingdom. Jesus preached the gospel; and unless and until this dawns upon us, we will not and cannot understand his ministry among men. Jesus preached the gospel—nothing more and nothing less.

What is the gospel? The gospel of the kingdom? And what is the kingdom of heaven that is now at hand?

The gospel is the plan of salvation, the plan ordained and established by the Father to enable his spirit children to advance and progress and become like him. It is all of the laws, truths, rites, ordinances, and performances by conformity to which men can save themselves with eternal exaltation in the mansions on high. It is the system that enables the sons of God to become gods. "It is the power of God unto salvation to every one that believeth." (Rom. 1:16.)

The gospel is the glad tidings of great joy that salvation is in Christ; that a gracious God has provided a Savior for his children; that fallen man can be ransomed from temporal and spiritual death. It is: "That he came into the world, even Jesus, to be crucified for the world, and to bear the sins of the world, and to sanctify the world, and to cleanse it from all unrighteousness; That through him all might be saved whom the Father had put into his power and made by him." (D&C 76:40-41.) It is: "That the Son of God hath atoned for original guilt," so that little children "are whole from the foundation of the world" (Moses 6:54), and that all who will repent and become as their little children shall be saved.

The gospel "is the plan of salvation unto all men, through the blood of [God's] Only Begotten." It recognizes that "all men, everywhere, must repent, or they can in no-

8

wise inherit the kingdom of God, for no unclean thing can dwell there, or dwell in his presence." (Moses 6:57-62.) It consists of hearkening unto the voice of God and believing in his Only Begotten; of forsaking the world and repenting of one's sins; of being baptized in water for the remission of sins; of receiving the gift of the Holy Ghost, so that the newly born saint may be sanctified and become pure and spotless; and of then enduring to the end and working the works of righteousness all one's days. "And this is my gospel—repentance and baptism by water, and then cometh the baptism of fire and the Holy Ghost, even the Comforter, which showeth all things, and teacheth the peaceable things of the kingdom." (D&C 39:6.)

Such is the gospel, the gospel of the kingdom of God, the gospel which admits men to the kingdom of God on earth—which is the Church—and to the kingdom of God in heaven—which is the celestial kingdom. When Jesus said, "The kingdom of heaven is at hand," he was announcing that the kingdom of God on earth, which is the Church of Jesus Christ, was then organized again among men.[1]

When Jesus preached the gospel, over and over again he said such things as these: 'The God of your fathers, who was worshipped by Abraham and Moses and all the holy prophets, hath sent me; I am his Son, by whom salvation comes. As I said unto Nicodemus, I am the Only Begotten; and as I said unto the woman of Samaria, I am the Messiah. Come unto me; believe in me; keep my commandments; join my church; be baptized and I will give you the Holy Ghost; walk in the paths of righteousness and my blood shall cleanse you from all sin. And having enjoyed the words of eternal life in this world, ye shall be inheritors of eternal life, even immortal glory in the world to come.'

Jesus did not come among men simply to teach ethical principles, to give parables, to present a higher and better way of life to downtrodden humanity. That he did all this, and more, none doubt. But Jesus came among men to atone for the sins of the world, to make salvation available through the shedding of his blood, and to teach those gospel laws by obedience to which all men can be saved in the kingdom of God. Jesus preached the gospel; so it is written, and so it is.

The Gospel accounts are not, and do not pretend to be, definitive expositions of the saving truths that comprise the gospel, nor do they pretend to record the doctrinal teachings of the Lord Jesus. Rather, they are fragmentary accounts of selected sayings and a few of his doings. "The Synoptic narratives"—Matthew, Mark, and Luke—are, as Edersheim expresses it, only "brief historical summaries, with here and there special episodes or reports of teaching inserted." (Edersheim 1:422-23.)

With these realities before us, we will be able to put the episodes and reports in their proper perspective and to learn why each one has been preserved for us. Parables, healings, teachings, sermons—all that our Lord said and did—can only be understood when considered in their relationship to that gospel—the fulness of the everlasting gospel—which Jesus came to teach.

Jesus Heals the Nobleman's Son
(John 4:46-54; JST, John 4:55-56)

Miracles are part of the gospel. Signs follow those that believe. Where the doctrines of salvation are taught in purity and perfection, where there are believing souls who accept these truths and make them a part of their lives, and where devout souls accept Jesus as their Lord and serve him to the best of their ability, there will always be miracles. Such ever attend the preaching of the gospel to receptive and conforming people. Miracles stand as a sign and a witness of the truth and divinity of the Lord's work. Where there are miracles, there is the gospel, the Church, the kingdom, and the hope of salvation. Where there are no signs and miracles, none of these desired blessings will be found. These realizations prepare us to consider the episodes and reports that have been preserved for us in the Gospels.

And so Jesus, coming back into Galilee, to a people many of whom are for the moment receptive and friendly, goes to Cana. His fame has preceded him; indeed, part of his fame had its beginning in this very Galilean village, for it was here that water became wine at his word. But now the Galileans also have in mind what he had done at the Feast of the Passover; and we cannot discount the possibility— shall we not say probability—that the glad tidings of his doings, of nine months' duration, through all Judea, have also come to their attention. He is being hailed by many for what he says he is, the One sent to teach and heal.

While Jesus was in Cana, perhaps staying at the home of Nathanael, there came to him from Capernaum, some twenty miles away, a nobleman whose son "was at the point of death." That this nobleman was an officer, either civil or military, in the court of Herod Antipas is reasonably certain; at least the word used by John to describe him is the same one Josephus and others used repetitiously to refer to officers in the service of that evil tyrant. In any event, the nobleman besought Jesus "that he would come down, and heal his son." What words of earnest entreaty were used we do not know. Their import must have been to induce the Master to travel to the bedside of the dying son, a thing that Jesus had no intention of doing.

To this assumption that the personal presence of the Healer was required to effect a cure, Jesus said: "Except ye see signs and wonders, ye will not believe." 'Except ye see me come and lay my hands on the head of your son, as ye are aware I have done to others, ye will not believe that he shall be healed. Do ye not know that it is written of me, "He sent his word, and healed them"?' (Ps. 107:20.) In spite of this gentle rebuke, the nobleman continued to plead: "Sir, come down ere my child die."

Having thus tested the growing faith of the influential suppliant, and finding that he knew in his heart that Jesus had power to heal those who lay at death's door, our Lord said: "Go thy way; thy son liveth." There was to be no gradual cure; distance meant nothing where the exercise of healing power was involved. Jesus spoke, and the event transpired. Without further assurance, knowing only that this Man's words must all be fulfilled, the nobleman "believed the word that Jesus had spoken unto him, and he went his way."

Whereas he had come in haste, anxious and perturbed, importuning and pleading that Jesus travel to Capernaum and heal his son, now, at peace within himself, he remained overnight in or near Cana. The next day as he traveled homeward he met his servants, who said, "Thy son liveth," and he learned that the fever had left him at the very hour when Jesus had spoken those same blessed words.

This is the first healing miracle that is set forth in detail in the Gospels. Those performed at the Feast of the Passover and throughout all Judea are not described or explained. This miracle—the second performed in Cana—adds a new dimension to Jesus' healing ministry that we have not seen up to this point. It is in fact a dual miracle: one that healed the body of the absent son, and one that cured unbelief and planted faith in the heart of the present father.

With reference to the dying boy, it bears witness that the Divine Healer is not limited by geographical location; that he speaks and disease flees; that the whereabouts of the suffering suppliant is of no moment; that God governs all things; that his power is everywhere. With reference to the father who sought the divine intervention, it bears witness that the growth of faith in the heart of an earthbound pilgrim, and the healing, as it were, of the soul of man, is as great a miracle as—nay, a far greater miracle than—the healing of the physical body.

Having heard the gospel taught, and believing that the Teacher could work miracles, the father came to Jesus. 'Come down to Capernaum and heal my son,' he pleaded. By declining to go down—as though his personal presence was required for a miracle!—Jesus tested the faith of the father; and finding that it remained unshaken, he healed the child at a word. The father, without more and before word came from his servants, knew that the healing power had operated and that his son lived. When this was confirmed a day later, John says: "Himself believed, and his whole house." We have seen, thus, the miracle of healing a disease-ridden body and the healing of a truth-seeking soul; we have seen a physical cure that raised a boy from the doors of death, and a spiritual cure that enabled a man to shake off the disease of unbelief that leads to spiritual death. Truly the Master Healer uses his power in a perfect way for the blessing and benefit of his mortal brethren!

NOTE

1. When the Lord called laborers into the vineyard in this dispensation and sent them out to do again what he had done in the day of his ministry, among other things he commanded them: "Open your mouths and they shall be filled, saying: Repent, repent, and prepare ye the way of the Lord, and make his paths straight; for the kingdom of heaven is at hand; Yea, repent and be baptized, every one of you, for a remission of your sins; yea, be baptized even by water, and then cometh the baptism of fire and of the Holy Ghost. Behold, verily, verily, I say unto you, this is my gospel; and remember that they shall have faith in me or they can in nowise be saved; And upon this rock I will build my church." (D&C 33:10-13.) "And ye shall go forth baptizing with water, saying: Repent ye, repent ye, for the kingdom of heaven is at hand." (D&C 42:7.)

Chapter 34

JESUS FULFILLS THE MESSIANIC PROPHECIES

Did not Moses prophesy unto them
concerning the coming of the Messiah,
and that God should redeem his people?
Yea, and even all the prophets who
have prophesied
ever since the world began—
have they not spoken more or less
concerning these things?
Have they not said that God himself
should come down among the children of men,
and take upon him the form of man,
and go forth in mighty power
upon the face of the earth?
(Mosiah 13:33-34.)[1]

To him give all the prophets witness,
that through his name whosoever
believeth in him
shall receive remission of sins.
(Acts 10:43.)[2]

Messianic Prophecies: Their Nature and Purpose[3]

We stand in old Jerusalem—the Holy City—the chosen spot where prophets teach Jehovah's word, and where, all too often, they die for the testimony of Jesus that is theirs. Isaiah is here—it is seven and a half centuries before Christ—and we hear him say: 'Rejoice, O Israel, for unto us a Child is born; unto us a Son is given. He is the Messiah, the Mighty God, the Prince of Peace. Behold, a virgin shall conceive; she shall bear this Son; and his name shall be called Immanuel, which means, God is with us, for God himself shall dwell as a Mortal Man.' This we hear and much more.

Then we stand on a Judean plain, a few short miles from the Holy City, where we see and hear such marvelous things that our bosom burns with living fire. We hear an angel, free from sin, announce the birth of David's kin. We hear the heavens resound as angelic choirs give glory to God and sing of peace among men of good will on earth. A Child is born; a Son makes flesh his tabernacle. His mother is none other than the Blessed Virgin of whom Isaiah and Nephi prophesied. It is as though we are seeing again what we saw before through prophetic eyes. Such is the nature of Messianic prophecies.

Again we mingle with the saints of old and hear their prophets speak in loving tones of the Messiah who is to come. Micah pictures for his hearers the little town of Bethlehem. 'Thou, Bethlehem Ephratah,' he says, 'out of thee shall come the Promised Messiah; though thou art little and insignificant among the cities of Judah, yet thy name shall be forever linked with the Lord Omnipotent, the Eternal God, for he shall be born in thee.'

We hear Jeremiah foretell the sorrow and lamentation that will be when Rachel weeps for the slain innocents in the days of Herod; we hear Hosea tell of the flight into Egypt so the Blessed Child will escape the sword that seeks his life; and we hear another prophetic voice testify: 'When he comes out of Egypt, he will go to Nazareth of Galilee, there to mature and grow and prepare; and ever thereafter he shall be called a Nazarene.'

Then we go to Bethlehem, find the caravanserie where the Eternal One lies in a manger, in that part of the camping place where the cattle are tethered. We see the flight into Egypt; and we rejoice at his return to the sacred home provided by Joseph and Mary among the Nazarenes. Again it is as though we had seen it all before; and so we had, for we had heard the Messianic utterances and known their meaning. And such is the nature of Messianic prophecies that those who go before know as surely and fully of the truth and divinity of that which is to be as do those who come after.

We see Jesus baptized at Bethabara in Jordan; we behold the heavens open and the Holy Spirit of God descend upon him, in bodily shape, with all the serenity and calmness of a dove. We hear his Forerunner's testimony: 'This is the Lamb of God, the Redeemer of the world, he who shall take upon himself the sins of all men on conditions of repentance'— and with it all we are not in Palestine; we are not standing on the banks of the Jordan; it is not January in A.D. 27. All that we see and hear is shown to us more than six hundred years before its destined occurrence, for we are with Nephi. We have been carried by the Spirit into an exceedingly high mountain where we behold in vision the very things that one day shall be when he who is the Spirit Lord shall become a mortal man.

Nor are we in any way surprised when we see it all over again, when Jesus comes to John to be baptized of him to fulfill all righteousness. The preview is the same as the performance. And such, be it known, is the nature of Messianic prophecies.

By the spirit of prophecy and revelation, as the visions of eternity rolled before them, and with a seeric insight known only to those who walk in the light of the Spirit, the ancient saints and their prophets and seers were as well informed

16

about Christ and his ministry, as are those of us who have come after. Their Messianic prophecies were as powerful and persuasive, and as filled with the doctrines of salvation, as are our Messianic testimonies. The only difference is that they spoke of what was revealed to them in advance, and we speak of what has been revealed to us after the events.

Messianic prophecies foretell all things that men must know concerning the Lord Jesus and his mortal ministry; all things concerning his birth and ministry and death; all things concerning his teachings and miracles and healing power; all things concerning the ransom he paid and the atonement he wrought; all things concerning all of these matters which men must know to cleanse their souls through his atoning blood. Messianic prophecies reveal Christ and his ministry and the salvation that is in him—before his coming.

We speak thus, with the illustrations here recited, to lay a foundation for the gracious words Jesus is about to speak in the synagogue in Nazareth of Galilee. Our Lord has come out of Judea, through Samaria, to Cana. While there he healed the son of the nobleman, though the dying boy was twenty miles away in Capernaum. Everywhere he has preached the gospel, and now he is in the synagogue on the Sabbath, and he is about to apply, in effect, all of the Messianic prophecies to himself.

Jesus Applies the Messianic Prophecies to Himself
(Luke 4:16-22)

Now we are with Jesus in Nazareth—a place of blessed memory to him—the Galilean city where he was subject to Joseph and Mary; the city founded in the hills and mountains of Galilee, from whose heights the Light of the World is now sending forth his rays; the city where he is known, where he learned the carpenter's trade, where he went to school and sat in the synagogue on the Sabbath.

He has come from Cana, where he turned water into

wine and where, at his spoken word, a boy in Capernaum received life and vitality and retreated from death's open door. His fame has preceded him; his fellow Nazarenes know of the Cana-Capernaum miracle, of what he did at the Feast of the Passover, of the miracles that were part of his early Judean ministry. He is no longer just one of a motley crowd; he has stepped forth as the Leader of men; he has disciples who follow in his footsteps and testify of his divinity; and he has begun to assume prerogatives that not even the great High Priest would dare to assume. None but he—none who came before, and none who followed after—had with violence driven the priestly courtiers from the temple courts, as though he himself were greater than the temple and all its ministers. None but he controlled the elements with such ease and had such wondrous power over disease and life and death. Nothing that Jesus shall do hereafter can be done in a corner; his light can never be hidden under a bushel; the eyes of all men shall be upon him as long as he lives; and his words are those which shall be prized above all others.

With Jesus we go to the synagogue on the Sabbath. Such is his custom, such is ours, and such is the custom of all the faithful in Israel. Synagogue worship is as mandatory as anything can be in the lives of the chosen people in this meridian day. Synagogues are sacred places where Jewish Israel resorts to pay their devotions to the Most High and to praise his name in sermon and prayer. In them we do not joke or laugh or eat or do aught that is irreverent or that detracts from the true spirit of worship. And it is worthy of note that what prevailed in synagogues anciently is what should prevail in our houses of worship today, for the Christian practice of frequent worship—of sermon and song and prayer and scriptural reading, in buildings set apart for such purposes—grew out of the Jewish dispensation that preceded ours. The apostles built upon the foundations of the past as they devised the procedures for their new day.

As we enter the stone synagogue, we admire the ornamentation over the lintel; perhaps it is "a seven-branched candlestick, an open flower between two Paschal lambs, or vine-leaves with bunches of grapes, or, as at Capernaum, a pot of manna between representations of Aaron's rod."[4] We observe the holy chest—a movable ark, as it were—in which the sacred rolls of the Law and the Prophets are kept. The holy lamp is burning, "in imitation of the undying light in the Temple." Before the ark are the seats of honor where the rulers of the synagogue sit, facing the people. There is a place for the one who is to lead the devotions and a desk from which the Law is read. It is all familiar and well suited to the needs and circumstances of the day.

As we seat ourselves, it is with full anticipation that the ruler of the synagogue will call on Jesus to deliver a discourse. Whenever "some great Rabbi, or famed preacher, or else a distinguished stranger, is known to be in the town," it is the custom to invite him to preach to the people. The "institution of preaching" is a way of life among the Jews, and popular preachers are sought for, and are given complete freedom to expound and teach, using "parables, stories, allegories, witticisms, strange and foreign words, absurd legends, in short, anything that might startle an audience." We anticipate that, as is the custom, "at the close of his address, the preacher" will refer "to the great Messianic hope of Israel," but little do we realize the power and import of the Messianic proclamation that is to be made this day.

The synagogue service commences. There are two prayers, then the reciting of the *Shema*—the three passages from the Pentateuch, in which the worshippers take upon themselves the yoke of the kingdom—and then another prayer. Then come eighteen eulogies or benedictions and yet other prayers. After these liturgical formalities, the minister takes out a roll of the Law, and seven persons are called upon to read successive portions. "A descendant of Aaron was always called up first to the reading; then followed a Levite, and afterwards five ordinary Israelites. . . . The reading of the Law was both preceded and followed by brief Benedictions."

It is now time for the reading of a section from the Prophets and for the discourse of the day. This is the portion of the service that we know that Jesus personally participated in. He "stood up for to read," Luke says, "And there was delivered unto him the book of the prophet Esaias." After the reading came the sermon. If, however, he followed the practice of the day, his participation involved more than reading from the Prophets and discoursing as he chose. "The person who read in the synagogue the portion from the Prophets, was also expected to conduct the devotions, at least in greater part," meaning, "part of the *Shema,* and the whole of the Eulogies."

If Jesus, as was the custom, and as other readers of the Prophets and preachers of the sermon would have done—if Jesus participated in full, he would have read such expressions as: "Thou art Jehovah, our God, and the God of our fathers, our King, and the King of our fathers, our Saviour, and the Saviour of our fathers, our Creator, the Rock of our Salvation, our Help and our Deliverer. Thy name is from everlasting, and there is no God beside Thee." "Blessed art Thou, Jehovah, Who quickenest the dead!" "Thou art Holy, and Thy name is Holy. Selah. Blessed art Thou Jehovah God, the Holy One." Such a participation on his part would in fact have fitted perfectly into the Messianic pronouncement he was about to make, for Jehovah was the Messiah, and the salvation promised Israel and all men by the One was the salvation that would be brought to pass by the Other.

But this we do know. Standing before the people, Jesus read from Isaiah one of the greatest of the sayings of that Messianic prophet. Probably he read in Hebrew—such was the practice—and then translated or "targumed" the passage into Aramaic. The targums were the oral translations or paraphrases of the written Hebrew. This would also account for the differences between Isaiah's record in the Old Testament, and the statements as given by Jesus and recorded by Luke.

The Spirit of the Lord is upon me, because he hath anointed me to preach the gospel to the poor; he hath sent me to heal the brokenhearted, to preach deliverance to the captives, and recovering of sight to the blind, to set at liberty them that are bruised, To preach the acceptable year of the Lord.

Such were the words he read. Then he sat down—as the custom was—to deliver the discourse. All eyes were upon him, and he began by saying unto them:

This day is this scripture fulfilled in your ears.

Thereafter, many "gracious words . . . proceeded out of his mouth," to which all present bore witness. What these words were we do not know, but in the very nature of things we can rest assured that they were a sermon on the text he had read. Providentially, we do know what Isaiah's words mean and how they apply to the One who read them that day in Nazareth, in the synagogue where he had worshipped as a youth, and among the people whom he knew and whose faces were familiar to him.

The Spirit of the Lord is upon me. Isaiah said: "The Spirit of the Lord God is upon me."[5] Being pure and without sin, Jesus always and ever possessed that Spirit which will not dwell in an unclean tabernacle, but which, conversely, always abides with those whose houses of clay make a fit abode for such a celestial presence. Further, the Holy Spirit descended upon him, like a dove, when he was baptized by John, which John was the one who also testified, as we have seen, that "God giveth not his Spirit by measure unto him." It is no wonder, then, as we have also seen, that when he came into Galilee it was "in the power of the Spirit."

He hath anointed me to preach the gospel to the poor. Isaiah has it: "The Lord hath anointed me to preach good tidings unto the meek." The Messiah comes in power; he is anointed, commissioned from on high; he comes in his Father's name, to do his Father's will, because his Father sent him; he speaks, not of himself, but of his Father. And his glorious message—it is the everlasting gospel, the plan of

21

salvation; it is the glad tidings of great joy that salvation is in Christ, that man shall gain the victory over the grave, that he has power to gain eternal life. And to whom does the message go? To the meek, to the God-fearing, to those who seek righteousness; and they, in general, are the poor among men.

He hath sent me to heal the brokenhearted. "He hath sent me to bind up the brokenhearted," Isaiah says. 'I am come to heal and to save. Let those whose spirits are depressed come unto me, and I will give them peace. Are there those who are crushed with the weight of their sins, who carry burdens of despair—let them come unto me. I will bear their burdens if they will repent. Though my own heart be broken, yet shall all those who believe in me be healed. I shall heal men spiritually even as you have seen me heal them physically.'

He hath sent me . . . to preach deliverance to the captives. "He hath sent me . . . to proclaim liberty to the captives." Messiah is a preacher; his words deliver men from the captivity of sin and the bondage of iniquity. He proclaims liberty to the sin-shackled soul. By his word—the everlasting gospel that he preaches—men in mortality and those in the spirit prison are made free.

He hath sent me . . . to preach . . . recovering of sight to the blind. There is no parallel passage in Isaiah, although the thought fits into the over-all sense and meaning acclaimed by ancient Israel's Messianic seer in the utterance he made. That is to say: Jesus, as he "targumed" Isaiah's meaning from Hebrew to Aramaic, did what only inspired interpreters can do: he expanded the words and interpreted the meaning of the original utterance. 'I am sent by the Father— not only to proclaim how deliverance from sin may be found, but to preach the recovering of spiritual sight to those who are blind spiritually. Through me they shall see out of obscurity, and out of darkness.' If a parallel passage for these added words is needed, it may be found in Isaiah's prophecy about the latter-day coming forth of the Book of

Mormon, for the promise is that through "the words of the book . . . the eyes of the blind shall see out of obscurity, and out of darkness." (Isa. 29:8.)

He hath sent me . . . to set at liberty them that are bruised. "He hath sent me . . . to proclaim . . . the opening of the prison to them that are bound." The prisoners shall go free! Messiah shall make it possible. Those who are bruised and bound and beaten and shackled in the dungeons of hell shall come forth. The word has gone forth; the prison doors shall open—be it for the prisoners of sin in this life, or, as another prophet has called them, the "prisoners of hope" in the life to come. (Zech. 9:12.) "Let the dead speak forth anthems of eternal praise to the King Immanuel, who hath ordained, before the world was, that which would enable us to redeem them out of their prison; for the prisoners shall go free." (D&C 128:22.)

He hath sent me . . . to preach the acceptable year of the Lord. "He hath sent me . . . to proclaim the acceptable year of the Lord." The acceptable year of the Lord! It is the year and the time when Messiah comes; when salvation is made available; when men have opportunity to learn what they must do to be saved in his everlasting kingdom. 'I now proclaim to you: This is the year; this is the set time; salvation is near; I am he; my word is truth; come and walk in the light of the Lord. Now is the time and the day of your salvation; this is the acceptable year.'

Then, by way of climax, having taught the doctrine with gracious words that could not be refuted, Jesus attests:

This day is this scripture fulfilled in your ears.

That is to say: 'I have read from Isaiah; I have set forth the meaning of his words; I have taught the doctrine. Now I testify that these words—and therefore all Messianic prophecies—are fulfilled in me; they apply to me; I am the one of whom the prophets spoke; I am he; I am the Messiah.'

Where such a witness is born, there are only two possible responses. One is complete acceptance, the other complete rejection. No one can argue with a testimony; it is not a debatable issue. It is there to be accepted or to be rejected. Jesus taught and testified, and as the full meaning of his gracious words sank into their hearts, his Nazarene friends made their choice. This Jesus they knew and had known from his infancy and youth. How can he be the Son of God? How can he be the Messiah? Their voice—to their eternal sorrow—was one of rejection, which they summarized in these words: "Is not this Joseph's son?" 'How then can he be the Messiah? We know him; he is one of us.'

The word fell on stony ground and found no soil in which to grow, and the seeds died without sprouting. It was a sad, dark day for Nazareth.

Jesus Is Rejected at Nazareth
(Luke 4:23-30)

As the spirit of rejection contained in their words—"Is not this Joseph's son?"—became the consensus of the synagogue throng, Jesus, feeling their reaction, turned from his proclamation of joy and deliverance to a proclamation of sorrow and damnation. That which might have been theirs was passing them by. And yet, opposed as they were to his claim of Messiahship, they could not explain away the reports of the wonders he had performed in Cana and Capernaum and Judea. 'We know he cannot be the Messiah—for he is Joseph's son—but what of the miracles? Can it be that he has performed them? And if the reports are true, why doesn't he show us, his friends and associates of many years, the same signs and wonders he has shown others?'

Jesus, reading their thoughts and feeling the sense of the meeting, yet remaining in complete command of the situation, continued his sermon. "Ye will surely say unto me this proverb, Physician, heal thyself: whatsoever we have heard done in Capernaum, do also here in thy country," he said. 'You have performed miracles in Cana and Capernaum, but none here, and yet you are a native of Nazareth. Why can't we see a sign, some great exhibition of your purported power? Don't you know that charity begins at home, that unless the physician heals himself of his own diseases we cannot believe he has power to heal others?' (*Commentary* 1:162.)

With bitter irony Jesus responds to the thoughts in their minds. "No prophet is accepted in his own country," he says. And as illustrations of blessings being withheld from the chosen people (the Nazarenes, as it were) and given to foreigners (those of other cities in Palestine, in this case), he referred to two accounts from Israel's history: that of Elijah, who blessed the Phoenician widow of Zarephath, and that of Elisha, who cleansed a Gentile of Syria.

After Elijah sealed the heavens that there was neither dew nor rain, but according to his word; after the brook Cherith, whereof he drank, failed for want of water; and after the ravens no longer brought him bread and flesh to eat, the Lord sent him to Zarephath in Zidon, to a widow woman, who was commanded to sustain him. Traveling thence, Elijah found the woman gathering two sticks for a fire, that she might take her last handful of meal and her last drops of oil and make them into a cake for herself and her son. Then she and her offspring faced certain death by starvation.

"Make me thereof a little cake first, and bring it unto me, and after make for thee and for thy son. For thus saith the Lord God of Israel, The barrel of meal shall not waste, neither shall the cruse of oil fail, until the day that the Lord sendeth rain upon the earth." The woman obeyed. Elijah's words were fulfilled. "And the barrel of meal wasted not, neither did the cruse of oil fail," and they all ate thereof for many days. And as though this were not enough, when the woman's son died, Elijah called him back from death, and his spirit came into his body again. All this was done for a woman of Phoenicia—who probably was not even of the house of Israel—because she had faith. (1 Kgs. 17.)

Naaman, a mighty man and captain of all the armies of Syria, was a leper. His wife had a servant, an Israelite maid who had been taken captive from her homeland. She said: "Would God my lord were with the prophet that is in Samaria! for he would recover him of his leprosy." Naaman in due course went down to Israel and was told by a messenger sent by Elisha: "Go and wash in Jordan seven times, and thy flesh shall come again to thee, and thou shalt be clean." Doing so, he became clean—a miracle wrought at a distance, as it were, somewhat like the healing of the nobleman's son by Jesus. (2 Kgs. 5.)

Elijah the prophet, who was taken up into heaven without tasting death, and Elisha, who poured water upon the hands of Elijah and upon whom his master's mantle fell—these mighty prophets, whose works were known to every Jew in Jesus' day—their miracles were performed selectively, for special individuals, not for the suffering hosts of their day. Where there is faith, there is the miracle; where there is no faith, no miracle is wrought. And if the prophets of old went outside the fold of Israel to find those worthy of their ministry, so Jesus would go outside Nazareth to find receptive souls who would believe in him and receive the blessings that he came to bestow. Should the people of Nazareth desire to see the wondrous works done elsewhere, then let them accept Him who now preached in their synagogue, and they too would receive the blessings of heaven. These things, in his infinite wisdom, Jesus taught them that day; from his more extended remarks, Luke has preserved for us these words:

> But I tell you of a truth, many widows were in Israel in the days of Elias, when the heaven was shut up three years and six months, when great famine was throughout all the land; But unto none of them was Elias sent, save unto Sarepta, a city of Sidon, unto a woman that was a widow. And many lepers were in Israel in the time of Eliseus the prophet; and none of them was cleansed, saving Naaman the Syrian.

Anger welled up in the hearts of his fellow Nazarenes.

26

Lucifer, not Jehovah, was their lord, as Jesus would one day tell the Jews in Jerusalem. Though they had given lip service—that very day, in that very synagogue—to the worship of Jehovah, yet they now, "filled with wrath," as Luke says, cast that very Jehovah out of their midst. They "thrust him out of the city"; they "led him unto the brow of the hill whereon their city was built." Why? "That they might cast him down headlong." The spirit of murder was in their hearts, and they sought the death of Jesus. His words they could not answer, his testimony they could not refute, but his voice—as they supposed—his voice they could silence.

Jesus had come unto his own, and his own received him not! The leaders of the people rejected his words when he preached in the temple at Passover time. The common people of Nazareth hardened their hearts against his words when he spoke to them in their synagogue. And so it would be throughout his whole ministry; save for a few believing souls, he was "despised and rejected of men" (Isa. 53:3); and eventually *his own* would lead him before Roman overlords, as they raised their voices in chants of "Crucify him, Crucify him."

How he escaped the wrath and murderous designs of the Nazarene mob is not recorded. Luke says simply: "But he passing through the midst of them went his way." "Perhaps His silence, perhaps the calm nobleness of His bearing, perhaps the dauntless innocence of His gaze overawed them. Apart from anything supernatural, there seems to have been in the presence of Jesus a spell of mystery and majesty which even His most ruthless and hardened enemies acknowledged, and before which they involuntarily bowed. It was to this that He owed His escape when the maddened Jews in the Temple took up stones to stone Him; it was this that made the bold and bigoted officers of the Sanhedrin unable to arrest Him as He taught in public during the Feast of Tabernacles at Jerusalem; it was this that made the armed band of His enemies, at His mere look, fall before Him to the ground in the Garden of Gethsemane. Suddenly, quietly,

He asserted His freedom, waved aside His captors, and over-awing them by His simple glance, passed through their midst unharmed. Similar events have occurred in history, and continue still to occur. There is something in defenceless and yet dauntless dignity that calms even the fury of a mob. 'They stood—stopped—inquired—were ashamed—fled—separated.' " (Farrar, p. 175.)

But now the Son of God would go elsewhere to continue his ministry.

NOTES

1. These are the words of Abinadi, spoken 150 years before our Lord's mortal birth.
2. This is the testimony of Peter, gained shortly after the crucifixion.
3. An extended analysis of the Messianic prophecies is found in *The Promised Messiah: The First Coming of Christ,* a companion volume to this work.
4. This data on synagogues is digested from Edersheim 1:430-50. See also chapter 10 of *The Mortal Messiah* (Book I).
5. All of the quotations are taken from Isa. 61:1-2.

Chapter 35

THE GALILEAN MINISTERS IN GALILEE

The land of Zebulun and the land of Naphtali,
... by the way of the sea,
beyond Jordan, in Galilee of the nations.
The people that walked in darkness
have seen a great light:
they that dwell in the land of the
shadow of death,
upon them hath the light shined.
(Isa. 9:1-2.)[1]

Jesus Dwells in Capernaum
(Matthew 4:13-16; JST, Matthew 4:12; Luke 4:31-32)

Palestine—Old Canaan—the Holy Land—the land where Jesus dwelt!

We find the Holy One of Israel, now dwelling in mortality, living among his Israelite kinsmen in the chosen land, the land promised them by Abraham their father. We find the Son of God dwelling among the chosen seed; among those to whose fathers the prophets had ministered in olden times; among those to whom the Law and the Prophets were as well known as is the light of the sun or as is

29

the falling of the rain to men in general. We find the Holy Messiah dwelling and doing and speaking and being—all as recorded in the Messianic utterances of the prophets who went before.

And how fittingly it all falls into place. Jesus' every word and act and movement weaves itself into a majestic tapestry, a work of art that was before planned by his Father, and whose beauty was revealed—a segment here and a golden thread there—to the prophets and saints who preceded our Lord in life.

He was born in Bethlehem—the City of David, the spot beloved by Israel's greatest king—for he was the Son of David, heir to his throne, the one on whose shoulders the government would rest. He was the King who should reign in righteousness, the one who should open and no man shut, and upon whom the Lord would hang all the glory of his Father's house. His birth must be where kings are born, in the City of David.

He grew to maturity, subject to Joseph and Mary, in an obscure Galilean village. In his youth he was exposed to the wholesome rugged life of the farm and the pasture and the shop. Obscure Nazareth preserved his obscurity until the time of his showing to Israel arrived. The manners and ways of a village set apart from the marts of trade and the centers of civilization enabled him to learn the way of the swallow and to rejoice in the beauties of the lilies.

Now his ministry is upon him. With a zeal scarce hinted at in the lives of others, he must now be about his Father's business. Where shall his dwelling be? Nazareth no longer serves his needs; the obscurity of the past must flee before the light he now sheds forth. He cannot live in Jerusalem, where priests and scribes and Pharisees and Sanhedrinists—whose influence is great—seek his life and plot his death. He will visit that Sodom-like city from time to time and testify to its people; and finally, he will go there, deliberately and consciously, to suffer many things of the elders and chief priests and scribes, and to be killed, and to rise again the third day. But for the next twenty-seven months or so of his life, he needs a home base from which he can work and whence his word can go forth.

And so—rejected at Nazareth—he now turns, as the Messianic prophecies foretold, to Capernaum, that city of sin on the shores of the Sea of Galilee. He leaves the ancient land of Zebulon, where Nazareth is, to live in the land of Naphtali. He has there a nobleman friend whose son he healed; it is the city of Peter's in-laws, and the future chief apostle himself has a home there. But what is more important, it is a logical center from which to travel to the cities and villages that must hear his voice and see his face; and the throngs of travelers who pass through it will hear of his words and his miracles and carry back to their home peoples the wondering queries of earnest truth-seekers.

Matthew tells us that "leaving Nazareth, he came and dwelt in Capernaum" to fulfill the Messianic word, which promises that a great light shall shine upon those who dwell in that part of "Galilee of the Gentiles." Luke says he went to Capernaum, entered their synagogue, taught them on the Sabbath day—perhaps precisely as he had done in Nazareth—and that "they were astonished at his doctrine: for his word was with power." His doctrine was the gospel; he spoke by the power of the Holy Ghost; and it was the light of his everlasting word that was shown forth, in Galilee, in all of Palestine, and in all nations and among all peoples where he or those sent of him should teach and minister.

"I Will Make You Fishers of Men"
(Luke 5:1-11; JST, Luke 5:2, 10; Matthew 4:18-22; JST, Matthew 4:18-21; Mark 1:16-20; JST, Mark 1:18)

About one year has passed since Andrew and Peter and the Beloved John (as well as Philip and Nathanael) all came to know that Jesus was the Christ, the Son of the living God. It was Andrew who then said to Peter: "We have found the Messias." It was Philip who then said: "We have found him,

31

of whom Moses in the law, and the prophets did write." And it was Nathanael who then testified: "Rabbi, thou art the Son of God; thou art the King of Israel."

Since then all of these brethren have been with Jesus in much of his ministry. They saw the water become wine, the moneychangers flee from the temple, the miracles wrought at the Passover and throughout all Judea. They know what Jesus said to Nicodemus and the woman of Samaria, nor is the episode involving the nobleman's son hidden from them. They were present or at least know what he said in the synagogue in Nazareth. By now they have spent hundreds, perhaps thousands, of hours conversing with and listening to the Master.

How much does a zealous convert learn about the gospel during his first year in the Church? How much would these brethren of apostolic stature learn as they ate and slept and walked and lived with the Master Teacher for weeks and months at a time? How many miracles had they witnessed? How many times and in what variety of ways had they heard him say he was the Messiah? We do not know when James (the brother of John) joined the group, but it is clear his knowledge and testimony was like that of the others.

These brethren were not novices; the gospel message was not new to them. They had testimonies of the truth and divinity of the work, and the resultant desires to serve God and keep his commandments were firmly planted in their hearts. But with it all, they still needed bread to fill their own bellies, fish to fill the mouths of their wives and children, money to support their families. They had not as yet been called into a full-time ministry; they were not yet living the law of consecration, under which all that they had and were was dedicated to the building up of the kingdom and the rolling forth of the work of Him whose special witnesses they would soon become.

It is in this setting, then, and with this understanding, that we find the brothers Andrew and Peter, and the sons of Zebedee, James and John, plying their trade as fishers of fish on the Sea of Galilee. Jesus their Lord comes into view on the shore. Seeing Peter and Andrew "casting a net into the sea," he said: "I am he of whom it is written by the prophets; follow me, and I will make you fishers of men." Probably he said more—perhaps much more; no doubt it would have recalled their numerous experiences with him of the past year. As to what happened, the inspired account says, "And they, believing on his words"—no doubt meaning all the words he had spoken to them over the months—"left their net, and straightway followed him."

Soon thereafter, he came upon James and John, in their father's ship, mending their nets. Jesus issued the call, "and straightway they left their father Zebedee in the ship with the hired servants, and went after him." These four apostles-to-be were preparing for their holy calling. No doubt they already were elders in the Melchizedek Priesthood—at least we know that at a much earlier time they were performing baptisms, which requires at least the Aaronic Priesthood, but now they were forsaking all to follow the Master. They were going forth on full-time missions; they were consecrating their time and means and talents to a greater work. They were to be fishers of men.

Luke gives us either a more amplified account of these calls or a recitation of a miraculous event that occurred immediately thereafter. Each of the two sets of brothers, in their own ships, had fished all night, as the custom was, and had caught nothing. It was morning; the ships were anchored, and the fishermen were ashore, washing their nets. Crowds so pressed in upon Jesus that he entered Peter's ship and asked him to "thrust out a little from the land." Then Jesus "sat down, and taught the people out of the ship." Again we do not know what he said, only that he preached the gospel.

When his sermon was ended, Jesus instructed Peter: "Launch out into the deep, and let down your nets for a draught." This Peter did, though he had toiled all night and caught nothing. Immediately, miraculously, the nets were so

33

full that they broke; with the help of James and John, both ships were filled, "so that they began to sink." Those who live by the law of consecration have their just needs and wants supplied, by divine power if need be.

Peter, falling at Jesus' knees, said: "Depart from me; for I am a sinful man, O Lord," so great was his astonishment "at the draught of fishes which they had taken." It was as though he had said: 'I am unworthy of this honor. A sinner such as I is not fit company for "the King, the Lord of hosts." Depart from me, that another more deserving may see thy countenance and behold thy person.' (*Commentary* 1:166.)

Jesus' response was kind and encouraging: "Fear not; from henceforth thou shalt catch men." A new day had dawned for Peter, James, John—the future First Presidency of the Church—and for Andrew, one of the Twelve. "And when they had brought their ships to land, they forsook all, and followed him."

That Glorious Sabbath in Capernaum
(Mark 1:21-34; Luke 4:31-41; JST, Luke 4:38; Matthew 8:14-17)

A day in the life of our Lord: one glorious, wondrous day in Capernaum, his own city; a Sabbath day—a day of mighty preaching, of doctrine that astonished, of casting out an unclean devil in the synagogue; a day when Peter's mother-in-law was raised from her sick bed, and when a congregation of persons, possessed by evil spirits and suffering from divers diseases, came to partake of the goodness of Him who "took our infirmities, and bare our sicknesses"!

It was the Sabbath. He entered into the synagogue. No doubt Simon and Andrew, and James and John, the two sets of brothers, were with him; as devout Jews they all knew their Sabbath place, and that place was in the synagogue of the Lord, the place where Jehovah was worshipped according to the best light and knowledge then found among mortals. What a favored and choice congregation assembled here in Capernaum, in the house of worship where archaeologists have found the ornamentation over the lintel, consisting of a pot of manna between representations of Aaron's rod; in the stone building where four future apostles and their families paid their devotions. And on this particular Sabbath the Son of God himself was to address the congregation. Word most assuredly had spread through the city of the claims he had made and the gracious words he had spoken so recently in the synagogue in Nazareth. Who would not have crowded into the rectangular building to hear the word of truth and breathe the spirit of worship on such a day?

After the liturgical and formal parts of the day's worship, Jesus speaks. Neither Mark nor Luke tell us what he said, though they both recount the effect of the sermon on the hearers. They tell us "his word was with power"; that the congregation was "astonished at his doctrine"—as well they might be when one of such stature and fame arises to announce he is the Messiah and that salvation comes by him, as he had done in Nazareth; and that he "taught them as one that had authority, and not as the scribes." Many believing souls must have been in the congregation, as witness what happened that evening in Capernaum; at least no tumult of opposition arose, and no one sought to put him to death, as had been the case among those of the city where once he dwelt.

Yet there was one in the synagogue upon whom the sermon had an astonishing effect; one who was so filled with animus and hatred that he welcomed into his body an unclean devil from the blackness of hell; one who was possessed by an unclean spirit who took complete control of all mortal functions. By the mouth of the man, the demon who hated both the truth and Him who is its author cried out: "Let us alone; what have we to do with thee, thou Jesus of Nazareth? art thou come to destroy us? I know thee who thou art, the Holy One of God."

Jesus' response was immediate, authoritative, unbending. He rebuked the devil. "Hold thy peace, and come out of him," he said, for the Son of Man neither sought nor accepted testimony of his divinity from an evil source. What matter it if "the devils also believe, and tremble"? (James 2:19.) What converting power attends the witness of Lucifer that Christ is the Holy One? Testimony should be borne by the power of the Holy Ghost or remain unspoken. What does it matter what the rebels from Sheol think or know about the laws of righteousness? Can a fountain bring forth both sweet and bitter water at the same place?

When the command came, this angel of the devil, this son of perdition, this unclean spirit, who like Lucifer his master was in opposition to all righteousness—this unclean spirit had no choice but to obey. With one final burst of hatred and venom, the unclean devil tore the man, threw him in agony in their midst, cried out with a loud and defiant voice, and then came out of his ill-gotten tenement.

The man was left limp and weak, but in a state to receive strength and light. The devil joined his fellow rebels who are continuing on earth the war commenced in heaven. And the people were amazed. Questioning among themselves, some asked: "What thing is this? what new doctrine is this? for with authority commandeth he even the unclean spirits, and they do obey him." Others acclaimed: "What a word is this! for with authority and power he commandeth the unclean spirits, and they come out." Is it any wonder that "the fame of him went out into every place of the country round about," and that all Galilee heard of his doctrine, his Messianic claims, and his power even over unclean spirits?

However much it may run counter to the carnal mind to read of men possessed of devils, and of other men who cast them out, such is one of the realities of mortal life. One-third of the hosts of heaven—all spirit children of our Eternal Father who is God—were cast out of heaven for rebellion. As angels of the devil and as sons of him who is Perdition, they stalk the earth, seeking whom they may destroy. Their condemnation: they are denied bodies; for them there is no further progression; they are miserable and seek the misery of all mankind; they are damned souls, without hope, forever. If, as, and when—subject to the restrictions and laws of our gracious God—they can gain temporary tenancy in a tenement of clay, they take up their habitation in the bodies of others.

We do not know how or under what circumstances such tenancy is permitted. That all things are governed and controlled by law, we do know; and we are left to suppose that in the day when the Incarnate Jehovah came among men, there must have been more persons who were susceptible to spirit possession than has been the case in other days. Perhaps somehow many of the Jews of that day—zealous, religiously inclined, yet going beyond the mark where spiritual things are concerned—got themselves into a state where evil spirits could enter their bodies. We do know from the Messianic utterance—"And he shall cast out devils, or the evil spirits which dwell in the hearts of men" (Mosiah 3:6)—that Jesus was destined, as he did, to cast out devils, and that this power was given to his apostles and seventies and, of course, is in the true church today.

After the synagogue service, He who had not where to lay his head, who—during the days of his active ministry at least—had no home of his own, went with Simon and Andrew to their abode to partake of the festive Sabbath meal. Such feasts at family gatherings were the most joyous occasions of the week. James and John were also guests in Peter's home on this memorable day.

Mark tells us that "Simon's wife's mother lay sick of a fever, and anon they tell him of her." Luke says she "was taken with a great fever; and they besought him for her." Jesus' specially selected disciples were married men with wives and children and families of their own, as his specially called servants should be in all ages. This is a household of faith; it is Peter's dwelling place; and all who dwell with him love the Lord and seek to walk uprightly before him. That they should importune the Master to heal one of their number is the most natural thing in the world.

37

And that Jesus should respond is what we all expect. He stood over her, rebuked the fever, took her by the hand, and lifted her up. "Immediately the fever left her, and she ministered unto them." What a joyous occasion this must have been. As the little group partook of the bounties of life, they also feasted spiritually; as they ate bread and fish, they rejoiced in the spiritual food set forth in the sermon of the morning; as they thought about the healed demoniac, there stood ministering to their every need a woman whose body but moments before had burned with fever. What marvels were being wrought in Israel!

Nor were the day's labors completed. From the morning session in the synagogue to the going down of the sun, the word went forth; all Capernaum heard what Jesus had preached; all learned that even the unclean devils departed at his word.

People began assembling at Peter's home. "All the city was gathered together at the door." Included with them were their sick and afflicted and diseased. Some were carried on litters; others were supported by loving arms; those with diseases of every sort came in faith, assured that miraculous cures awaited them. At evening after sunset, Jesus "laid his hands on every one of them, and healed them." And at his word, the devils came out of many, saying, "Thou art Christ the Son of God," and he rebuked them and "suffered them not to speak: for they knew that he was Christ."

Jesus Tours and Preaches in Galilee
(Matthew 4:23-25; JST, Matthew 4:22; Mark 1:35-39; Luke 4:42-44; JST, Luke 4:42)

When the night came the labors of the day ceased; the wise words and healing power stopped for a moment. Needed sleep and rest were sought, but not for long. "In the morning, rising up a great while before day, he went out, and departed into a solitary place, and there prayed."

How often Jesus prays! If it were not a basic tenet of true

38

religion that private prayers are personal; that they are between the earthly suppliant and the Divine Father; that they should be known only by him who speaks and Him who hears—if it were not for these things, we would covet a knowledge of what the Son of the Father said to the Father of the Son on this and numerous other occasions. We can suppose that the voice of prayer poured out words of thanksgiving for the grace and guidance of that Capernaum Sabbath, which is scarcely over, and sought wisdom and direction for the continuing labors that lay ahead.

Jesus did not remain long in the desert solitude. Simon and the disciples followed after him. "All men seek for thee," Peter said, as the multitudes came pleading and importuning that he remain with them.

They, however, had heard the word. His voice had testified in their synagogue; the witness of his divine Sonship had been borne in their presence; he had preached the gospel, opened the door to further investigation, and demonstrated his power by the healings and the miracles. The responsibility was now theirs to obtain baptism, to join the sheepfold of the Good Shepherd, and to live as becometh saints. Jesus must go elsewhere and give others a like opportunity.

"I must preach the kingdom of God to other cities also," he said, "For therefore am I sent." And preach it he did, in Galilee (except for a brief attendance at his second Passover), for almost two years, for about twenty-one months. By then it will be October, A.D. 29, and he will go to the Feast of Tabernacles to commence his later Judean ministry. But now he is starting his first tour of Galilee, preaching, healing, doing good, and working righteousness. Those with diseases and torments are healed; the lunatics and the paralytics are made well; devils are cast out; and multitudes follow him, "from Galilee, and from Decapolis, and from Jerusalem, and from Judæa, and from beyond Jordan." His fame knows no limit, and men flock to him from every political jurisdiction.

Truly this is that which Nephi foresaw. "I . . . beheld the Lamb of God going forth among the children of men," he said. "And I beheld multitudes of people who were sick, and who were afflicted with all manner of diseases, and with devils and unclean spirits; and . . . they were healed by the power of the Lamb of God; and the devils and the unclean spirits were cast out." (1 Ne. 11:31.)

NOTE

1. The marginal reading for the introductory portion of this Messianic prophecy is: "In the former time he brought into contempt the land of Zebulon and the land of Naphtali, but in the latter time hath he made it glorious," meaning that in the coming day when the Lord Jesus would dwell there, it would be glorious because the light of his countenance would shine upon the people.

Chapter 36

JESUS USES MIRACLES TO SPREAD THE WORK

Jesus was touched with a feeling
of their infirmities. Those cries pierced
to His inmost heart;
the groans and sighs of all that
collective misery
filled His whole soul with pity.
His heart bled for them;
He suffered with them;
their agonies were His;
so that the Evangelist St. Matthew
recalls in this place,
with a slight difference of language,
the words of Isaiah,
"Surely He bore our griefs and carried
our sorrow." (Farrar, p. 182.)[1]

A New Dimension to Jesus' Miracles

Miracles stand out as one of the chief identifying characteristics of the mortal ministry of the Messiah. His Messianic witnesses—Isaiah, Nephi, King Benjamin, and others—

spoke plainly of the throngs who would be healed by his word. We have now seen these throngs in Judea and throughout all Galilee. All of Palestine knows that here is a man who heals the sick in such a measure as was never before known in Israel. The raising of great multitudes from their beds of affliction and the casting out of many unclean spirits from many contorted and abused souls cannot be hidden from the people. Nor was it intended that it should be. Jesus' miracles bore testimony of his divinity and to the truth of the words he spoke.

Primarily, however, our Lord in his ministry is preaching the gospel of the kingdom; he is announcing to all men what they must do to gain peace in this life and eternal life in the world to come; he is proclaiming that a gracious Father ordained and established a plan of salvation that will enable the whole family of earth to advance and progress and become like their Creator; he is testifying that he is the Promised Messiah, the Savior and Redeemer, through whom salvation comes. "Whoso believeth in me, and is baptized, the same shall be saved; and they are they who shall inherit the kingdom of God. And whoso believeth not in me, and is not baptized, shall be damned." (3 Ne. 11:33-34.) This is his message; this summarizes what men must believe and what they must do. Jesus came to save sinners, and salvation comes through repentance and baptism and continued devotion to the truth. Unless we keep this perspective clearly before us, we will not and cannot keep in their perspective the disjointed collection of episodes from his life that have been preserved in the inspired writings now extant.

The miracles he is constantly performing are visible evidences in the eyes of all, believers and nonbelievers alike, that he has more than mortal power. They are proof, as it were, that his words are true. Can a deceiver and false teacher open blind eyes and unstop deaf ears? Miracles and true teachings always go hand in hand; signs follow those that believe—in their purity and perfection—the truths of the everlasting gospel.

We have little conception of the number of healings Jesus wrought. Multitudes thronged his way day after day, bringing their diseased and deformed, their lame and decrepit, their deaf and their blind. All these were healed as faith and desire warranted. Even their dead were subject to Jesus' will.

No attempt is made by the Gospel authors to record Jesus' many miracles. Only selected samples are set forth in the scriptures. The obvious plan of the inspired authors is to preserve illustrations of his purposes and powers, and surely the wide variety of healings and miraculous performances that they chose to record do attest to his power and control over all things.

After that glorious Sabbath in Capernaum when he cast out devils and healed all manner of diseases and torments, we find him touring throughout all Galilee "healing all manner of sickness and all manner of disease among the people." About three months pass, during which period the synoptists select, for analysis and exposition, only two of his miracles. These are the healing of a leper somewhere in Galilee and the healing of one sick with palsy when Jesus comes back to Capernaum.

Both of these manifestations of divine power add a new dimension, not so far seen, to his miraculous performances: the healing of the leper because of the nature of the disease, the secrecy he enjoined upon the recipient of his blessing, and the stipulation that the healed person conform to the provisions of the law of Moses; and the curing of the paralytic because it was preceded by a forgiveness of sins, showing that Jesus was Jehovah, who alone can forgive sins. Each of these miracles was performed not alone for the benefit and blessing of the suffering Israelite whose body was affected, but as a witness to the growing group of opponents that he whom they opposed came from God and had divine power. The wicked and rebellious in Israel, word upon word and miracle after miracle, were being left without excuse; their sins were being bound securely upon their own heads; the Light they were rejecting was shining forth everywhere in word and in deed.

He Heals a Leper
(Mark 1:40-45; JST, Mark 1:40; Luke 5:12-16; JST, Luke 5:14; Matthew 8:2-4; JST, Matthew 8:2)

Healings there have been in profuse abundance, but none—up to this point and as far as we know—has involved a leper, "a man full of leprosy." None has dealt with a body and soul plagued with a living death, one whose body was in process of rotting, decaying, and returning to the dust to gain merciful surcease from the torments of the flesh. Before the Second Coming, "the Lord God will send forth flies upon the face of the earth, which shall take hold of the inhabitants thereof, and shall eat their flesh, and shall cause maggots to come in upon them; . . . and their flesh shall fall from off their bones, and their eyes from their sockets." (D&C 29:18-19.) Before and at the time of his First Coming, there were many in Israel who were lepers, possessors of such a vile and degenerating disease that they were anathema to everyone and a curse to themselves. Except for the extent of the coming latter-day plague, it can scarcely be worse than the hell and torment and physical affliction suffered by the lepers of Jesus' day.

Leprosy is an evil and wicked disease. "The symptoms and the effects of this disease are very loathsome. There comes a white swelling or scab, with a change of the color of the hair . . . from its natural hue to yellow; then the appearance of a taint going deeper than the skin, or raw flesh appearing in the swelling. Then it spreads and attacks the cartilaginous portions of the body. The nails loosen and drop off, the gums are absorbed, and the teeth decay and fall out; the breath is a stench, the nose decays; fingers, hands, feet, may be lost, or the eyes eaten out. The human beauty has gone into corruption, and the patient feels that he is being eaten as by a fiend, who consumes him slowly in a long remorseless meal that will not end until he be destroyed. He is shut out from his fellows. As they approach he must cry, 'Unclean! unclean!' that all humanity may be warned from his precincts. He must abandon wife and child. He must go to live with other lepers, in disheartening view of miseries similar to his own. He must dwell in dismantled houses or in the tombs."[2]

"It began with little specks on the eyelids, and on the palms of the hand, and gradually spread over different parts of the body, bleaching the hair white wherever it showed itself, crusting the affected parts with shining scales, and causing swellings and sores. From the skin it slowly ate its way through the tissues, to the bones and joints and even to the marrow, rotting the whole body piecemeal. The lungs, the organs of speech and hearing, and the eyes were attacked in turn, till, at last, consumption or dropsy brought welcome death." (Geikie, pp. 390-91.)

Leprosy in biblical times, in addition to its desolating physical effects, was looked upon as the symbol of sin and uncleanness, signifying that as this evil disease ate away and destroyed the physical body, so sin eats away and corrupts the spiritual side of man. This did not mean that the disease borne by any individual attested that he was a worse sinner than his fellows, only that the disease itself was a symbol of the ills that will befall the ungodly and rebellious. It had been chosen as such a symbol, however, because it was considered to be the worst of all diseases, one that could not be cured except by direct divine intervention. There were instances in the Old Testament—Miriam, Gehazi, and Uzziah—in which rebellious persons were cursed with leprosy as a punishment for their evil deed.

And so we find the Galilean, preaching the gospel in his beloved Galilee, in an unnamed city, when a man "full of leprosy" — one in the last stages of the plague; one who is affected from head to toes, in all parts of his body; one for whom a dropsical death is not far distant—who, seeing Jesus, falls on his face, worships him, and says: "Lord, if thou wilt, thou canst make me clean."

45

Here is a man of faith. There is no question as to whether Jesus can heal him—only will the Great Healer use his power in this case. Indeed, here is man of great faith, for it would take an almost unbounded spiritual assurance to have the confidence of a restoration of health from a disease so dread. And was it not the recognized teaching of all the Rabbis of the day that leprosy was incurable? For such an affliction to leave the flesh of man had scarcely been heard of since the day of Naaman the Syrian.

Jesus is compassionate. With no thought of the Levitical uncleanness that results from touching a leper, he reaches forth his hand, touches the suffering suppliant—which physical contact is mentioned by all three of the synoptists—and, almost as the echo of the entreaty, says: "I will; be thou clean."[3] Immediately, instantaneously, as it were, the leper is cleansed, his leprosy departs, and the miracle is wrought. Nothing is too hard for the Lord.

There were times when Jesus deliberately performed miracles to attract attention and to force, as it were, unbelieving hearers to give credence to his words. On this occasion, for reasons not recited, he chose to give a pointed charge to the cleansed leper to "tell no man" of the healing that had come to him. "See thou say nothing to any man," he commanded, "but go thy way, shew thyself to the priest, and offer for thy cleansing those things which Moses commanded, for a testimony unto them."

It may be that at this time, when men were flocking to him in such great numbers, further fame and notoriety would have hindered him in his travels and preaching; or that such a notable miracle would fan the flames of persecution that already were beginning to burn with an intense flame; or that if the priests in the temple in Jerusalem—whence the cleansed leper must now go to seek Levitical cleanness—knew the source of the healing power, it would have been difficult to obtain the ceremonial absolution required.

Jesus, at this point, was still requiring his converts to

keep the law of Moses. After his passion and crucifixion it would be different; then "the law of commandments contained in ordinances" would be "abolished in his flesh" (Eph. 2:15); then "the handwriting of ordinances, or better, "the bond written in ordinances," would be nailed "to his cross." (Col. 2:14.) But now the healed leper must report to the priest, be shaved and examined, be quarantined for seven days, wash his clothes, offer the required sacrifices, and have the blood sprinkled and all the rites performed as set forth in Leviticus 14.

But the great thing that had happened to him was too good to keep. "He went out, and began to publish it much, and to blaze abroad the matter, insomuch that Jesus could no more openly enter into the city, but was without in desert places: and they came to him from every quarter." He, however, "withdrew himself into the wilderness, and prayed."

He Forgives and Heals One Sick with Palsy
(Mark 2:1-12; JST, Mark 2:1-3, 7, 9; Luke 5:17-26; JST, Luke 5:19-20, 23-24; Matthew 9:2-8; JST, Matthew 9:2, 4-6, 8)

Jesus is now back in Capernaum after a long Galilean tour of teaching and healing. The flames of his fame—fanned by his words, fed by the flow of miracles—are blazing forth in every part of Palestine. Never was a man's name on as many Palestinian tongues as is this Man's. His doctrine, his deeds, his doings—all that he says and every good thing that he does—are discussed in every home, at every festive meal, in every synagogue. The believing among the sick and the penitent among the afflicted seek him with a hope of being healed; those who hunger and thirst after righteousness hang on his every word and find peace to their souls as they live in harmony with his teachings; the rulers and the rebellious rate him as an evil troublemaker and seek ways to entrap and defame and even to slay him.

In Capernaum he stays with Peter, and he is now in the

home of that chief of his apostolic witnesses. Throngs crowd around. The house, apparently a large one, is filled; the living quarters, the guest chamber, the bedrooms, all are crowded with people; and throngs of others are massed around the door and out into the street. Scribes and Pharisees and "doctors of the law" have assembled there "out of every town of Galilee, and Judea, and Jerusalem." Jesus is seated, as the custom is, and is teaching his hearers. Mark, who records what he learned from Peter, and whose account of the wondrous happenings we are about to witness is the most complete, says: "He preached the word unto them." Jesus is preaching the gospel; he is speaking of his Father, of the plan of salvation, of the atoning sacrifice upon which all else rests; he is setting forth the need to repent and be baptized and receive the Holy Ghost and to work the works of righteousness. He is preaching the everlasting word, the word of truth and salvation, the word of the gospel. Such is the course he will follow everywhere.

Four men approach the house. They are carrying a litter or pallet whereon lies one sick of the palsy, one who is paralyzed, who cannot speak, and who of himself is helpless; yet he is a man of faith who has made known his desire to be deposited in the Divine Presence that perchance the one in whom his faith is centered will exercise his healing power in the paralyzed one's behalf. Unable to pass through the throng with their human burden, the four men ascend to the roof, probably by the usual outside stairs found on nearly every house. On the roof they do what is neither difficult nor uncommon; they make an opening in the thatch-type roof, and through it they lower the suffering suppliant into the presence of Jesus.

Our Lord ceases his sermon; all eyes are upon him and the paralytic, whose eyes make the entreaty that his voice cannot. Here, as planned by a Providence that foreknows all things, is a teaching situation seldom equaled in the annals of the Lord's dealings with his people. Before Jesus lies one sick of the palsy who has faith to be healed, and who seeks the blessed word that will make him well. The scribes and the Pharisees and the doctors are all present to see and become witnesses of the power of God. Shall our Lord go forward with the healing, as he has done in many other instances, and as we might suppose he would do now?

Jesus' choice is not to do so. Here also is a man, lying on a litter, who is qualified and entitled, by faith, to have his sins remitted. No verbal request, either for healing or for forgiveness, has been made to the Master; yet the desire of the incapacitated one is apparent. Jesus knows exactly what ought to be done. The man should be healed and forgiven; his faith has prepared him for both blessings. If Jesus should say to him first, 'Be thou made whole,' and then, 'Thy sins are forgiven thee,' the miraculous performance would be another example of his divine power—of which there already was an uncounted number—and the physically decrepit person would, of course, be healed physically and spiritually. Such is a possible course of procedure.

On the other hand, if Jesus should first forgive the man's sins—since none but God can forgive sins—such an act would be an announcement that he was God; then, if he commanded the sick person to rise up and walk, it would be proof that his claim to divinity was true. The teaching situation is ideally prepared, and the Master Teacher knows the course to pursue.

"Son, be of good cheer," he says. And what greater cheer and joy can come into a human heart than that which results from a remission of sins, from an assurance that one is free from earth stains, free from the bondage and sorrow that binds all sin-shackled souls? Then come the glad tidings: "Thy sins be forgiven thee," which act in itself is a greater blessing than to be made whole physically, for all men will attain physical perfection in the resurrection, but only those who are free from sin will go on, in that day, to eternal life in the kingdom of God. As part of the announced freedom from sin for the paralyzed one, Jesus then commands: "Go thy way and sin no more."

The great drama is being acted out by the greatest Dramatist of them all. Jesus has forgiven a man's sins. Luke's account puts the blessed words in the present tense: "Man, thy sins are forgiven thee." Immediately rebellion wells up in the hearts of the ever-present rebels. "Why doth this man thus speak blasphemies?" they think. "Who can forgive sins but God only?"

In part, their thinking is correct. None but God can forgive sins, and if this man is not God, then the words he has spoken are blasphemy, and according to divine law, the penalty for such is death. If, however, this man is the Messiah, then the prerogative he has assumed is proper, and it is within his province to loose on earth and have it loosed eternally in the heavens. Messiah can forgive sins because Messiah is God.

Before viewing the remainder of the drama here opening to our view, we must remind ourselves of how the law of forgiveness operates, for the Lord, who himself ordained the laws, is also himself bound to uphold and sustain and conform to them. The Lord forgives sins, but he does it in harmony with the laws he ordained before the world was.

All men sin and fall short of the glory of God; all need repentance; all need forgiveness; and all can become free from sin by obedience to the laws and ordinances that comprise the cleansing process. For those who have not accepted the gospel—the everlasting word that Jesus was this day preaching in Peter's house—the course of forgiveness is to believe in the Lord Jesus Christ, to repent, to be baptized by immersion for the remission of sins, and to receive the gift of the Holy Ghost by the laying on of hands. The Holy Ghost is a sanctifier, and those who receive the baptism of fire have sin and evil burned out of their souls as though by fire.

For those whose sins have thus been remitted and who sin after baptism—as all baptized souls do—the path to forgiveness consists of repenting and renewing the covenant made in the waters of baptism. Godly sorrow for sin, complete abandonment of the wrongful acts, confession to the

Lord and to the church officers where need be, restitution if such is possible, and renewed obedience—these are all part of the cleansing process for those who, after baptism, fall from the strait and narrow path leading to eternal life. By doing these things and by then partaking worthily of the sacrament, so that the Spirit of the Lord will come again into the lives of the penitent persons, members of the kingdom gain forgiveness of sins.

We are not told whether the paralytic here forgiven by Jesus was a member of the Church or not. The overwhelming probability is that he was, and that Jesus was now forgiving his sins anew, as he did many times to Joseph Smith and the early elders of his latter-day kingdom.[4] "Where members of the Church are concerned, there is a very close connection between manifestations of healing grace and the forgiveness of sins. When the elders administer to faithful saints, the promise is: 'And the prayer of faith shall save the sick, and the Lord shall raise him up; and if he have committed sins, they shall be forgiven him.' (James 5:15.) The very fact that a member of the kingdom has matured in the gospel to the point that he has power through faith in Christ to be healed, means that he also has so lived that he is entitled to have his sins remitted. Since all men repeatedly sin they must all gain successive remissions of their sins, otherwise none would eventually stand pure and spotless before the Lord and thus be worthy of a celestial inheritance." (*Commentary* 1:179.)

Now let us return to the worldly wise who reasoned in their hearts that Jesus' act of forgiveness was blasphemy. For that matter, they reasoned, how could anyone know if the paralytic's sins were remitted? Forgiveness of sins is not something that can be seen or felt or tasted by an outside observer. And weren't the only provisions for forgiveness accomplished by the priests through the sin offerings, the trespass offerings, and the other sacrificial performances, especially those on the day of atonement?

"Wherefore is it that ye think evil in your hearts?" Jesus

51

asked, for he knew their thoughts. "Why reason ye these things in your hearts? Is it not easier to say to the sick of the palsy, Thy sins be forgiven thee; than to say, Arise, and take up thy bed and walk?" His logic was perfect. 'Does it require more power to forgive sins than to make the sick rise up and walk?' Then came the healing word: "But, that ye may know that the Son of Man hath power upon earth to forgive sins, I said it. And he said unto the sick of the palsy, I say unto thee, Arise, and take up thy couch, and go unto thy house."

Thereupon strength came into the limbs and legs and organs of the paralyzed one. Speech returned; full physical capacity, for his age and circumstances, came again. He obeyed the divine counsel, took up his couch, and went his way, rejoicing and glorifying God.

And what of the others who were present? The proof of Messiahship could not be controverted. He who claimed to forgive sins—which all agreed none but God could do—had proved his divine power by turning the living death of palsy into the joyous life of physical health and spiritual cleanness. Following this display of power, the polarization of the people increased. All were amazed; the doctors of the law were, as such lawyers almost always are, unconvinced, disbelieving, rebellious. Yet "many glorified God, saying, We never saw the power of God after this manner."

Jesus had accomplished that which he set out to do.

NOTES

1. Though Canon Farrar wrote these eloquent words with reference to the multitudes who came to Peter's home to be healed on that glorious Sabbath evening in Capernaum, they apply in principle to all of our Lord's healings. Isaiah's actual Messianically spoken words were: "Surely he hath borne our griefs, and carried our sorrows" (Isa. 53:4); and what Matthew said was: "Himself took our infirmities, and bare our sicknesses" (Matt. 8:17). Isaiah's clear meaning is that the Messiah takes upon himself the sins—and hence the griefs and sorrows, for these come because of sin—of all men on condition of repentance. Matthew simply assumes his apostolic prerogative to give added meaning to Isaiah's words by applying them—properly—to the physical healings that are a type and pattern of the spiritual healings wrought through the infinite and eternal atonement of Him who ransoms men both temporally and spiritually.

2. Quoted from Deems, *Light of the Nations*, p. 185. See *Commentary* 1:173-74.

3. As to Jesus' touching the leper, Farrar says: "It was a glorious violation of the *letter* of the Law, which attached ceremonial pollution to a leper's touch; but it was at the same

time a glorious illustration of the *spirit* of the Law, which was that mercy is better than sacrifice. The hand of Jesus was not polluted by touching the leper's body, but the leper's whole body was cleansed by the touch of that holy hand. It was even thus that He touched our sinful nature, and yet remained without spot of sin." (Farrar, p. 208.)

4. D&C 29:3; 36:1; 50:36; 60:7; 62:3; 64:3; 108:1; 110:5.

Chapter 37

JESUS BRINGS A NEW GOSPEL DISPENSATION

Behold, I say unto you
that all old covenants have I caused
to be done away
in this thing; and this is a new
and an everlasting covenant,
even that which was from the beginning.
Wherefore, although a man should be baptized
an hundred times it availeth
him nothing, for you cannot enter in
at the strait gate by the law of Moses,
neither by your dead works.
For it is because of your dead works
that I have caused this last covenant
and this church to be built up unto me,
even as in days of old.
Wherefore, enter ye in at the gate,
as I have commanded,
and seek not to counsel your God.
(D&C 22:1-4.)[1]

Jesus Calls Sinners to Repentance
(Mark 2:13-17; JST, Mark 2:11; Luke 5:27-32; JST, Luke 5:27; Matthew 9:9-13; JST, Matthew 9:10, 13)

Jesus is in process of restoring the gospel for his day and dispensation. So far we have seen him reveal new doctrine, call and ordain new officers, approve the baptism of John, and perform like baptisms of his own. We are aware that his new converts have the promise that in due course they will receive the gift of the Holy Ghost, which will guide them into all truth. We know that he will continue to reveal doctrine, to expound eternal truths, and to call officers to govern the affairs of his earthly kingdom. In due course he will call his Twelve special witnesses and give them the keys of the kingdom, so they can regulate all things incident thereto, to say nothing of having power to bind on earth and seal in heaven.

At the moment, however, we are with him as he calls Matthew, attends a feast in that publican's home, and speaks of his mission to call sinners to repentance. As an outgrowth of this episode we shall hear him tell why the wine of new revelation cannot be poured into the old bottles of Mosaic formalism. The place of our present happening is near Capernaum, on the Sea of Galilee.

Matthew is a publican, and publicans, as a group, are a vile, corrupt, and evil lot. They are classed with sinners and harlots. Even Jesus, in speaking of a brother caught in trespass who rebels against the discipline of the Church, says: "Let him be unto thee as an heathen man and a publican." (Matt. 18:17.) And a famous Gentile rejoinder to the question "Which are the worst kind of wild beasts?" is: "On the mountains, bears and lions; in cities, publicans and pettifoggers." The Jews had a proverb: "Take not a wife out of the family where there is a publican, for they are all publicans." (Farrar, p. 188, n. 1.)

Publicans are tax collectors; they represent Rome and are a symbol of the tyranny and oppression of the Gentile yoke. Partiality, avarice, greed, exacting more than is lawful, and petty oppression are deemed, in the public mind, to be a way of life with them. "The rabbis ranked them as cutthroats and robbers, as social outcasts, as religiously half-excommunicated." (*Commentary* 1:181.) It is assumed their wealth comes from rapine and their business is the business of extortioners.

It is to this class of people that Matthew belongs. Manifestly the claims made against them are exaggerated and do not apply to all individual tax collectors. And we know nothing of Matthew's way of life before he forsook all to follow Jesus. It is assumed that he forsook great wealth, even as Lehi and his family did when they went out from Jerusalem to be led of the Lord to their promised land, now known as America.

Matthew may have been a bright light among associates, most of whom were greedy and extortionate, or, if there were faults in his character, we must assume he repented in sackcloth and ashes before his call to the ministry. The earlier calls, also on the shores of the Galilean sea, of Simon and Andrew and of James and John were calls of men whose association with Jesus had extended over a long period. Those brethren were probably as well versed in the new theology and the new way of life as any then living in Galilee. It is natural to assume that Matthew had a similar background; his association with the Master must have been considerable before his call. Was he present that day in the synagogue when the demoniac was healed? Had he traveled with Jesus through the cities and towns of Galilee, hearing his words and seeing his miracles? Was he crowded into Peter's home when the Son of Man chose to remit the sins of the paralytic and then commanded him to take up his bed and walk? All we know is that after Jesus left the home of Peter, having there taught the word and healed the paralytic, he went to the seaside. The multitude followed, and he continued to teach; precious words yet poured forth from his lips to find lodgment in receptive ears.

There on the seashore he saw Matthew the publican, called also "Levi the son of Alpheus, sitting at the place where they receive tribute, as was customary in those days." Jesus said, "Follow me. And he left all, rose up, and followed him." Truly, as the scripture saith, "the gifts and calling of God are without repentance" (Rom. 11:29), meaning the Lord takes a Paul, an Alma, or a Matthew, as he chooses, because that called servant was prepared and foreordained from the premortal eternities to perform the labors to which the call extends. Manifestly all such do repent and make themselves worthy in all respects for the divine labor that is then theirs.

Sometime after his call, Matthew appoints a great feast in his house in honor of Jesus; perhaps also it is a farewell feast for his fellow publicans, for they are there in great numbers. Matthew himself says "many publicans and sinners came and sat down" with Jesus and his disciples. The social outcasts of society are celebrating—sinners being among them—and the Son of God and his newly called disciples sit in their midst, eat the food, and partake of the hospitality. Beholding such a scene, the scribes and Pharisees murmur. Why, they query, do Jesus and his disciples eat and drink with publicans and sinners? The questions are put to the disciples, but the answers come from Him who sets the tone of those festivities which we must believe he found enjoyable.

"They that be whole need not a physician, but they that are sick," he says. Such is the proverb of the day, which Jesus here uses with a veiled sarcasm, as though he had said, 'You self-righteous Pharisees think you have no need of my healing doctrine, and so I go to these sick publicans and sinners to make them whole.' Actually, of course, no one needed a physician more than the spiritually sick Pharisees.

"But go ye and learn what that meaneth, I will have mercy, and not sacrifice: for I am not come to call the righteous, but sinners to repentance." The Pharisaic religion was one of ritualistic forms, of rules and ceremonies, of rites and sacrifices; it was a religion that held them aloof from publicans and sinners. Jesus is here telling them that if they knew that mercy, love, charity, and all the attributes of godliness were more important than their ritualistic performances, they too would eat and drink with sinners and seek to do good to all men.

Truly, Jesus came to save sinners; and if he can take a Paul, an Alma, and a Matthew from their lowly spiritual states and raise them to apostolic and prophetic stature, surely he can pour out good things on the spiritual publicans of the world, to the end that all who will repent shall find salvation in his Father's kingdom.

Jesus Brings New Revelation to a New Church
(Matthew 9:14-17; JST, Matthew 9:15, 18-21; Mark 2:18-22; JST, Mark 2:16-17; Luke 5:33-39; JST, Luke 5:36)

At this point, as the feast continues in the home of the now spiritually refreshed publican Levi-Matthew, the disciples of John the Baptist add their voices of complaint to those of the scribes and Pharisees. "While he was thus teaching"—that is, at the very moment when Jesus asserted that he had come to call sinners to repentance; to call them from their old Mosaic way of life to a new gospel order—the disciples of John, who also had preached a new order of repentance and a new baptism for the remission of sins, came to him and asked: "Why do we and the Pharisees fast oft, but thy disciples fast not?"

Fasting was a fetish with the Pharisees. There were times when they fasted twice a week, regularly, religiously, and with holy zeal, as they supposed.[2] They paid tithes with such scrupulous attention to detail that they even gave a tenth part of the herbs that grew in pots on their windowsills. They attended to every sacrificial detail with such ritualistic attention that scarcely a single drop of blood was sprinkled other than at the appointed place. And John's disciples—for their master was cut in the Pharisaic mold, and had in fact been sent to wind up the affairs of the dying dispensation of

58

Mosaic formalisms—partook of some of the characteristics of their Pharisaic kinsmen. They fasted—perhaps as religiously as the Pharisees themselves, for the last accepted adherents to the old order were expected to live that law to the full, that it might be fulfilled in glory as the day approached when it would be replaced in full by the new gospel order.

Fasting as such is not to be condemned. In its place, and within the bounds set by Him who incorporated it as part of his eternal system, it is to be commended. Mortals can never attain the unity with Deity that it is their privilege to gain without fasting and prayer. Whether the Pharisaic fasts met with divine approval is quite another thing, however. Their fathers had been condemned for fasting for evil purposes. "Behold, ye fast for strife and debate, and to smite with the fist of wickedness," Isaiah had said to them. "Ye shall not fast as ye do this day, to make your voice to be heard on high," he had said. "Is it such a fast that I have chosen?" the Lord Jehovah asked of his people.

And that they might know the standards attending the true law of the fast, Jehovah had said to them: "Is not this the fast that I have chosen? to loose the bands of wickedness, to undo the heavy burdens, and to let the oppressed go free, and that ye break every yoke? Is it not to deal thy bread to the hungry, and that thou bring the poor that are cast out to thy house? when thou seest the naked, that thou cover him; and that thou hide not thyself from thine own flesh?" (Isa. 58.) How far removed the Pharisaic fasts were from these standards is clear to all who have studied the gospel accounts.

How apt, then, was Jesus' reply to John's disciples, disciples who were devout, who had been properly baptized, and who should now be following Jesus rather than John, as John himself had taught them. "Can the children of the bridechamber fast, while the bridegroom is with them?" he asked. His answer: "As long as they have the bridegroom with them, they cannot fast." Jesus, the Bridegroom, is with them; why should they mourn or fast? Is it not, rather, a time to rejoice? And are not Jesus' words a needed reminder and a gentle rebuke to John's disciples? Do they not remember that John himself—knowing that Jesus baptized more disciples than did the Baptist—had said that he, John, was the friend of the Bridegroom, whose joy was full because he heard the Bridegroom's voice? Have they forgotten that John testified that he must decrease while the Bridegroom increased? Why then—and this is the rebuke, if such there be in Jesus' reply—why then did not John's disciples forsake the imprisoned Baptist and follow the One whose way their master had prepared?

Then, with seeric insight—seeing what was to be more than two years hence; seeing what would be when one without sin hung on a cross between two sinners—Jesus said: "But the days will come, when the bridegroom shall be taken away from them, and then shall they fast in those days." But their fast will not be to smite with the fist of wickedness, but, rather, to draw near unto that Lord who has gone, for a moment, from them, but who will return in power and great glory at the appointed time.

At this point, the Pharisees interjected themselves again into the discussion. Knowing that John—who fasted as they did, and who to that extent was a man who followed their system—had baptized for the remission of sins, they assayed to make themselves the equal or superior of John by asking: "Why will ye not receive us with our baptism, seeing we keep the whole law?" They did all that John did, as they supposed, and they did more; they had *all* the rites and ordinances and performances and rituals handed down from Moses of old; and they kept them, so they thought.

"But Jesus said unto them, Ye keep not the law. If ye had kept the law, ye would have received me, for I am he who gave the law." No man can truly keep the law of Moses without believing in Christ, for that was the whole intent and purpose and design of the law. Jehovah gave it to help his people believe in the Messiah who was to come, who would, as the Lamb of God, sacrifice himself for the sins of the world. Men may go through the rites and performances of the law; they may exalt its letter and kill its spirit; they may think they keep the law of Moses—but they do not and cannot unless and until they know that all that they are doing centers in Christ and that he is the Savior. In that event they would receive him when he comes, for he is the Lord Jehovah who gave the law. How pointedly and expressly, without reservation or qualification, over and over again, the Lord Jesus testifies of his Messiahship!

"I receive not you with your baptism, because it profiteth you nothing," he continues. "For when that which is new is come, the old is ready to be put away." 'I have come with the new order; all old covenants have I caused to be done away; the new baptism of John and the baptism which I perform is a new and an everlasting covenant, even that which was from the beginning. Your baptism profiteth nothing because it is now performed without authority; John is the legal administrator of your dying dispensation. Though you should be baptized an hundred times, it availeth you nothing, for you cannot enter in at the strait gate by the law of Moses, neither by your dead works. When the new law comes the old law leaves. When the gospel, which was from the beginning, is restored, the law of Moses is fulfilled. It is because your works are dead works that I am bringing a new covenant. I am come to build up my church as in days of old, for my church has been on earth, from time to time, even before Moses. Wherefore, enter ye in at the gate, as I have commanded, and seek not to counsel your God.'

These things spoke Jesus in plainness. Then he added this parable: "No man putteth a piece of a new garment upon an old; if otherwise, then both the new maketh a rent, and the piece that was taken out of the new agreeth not with the old. And no man putteth new wine into old bottles; else the new wine will burst the bottles, and be spilled, and the bottles shall perish. But new wine must be put into new bottles; and both are preserved."

"What, new baptism in an old church, new revelation in a dying kingdom, new doctrine in an apostate organization! Could Jesus add Christian ordinances, with their spirit and power, to the dead formalism and ritual of the Mosaic procedures? Could new wine be put in old bottles (animal skins used as containers) without breaking the bottles and losing both the old and the new?" (*Commentary* 1:186.)[3] Jesus came to restore, not just to reform. His mission was to fulfill the old order and commence the new; he came to tramp out the dying embers of Mosaic performances and ignite the living flames of the gospel fire in the hearts of men.

We suppose that Jesus now said something more to John's disciples about their obligation to leave the dead past and come to the living present; yet he spoke to them with more tenderness and compassion than he did to the Pharisees, for John's followers were in process of preparing themselves to receive the One of whom John had testified. "No man also having drunk old wine straightway desireth new," Jesus said to them, "for he saith, The old is better." That is: 'In following John, who was sent of my Father to prepare the way before me, you have conformed to the law of Moses. Now, however, a greater than Moses is here, even the Messiah, and as John taught, you must now follow him, even though it is difficult for you to "straightway" turn from your old teachings and accept the new.' (*Commentary* 1:186.)

Thus Jesus called a lowly publican to a station of apostolic excellence; thus he taught that he came to call sinners to repentance; thus he rejected Pharisaic baptisms and claims of righteousness-born-of-the-law; thus he invited John's disciples to complete their conversion and follow him; and thus he testified that as the Messiah he had come to restore the gospel and build the city of salvation on a new foundation, not within the crumbling walls of an ancient order whose sun had set.

NOTES

1. This is a revelation given to the Prophet Joseph Smith in April 1830, just after the organization of The Church of Jesus Christ of Latter-day Saints. Some persons who had already been baptized in the sectarian churches of the day desired to enter the newly established church and kingdom of God on earth without rebaptism. This is the Lord's answer to them. The new kingdom was being established, "even as in days of old," and the same principles as applied then were still in force. There must be new revelation, new divine authority, new officers, just as it was when Jesus came to replace the old Mosaic order in his day.

2. "Private fasts would, of course, depend on individuals, but the strict Pharisees were wont to fast every Monday and Thursday during the weeks intervening between the Passover and Pentecost, and again, between the Feast of Tabernacles and that of the Dedication of the Temple. It is to this practice that the Pharisee in the parable refers [Luke 18:12] when boasting: 'I fast twice in the week.' " (Edersheim, *The Temple,* pp. 197-98.)

3. "He told them, in words of yet deeper significance, though expressed, as so often, in the homeliest metaphors, that his religion is, as it were, a robe entirely new, not a patch of unteazled cloth upon an old robe, serving only to make worse its original rents; that it is not new wine, put in all its fresh fermenting, expansive strength, into old and worn wineskins, and so serving only to burst the wine-skins and be lost, but *new* wine in *fresh* wineskins. The new spirit was to be embodied in wholly renovated forms; the new freedom was to be untrammelled by obsolete and long meaningless limitations; the spiritual doctrine was to be sundered for ever from the elaborate externalism of cancelled ordinances." (Farrar, p. 267.)

Chapter 38

THE SECOND PASSOVER OF JESUS' MINISTRY

My Father worketh hitherto, and I work. . . .
God was his Father. . . .
The Father loveth the Son. . . .
All men should honour the Son,
even as they honour the Father. . . .
The Father hath . . . given to the Son to have life
in himself. . . . the Father hath sent me. . . .
I am come in my Father's name.
(John 5:1-47.)[1]

Jesus Heals a Man on the Sabbath
(John 5:1-16; JST, John 5:3, 6, 9)

We are with Jesus in Jerusalem. It is Passover time, the second such feast of his ministry, and his disciples are with him, for they, like he, are under obligation, imposed by Jehovah, to appear three times each year before the Lord in the temple. Our Gospel author, John in this case, does not name the feast, and many volumes have been written to sustain one view or another as to what feast it is.

And we repeat that no one is able to make a harmony of the Gospels or to list chronologically the events of Jesus' life.

Matthew, Mark, Luke, and John did not do it, and the accounts they have left us do not agree among themselves. Every reputable scholar who has made an independent study of the issues involved has found himself at loggerheads, in large or small part, with every other analyst. In this present work we are following—primarily but not entirely—the chronology of President J. Reuben Clark, Jr., who often disagrees with Elder James E. Talmage, just as Edersheim does with Farrar, or as Mark does with Luke, or as every independent analyst does with some or all of his fellows. Choices must be made; every writer must make his own, and it is doubtful if any author—nay, it is a surety that no author—has made right choices in all cases.

As to the present feast, suffice it to say that it fits as well into the chronology here as elsewhere, and it is logical to assume that Jesus—as yet not subject to the total harassment of scribes, Pharisees, and Sanhedrinists—would appear again in the Passover crowds to make the doctrinal declarations relative to him and his Father that we are about to hear.

It is the Sabbath, that holy day when servile work ceases and the children of Jehovah—those who have become his sons and his daughters through the waters of baptism—assemble to worship the Lord and renew their covenants. But worship of the Father, in spirit and in truth, is almost a thing of the past among them. Those who use the sacred Sabbath to gain spiritual refreshment are few in number. In the true and eternal sense, the Sabbath is universally desecrated among them through disuse, through failure to use it as a day for confessing their sins in the holy convocations, and through neglecting to partake of the spiritual food prepared on that day, by a gracious God, to give to all those who hunger and thirst after righteousness.

But oh, how the rigid religious formalists have compensated for their Sabbath failures and desecrations! In place of the holy and hallowed day that should have been, theirs is a Sabbath of ritualistic restrictions that defy sense and mock reason. The absurdities of Sabbath observance—shall we call it a temporal observance that replaced the spiritual worship that should have been?—these absurdities, referred to in chapter 11 herein, all were assumed to center in the decree of Deity: "In it thou shalt not do any work." (Ex. 20:10.) This was something the scribes and Pharisees could get their teeth into. Worship in spirit and in truth might be beyond their spiritual capacity, for the things of God are known only by the power of the Spirit, but carrying no burden on the Sabbath day—that was another matter. Burdens could be seen and weighed and defined and anathematized. If a man picked up sticks on the Sabbath, he could be stoned. If he carried his couch of affliction, he could be damned. Man was made for the Sabbath, and for the Sabbath he must live. This was what set the Jews apart from all mankind, and so set apart they would remain; or, at least such was what they assumed and how they felt.

And so on this particular Passover Sabbath, we see Jesus near the sheep market, at the side of the pool Bethesda, which means "House of Mercy." By this pool—evidently a mineral spring of some sort whose waters bubbled intermittently as escaping gases broke the surface—there stands a large structure with five porches. "In these lay a great many impotent folk," some blind, others halt, paralytic, or withered, all "waiting for the moving of the water." No doubt these waters had—as hot mineral springs do in our day—some curative and healing powers, which gave rise to a legend, among the superstitious and spiritually illiterate Jews, that "an angel went down at a certain season into the pool, and troubled the water," and that "whosoever then first after the troubling of the water stepped in was made whole of whatsoever disease he had."

On a pallet on one of the porches lies an impotent man, lame with paralysis, who has so suffered for thirty-eight years, almost as long as the whole history of Israel from the going through of the Red Sea to the crossing of Jordan. Jesus sees the paralytic sufferer, knows how long he has been thus, and picks him out from all the rest—for reasons best known to himself, but unquestionably involving the man's faith and spiritual stature—as the object of his divine healing power. With a heart full of compassion, our Galilean Friend asks: "Wilt thou be made whole?"

Not knowing the source of the inquiry; unaware that it was the Son of God who spoke; not realizing that the questioning voice came from Him who had cleansed lepers, cast out devils, and healed all manner of diseases, the impotent man answered: "Sir, I have no man, when the water is troubled, to put me into the pool: but while I am coming, another steppeth down before me."

Without more ado, Jesus says: "Rise, take up thy bed, and walk." "It was spoken in an accent that none could disobey. The manner of the Speaker, His voice, His mandate, thrilled like an electric spark through the withered limbs and the shattered constitution, enfeebled by a lifetime of suffering and sin. After thirty-eight years of prostration, the man instantly rose, lifted up his pallet, and began to walk. In glad amazement he looked round to see and to thank his unknown benefactor; but the crowd was large, and Jesus, anxious to escape the unspiritual excitement which would fain have regarded him as a thaumaturge alone, had quietly slipped away from observation." (Farrar, p. 286.)

A miracle is thus wrought, such a one as is seldom seen. After thirty-eight years of paralytic impotence, a man known to have spent long hours on a pallet in the porches by the pool of Bethesda—desiring and hoping and praying to be healed—in an instant arises; full strength comes into his whole body; he walks—yea, more: he carries his bed. He is seen by the multitude, many of whom no doubt rejoice with him at the new vigor and vitality exuding from every pore of his once pain-ridden flesh.

But what do the leaders of Jewry see? Is it a wondrous work of manifest goodness? No, not in any manner of speaking. What they see is a man, unlearned and ignorant in the niceties of their legalistic restrictions attending Sabbath life, desecrating that holy day, as they suppose, by bearing a burden thereon. "It is the sabbath day," thunders the Pharisaic voice, "it is not lawful for thee to carry thy bed." 'Let it lie in the street; discard it; sit thou here until the morrow; no matter the inconvenience—but carry this bed of straw, this blanket, upon which you are wont to lie, never!'

And their words, spoken not so much against the healed one as against the One who healed, shall testify forever, before the judgment bar, of the degeneracy and baseness of their religion. How awful it is when true religion sinks into superstition; when the witch hunters in search of heresy find it—not in a departure from the ancient doctrinal moorings, but in the breaking of their own petty formalisms.

In reply, rejoicing in his newfound health, the packer of the pallet says: "He that made me whole"—he who wrought this wondrous miracle; he who is a great prophet and has such wondrous power with God that at his word I walk—"the same said unto me, Take up thy bed, and walk." 'Come, rejoice with me, for a great miracle has been wrought.'

But they, as part of their inquisitorial machinations, pried still further: "What man is that which said unto thee, Take up thy bed, and walk?" Not: 'Who has worked this miracle? Who has such power with God? What mighty prophet is in our midst? Is he not the Messiah; or, will he not lead us to the Deliverer?' No; nothing of this sort; only— 'Who hath counseled thee to break the Sabbath, for which offense our law says a man is worthy of death.'

Strangely, at the moment, the healed one knew not who his benefactor was. Only after Jesus found him in the temple later—we suppose worshipping and thanking the Lord for his new health—did the man from Bethesda's porches learn the source of his blessing. Jesus then said to him, "Behold, thou art made whole: sin no more, lest a worse thing come unto thee"—not meaning to teach that disease and affliction are always the result of sin, only that in this case the man had disobeyed some law that caused his affliction of long standing to imprison his body.

Thereafter the man told the Jews it was Jesus who had healed him—not, we assume, out of any malice toward the Master, but in the hope that the name of Jesus would be revered for the good deed he had done. After all, it was Jesus who selected, from among many blind and halt and withered and diseased persons, the single one to be healed; and surely he would have chosen the one whose spiritual worth caused him to merit the blessing. And it is not too much to suppose that the man and others whom he could influence joined the Church and were true to all subsequent trusts.

At this point in his account, John tells us: "Therefore did the Jews persecute Jesus, and sought to slay him, because he had done these things on the sabbath day."

What had he done? He had spoken a few words—perhaps a dozen in all—which in itself was certainly no more work than the long sermons delivered each Sabbath in the synagogues by the Rabbis. What work had Jesus done, unless the fact of healing itself was to be construed as work because divine power was exercised to change the body of the afflicted person?

The Sabbath healing of the impotent man clearly was an excuse, not a reason, for the forthcoming persecution. When men thirst for the blood of the prophets, it is not because of a reasoned judgment, arrived at by judicial deliberations. Persecution is carried out under the spell of emotion and hatred. And the voice of emotion on this day is crying: 'Here is the Son of God. Satan knows it, and he is our master. We must rid the nation of this menace at all costs; he will destroy our craft. Slay him. Crucify him. His blood be upon us and our children.'

Jesus Proclaims His Divine Sonship
(John 5:17-24)

What answer will Jesus give to the charge—absurd and unrealistic as it is—that he, the Lord of the Sabbath, has violated his own holy day by working thereon? In fact, he has carried no burden nor performed any servile service; he has not even overstepped any of the rigid rabbinic restrictions, not so much as the lifting of a finger on that day when men must cease from their labors. If it is a Sabbath violation to exercise the power of faith—and such is done by words and mental exertion only; if he is an accessory to the offense of another in that he said, "Take up thy bed, and walk," thus defying the scribal code of Sabbath formalisms, then, yes, he is showing contempt for the legalisms of the lawyers and the prohibitions of the doctors.

But, no matter, his concern is not to debate Sabbath rules. He has healed a man and gained a congregation of hearers; now he will bear to them a testimony that will open or close the door of salvation, depending upon its acceptance or rejection. For the purposes at hand, we will assume, as he himself seems to have done, that he has worked on that day when no work is to be done. To the charges of the Jewish leaders that he has violated their Sabbath, he says: "My Father worketh hitherto, and I work."

'True, this is the Sabbath; true, I have worked on this holy day. I have spoken healing words; and my Father, who is God, has done the work—it is his power by which the impotent man is healed. I have worked on the Sabbath, and my Father has worked on the Sabbath; is it not proper to do the Lord's work on the Lord's day? There is an eternal and unending law of work that is greater than the Sabbath. My Father and I both work everlastingly; our creative and redemptive labors go on forever for innumerable hosts on worlds without number. Why should the mere healing of one suffering soul cause such consternation among you?'

There was no misunderstanding on anyone's part as to this bold proclamation. Jesus is admitting Sabbath disobedience and adding blasphemy (as they suppose) to his arraignable offenses. "Therefore the Jews sought the more to kill him, because he not only had broken the sabbath, but said also that God was his Father, making himself equal with God."

"Equal with God!"—awful blasphemy or awesome truth!—one or the other. There is no middle ground, no room for compromise; there are no principles to compose: either Jesus is divine or he is blaspheming!

"Equal with God!"—not, as yet, in the infinite and eternal sense, but in the sense of being one with him, of being his natural heir, destined to receive, inherit, and possess all that the Father hath.

"Equal with God!"—not that he was then reigning in glory and exaltation over all the works which their hands had made, but in the sense that he was God's Son, upon whom the Father had placed his own name and to whom he had given glory and honor and power.

Then in solemn tones came words of infinite import, words whose full meaning can only be understood by the power of the Spirit—and shall we not suppose that one of the purposes of the Bethesda healing was to gain a congregation and set the stage for such a heaven-inspired statement as this?—then came from the lips of Jesus, who had a perfect knowledge of his divine paternity, this proclamation:

"The Son can do nothing of himself" ('I am come in my Father's name; aside from him I have no power; it was his power that healed the impotent man; all that I do has his approval') "but what he seeth the Father do" ('and further, I do only what I have seen the Father do, for he has revealed all his doing to me; I have seen his works') "for what things soever he doeth, these also doeth the Son likewise" ('and I do what he does, he heals the sick and so do I; I tread in his tracks for I am his Son.')[2]

"For the Father loveth the Son" (because the Son obeys the Father) "and sheweth him all things that himself doeth" ('I have seen in vision all the works of the Father; I have seen what he did in ages past; what he does even now; and he has manifest to me his future works, even "all things that himself doeth') "and he will shew him greater works than these, that ye may marvel" ('and the Father will manifest, through me, greater works than the healing of the impotent

71

man, causing you to marvel that one who ministers among you can perform such infinite and eternal works').

Then Jesus alluded to these greater works which he would do in his Father's name—the atoning sacrifice, the resurrection, the very day of judgment itself—by saying: "For as the Father raiseth up the dead, and quickeneth them; even so the Son quickeneth whom he will." 'By the power of the Father all men shall come forth in immortality, but it is I who shall bring it to pass. It is I who shall call the dust from the graves to form again a habitation for the spirits of men; I shall quicken whom I will, when I will; by me the resurrection cometh; I am the Resurrection and the Life.'

"For the Father judgeth no man, but hath committed all judgment unto the Son." 'And when all men have passed from death to life, they shall stand before me—before the pleasing bar of the Great Jehovah—to be judged according to the deeds done in the flesh; for the Father hath committed all judgment into my hands. He, himself, judgeth no man; but my judgment shall be his judgment.'

And all this is to be "that all men should honour the Son, even as they honour the Father. He that honoureth not the Son honoureth not the Father which hath sent him." 'Beware therefore how ye treat me. Because I shall work out the infinite and eternal atonement; because I shall break the bands of death and gain the victory over the grave; because all men shall stand before me to be judged, you should honor me as you honor the Father, whose Son I am, and whose power makes all this possible. And if you do not honor me, you do not honor the Father, who you say is your God, because the Father hath sent me: I am his Son, and I do Only what he commands—all in his name and by his power.'[3]

Jesus' proclamation of his divine Sonship; his plain statements that God is his Father; his witness that he and his Father both work, he doing the Father's work here on earth; his acts and words that made him equal with God; his declarations that the Father had revealed all things to him, and that he of himself could do nothing; his assertion that the Father loved him; his doctrinal teachings that the resurrection itself comes because of him, and that he it is who shall judge all men; his command to men to honor him as they honor the Father, coupled with the decree that those who do not honor the Son do not honor the Father—all this leads to one glorious conclusion. It is: Salvation is in Christ. He is the One to whom we must look to gain eternal life. He is the Author and Finisher of our faith. He is our Redeemer, Savior, Lord, and King.

And so, having taught all that we have here recited, and no doubt much more to the same effect—for the Gospel authors only give extracts and digests of his numerous sayings—this blessed Lord Jesus then said: "He that heareth my word, and believeth on him that sent me, hath everlasting life, and shall not come into condemnation; but is passed from death unto life." 'He who believes and obeys my words, who believeth in me and my Father, shall have exaltation and shall not be damned; yea, such already have passed from spiritual death to spiritual life, for they have been born again.'

Jesus Saves the Living and the Dead
(John 5:25-30; JST, John 5:29-31)

We have heard such a sermon as seldom has been preached on earth or in heaven; our ears have caught the words spoken by the Son of God that he is the Savior of all men. Jesus has announced his divine Sonship and centered the whole plan of salvation in his person. All men who believe in him shall be saved; those who reject him shall be damned. But what of those who never hear a whisper of his name while they dwell as mortals? What of the nations and kingdoms of the past whose inhabitants never heard of Christ and the salvation that is in him? Is there no hope for those who have not been privileged to listen to a prophet's voice and hear the word of God?

73

Having assured the living that eternal life is theirs if they believe his word and live his law; having announced his status as the Judge of all, this Jesus, to whom nothing is impossible, enlarges the vision of all who will see and announces how even the dead can obtain an inheritance with him and his Father. "The hour is coming, and now is" (it is to be in this very age in which you live, he says), "when the dead shall hear the voice of the Son of God: and they that hear shall live." 'I shall preach the gospel to the dead, to those in the spirit prison; I shall visit them; they shall hear my voice; and those who believe and obey shall be saved. They shall be judged according to men in the flesh, but live according to God in the spirit. My Father is no respecter of persons; those who do not have opportunity to hear the word of truth in this life shall get it in an appointed time between death and the resurrection.'[4]

We suppose that our Lord's Jewish detractors by this time are completely overawed. How could it be otherwise, so comprehensive are the concepts of which he speaks, so infinite their application! But Jesus continues: "For as the Father hath life in himself; so hath he given to the Son to have life in himself." 'The Father is an immortal, exalted, resurrected being, who cannot die. He is the Creator of the lives of men. Life dwells in him independently; he has life in himself; all things live because of him. He is the source of life, and the one who upholds, preserves, and continues it. And he has given this same power to the Son; the Son inherits from the Father; an immortal Father passes on to his mortal Son the power of immortality; it comes as a natural inheritance.'

"And hath given him authority to execute judgment also," Jesus continues, "because he is the Son of man." Why will Jesus be the Judge of the living and the dead? Because he is the Son of Man of Holiness—the Son of an Immortal Man, a Holy Man, who is God—because he is the Son of God who has received the power to do all things, from his Father whose right it is to grant such infinite power.

Marvel not at this: for the hour is coming, in the which all that are in the graves shall hear his voice, And shall come forth; they who have done good, in the resurrection of the just; and they who have done evil, in the resurrection of the unjust. And shall all be judged of the Son of Man. For as I hear, I judge, and my judgment is just; For I can of mine own self do nothing; because I seek not mine own will, but the will of the Father who hath sent me.

Strong doctrine this! 'I, Jesus, shall call forth all that are in their graves, but every man in his own order. All shall live again; the resurrection is as universal as death; as all men die, through Adam, so all shall live again, through me. But some shall come forth in the resurrection of the just to receive eternal life; others shall come forth in the resurrection of the unjust to receive eternal damnation. All shall be judged by me and assigned their places in the realms that are prepared, and my judgment shall be just because I shall conform to the will of my Father who sent me.'[5]

Jesus Obeys the Divine Law of Witnesses
(John 5:31-47; JST, John 5:32-35, 37-39, 41, 46)

Seldom, if ever, has such plain and powerful and persuasive witness been borne of the divine Sonship of the Lord Jesus as has just fallen from his own lips. 'God is my Father; I am his Son; I am equal with him. I give eternal life to those who believe in me. Even the dead shall hear my voice and be judged by my law. I have life in myself and shall atone for the sins of the world. I shall open the graves of all men, call them forth in immortality, judge them, and assign them an inheritance in the worlds to be. I do the will of my Father who sent me, and all men should honor me as they honor my Father.'

Seldom, if ever, has so much been said in words as few as the Mortal Messiah is here saying to his own nation. The word has been given; the truth has been spoken; the testimony has been borne; and now—in the providences of the One who sent his Son to say these very things—the responsibility rests with the hearers to believe or disbelieve, to obey or disobey, to come unto Christ or continue in their "Gentile" ways.

How shall these Jews who hear his voice and see the wonders wrought by his hand—how shall they know if he has spoken the truth? Are they at liberty to consider him to be a confused babbler whose mind is deranged? Or an unfortunate soul possessed by demons who speak by his mouth? Or a sincere—though deluded and deceived—false prophet who speaks without divine approval? Are they bound to believe the words of this Galilean troublemaker who breaks their Sabbath and castigates their priests and scribes? Must they believe his message simply because he says it is so?

Jesus has delivered his message; a spirit of disbelief envelops the whole congregation of hearers. He has spoken by the power of the Spirit, but their souls have not been quickened by that same divine influence. Now he must tell them that pursuant to their own law—the divine law of witnesses given by Jehovah to their fathers—they must either accept his words or be damned. This law, as they well know, is that the Lord always sends his word by witnesses who testify of its truth and divinity; that one witness alone, though he speaks the truth, is not enough to bind his hearers; that two or more witnesses always unite their voices to make the divinely borne testimony binding on earth and sealed everlastingly in the heavens; and that, thus, in the mouth of two or three witnesses every word shall be established.[6]

> If I bear witness of myself, yet my witness is true. For I am not alone; there is another who bearest witness of me, and I know that the testimony which he giveth of me is true. Ye sent unto John, and he bare witness also unto the truth. And he received not his testimony of man, but of God, and ye yourselves say that he is a prophet, therefore ye ought to receive his testimony. These things I say that ye

might be saved. He was a burning and a shining light, and ye were willing for a season to rejoice in his light.

John and Jesus—missionary companions, as it were— both taught the same truths and bore the same witness. Jesus was not alone. There was another, the son of Zacharias, who received his own testimony from God, and who bore it, unequivocally, with fire and fervor, for he was a burning and shining light. There was nothing hidden or secret about John's witness. "Behold, the Lamb of God, which taketh away the sin of the world," he said. (John 1:29.) These very Jews had received John as a prophet. How then can they reject his testimony? And if that testimony was the same as Jesus bore, how can the words of Him of whom John testified be rejected? Jesus did not stand alone; John was his companion, and the Jews, by their own law, were bound to believe the message and accept the Messenger.

> *But I have a greater witness than the testimony of John; for the works which the Father hath given me to finish, the same works that I do, bear witness of me, that the Father hath sent me. And the Father himself who sent me, hath borne witness of me. And verily I testify unto you, that ye have never heard his voice at any time, nor seen his shape; For ye have not his word abiding in you; and him whom he hath sent, ye believe not.*

But there is more. The Father himself—that Holy Being whose shape they have not seen; that Holy Man who has a body of flesh and bones—has also borne witness of the Son. By his own voice, heard on the banks of Jordan, the Father had said, "This is my beloved Son, in whom I am well pleased. Hear ye him." (JST, Matt. 3:46.) By the power of the Holy Ghost, shed forth upon Anna and Simeon and Nathanael and Philip and a host of others, the Father had planted his witness of the divinity of his Son in receptive human hearts.

All these testimonies—borne by Jesus, by John, by the Father, by those upon whom the Holy Spirit rested, and by

77

the miracles that Jesus wrought—all were current and up to date; they were the living witnesses, borne by living persons, in the living present. To them Jesus now added all the testimonies and all the witnesses found in holy writ.

Search the scriptures; for in them ye think ye have eternal life: and they are they which testify of me.[7]

That is to say: 'Ye think ye shall inherit eternal life because of Moses and his law, but search the scriptures and learn that they testify of me and the salvation which I bring. I am the Messiah. Learn what is said about me in the Psalms and the prophets; know that all the prophets spoke of me and my ministry.'[8]

Prejudice and passion and pettiness, these three—born of unreasoning emotion—are the things that destroy men's souls. "And ye will not come to me that ye might have life, lest ye should honor me," Jesus said.

'Lest ye should honor me!' How petty; how childish; how unworthy of the seed of Abraham! Forsake salvation rather than rise above the emotional prejudices that say: 'A Galilean Carpenter cannot be the Son of God. Everyone knows he is Joseph's son; and further, no good thing cometh out of Galilee.'

"I receive not honour from men." 'Think not that ye can honor me; who among you can add to what my Father has already given me? What wealth can you give to the One whose all things are? What degrees can you confer that will add educational luster to the Author or Truth who knows all things by the power of the Spirit? What political power or influence can men add to him who already sways the universe by his voice?'

"But I know you, that ye have not the love of God in you." Jesus knew their hearts; also, they had not the love of God in them, because they did not love his Son. 'He that loveth the Father loveth also the Son; none love either the Father or the Son unless they keep their commandments.'

"I am come in my Father's name, and ye receive me not: if another shall come in his own name, him ye will receive."

Jesus bears his Father's name and is empowered, thus, to speak in the first person as though he were the Father.[9] Carnal men who come in their own name, having no divine message to deliver, find ready acceptance from other carnal men.

"How can ye believe, which receive honour one of another, and seek not the honour that cometh from God only?" A desire to know the truth precedes a testimony. Men must seek the honors—revelations, visions, companionship of the Holy Spirit, and the like—which it is the Father's good pleasure to confer; otherwise such are not obtained. As long as men's hearts are centered on the things of the world and the honors of men, they never seek the blessings of eternity with that fervor and devotion which leads to the receipt of spiritual gifts. What greater honor can a man receive than that which comes from God? Is it not glory and honor in the celestial kingdom that all true believers seek?

Do not think that I will accuse you to the Father; there is Moses who accuseth you, in whom ye trust. For had ye believed Moses, ye would have believed me: for he wrote of me. But if ye believe not his writings, how shall ye believe my words?

The Lord and his prophets are one, and no one can believe in Christ and reject his prophets. "Believe in Christ and deny him not," Nephi said, "for by denying him ye also deny the prophets and the law." (2 Ne. 25:28.) And those who truly believe the words of the prophets believe also in Christ, for it is he of whom all the prophets testify.[10]

And all these things spake Jesus in Jerusalem, at the Feast of the Passover, after he healed the impotent man at the pool of Bethesda; and many other things did he say that bore witness that he is the Son of God by whom salvation comes, and that all men must come unto him and worship the Father in his name if they are to gain eternal life and sit down with Abraham, Isaac, and Jacob in the kingdom of God.

NOTES

1. The views of the modern religious-atheists—who profess to believe in Christ but say he never personally claimed to be divine—to the contrary notwithstanding, we find Jesus, everywhere and always, as in this case, attesting to the personal relationship between him and the great Elohim.

2. The great concept set forth in John 5:19-20 is beyond human comprehension. It is the doctrine that "Jesus is the replica of his Father—thinking, saying, doing, achieving, attaining, as the Father has done before." (*Commentary* 1:191.) That all of this is infinite in scope and universal in application is seen from the Prophet Joseph Smith's Spirit-guided utterances in the King Follett sermon. "It is the first principle of the Gospel to know for a certainty the Character of God," the Prophet said, "and to know that we may converse with him as one man converses with another, and that he was once a man like us; yea, that God himself, the Father of us all, dwelt on an earth, the same as Jesus Christ himself did; and I will show it from the Bible. . . .

"What did Jesus say? . . .The Scriptures inform us that Jesus said, As the Father hath power in Himself, even so hath the Son power—to do what? Why, what the Father did. The answer is obvious—in a manner to lay down His body and take it up again. Jesus, what are you going to do? To lay down my life as my Father did, and take it up again. Do we believe it? If you do not believe it, you do not believe the Bible. . . .

"What did Jesus do? Why; I do the things I saw my Father do when worlds came rolling into existence. My Father worked out his kingdom with fear and trembling, and I must do the same; and when I get my kingdom, I shall present it to my Father, so that he may obtain kingdom upon kingdom, and it will exalt him in glory. He will then take a higher exaltation, and I will take his place, and thereby become exalted myself. So that Jesus treads in the tracks of his Father, and inherits what God did before; and God is thus glorified and exalted in the salvation and exaltation of all his children. It is plain beyond disputation, and you thus learn some of the first principles of the Gospel, about which so much hath been said." (*Teachings of the Prophet Joseph Smith*, pp. 345-48.)

3. "Two exalted personages, the Father and the Son, are one—one in purpose, plan, and power; one as to character, perfections, and attributes; one in all things; and therefore one in the receipt of worship and honor. In the true sense no one can believe in or know the one without having the same belief and knowledge of the other; nor can one be accepted and the other rejected. They are one." (*Commentary* 1:192-93.)

4. This visit of the Messiah to the spirits in prison—which occurred while his body lay in the Arimathean's tomb—was one in which he preached the gospel, organized his church, and sent forth his representatives to teach the truths of salvation to the hosts of the dead. There is scarcely a more glorious doctrine than that of salvation for the dead. All those who die without a knowledge of the gospel, who would have received it with all their hearts, shall receive it in the spirit world, and, having obeyed its laws, shall be heirs of full salvation. In reality, " 'God is not the God of the dead, but of the living' (Matt. 22:32), for all live unto him; all are alive in his eyes, whether their spirits are temporarily housed in mortal tabernacles or imprisoned in the spirit sphere awaiting the day of the resurrection. And the salvation of all men—living or dead (as men count death)—is centered in and comes because of the Son." (*Commentary* 1:193.)

5. "John 5:29 is the verse Joseph Smith and Sidney Rigdon were studying and pondering—in the course of their work on the Inspired Version of the Bible—when the eyes of their understanding were opened and they received the vision of the degrees of glory (D&C 76). This vision and other revelations teach that "salvation grows automatically out of the resurrection, and the coming forth in the resurrection constitutes the receipt of whatever degree of salvation has been earned. By one degree of obedience or another, all men, in this life, develop either celestial, terrestrial, or telestial bodies (or in the case of those destined to be sons of perdition, bodies of a baser sort). In the resurrection all men receive back again 'the same body which was a natural body,' whether it be celestial, terrestrial, or what have you. That body is then quickened by the glory attending its particular type, and the person receiving the body then goes automatically, as it were, to the kingdom

of glory where that degree of glory is found. (D&C 76; 88: 16-33; 1 Cor. 15:35-38; *Mormon Doctrine*, pp. 573-579.)" (*Commentary* 1:196.)

6. 2 Cor. 13:1; Deut. 17:6; 19:15; Matt. 18:15-16; John 8:12-29.

7. "Man's hope of gaining salvation is in direct proportion to his knowledge of God and the laws of salvation. No man can be saved in ignorance of Jesus Christ and the laws of the gospel. Man is saved no faster than he gains knowledge of God and the saving truths recorded in the scriptures. A fountain cannot rise above its source; a people cannot live laws of which they are ignorant, nor believe in a Christ about whom they know little or nothing. The Lord expects his people to learn the doctrines of salvation. 'Search these commandments' (D&C 1:37), is a decree which applies in principle to all revelations of all ages." (*Commentary* 1:201.)

8. "Who bears testimony that Jesus is indeed the Christ?

"(1) Jesus himself, repeatedly, bluntly, plainly, over and over again testified of his own divine Sonship;

"(2) His Father, by his own voice out of heaven, by personally coming to earth to introduce the Son, and by sending the Holy Ghost to speak to the spirits of the contrite;

"(3) The Holy Ghost, the Spirit member of the Godhead, whose mission is to bear record of the Father and the Son;

"(4) The works performed by Jesus in his mortal ministry, including his miracles, teachings, resurrection, and atoning sacrifice which made immortality and eternal life a reality;

"(5) Prophets and apostles of all ages—Moses, John, Peter, Nephi, Joseph Smith, the elders of Israel, a great host which no man can number; and

"(6) The scriptures and recorded revelations of the past and present." (*Commentary* 1:198-99.)

9. It is on this basis—that of divine investiture of authority—that some scriptures call Christ the Father. Other passages call him the Father in the sense of Creator or of being the Father of those—born again as they are—who believe the gospel. See *Mormon Doctrine*, 2nd ed., p. 130.

10. "Though the Jews trusted in Moses, they were damned for rejecting the great lawgiver's testimony concerning the Messiah. Similarly, though modern sectarians trust in Peter, falsely supposing they believe what that ancient apostle taught, they shall be damned for refusing to accept Peter's testimony about the restoration of all things in the last days. (Acts 3:19-21.) In the same sense that Moses stands as the accuser of the Jews, so Peter, James, and John and the apostles of old will stand as the accusers of an apostate Christendom. . . . Similarly, if men today believed in Christ and the apostles of old, they also would believe in Joseph Smith, the Book of Mormon, and the restoration of the gospel. (*Mormon Doctrine*, pp. 75-77.)" (*Commentary* 1:202.)

Chapter 39

JESUS: "LORD ... OF THE SABBATH"

Thus saith the Lord; Take heed
to yourselves, and bear no burden
on the sabbath day, nor bring it in
by the gates of Jerusalem;
Neither carry forth a burden
out of your houses on the sabbath day,
neither do ye any work,
but hallow ye the sabbath day,
as I commanded your fathers. . . .
And it shall come to pass,
if ye diligently hearken unto me,
saith the Lord, to bring in
no burden through the gates
of this city on the sabbath day,
but hallow the sabbath day,
to do no work therein;
Then shall there enter into the gates
of this city kings and princes
sitting upon the throne of David,
riding in chariots and on horses,

they, and their princes,
the men of Judah, and the inhabitants
of Jerusalem: and this city
shall remain for ever. . . .
But if ye will not hearken unto me
to hallow the sabbath day,
and not to bear a burden, even entering
in at the gates of Jerusalem
on the sabbath day; then will I kindle
a fire in the gates thereof,
and it shall devour the palaces
of Jerusalem, and it shall not
be quenched. (Jer. 17:21-27.)[1]

"The Sabbath Was Made for Man"
(Matthew 12:1-8; JST, Matthew 12:4; Mark 2:23-28; JST, Mark 2:22, 26-27; Luke 6:1-5)

Jesus is back in Galilee with his disciples; the Passover is past; the little band has walked the wearisome miles from Jerusalem to the rugged hill country where he loved so much to be. Behind them in the capital of Jewry are the rulers of the people—the leading Rabbis, the scribes, the San-hedrinists—smarting under the rebukes received from Jesus at the Passover; debating the doctrines delivered in the Bethesda sermon; and stirring up animosity and hatred against him, both on the pretext of Sabbath desecration and because he made himself equal with God.

Again, here in Galilee, the Sabbath issue arises to plague Jesus and his disciples and to hinder the spread of truth. 'How can this man be a true prophet if he and those who follow him violate our sacred Sabbath laws? Many among our fathers laid down their lives rather than raise the sword, even in self-defense, on the Sabbath. If a man breaks our laws, defies our traditions, desecrates our holy day, how can he be a leader, a light, or a guide among us?' So went their reasoning. No matter that he went about doing good and working miracles! This matter of Sabbath observance was of overriding import; it took precedence over all else; had not the scribes and Pharisees so ordained?[2]

Thus we see Jesus and his friends walking "through the corn fields on the sabbath day." They are hungry; his disciples pluck the ears of corn, rub them in their hands, and eat the grains of barley. In Palestine the barley harvest begins immediately after the Passover. Jesus himself makes no attempt to satisfy his own hunger; only the disciples are engaged in the act, which on any other day would have been proper in the Pharisaic eye. "When thou comest into the standing corn of thy neighbour, then thou mayest pluck the ears with thine hand; but thou shalt not move a sickle unto thy neighbour's standing corn." (Deut. 23:25.) It was the divine intent that any in Israel—for they were all brethren, and all things were the Lord's—might freely satisfy his hunger by eating his neighbor's grain.

By this one Sabbath-performed act, our Lord's fellow travelers were guilty of two violations, not of biblical, but of Rabbinic law. They had both reaped and harvested. The plucking of the ears of corn constituted reaping, and the rubbing off of the husks fell under the sabbatical prohibition against sifting in a sieve, threshing, sifting out fruit, grinding, or fanning. Each of these sins merited punishment and required a sin offering on the great altar in the house of the Lord in Jerusalem.

Spying eyes—viewing, we suppose, with prosecutorial pleasure—observed the two sins, which they could argue were capital offenses. Perhaps these peering Pharisees were following to see if the disciples of the New Order would walk more than the two thousand cubits allowed by the Rabbinic restrictions on the Sabbath day; perhaps they hoped to witness the sins of harvesting and threshing. Seeing what they did, they complained to Jesus: "Thy disciples do that which is not lawful to do upon the sabbath day."

The charge was lodged, not against Jesus, but against his

friends. When they had accused him of violating the Sabbath by healing the impotent man at Bethesda, he admitted the charge and testified that both he and his Father worked on that day, and that without God's approval he could not have commanded the man, who for thirty-eight years had taken no step and lifted no burden, to arise, carry his couch, and walk. But this time his response was one of defense and vindication. His disciples had done no wrong, he said. Even by their own traditions Sabbath observance was superseded by a higher law in proper cases.

"Have ye not read so much as this"—'with all your learning has it not come to your attention'—"what David did, when himself was an hungered, and they which were with him; How he went into the house of God, and did take and eat the shewbread, and gave also to them that were with him; which it is not lawful to eat but for the priests alone?" 'Surely even you know'—is there not a touch of irony here?—'even you know that your law calls for men to eat on the Sabbath, and that danger to life and being on the Lord's errand supersede the Sabbath law. Since David was guiltless in taking the very Bread of the Presence from off the holy table, think ye that my disciples will be condemned for rubbing a few grains of barley in their hands to make them more palatable?'

And further: "Have ye not read in the law, how that on the Sabbath days the priests in the temple profane the Sabbath, and [even] ye say they are blameless?" 'Do not the priests labor for many hours in offering sacrifices on the Sabbath day? And yet ye yourselves say they are blameless.' "But I say unto you, That in this place is one greater than the temple." 'As the priests who serve in the temple are blameless because their labors on the Sabbath day are for the salvation of men, so are my disciples, who serve me, blameless, for I am the Living Temple, through whom salvation comes.'

"If their own Rabbis had laid it down that there was 'no Sabbatism in the Temple;' that the priests on the Sabbath might hew the wood, and light the fires, and place hot fresh-baked shewbread on the table, and slay double victims, and circumcise children, and thus in every way violate the rules of the Sopherim about the Sabbath, and yet be blameless— nay, if in acting thus they were breaking the Sabbath at the bidding of the very Law which ordains the Sabbath—then if the Temple excuse *them,* ought not something greater than the Temple to excuse these? And there was something greater than the Temple here." (Farrar, pp. 336-37.)

"But if ye had known what this meaneth," Jesus continued, drawing his quotation from Hosea, "I will have mercy, and not sacrifice, ye would not have condemned the guiltless."

To ancient Israel—bound down with tradition; buried in formalism; following the letter and not the spirit of the law; not envisioning the meaning, nor the symbolism, nor the purport of their sacrifices—the Lord Jehovah, by the mouth of Hosea, proclaimed: "I desired mercy, and not sacrifice; and the knowledge of God more than burnt offerings." (Hosea 6:6.)

Micah, struggling to combat the same "form of godliness" that was devoid of the true spirit of worship, was even more severe in his denunciations—not, of course, of the true order of sacrifice, but of its perverted substitutes. A denunciation of false baptisms performed without authority is no condemnation of true ones done at the Lord's behest. "Wherewith shall I come before the Lord, and bow myself before the high God?" Micah asks. "Shall I come before him with burnt offerings, with calves of a year old? Will the Lord be pleased with thousands of rams, or with ten thousands of rivers of oil?" Is it sacrifices performed as an end in themselves that please him? "Shall I give my firstborn for my transgression, the fruit of my body for the sin of my soul?" he asks, alluding to the knowledge had by the ancients that the Firstborn of the Father, the fruit of the body of the great God, would be offered as a sacrifice for sin. "He hath shewed thee, O man, what is good; and what doth the Lord require of thee, but to do justly, and to love mercy, and to walk humbly with thy God?" (Micah 6:6-8.)

There is a higher law. Mercy is greater than sacrifice. The "letter," as it were, of sacrificial performances, or of Sabbath observance, or of tithe paying, or of keeping the Word of Wisdom, or of any act or performance, "killeth"; only the spirit giveth "life." Sabbath restrictions are not to be compared with Sabbath acts involving mercy and goodness and grace. The lesser law is superseded by the higher. "The Sabbath was expressly designed for mercy, and therefore not only might all acts of mercy be blamelessly performed thereon, but such acts would be more pleasing to God than all the insensate and self-satisfied scrupulosities which had turned a rich blessing into a burden and a snare." (Farrar, p. 337.)

"In truth, the reason why David was blameless in eating the shewbread was the same as that which made the Sabbath-labour of the priests lawful. The Sabbath-Law was not one merely of rest, but of rest for worship. The Service of the Lord was the object in view. The priests worked on the Sabbath, because this service was the object of the Sabbath; and David was allowed to eat of the shewbread, not because there was danger to life from starvation, but because he pleaded that he was on the service of the Lord and needed this provision. The disciples, when following the Lord, were similarly on the service of the Lord; ministering to Him was more than ministering in the Temple, for He was greater than the Temple. If the Pharisees had believed this, they would not have questioned their conduct, nor in so doing have themselves infringed that higher law which enjoined mercy, not sacrifice." (Edersheim 2:58.)

> Wherefore the Sabbath was given unto man for a day of rest; and also that man should glorify God, and not that man should not eat;
>
> For the Son of man made the Sabbath day, therefore the Son of man is Lord also of the Sabbath.

The Sabbath day—wondrous, glorious day! A day of

rest; a day of peace; a day of worship; a day to glorify God! The Sabbath day—a time to offer to the Lord the sacrifice of a broken heart and a contrite spirit; a time to pay our devotions to the Most High, to offer up our sacraments, and to confess our sins! "And on this day thou shalt do none other thing, only let thy food be prepared with singleness of heart that thy fasting may be perfect, or, in other words, that thy joy may be full." (D&C 59:13.)

"For the Son of man made the Sabbath day." 'I am the God of Israel, the great Jehovah, your Messiah, the one who made the Sabbath day, giving it to Moses on Sinai; therefore, I am Lord also of the Sabbath and can specify in my own name what constitutes proper Sabbath observance.' (*Commentary* 1:204-5.)

Thus, Jesus tied the Sabbath into his own divine Sonship. And we must know—as the scribes, Pharisees, and Sanhedrinists who opposed him knew—that by objecting to his Sabbath conduct, or that of his disciples, they were in fact objecting to his Messiahship.

Jesus Heals a Withered Hand on the Sabbath
(Matthew 12:9-15; JST, Matthew 12:13; Mark 3:1-6; Luke 6:6-11)

On yet another Galilean Sabbath, Jesus enters a synagogue, as is his wont, and teaches the people. Would that we knew what words he spoke! Spies are present. "Henceforth, at every turn and every period of His career—in the cornfields, in synagogues, in feasts, during journeys, at Capernaum, at Magdala, in Perea, at Bethany—we find Him dogged, watched, impeded, reproached, questioned, tempted, insulted, conspired against by these representatives of the leading authorities of His nation, of whom we are repeatedly told that they were not natives of the place, but 'certain which came from Jerusalem.'" (Farrar, p. 334.)

He has aforetime healed in synagogues on the Sabbath, and but recently has vindicated his disciples for harvesting and threshing a few grains of barley on that holy day. His enemies, however, at the direction of the Jewish leaders in Jerusalem, are building up a case against him. By the sheer weight of the evidence, by accumulating numerous instances of supposed wrongdoing, they seek to justify their murderous designs. Will he heal on this Sabbath as he has done on others?

There is in the synagogue a man with a withered hand, an underdeveloped hand, a hand without strength or facility, hanging on an arm and a wrist that may not have been wholly normal. Whether the man is there of his own accord to worship with his fellow Galileans, or was enticed to come as an unwitting dupe, that the guile-filled Pharisees might have aught with which to challenge the Master Healer, is not apparent. Perhaps it is the latter, for the Pharisees, "that they might accuse him," ask: "Is it lawful to heal on the sabbath days?"

This question, proposed by captious scribes and quarrelsome Pharisees, seems simple enough to us; but in their cultural and social circumstances it grew out of a maze of Rabbinic debate, uncertainty, and absurdity. Indeed: "So much unclearness prevails as to the Jewish views about healing on the Sabbath, that some connected information on the subject seems needful. We have already seen, that in their view only actual danger to life warranted a breach of the Sabbath-Law. But this opened a large field for discussion. Thus, according to some, disease of the ear, according to some throat-disease, while, according to others, such a disease as angina, involved danger, and superseded the Sabbath-Law. All applications to the outside of the body were forbidden on the Sabbath. As regarded internal remedies, such substances as were used in health, but had also a remedial effect, might be taken, although here also there was a way of evading the Law. A person suffering from toothache might not gargle his mouth with vinegar, but he might use an ordinary toothbrush and dip it in vinegar. The Gemara here adds, that gargling was lawful, if the substance was afterwards swallowed. It further explains, that affections extending from the lips, or else from the throat, inwards, may be attended to, being regarded as dangerous. Quite a number of these are enumerated, showing, that either the Rabbis were very lax in applying their canon about mortal diseases, or else that they reckoned in their number not a few which we would not regard as such. External lesions also might be attended to, if they involved danger to life. Similarly, medical aid might be called in, if a person had swallowed a piece of glass; a splinter might be removed from the eye, and even a thorn from the body." (Edersheim 2:59-60.)

But Jesus rises above the dust of Rabbinic battles; he is not concerned with their petty prohibitions, their childish rules, their endless debates. "What man shall there be among you," he asks, "that shall have one sheep, and if it fall into a pit on the sabbath day, will he not lay hold on it, and lift it out?" On this point also the Rabbinic debates raged; was it lawful to save the sheep, or not? In practice the people found ways of doing so. And so Jesus continues, "How much then is a man better than a sheep? Wherefore it is lawful to do well on the sabbath days."

At this point Jesus says to the man with the withered hand, "Stand forth," which he does. To the spies from Jerusalem, he rephrases their own tempting accusation: "Is it lawful to do good on the sabbath days, or to do evil? to save life, or to kill?" If their answer is affirmative, how can they condemn Jesus for Sabbath healings? If it is negative, they are condoning murder by neglect. They hold their peace and say nothing.

Then Jesus "looked round about on them with anger," his soul stirred with righteous indignation, he being "grieved for the hardness of their hearts," and he said to the man, "Stretch forth thine hand." The man obeyed, and his hand was restored; it became whole like unto the other one.

Among the Godfearing and the righteous such a miracle would have raised shouts of praise and thanksgiving that God dealt so graciously with suffering mortals. Not so among these enemies of Him who came down from heaven to heal men physically and to save them spiritually. Rather, "they were filled with madness" and took counsel with the hated Herodians—those half-apostate Jews who dealt traitorously toward their own people, and who stood for all that Roman tyranny imposed upon the chosen race—they took counsel with such misdirected recreants as to how they might destroy him. It was the ages-old scene of enemies forgetting their own differences and joining hands to fight the truth and Him who is its source.

While they held their council, planning how to destroy him, Jesus withdrew, leaving them to their own evil devices. His time had not yet come; much preaching lay ahead, and many miracles were yet to be wrought.

Some Gentiles Hear and Believe and Are Healed
(Matthew 12:15-21; Mark 3:7-12)

To what extent did Jesus preach and minister and heal among the Gentiles? Was the Holy One of Israel, while incarnate among men, destined to proclaim his message in other than Israelite ears?

As a general principle, we know from many passages that he was sent only to the lost sheep of the house of Israel; that during his lifetime he limited his preaching, and that of his disciples, to the members of the one chosen race; and that even after his resurrection, the other sheep whom he visited were Israelitish Nephites, not Gentiles whose blood lineage came from other than Abraham, Isaac, and Jacob. (See *Commentary* 1:207-9; 325; 488.)

There are, of course, many Old Testament prophecies, as Paul's writings so amply attest, that foretell the taking of the message of salvation to the Gentiles. One of these that is purely Messianic comes to us from the pen of Isaiah and contains these words: "Behold my servant, whom I uphold; mine elect, in whom my soul delighteth; I have put my spirit upon him: he shall bring forth judgment to the Gentiles. He shall not cry, nor lift up, nor cause his voice to be heard in the street. A bruised reed shall he not break, and the smoking flax shall he not quench: he shall bring forth judgment unto truth. He shall not fail nor be discouraged, till he have set judgment in the earth: and the isles shall wait for his law." (Isa. 42:1-4.)

Matthew sees in what Jesus now does at least a partial fulfillment of Isaiah's prophecy. While the Herodians and Pharisees sit in council devising ways and means to destroy him, Jesus departs, apparently into the Decapolis area, to continue his preaching and healing ministry among a more receptive people. And those to whom he goes are in large measure Gentiles. Mark tells us whence they came. He says multitudes came from Galilee, and from Judea, and from Jerusalem. In addition, multitudes came from Idumea, and from beyond Jordan, and from Tyre and Sidon—all areas measurably inhabited by Gentiles. Being on the shore of the Sea of Galilee, and because the throngs press upon him in such great numbers, seeking just to touch his person, Jesus has his disciples provide a small ship to remove him from the press of the people. Through it all he teaches much, heals many, and casts out numerous unclean spirits. Those by whose mouths unclean spirits spoke testified, "Thou art the Son of God," and Jesus charged them "that they should not make him known." As his custom was, he desired no witness from devils, only from those whose testimony came from on high.

It is to Matthew that we turn to learn the identity of many in the surging throngs. He tells us that all this happened in fulfillment of Isaiah's Messianic prophecy, which he quotes in a paraphrased or targumed form, concluding with the affirmation: "And in his name shall the Gentiles trust."

Truly, Jesus came to "shew judgment to the Gentiles" as well as to gather in the lost sheep of Israel. Though his great commission was not to raise his voice in Gentile ears nor to strive personally to bring them into the Israelite fold, yet as

Jew and Gentile mingled in the multitudes who sought his goodness, many Gentiles would believe and his healing power would bless them. Many of the bruised reeds who were weak in faith, and the smoking flax who were afflicted in body—whom Jesus taught and healed—were of Gentile blood. As Matthew testified, Jesus here labored with those outside the fold of Jacob, and his labors prefigured the great Gentile harvest that one day would sweep the world.

NOTES

1. It should come as no surprise to find that an apostate people, with this and numerous other Old Testament sabbatical injunctions before them—being devoid as they were of the Spirit of the Lord—had turned the worship of a holy being into the worship of what they esteemed to be a holy day. Jewish Sabbath observance in Jesus' day—founded upon and growing out of prophetic utterances, such as this one from Jeremiah—was not all bad; within it lay the potential of true worship; its fault came because of the quenching of the Spirit and the igniting of the fires of rigid formalism.

"The Judaism of that day substituted empty forms and meaningless ceremonies for true righteousness; it mistook uncharitable exclusiveness for genuine purity; it delighted to sun itself in the injustice of an imagined favouritism from which it would fain have shut out all God's other children; it was so profoundly hypocritical as not even to recognise its own hypocrisy; it never thought so well of itself as when it was crushing the broken reed and trampling out the last spark from the smoking flax; it thanked God for the demerits which it took for virtues, and fancied that He could be pleased with a service in which there was neither humility, nor truthfulness, nor loyalty, nor love." (Farrar, p. 330.)

2. See chapter 11 (Book I) for a brief summary of Jewish Sabbath practices. "The Sabbath was a Mosaic, nay, even a primeval institution, and it had become the most distinctive and the most passionately reverenced of all the ordinances which separated the Jews from the Gentiles as a peculiar people. It was at once the sign of their exclusive privileges, and the centre of their barren formalism. Their traditions, their patriotism, even their obstinacy, were all enlisted in its scrupulous maintenance. . . . They had suffered themselves on that day to lose battles, to be cut in pieces by their enemies, to see Jerusalem itself imperilled and captured. Its observance had been fenced round by the most painfully minute, the most ludicrously insignificant restrictions. . . . According to the pedantic school of Shammai, no one on the Sabbath might comfort the sick or enliven the sorrowful. Even the preservation of life was a breaking of the Sabbath; and, on the other hand, even to kill a flea was as bad as to kill a camel. Had not the command to 'do no manner of work upon the Sabbath day' been most absolute and most emphatic? had not Moses himself and all the congregation caused the son of Shelomith to be stoned to death for merely gathering sticks upon it? had not the Great Synagogue itself drawn up the thirty-nine *abhoth* [primary rules] and quite innumerable *toldoth* [derivative rules], or prohibitions of labours which violated it in the first or in the second degree?" (Farrar, pp. 330-32.)

SECTION V

THE TWELVE,
THE SERMON ON THE
MOUNT,
AND THE RISING
PHARISAIC OPPOSITION

THE TWELVE, THE SERMON ON THE MOUNT, AND RISING PHARISAIC OPPOSITION

Thou, O God, hast prepared
of thy goodness for the poor.
The Lord gave the word:
great was the company
of those that published it.
(Ps. 68:10-11.)

Jesus now calls unto him the Twelve—holy men; men of faith and valor; men who will serve and suffer and bleed and die for him—and upon them he confers the holy apostleship. From henceforth they shall be his special witnesses, to teach his doctrine and testify of his divine Sonship before all men.

To them—and to a great multitude—he preached the Sermon on the Mount. The Lord gave the word! Such a sermon as none but he could preach fell from his lips.

And great was the company of those that published it! Jesus, the Twelve, Mary Magdalene and other faithful women, a great host of disciples—all traveling through every city and village of Galilee—spread the word that salvation is in Christ and that all men must come unto him, repent of their sins, and keep his commandments, to gain peace in this world and eternal life in the world to come.

Jesus heals the son of a Gentile centurion, and accepts an anointing from a repentant sinner in Simon's house; he raises from death a widow's son near Nain; he acclaims John the Baptist as one than whom there is no greater prophet; and he casts a demon out of one who is deaf and blind, thus also opening his eyes and unstopping his ears.

Then the spies from the Sanhedrin launch their assaults anew. He is accused of being Satan incarnate, of casting out devils, and of performing miracles by the power of Beelzebub, the prince of devils.

He excoriates his adversaries; speaks of pardoning grace and the unpardonable sin; condemns those who seek signs, identifying them as adulterers; and extends the limits of his family to include all those who do the will of his Father who is in heaven.

The Lord gave the word! His preachers—a great and mighty host—did and do publish it to all men everywhere. It is the word of salvation, his everlasting gospel.

Chapter 40

JESUS CHOOSES THE TWELVE

Mine apostles, the Twelve,
which were with me in my ministry
at Jerusalem,
shall stand at my right hand
at the day of my coming
in a pillar of fire,
being clothed with robes
of righteousness,
with crowns upon their heads,
in glory even as I am. (D&C 29:12.)[1]

Apostles: Their Position and Powers

Jesus is now going to call the Twelve: twelve men who will be his witnesses; who will bear, with him, the burdens of the kingdom; who will accept martyrdom and defy the rulers of the world; and who, save Judas the traitor and John the Beloved, shall seal their testimonies with their own blood.

The day has arrived and the hour is at hand to build, on the foundation he has laid, that glorious structure: the Church and kingdom of God on earth. A year and a half has elapsed since he was baptized by John, since his formal ministry began. It is the summer of A.D. 28; in less than two years (April of A.D. 30) he will finish his mortal labors, ascend unto his Father, and leave the Twelve to preach the gospel in all the world and to build up that church and kingdom which will administer salvation to all who believe and obey.

Truly, "God hath set some in the church" to be living witnesses of the truth and divinity of the work; to regulate all the affairs of the kingdom; to serve, by their very presence, as conclusive proof that the Lord's hand is in his earthly work. Who and what identifies the true church? The Holy Book responds: "First apostles, secondarily prophets, thirdly teachers"—such is the divine order of priority— "after that miracles, then gifts of healings, helps, governments, diversities of tongues." (1 Cor. 12:28.)

Truly, the Lord has given "some, apostles; and some, prophets; and some, evangelists; and some, pastors and teachers; For the perfecting of the saints, for the work of the ministry, for the edifying of the body of Christ: Till we all come in the unity of the faith." These officers, as the Holy Book also records, are placed in the true church, "That we henceforth be no more children, tossed to and fro, and carried about with every wind of doctrine, by the sleight of men, and cunning craftiness, whereby they lie in wait to deceive." These agents of the Lord, "speaking the truth in love," guide and direct the Lord's affairs on earth. (Eph. 4:11-15.)

Truly, where there are apostles and prophets, called of God and endowed with power from on high, there is the true church and kingdom; and where these are not, there the Lord's work is not established among men. And so we come to that point in time when Jesus, setting up anew for his day and dispensation the organization designed to administer salvation to mortals, is prepared to call the Twelve.

Apostles of the Lord Jesus Christ—mighty men of faith; pillars of personal righteousness; chosen spirits who were before ordained to walk with Christ, teach his doctrine, and testify of his divine Sonship!

These are they whom Lehi saw—following one whose "luster was above that of the sun at noon-day"—they whose own "brightness did exceed that of the stars in the firmament. And they came down and went forth upon the face of the earth." (1 Ne. 1:9-11.) These are they who were among "the noble and great ones" seen by Abraham, who were chosen to be rulers before they were "born." (Abr. 3:22-23.) As with Jeremiah, their fellow servant—before they were formed "in the belly," and before they came "forth out of the womb"—the Lord had known them, and "sanctified" them, and "ordained" them to be prophets and apostles "unto the nations." (Jer. 1:5.) There was no happenstance in their calls; they had been foreordained by Him who knows all things and who had prepared them from all eternity to be his ministers in the meridian day.

Witnesses of the Redeemer—humble folk; weak and simple Galileans, unlearned in Rabbinic lore; but men who could be taught from on high, whose souls will vibrate as the revelations of eternity pour in upon them!

How aptly it is written of them, and of Heaven's emissaries in all ages: "Ye see your calling, brethren, how that not many wise men after the flesh, not many mighty, not many noble, are called: But God hath chosen the foolish things of the world to confound the wise; and God hath chosen the weak things of the world to confound the things which are mighty; And base things of the world, and things which are despised, hath God chosen, yea, and things which are not, to bring to nought things that are: That no flesh should glory in his presence." (1 Cor. 1:26-29.)

His apostolic friends—men who will walk with him through his mortal trials; who will feel the scourge and carry a cross; who are appointed unto suffering and persecution and death!

"I think that God hath set forth us the apostles last, as it were appointed to death: for we are made a spectacle unto the world, and to angels, and to men. We are fools for Christ's sake, but ye are wise in Christ; we are weak, but ye are strong; ye are honourable, but we are despised. Even unto this present hour we both hunger, and thirst, and are naked, and are buffeted, and have no certain dwelling place; And labour, working with our own hands: being reviled, we bless; being persecuted, we suffer it: Being defamed, we intreat: we are made as the filth of the world, and are the offscouring of all things unto this day." (1 Cor. 4:9-13.)

Noble souls—unknown, unlearned, and unlettered now, as it were; but men who, as the world's greatest crusaders, will attain endless fame and receive eternal renown; whose names shall be engraved forever in the walls of the Holy City!

As there are twelve tribes in Israel, so there are twelve apostles for all Israel and the world; as Jehovah gave his saving truths to the twelve sons of Jacob and their seed, throughout their generations, so Jesus is placing in the hands of his twelve friends the saving truths and powers for their day; and as the names of the twelve tribes of Israel are written on the twelve gates of the Holy Jerusalem, which shall descend from God out of heaven, so are the names of the twelve apostles of the Lamb written on the twelve foundations of the walls of that celestial city. (Rev. 21:10-14.) Surely it shall be with the Jewish Twelve as it is with the Nephite Twelve—and as it shall be with the latter-day Twelve, as also with all the saints who are true and faithful: "Behold, they are righteous forever; for because of their faith in the Lamb of God their garments are made white in his blood." (1 Ne. 12:10.)

The Twelve Apostles of the Lamb—legal administrators who shall in due course hold the keys of the kingdom; who shall have power to bind on earth and seal in heaven; who shall stand in the place and stead of the Lord Jesus when he returns to his Father to reign in eternal glory forever!

The Twelve Apostles of the Lamb—the choicest and noblest spirits available to the God of Heaven to do his work in that day; the friends of his Son; those who shall see visions, receive revelations, and work wonders—such are the ministers whom Jesus is about to choose, to ordain, and to instruct! What a glorious day this is in the cause of truth and righteousness!

Jesus Calls Eleven Galileans and One Judean
(Mark 3:13-21; JST, Mark 3:16; Matthew 10:2-4; Luke 6:12-16)

When the servants of the Lord go forth to choose others to labor on the Lord's errand and to engage in his ministry, they have one goal and one only: to find those whom the Lord has already chosen to serve in whatever capacities are involved. Their constant prayer on those occasions is: "Lord, show unto thy servants whom thou hast chosen to do this work or fill these offices." All of the legal administrators in the earthly kingdom "must be called of God, by prophecy, and by the laying on of hands, by those who are in authority, to preach the Gospel and administer in the ordinances thereof." (A of F 5.)

It is the Lord's work and not man's, and the Lord knows whom he wants to serve in all places in his kingdom. No man, of himself, can build up the kingdom; it is only when the earthly servants get the spirit of revelation, and do thereby the things the Lord wants done, that the work prospers to the full. And as with us, so also with the Lord Jesus, who came not to do his own will, but that of his Father who sent him. We heard him say at the Passover in Jerusalem after healing the impotent man at the pool of Bethesda: "I can of mine own self do nothing; . . . because I seek not mine own will, but the will of the Father which hath sent me." (John 5:30.)

Now Jesus is to choose the Twelve—the holy apostles who were foreordained in the councils of eternity to tread in his tracks and bear witness of his name in all the world—the Twelve whose spiritual talents, developed before they were born, will enable them to build up the kingdom and withstand the pressures of the world. Whom shall he choose? He must find those whom Nephi saw in vision six hundred years before; he must select those whom he himself first called to this high and holy ministry when he and they mingled among the noble and great spirits, seen by Abraham, who were destined to be the Lord's rulers among mortal men. These foreordained ones must be found; there must be no mistakes made.

Thus we see Jesus (for the time for calling the Twelve is now) go out alone into a mountain to pray. All night long his petitions ascend to his Father; during the long hours of darkness he communes with the one who sent him and whose will he came to do. He needed—as we need during the long and dark days of life—direction from on high. He received answer to his prayer; and someday, perhaps, when our spiritual capacity enables us to know and feel what else was involved in this and other prayers of the Son of God, we shall gain that knowledge. For now, we know only that "when it was day, he called unto him his disciples: and of them he chose twelve, whom also he named apostles."

All true believers are disciples; all who keep his commandments and who follow him as he follows his Father are his disciples; the apostles, as here designated, are those chosen disciples who are ordained to the office of apostle in the Melchizedek Priesthood and who receive and use the keys of the kingdom of God on earth. There are or may be disciples without number, but those acting in the holy apostleship are twelve in number at any given time; they are the governing officers over the disciples.

Those chosen by Jesus on this memorable morning are named, as a group, four times in the New Testament—by Matthew, by Mark, and twice by Luke, once in his Gospel and once in the Acts of the Apostles. No two of these listings give the same order of seniority, and in some instances the name applied to the same person varies. All of the lists place Peter first, and the three that mention Judas place him last. The account in Acts lists only the eleven, as Judas by then had served his purpose and sealed his traitorous conduct with a suicidal death.

From other sources we know that Peter, James, and John

were the preeminent three, and were in fact the First Presidency of the Church in that day, although we have no way of knowing whether they served as a separate quorum apart from the others of the Twelve as is the case today. They may well have done, since "the keys of the kingdom" that they restored in this dispensation "belong always unto the Presidency of the High Priesthood" (D&C 81:2), meaning they are always, in all dispensations, held by the First Presidency of the Church.

Our present knowledge of the original Twelve is scanty; some things cannot be other than speculative at this time, and a true understanding of their lives and ministries—of their kinships and works, of the sermons they preached and the miracles they wrought—must await the day when all things are revealed.[2] It may be that all of them wrote Gospels that someday will come forth for the enlightenment and salvation of men, Gospels that will come forth in a day when men are prepared, by faith and good works, and have attained the spiritual stature to be worthy to study their holy words.

Without falling into the not-uncommon trap of creating a whole personality, or of pontificating a complete life-style, or of naming with finality all of the characteristics and attributes of a person, simply because we have a known sliver of information about him, we can with some assurance note at least the following about the Twelve whom Jesus called. We shall take Mark's order of seniority, since he was the disciple of Peter and is believed to have set forth views and feelings and factual knowledge received personally from the Chief Apostle.

1. *Simon Peter.*

This noble soul—chief of the apostles, valiant, courageous, conforming; as rugged and forceful as Elijah, who called down fire from heaven, and slew the priests of Baal with the sword; as submissive and spiritual as Samuel, who attuned his ear to hear the voice of God—Simon Peter was called by Jesus to preside over the earthly kingdom, to lay the foundation and build up that church which alone would administer salvation for that day and dispensation.

We shall see him in many settings: forsaking all to follow Jesus; testifying of his divine Sonship in the coast of Caesarea Philippi; severing the ear of Malchus with a sword in Gethsemane; denying that he knows who Christ is in the courtyard of Caiaphas, the high priest; accusing the Jews, to their face, of murdering the Lord; penning the most sublime language in the New Testament; being crucified, head downward, for the testimony of Jesus that was his; coming in resurrected glory in 1829 to restore priesthood and keys and call men again to the holy apostleship.

He is described as being "generous, impetuous, wavering, noble, timid," of being "thoroughly human," and of having a "most lovable disposition." He was all this and more. There has seldom been such a mighty man as he on earth. "It would be hard to tell," says one analyst, "whether most of his fervour flowed through the outlet of adoration or activity. His full heart put force and promptitude into every movement. Is his Master encompassed by fierce ruffians?— Peter's ardour flashes in his ready sword, and converts the Galilean boatman into the soldier instantaneous. Is there a rumor of a resurrection from Joseph's tomb?—John's nimbler foot distances his older friend; but Peter's eagerness outruns the serene love of John, and past the gazing disciple he rushes breathless into the vacant sepulchre. Is the risen Saviour on the strand?—his comrades secure the net, and turn the vessel's head for shore; but Peter plunges over the vessel's side, and struggling through the waves, in his dripping coat falls down at his Master's feet. Does Jesus say, 'Bring of the fish ye have caught?'—ere any one could anticipate the word, Peter's brawny arm is lugging the weltering net with its glittering spoil ashore, and every eager movement unwittingly is answering beforehand the question of the Lord, 'Simon, lovest thou me?' And that fervour is the best, which, like Peter's, and as occasion requires, can ascend in ecstatic ascriptions of adoration and praise, or follow

Christ to prison and to death; which can concentrate itself on feats of heroic devotion, or distribute itself in the affectionate assiduities of a miscellaneous industry." (Dr. Hamilton, cited in Farrar, pp. 195-96.)

2. *James.*

The whims of chance and the happenstance of history leave us little knowledge that is unique and personal about the second man in seniority in that earthly kingdom of the One who chose and placed in their order those whom he had foreordained unto those very positions in the councils of eternity. James and his brother John, their father Zebedee, and Simon and Andrew were partners in a prosperous fishing business. They owned boats and employed servants. They forsook all to follow Jesus, and James was the first apostolic martyr in the meridian dispensation. He was beheaded by Herod Agrippa just before the Passover in A.D. 44. With Peter, his file leader, and John, his brother, he served in the Council of Three whose destiny called them to preside over the others of the Twelve and over the whole earthly kingdom of their Lord. It was these three who alone were present when Jesus raised the daughter of Jairus from death; they alone of the Twelve ascended the Mount of Transfiguration to receive keys and powers from Elias, Moses, and Jesus, and to hear the Heavenly Voice acclaim that the Beloved Son was then dwelling on earth; they were the ones chosen to be nearby when the sins of all men were laden on the Nazarene's back as he sweat great drops of blood in Gethsemane; and it was they, in June 1829, who ministered with life-giving power to their mortal fellowservants.

3. *John.*

We come now to John: to John the disciple of the Baptist—who forsook the forerunner, to follow Him of whom the witness said, "Behold the Lamb of God, which taketh away the sin of the world" (John 1:29); to John the Beloved—the disciple whom Jesus loved, and who, at the last supper, leaned on the Master's breast; to John the Revelator—who was banished to Patmos where he saw the visions of eternity and wrote the book of Revelation; to John—the author of the Gospel of that name, a gospel oriented to the saints, and of three other New Testament epistles; to John—generally esteemed to be a mystic, though he and James are called by Jesus Boanerges, or Sons of Thunder, because they were rugged and forceful characters, like Elijah, who would have called down fire from heaven upon their enemies; to John—the translated one, who alone of all the Twelve chose to live on earth until the Second Coming that he might bring souls unto salvation; to John—an apostle of love, than whom there have been few greater on earth. He is known to us for his inspired writings, his heavenly visions, and his incomparable centuries-long missionary work. It was he to whom Jesus, hanging in agony upon the cross, entrusted the care of the Blessed Virgin, and who enjoyed as close an intimacy with the Lord as any man who ever lived.

4. *Andrew.*

In the veins of Andrew surged the same believing blood that made his brother Peter a valiant witness of the truth. They were sons of Jona, fishing partners, and friends of Zebedee's children. Andrew and John the apostle were disciples of the Baptist, who, believing his witness of the Messiah, forsook the son of Zacharias to follow Jesus. After one day with our Lord, Andrew gained a witness of his divinity, found his brother, the future president of the Church, and said: "We have found the Messias." (John 1:41.) Andrew was with Peter when the Lord found them casting a net into the still Galilean waters, and said: "Follow me, and I will make you fishers of men." (Matt. 4:19.) He is mentioned in connection with several New Testament episodes and, according to tradition, was crucified at Patrae in Achaia.

5. *Philip.*

Jesus found Philip, apparently searched for him, at Bethsaida, the city where Andrew and Peter then lived. This early-found disciple was with Jesus at the marriage feast in Cana and is mentioned several other times. His most noted conversation of which we have record was the plea, "Lord, shew us the Father, and it sufficeth us," in reply to which he received the mild rebuke: "Have I been so long time with you, and yet hast thou not known me, Philip? he that hath seen me hath seen the Father; and how sayest thou then, Shew us the Father?" (John 14:8-9.) Of his ministry after Jesus' ascension we know nothing.

6. *Bartholomew.*

Called also Nathanael, he is described by Jesus as an Israelite without guile; his witness from the beginning, as first spoken to Jesus, was: "Rabbi, thou art the Son of God; thou art the King of Israel." (John 1:49.) He received from Jesus the promise that he would see the heavens open and angels ascending and descending upon the Son of Man. We know little else of him but doubt not that the divine promise found fulfillment at the appointed time.

7. *Matthew.*

In his capacity as a special witness, Matthew took it upon himself to write of the generation, birth, ministry, passion, resurrection, and exaltation of the Lord Jesus. His spiritual talents and literary craftsmanship enabled him to record— more particularly for Jewish readers, who believed the prophets and pondered their Messianic utterances—many of the words and deeds of the one he knew to be the Son of God. Also known as Levi the son of Alpheus, he was a publican, one of that hated and despised group of Roman tax collectors; apparently he was well-to-do, as he gave a great feast in his own home to introduce many publicans and sinners to Jesus. The numerous quotations in his Gospel from the Old Testament identify him as a scriptural scholar and a trained theologian. His collecting and collating of the numerous events preserved for us in his Gospel establish him as a historian and preserver of that knowledge which Christ came to deliver to men. Aside from the obvious diligence manifest and the labors involved in preparing his written testimony, we know nothing of his ministry after the ascension of the Lord.

8. *Thomas.*

Clearly this holy man, known also as Didymus, was one of the most valiant and courageous of the Twelve, one whose sure witness of the divine Sonship is recorded in fervent and worshipful words. When others of the Twelve counseled Jesus not to go into Judea, where the Jews then sought his life and where Lazarus lay in need of divine help, it was Thomas who said, "Let us also go, that we may die with him." (John 11:16.) When Jesus told the Twelve that he was going to prepare a heavenly place for them and that they knew the way to obtain such a high status, it was Thomas who dared to say: "Lord, we know not whither thou goest; and how can we know the way?" (John 14:5), which brought forth the great pronouncement that Jesus was the way, the truth, and the life. And it was Thomas—absent when the others, in the upper room, felt the prints of the nails, thrust their hands into the riven side, and saw the resurrected Lord eat before them—it was Thomas, not understanding the corporeal nature of the resurrection, who expressed disbelief, only to have Jesus appear eight days later and say: "Thomas, Reach hither thy finger, and behold my hands; and reach hither thy hand, and thrust it into my side: and be not faithless, but believing." Then came from Thomas the inspired witness: "My Lord and my God" (John 20:27-28), which we may be assured he continued to bear as long as mortal breath was his.

9. *James.*

Of this James we know only that he was the son of Alpheus, and that he was ordained to the holy apostleship. That he was of apostolic stature, bore true witness, and taught sound doctrine is implicit in the known system governing the apostolate. Our lack of knowledge about him shows only the inadequacy of the accounts that have been preserved for us.

10. *Judas.*

Luke calls him "Judas the brother of James," and Matthew names him as "Lebbeus, whose surname was Thaddeus." As to his works and ministry we are not advised, and conclude only that he was of like spiritual stature with his brethren of the Twelve.

11. *Simon Zelotes.*

Of this member of the Twelve we know only that he was at one time one of the party of Zealots, but this fact of itself speaks volumes. The Zealots were a Jewish sect whose avowed purpose was to uphold the Mosaic ritual and stand as guardians of the law. Simon must have been a valiant leader in this politico-nationalistic movement, for Matthew, Mark, and Luke, all three, in identifying him append the name of the sect to his personal name. Luke calls him Simon Zelotes; Matthew and Mark call him Simon the Canaanite. In the original records the term Canaanite, in this instance, is the Syro-Chaldaic equivalent of the Greek word that has been translated into English as Zelotes.[3]

12. *Judas Iscariot.*

Eleven of the Twelve were Galileans; Judas only was from Judea, his name signifying, as it is supposed, that he came from Kerioth, a small town of the tribe of Judah. Ish Kerioth (Iscariot) signifies "a man of Kerioth." He was the steward and almoner for Jesus and the other disciples, receiving and dispensing, to the poor and otherwise, such monies as came into their hands. We suppose he had a testimony and followed Jesus willingly, although he well could have done so with ulterior motives—for money and power—and with evil intent. Certainly Satan was his chief master; greed and avarice dwelt in his heart; he was dishonest in caring for the monies placed in his hands; and for thirty pieces of silver he planted the traitor's kiss. Thereafter he hanged himself at Aceldama, the field of blood, which is on the southern slope of the valley of Hinnom outside Jerusalem. In the process he fell headlong, burst asunder, his bowels gushed out, and his spirit went to associate with Lucifer in that realm where traitors to the truth suffer the agonies of the damned.

These, then, are the Lord's Twelve—all save one are holy

and righteous men—the ministers called to bear witness of his holy name and build up his earthly kingdom, first among the Jews, and then among the Gentiles.[4] They were called of God by prophecy; power from on high was imparted by the laying on of hands; they all held the holy Melchizedek Priesthood; and each was ordained to the office of an apostle therein. "Ye have not chosen me"—men do not call themselves to the ministry!—"but I have chosen you, and ordained you," Jesus said. (John 15:16.) Of their call Mark, reflecting Peter's teaching, said: "He ordained twelve, that they should be with him, and that he might send them forth to preach, And to have power to heal sicknesses, and to cast out devils."

In due course Jesus will give, first to Peter, James and John, and then to all of the Twelve, the keys of the kingdom of heaven; these keys will enable them to preside over the earthly kingdom and direct all its affairs, to say nothing of that divine and eternal power which transcends the bounds of earth and endures beyond this mortal vale—the power to bind and seal on earth and in heaven. These keys enable the Lord's servants on earth to seal men up unto eternal life, on the one hand, and, on the other, "to seal them up unto the day when the wrath of God shall be poured out upon the wicked without measure." (D&C 1:9.)

For the meridian dispensation, vacancies in the Twelve were filled as they occurred. By the spirit of revelation, the Eleven chose Matthias—one who had companied with them all the time that the Lord Jesus went in and out among them—to serve in the place of Judas. This thirteenth apostle was "ordained" to be a witness with the others of the resurrection and to bear with them the burdens of the kingdom. The pattern being thus set, vacancies in the Quorum of the Twelve were filled until that day when the man-child "was caught up unto God and his throne," and the long night of apostate darkness descended upon the earth. (*Commentary* 3:513-19.)[5]

NOTES

1. These words are part of the heavensent pronouncement that these very Twelve shall "judge the whole house of Israel," so glorious, so high, and so exalted is their station.

2. There are reasons to believe that others of the original Twelve than Peter and Andrew, James and John, were related, and that some of them were cousins of Jesus, but of these things we cannot be sure. With our present source material only, it remains a fascinating but somewhat fruitless field of inquiry. Perhaps these two quotations, one from Farrar, the other from Edersheim, which do not themselves agree, will help those readers whose inclinations lie in this genealogical field to envision something of what is involved.

"Simon and Andrew the sons of Jonas, James and John the sons of Zabdia, and Philip, were of the village of Bethsaida. [As we have heretofore seen, Philip was *at* Bethsaida, not *of* Bethsaida, when Jesus first called him.] If Matthew be the same as Levi [and of this there is almost complete agreement], he was a son of Alpheus, and therefore a brother of James the Less and of Jude, the brother of James, who is generally regarded as identical with Lebbeus and Thaddeus. They belonged in all probability to Cana or Capernaum, and if there were any ground for believing the tradition which says that Mary, the wife of Alpheus or Klopas, was a younger sister of the Virgin, then we should have to consider these three brothers as first-cousins of our Lord. Nathanael or Bartholomew was of Cana in Galilee. Thomas and Simon Zelotes were also Galileans. Judas Iscariot was the son of a Simon Iscariot, but whether this Simon is identical with the Zealot cannot be determined." (Farrar, pp. 190-91.) This analysis makes Matthew, James the Son of Alpheus, and Jude brothers, and possible cousins of Jesus.

"The difficulties connected with tracing the family descent or possible relationship between the Apostles are so great, that we must forego all hope of arriving at any certain conclusion. . . . Some points at least seem clear. First, it appears that only the calling of those to the Apostolate is related, which in some sense is typical, viz. that of Peter and Andrew, of James and John, of Philip and Bartholomew (or Bar Telamyon, or Temalyon, generally supposed the same as Nathanael), and of Matthew the publican. Yet, secondly, there is something which attaches to each of the others. Thomas, who is called Didymus (which means 'twin'), is closely connected with Matthew, both in St. Luke's Gospel and in that of St. Matthew himself. James is expressly named as the son of Alpheus or Clopas. This we know to have been also the name of Matthew-Levi's father. But, as the name was a common one, no inference can be drawn from it, and it does not seem likely that the father of Matthew was also that of James, Judas, and Simon, for these three seem to have been brothers. Judas is designated by St. Matthew as Lebbeus, from the Hebrew *lebh,* a heart, and is also named, both by him and by St. Mark, Thaddeus. . . . St. Luke simply designates him Judas of James, which means that he was the brother (less probably, the son) of James. Thus his real name would have been Judas Lebbeus, and his surname Thaddeus. Closely connected with these two we have in all the Gospels, Simon, surnamed Zelotes or Cananean (not Canaanite), both terms indicating his original connection with the Galilean Zealot party, the 'Zealots for the Law.' His position in the Apostolic Catalogue, and the testimony of Hegesippus, seem to point him out as the son of Clopas, and brother of James, and of Judas Lebbeus. These three were, in a sense, cousins of Christ, since, according to Hegesippus, Clopas was the brother of Joseph, while the sons of Zebedee were real cousins, their mother Salome being a sister of the Virgin. Lastly, we have Judas Iscariot, or *Ish Kerioth,* 'a man of Kerioth,' a town in Judah. Thus the betrayer alone would be of Judean origin, the others all of Galilean." (Edersheim 1:521-22.) This analysis makes James the Less, Judas, and Simon Zelotes brothers and cousins of Christ through Joseph. James and John are listed as blood-cousins through Mary.

It is worthy of note that among the Nephite Twelve, Nephi and Timothy were brothers, as also were Mathoni and Mathonihah, and that Jonas was a son of Nephi. (3 Ne. 19:4.)

In the first Twelve called in this dispensation, Parley P. and Orson Pratt were brothers, as were Luke S. and Lyman E. Johnson. Joseph Smith, the Prophet, and Hyrum Smith, the Patriarch, were brothers; their brother William served in the Twelve, and their father, Joseph Smith, Sr., was the first Patriarch to the Church. Brigham Young, Jr., a son of President Brigham Young, was one of the Twelve. George A. Smith, John Henry Smith, and George Albert Smith constitute three generations of apostles, as do Franklin D. Richards, George F. Richards, and LeGrand Richards, and Amasa, Francis M., and Richard R. Lyman. President Joseph F. Smith and two of his sons, Hyrum Mack and Joseph Fielding, served in the Twelve. Lorenzo and Erastus Snow were related. John Taylor and his son John W., Wilford Woodruff and his son Abraham O., Matthias F. Cowley and his son Matthew, and George Q. Cannon and his son Sylvester were all apostles. Joseph F. Merrill was a son of Marriner W. Merrill, Ezra Taft Benson a great-grandson of the original Ezra T. Benson, and Stephen L Richards a grandson of Willard Richards. President Spencer W. Kimball is a grandson of Heber C. Kimball, and Gordon B. Hinckley a nephew of Alonzo A. Hinckley—plus the fact that there are many instances of cousins and more distantly related family members, all called to positions of apostolic power. Truly, faith runs in families, in all dispensations.

3. Referring to a work by Bruce, *Training of the Twelve,* Farrar, in a footnote, comments: "Bruce happily remarks that the choice of an ex-Zealot as an Apostle, giving grounds for political suspicion, is another sign of Christ's disregard of mere prudential wisdom. Christ wished the apostles to be the type and germ of the Church; and therefore we find in it a union of opposites—the tax-gatherer Matthew, and the tax-hater Simon— the unpatriotic Jew who served the alien, and the patriot who strove for emancipation." (Farrar, p. 192.)

4. In our dispensation, the Twelve Apostles are also called to be "special witnesses of the name of Christ in all the world," and "to build up the church, and regulate all the affairs of the same in all nations," but the order of priority where Jews and Gentiles are concerned is reversed. For our day, the gospel goes "first unto the Gentiles and secondly unto the Jews." (D&C 107:23, 33.)

5. "All of the brethren in the Church who knew by personal revelation that Jesus was the Christ, meaning all who had testimonies given by the Holy Ghost of his divine Sonship, were witnesses of the Lord. Such were Stephen, Philip, Prochorus, Nicanor, Timon, Parmenas, Nicolas, Ananias, John Mark, Simeon, Lucius, Manaen, Judas Barsabas, Silas, Timotheus, Apollos, Sopater, Aristarchus, Secundus, Gaius, Tychicus, Trophimus, Agabus, Mnason—all of whom are mentioned in Acts and are variously referred to as prophets, teachers, and disciples, but none of whom are called apostles. Only Barnabas, Paul, Matthias, James the Lord's brother, and the original Twelve are singled out to carry the apostolic appelation. The clear inference thus is that the name is being reserved for those who were ordained to the office of apostle in the Melchizedek Priesthood and therefore that Paul and Barnabas were members of the Council of the Twelve, having filled vacancies in the normal course of events. President Joseph Fielding Smith has written: 'Paul was an ordained apostle, and without question he took the place of one of the other brethren in that Council.' (Joseph Fielding Smith, *Doctrines of Salvation* 3:153.)" (*Commentary* 2:131.)

Chapter 41

THE SERMON ON THE MOUNT

His name shall endure for ever:
his name shall be continued as long as the sun:
and men shall be blessed in him:
all nations shall call him blessed.
Blessed be the Lord God,
the God of Israel,
who only doeth wondrous things.
And blessed be his glorious name for ever:
and let the whole earth be filled
with his glory. (Ps. 72:17-19.)

Come, ye blessed of my Father,
inherit the kingdom prepared for you
from the foundation of the world.
(Matt. 25:34.)

The Sermon on the Mount—Its Nature and Delivery

It is now our privilege to hear anew the Sermon on the Mount, the Sermon on the Plain, the Sermon in Bountiful— for they are all one; all contain the same truths; all fell from the same lips; all were spoken by the power of the same Spirit. We shall not hear the whole sermon, for no man, of whom we know, has been so privileged since the holy words fell from the lips of Him who chose in his own right, rather than by the mouths of his servants the prophets, to present such a wondrous compilation of the divine truth in a single sermon. But we shall both hear the words and feel the spirit of the portion that has come down to us in Holy Writ.

There may have been greater sermons preached to selected congregations of spiritual giants—as, for instance, at Adam-ondi-Ahman when the first man assembled together the high priests and patriarchs of his dispensation, along with other righteous saints of like spiritual capacity—there may have been other sermons preached to spiritual giants who could comprehend more of the truths of eternity than the general run of mankind. The Sermon on the Mount, however, was preached to instruct and counsel the newly ordained apostles; to open the door of spiritual progress for all newly called members of the Church and kingdom of God on earth; and to stand as a beacon inviting men of good will of every doctrinal persuasion to come to the Fount of Wisdom and learn those things which will assure them of peace in this world and eternal glory in the world to come.

This sermon is a recapitulation, a summary, and a digest of what men must do to gain salvation; and the eternal concepts in it are so stated that hearers (and readers) will get out of it as much as their personal spiritual capacity permits. To some it will point the way to further investigation; to others it will confirm and reconfirm eternal truths already learned from the scriptures and from the preachers of righteousness of their day; and to those few whose souls burn with the fires of testimony, devotion, and valiance, it will be as the rending of the heavens: light and knowledge beyond carnal comprehension will flow into their souls in quantities that cannot be measured. Every man must judge and determine for himself the effect the Sermon on the Mount will have upon him.

As the words of the sermon are spoken, anew, as it were, in our ears, there are some basic and simple realities of which we must be aware. The Sermon on the Mount has never been recorded in its entirety as far as we know; at least no such scriptural account is available to us. What has come to us is a digest; the words in each account that are attributed to Jesus are, in fact, verbatim recordings of what he said, but they are not all that he said by any means. He may have expounded on each point at extended length, with the Gospel historians who preserved his sayings being guided by the Spirit to write only those words which, in the infinite wisdom of Him who knoweth all things, should have been incorporated into their scriptural accounts. It may well be that the most perfect and elaborate sermon was delivered to the Nephites, for their congregation was composed only of spiritually attuned souls. Without question, when Matthew records a thought in one set of words and Luke does so in different language, both are preserving the verbatim utterances of the Lord. He said what both of them attribute to him as part of the whole sermon. The recording witnesses of his words simply chose to preserve different spoken sentences to present the eternal concepts involved.

And, finally, in this connection: The Sermon on the Mount is not an assemblage of disjointed sayings, spoken on diverse occasions, that have been combined in one place for convenience in presentation, as some uninspired commentators have speculated. It is rather selected sayings, all spoken by Jesus on one day, following the ordination of the Twelve; it is that portion of his words, spoken on that occasion, which the Spirit knew should be preserved for us and for all men who seek truth. It may well be that the sealed portion of the Book of Mormon contains more of the sermon than is now found in Third Nephi, and it may well be that future revelations—accounts of others of the apostles, for instance—will bring to light more that was said on the mountainous plain near Capernaum where Jesus spoke the Spirit-guided words to his Jewish friends.

No doubt what we receive in the future—as to this and all other scriptural expansions—will depend upon our spiritual maturity. When we exercise faith like unto the brother of Jared, we will learn by revelation what he knew, and feel by the power of the Spirit what he felt. Until then let us start with what we have, the glorious truths recorded in Matthew 5, 6, and 7; in Luke 6; and in 3 Nephi 12, 13, and 14; and let us lay the foundation for that knowledge and that perfection of life which it is ours to receive because we have what we have—the glorious Sermon on the Mount as now constituted.

Jesus Speaks the Beatitudes
*(3 Nephi 12:1-12; Matthew 5:1-12; JST, Matthew 5:3-5, 8, 10-12, 14;
Luke 6:17-26; JST, Luke 6:20-21, 23)*

Jesus came in resurrected glory to a great multitude of the Nephites who were assembled round about the temple in the land Bountiful. At his invitation they all thrust their hands into his side and felt the print of the nails in his hands and in his feet, and all cried out with one accord: "Hosanna! Blessed be the name of the Most High God!" From among them Jesus chose Twelve, whom he ordained apostles, and to whom he gave power to proclaim his gospel, to baptize, to confer the gift of the Holy Ghost, and to do all things needful for the salvation of that remnant of the house of Israel.

To these Twelve and to the whole congregation Jesus taught his gospel, including faith, repentance, baptism of water and of the Spirit, and the keeping of the commandments of God. (3 Ne. 11.) Then, stretching forth his hand to the multitude, he began to deliver the Sermon in Bountiful, which was the Sermon on the Mount, as we conclude from Matthew's account, or the Sermon on the Plain, as we reason from Luke's recording of the same persuasive words.[1] His initial declarations in this sermon have been appropriately called the Beatitudes. To beatify is to make supremely happy or to announce that a person has attained the blessedness of heaven. Beatitude is a state of utmost bliss, and the Beatitudes are our Lord's declarations of the blessedness and eventual eternal glory of those who obey the various principles recited in them. May we now, with beatific vision, as it were, seek to envision the meaning of Jesus' blessed pronouncements on blessedness.

Blessed are ye if ye shall give heed unto the words of these twelve whom I have chosen from among you to minister unto you, and to be your servants; and unto them I have given power that they may baptize you with water; and after that ye are baptized with water, behold, I will baptize you with fire and with the Holy Ghost; therefore blessed are ye if ye shall believe in me and be baptized, after that ye have seen me and know that I am.

And again, more blessed are they who shall believe in your words because that ye shall testify that ye have seen me, and that ye know that I am. Yea, blessed are they who shall believe in your words, and come down into the depths of humility and be baptized, for they shall be visited with fire and with the Holy Ghost, and shall receive a remission of their sins.

These are the basic Beatitudes; these are the initial words of blessing; these are the beatific promises that precede all others; out of them all other blessings come. Before the blessedness of heaven; before the beatific state of supreme happiness; before the glory of utmost bliss can be gained; before we progress on the strait and narrow path leading to eternal life—before nearly all else, we must believe in the Lord Jesus Christ; we must give heed to the apostles and prophets who minister in his name; we must come down in the depths of humility and be baptized in his holy name; we must be visited with fire and with the Holy Ghost and receive a remission of our sins; and we must then walk in the light of the Spirit. It is only after the blessings promised in these beginning Beatitudes have been received that we can obtain the things promised in the Beatitudes that follow.

Jesus' beginning beatific statements in the Sermon on the Mount, as delivered on the mountainous plain near Capernaum, were similar to those made to the Nephites. Having spent the night on the mountain in prayer, Jesus chose the

119

Twelve, ordained them, and gave them the same powers and commission received by their Nephite fellow laborers. Then, Luke says, "he came down with them, and stood in the plain," meaning a high plateau area near where he, alone, had communed during the night with his Father.

Assembled before him were a host of disciples and a great multitude of people. Disciples and investigators had come together "out of all Judea and Jerusalem, and from the sea coast of Tyre and Sidon." They came to hear and heed, to be healed of their diseases, to bask in the divine Presence, to be fed spiritually. It was a day of miracles. Those vexed with unclean spirits were healed; multitudes thronged near seeking merely to touch him; faith was in every heart; he responded to their pleas; and "virtue went out of him, and healed them all." The account seems to indicate that thousands were present. He healed them all! All were given health of body and enlightenment of soul. The kinds and severities of their afflictions are not named, simply that he healed them all.

On other occasions, the healing of lepers, the opening of blind eyes, the restoring of withered legs and arms, the raising of dead bodies from their biers and graves—all are recounted in detail. But the great event of this day was not the miracles, but the sermon; and so, in the setting of faith where all present were healed, in a setting where the Spirit of the Lord was present, Jesus began the Sermon on the Plain. These beginning Beatitudes then fell from his lips:

> *Blessed are they who shall believe on me; and again, more blessed are they who shall believe on your words, when ye shall testify that ye have seen me and that I am.*
>
> *Yea, blessed are they who shall believe on your words, and come down into the depth of humility, and be baptized in my name; for they shall be visited with a fire and the Holy Ghost, and shall receive a remission of their sins.*

Believe in Christ; believe in the words of the apostles; come down in the depths of humility; be baptized; receive the gift of the Holy Ghost; gain a remission of sins—all of which must happen if men are to be led into all truth—and then comes an understanding of all the Beatitudes. It was in such a setting—a setting of faith, of belief in the Son of God; a setting of miracles and healings and worship—that Jesus spoke the Sermon on the Mount both in Galilee and in the land Bountiful.

And he lifted up his eyes on his disciples, and said, Blessed are the poor; for theirs is the kingdom of God.

Yea, blessed are the poor in spirit, who come unto me; for theirs is the kingdom of heaven.

We'll go to the poor, like our Captain of old,
And visit the weary, the hungry, and cold;
We'll cheer up their hearts with the news that he bore,
And point them to Zion and life evermore.[2]

"To the poor the gospel is preached." (Luke 7:22.) "Hath not God chosen the poor of this world rich in faith, and heirs of the kingdom which he hath promised to them that love him?" (James 2:5.) The poor in spirit! If they come unto Christ, salvation is theirs; and it is so often easier for those who are not encumbered with the cares and burdens and riches of the world to cast off worldliness and set their hearts on the riches of eternity than it is for those who have an abundance of this world's goods.

Blessed are they who weep now; for they shall laugh.

And again, blessed are all they that mourn, for they shall be comforted.

Those who are bereft of loved ones, having learned the purposes of the Lord in the brief separation called death, shall be comforted. The peace that passeth understanding shall rest upon all those who have a knowledge of the plan of salvation. What greater comfort is there than to know that lost loved ones shall be returned to the family unit, and that all the saints shall reign in joy and peace forever? And further: When He comes again whose right it is to rule, he "shall wipe away all tears from their eyes; and there shall be no more death, neither sorrow, nor crying, neither shall there be any more pain." (Rev. 21:4.) They that mourn shall be comforted!

Blessed are the meek: for they shall inherit the earth.

As things are now constituted, the meek do not inherit the earth; even He who said of himself, "I am meek and lowly in heart" (Matt. 11:29) had in fact no place of his own to lay his head. This world's goods were of little moment to him, and he had neither gold nor silver nor houses nor lands nor kingdoms. Peter was even directed to catch a fish in whose mouth a coin was lodged, that a levied tax might be paid for the two of them. The meek—those who are the God-fearing and the righteous—seldom hold title to much of that which appertains to this present world. But there will be a day when the Lord shall come to make up his jewels; there will be a day when Abraham, Isaac, and Jacob, and the faithful of ancient Israel shall dwell again in old Canaan; and there will be also an eventual celestial day when "the poor and the meek of the earth shall inherit it." (D&C 88:17.)

Blessed are they who hunger now; for they shall be filled.

And blessed are all they that do hunger and thirst after righteousness; for they shall be filled with the Holy Ghost.

Filled with the Holy Ghost! As starving men crave a crust of bread, as choking men thirst for water, so do the righteous yearn for the Holy Ghost. The Holy Ghost is a Revelator; he is a Sanctifier; he reveals truth, and he cleanses human souls. He is the Spirit of Truth, and his baptism is one of fire; he burns dross and evil out of repentant souls as though by fire. The gift of the Holy Ghost is the greatest of all the gifts of God, as pertaining to this life; and those who enjoy that gift here and now, will inherit eternal life hereafter, which is the greatest of all the gifts of God in eternity.

Blessed are the merciful: for they shall obtain mercy.

Mercy is for the merciful. In that great day of restoration

and judgment, when every man is rewarded according to the deeds done in the flesh, those who have manifest mercy to their fellowmen here will be treated mercifully by the Merciful One. Those who have acquired the godly attribute of mercy here shall have mercy restored unto them again in that bright day.[3]

And blessed are all the pure in heart; for they shall see God.

How glorious is the voice we hear from him! Man may see his Maker! Did not Abraham, Isaac, and Jacob see the Lord? Did not Moses and Aaron, Nadab and Abihu, and seventy of the elders of Israel see the God of Israel, under whose feet was a paved work of a sapphire stone? Was it not thus with Isaiah and Nephi, with Jacob and Moroni, and with mighty prophets without number in all ages? Is God a respecter of persons who will appear to one righteous person and withhold his face from another person of like spiritual stature? Is he not the same yesterday, today, and forever, dealing the same with all people, considering that all souls are equally precious in his sight? Did not Moses seek diligently to sanctify his people, while they were yet in the wilderness, that they might see the face of God and live? Does not the scripture say that the brother of Jared had such a perfect knowledge of God that he could not be kept from seeing within the veil? Why then should not the Lord Jesus invite all men to be as the prophets, to purify themselves so as to see the face of the Lord?

It is written: "Verily, thus saith the Lord: It shall come to pass that every soul who forsaketh his sins and cometh unto me, and calleth on my name, and obeyeth my voice, and keepeth my commandments, shall see my face and know that I am." (D&C 93:1.) How glorious the concept is! What a wondrous reality! The pure in heart—all the pure in heart—shall see God!

And blessed are all the peacemakers; for they shall be called the children of God.

The gospel of peace makes men children of God! Christ

came to bring peace—peace on earth and good will to men. His gospel gives peace in this world and eternal life in the world to come. He is the Prince of peace. How beautiful upon the mountains are the feet of them who preach the gospel of peace, who say unto Zion: Thy God reigneth! Let there be peace on earth, and let it begin with his saints. By this shall all men know the Lord's disciples: They are peacemakers; they seek to compose difficulties; they hate war and love peace; they invite all men to forsake evil, overcome the world, flee from avarice and greed, stand in holy places, and receive for themselves that peace which passeth understanding, that peace which comes only by the power of the Spirit.

And these are they who are adopted into the family of God. They become the sons and daughters of him whose we are. They are born again. They take upon themselves a new name, the name of their new Father, the name of Christ. Those who believe in him have power to become his sons and his daughters. Truly the peacemakers shall be called the children of God!

Blessed are ye, when men shall hate you, and when they shall separate you from their company, and shall reproach you, and cast out your name as evil, for the Son of man's sake. Rejoice ye in that day, and leap for joy; for behold your reward shall be great in heaven; for in the like manner did their fathers unto the prophets.

Blessed are all they that are persecuted for my name's sake; for theirs is the kingdom of heaven. And blessed are ye, when men shall revile you, and persecute you, and shall say all manner of evil against you falsely, for my sake. For ye shall have great joy, and be exceeding glad; for great shall be your reward in heaven; for so persecuted they the prophets which were before you.

How could it be said better? Jesus is speaking to the members of his earthly kingdom. In our day that kingdom is The Church of Jesus Christ of Latter-day Saints. It is composed of those who have taken upon them the name of Christ—covenanting in the waters of baptism to honor that name and to do nothing that will hold it up to contempt or ridicule. It is composed of those who have forsaken the world; who have crucified the old man of sin; who have become humble, meek, submissive, willing to conform to all that the Lord requires of them.

And, of course, the world loves its own and hates the saints. The world is the carnal society created by evil men; it is made up of those who are carnal and sensual and devilish. Of course the world persecutes the saints; the very thing that makes them saints is their enmity toward the things of the world. Let the ungodly and the evildoers reproach the Lord's people; let them cry transgression against his saints; let persecution rage against those who bear the Lord's name; let true believers be reviled and evilly spoken of—all for his name's sake. So be it!

Do they face trials of cruel mockings and scourgings? Are they stoned, sawn asunder, slain with the sword? Are they destitute, afflicted, tormented? Are they cast into dens of lions and furnaces of fire? Are they slain in gladiatorial arenas, lighted as torches on the walls of Rome, crucified head downward? Are they driven from Ohio to Missouri, and from Missouri to Illinois, and from Illinois to a desert wilderness—leaving their Prophet and Patriarch in martyrs' graves? No matter! They do not live for this life alone, and great shall be their reward in heaven.

Such are the Beatitudes—insofar as they have been preserved for us—those blessed statements about blessedness. As with all our Lord's sayings, they were unlike and superior to the Rabbinical beatitudes of the day.[4] No doubt Jesus made many more beatific declarations either in this sermon or on other occasions. Such of his statements as "It is more blessed to give than to receive" would take on the nature of a true beatitude if it were phrased thus: "Blessed are all they who give all they have for the building up of the Lord's kingdom on earth, for they shall receive the riches of eternity in the world to come."

Quite properly we glory in the Beatitudes, as Jesus

himself gloried in them. Edersheim says they are the New Testament counterpart of the Ten Commandments, and that they "present to us, not the observance of the Law written on stone, but the realization of that Law which, by the Spirit, is written on the fleshly tables of the heart." (Edersheim 1:529.) But as we glory in their greatness—and all the blessings thereunto appertaining—we must not overlook the fact that Jesus appended to them certain curses, curses for those who continue to live after the manner of the world and who do not walk in that course which leads to blessedness.

But woe unto you that are rich! for ye have received your consolation.

Woe unto you that are full! for ye shall hunger.

Woe unto you that laugh now! for ye shall mourn and weep.

Woe unto you, when all men shall speak well of you! for so did their fathers to the false prophets.

If there is a blessing, there must needs be a cursing. There can be no light without darkness, no good without evil, no blessed heights of glory and honor unless there are also cursed depths of despair and damnation.

If the pure in heart shall see God, those whose hearts are impure shall be shut out of his presence. If the peacemakers shall be called the children of God, those who foment war shall be the children of Lucifer their father. If those who hunger and thirst after righteousness shall be filled with the Holy Ghost, those whose appetites are fed on carnal and evil food shall be filled with a worldly spirit that breeds evil deeds. And so on with reference to all of the Beatitudes. All things have their opposites, and there must needs be an opposition in all things.

Woe, then, unto the rich, Jesus says, the rich whose hearts are set on the things of this world; on the gold in the mountains and the cattle on the hills; on the merchant's goods and the spices coming in on a thousand ships—for they have already received their consolation, the consolation and rewards of this life, rather than the riches of eternity.

Woe unto those whose bellies are full; who have laid up provisions in granaries and storehouses; who have been concerned only with feeding the body—for their spirits, being unfed, shall hunger.

Woe unto those who laugh now, as they rejoice in the things of this world—for they shall mourn and weep in the day of judgment.

Woe unto those who are held in high esteem by worldly and evil people; who revel in the praise of ungodly men; who gain the plaudits of carnal people—for in such manner were the false prophets treated in days of old.

"Ye Are the Light of the World"
(*Matthew 5:13-16; JST, Matthew 5:15-18; 3 Nephi 12:13-16*)

We repeat: The Sermon on the Mount, including the Beatitudes, was delivered to true believers; to the Twelve Apostles of the Lamb (it was their ordination sermon); to the saints of the Most High God; to members of the Church of Jesus Christ; to people who had been baptized and who were in process of seeking the riches of eternity. To them—after holding out the blessed and sanctified wonders of gospel obedience, as these are stated in the Beatitudes—Jesus now says: "Ye are the salt of the earth. . . . Ye are the light of the world." That is to say: 'Ye are the choicest and best people on earth; and ye must now be an example to all men, that others, seeing your good works, shall come unto me and glorify your Father who is in heaven.' Our Lord's words, insofar as they have been preserved for us, are:

Verily, verily, I say unto you, I give unto you to be the salt of the earth; but if the salt shall lose its savor, wherewith shall the earth be salted? the salt shall thenceforth be good for nothing, but to be cast out, and to be trodden under foot of men.

Verily, verily, I say unto you, I give unto you to be the light of the world; a city that is set on a hill cannot be hid.

Behold, do men light a candle and put it under a

bushel? Nay, but on a candlestick; and it giveth light to all that are in the house.

Therefore, let your light so shine before this world, that they may see your good works, and glorify your Father who is in heaven.

Salt and light, symbols of the saints: salt because it has a seasoning, purifying, preserving power; light because it manifests the good works and wise words of the true believers! The saints, as the salt of the earth, are set forth to season their fellowmen, to keep society free from corruption, to help their fellow beings become wholesome, pure, and acceptable before the Lord.[5] The saints, as the light of the world, are to set an example of good works and charitable deeds, so they may say to all men, as does their Master, 'Follow thou me; and I will lead you in sure paths here and to heights above the clouds hereafter.'[6]

That Christ is the Light of the World, no Christian doubts; what Jesus is now saying is that all his disciples should be even as he is. That upright people who keep the commandments are the salt of the earth, none question; but we might add that the Lord Jesus himself is the Salt of the Earth. The seasoning, sanctifying, edifying, preserving, uplifting influence of his gospel keeps all the obedient from corruption and decay and sorrow.

If the saints lose their seasoning power and no longer set examples of good works, they are thenceforth as other worldly people to whom salvation is denied. The saints are as a city set on a hill that is open to the view of all. Their good works lead others to the truth and to glorify their Creator, their Redeemer, and the Holy Spirit who testifies of the truth of all things.

NOTES

1. "The plain" of Luke 6:17 is better rendered "level spot," which translation brings the account into complete harmony with Matthew's statement that the sermon was delivered in a mountain, meaning on a level plateau in a mountainous area.

2. "Ye Elders of Israel," *Hymns*, no. 44.

3. This principle applies to mercy and every godly attribute, as also to carnality and devilishness and every evil thing, as Alma has so well said: "The meaning of the word restoration is to bring back again evil for evil, or carnal for carnal, or devilish for devilish— good for that which is good; righteous for that which is righteous; just for that which is just; merciful for that which is merciful. Therefore, my son, see that you are merciful unto your brethren; deal justly, judge righteously, and do good continually; and if ye do all these things then shall ye receive your reward; yea, ye shall have mercy restored unto you again; ye shall have justice restored unto you again; ye shall have a righteous judgment restored unto you again; and ye shall have good rewarded unto you again. For that which ye do send out shall return unto you again, and be restored; therefore, the word restoration more fully condemneth the sinner, and justifieth him not at all." (Alma 41:13-15.)

4. This applies to all that Jesus did and said—it was unlike and superior to the prevailing preachments and performances in the same fields. For instance, there are in the Talmud many graphic statements and wise sayings that, quoted out of context, have been interpreted by some to mean that the Talmud is an inspired work comparable to the New Testament. But, as Edersheim expresses it: "Take these in their connection and real meaning, and what a terrible awakening! Who, that has read half-a-dozen pages successively of any part of the Talmud, can feel otherwise than by turns shocked, pained, amused, or astounded? There is here wit and logic, quickness and readiness, earnestness and zeal, but by the side of it terrible profanity, uncleanness, superstition, and folly. Taken as a whole, it is not only utterly unspiritual, but anti-spiritual. . . . Taken not in abrupt sentences and quotations, but as a whole, it is so utterly and immeasurably unlike the New Testament, that it is not easy to determine which, as the case may be, is greater, the ignorance or the presumption of those who put them side by side. . . . He who has thirsted and quenched his thirst at the living fount of Christ's Teaching, can never again stoop to seek drink at the broken cisterns of Rabbinism." (Edersheim 1:525-26.)

5. "When men are called unto mine everlasting gospel, and covenant with an everlasting covenant," the Lord says, "they are accounted as the salt of the earth and the savor of men; They are called to be the savor of men; therefore, if that salt of the earth lose its savor, behold, it is thenceforth good for nothing only to be cast out and trodden under the feet of men." (D&C 101:38-40. See also D&C 103:9-10.)

6. "Behold I am the light; I have set an example for you," Jesus said to the Nephites. Then of their obligation, he added: "Hold up your light that it may shine unto the world. Behold I am the light which ye shall hold up—that which ye have seen me do." (3 Ne. 18:16, 24.)

Chapter 42

JESUS DISCOURSES ON THE LAW OF MOSES

The law is fulfilled
that was given unto Moses.
Behold, I am he that gave the law,
and I am he who covenanted with my people Israel;
therefore, the law in me is fulfilled,
for I have come to fulfil the law;
therefore it hath an end.
Behold, I do not destroy the prophets,
for as many as have not been fulfilled in me,
verily I say unto you,
shall all be fulfilled.
And because I said unto you
that old things have passed away,
I do not destroy that which hath been spoken
concerning things which are to come.
For behold, the covenant
which I have made with my people
is not all fulfilled;
but the law which was given unto Moses
hath an end in me.
Behold, I am the law, and the light.
Look unto me, and endure to the end,

and ye shall live; for unto him
that endureth to the end
will I give eternal life.
Behold, I have given unto you the commandments;
therefore keep my commandments.
And this is the law and the prophets,
for they truly testified of me.
(3 Ne. 15:4-10.)[1]

Jesus Fulfills and Honors the Law
(Matthew 5:17-20; JST, Matthew 5:19-21; 3 Nephi 12:18-20, 46-47)

Jesus has now spoken the Beatitudes; he is about to go forward in his glorious mountain sermon with some very plain statements about the law of Moses. A sweet spirit has filled our souls as we have heard and felt the sublime truths given in the Beatitudes. We cannot, however, avoid contrasting that which occurred on the Mount of Beatitudes with the heavenly manifestations displayed on Mount Sinai when the law itself was given.

Jesus as Jehovah spoke to Moses amid the fires and thunders and quakings of Sinai; smoke ascended as from a furnace; all Israel trembled at the display; and the Lord, in majesty, with a finger of fire, wrote his holy law for that man whom he had chosen to lead his people. Below were the camps of Israel, with their lowing cattle and bleating sheep, and with all the confusion of moving multitudes.

The law then given was a law of eternal verities—first, the gospel itself, which the people rejected, and, later, the lesser law; a law, however, that changed the course of history forever; a law that revealed Jehovah to his people and commanded them—at sword's point, as it were—to worship him or be damned. The crescendo of sounding trumpets proclaimed: 'Thou shalt not worship false gods, or violate the Sabbath, or commit adultery, or kill, or do any wickedness.' It set forth, as illustrated in Exodus 21 and 22, the minutia

131

and detail and strictness and severity of the divine will where his slave-like people were concerned. For instance: "He that curseth his father, or his mother, shall surely be put to death. . . . Thou shalt give life for life, Eye for eye, tooth for tooth, hand for hand, foot for foot, Burning for burning, wound for wound, stripe for stripe. . . . If an ox gore a man or a woman, that they die: then the ox shall be surely stoned, and his flesh shall not be eaten; but the owner of the ox shall be quit. But if the ox were wont to push with his horn in time past, and it hath been testified to his owner, and he hath not kept him in, but that he hath killed a man or a woman; the ox shall be stoned, and his owner also shall be put to death." And so on and so on and so on.

Jehovah as Jesus spoke to the Twelve and to the multitude in the calm serenity of a summer morning, on a grassy plateau on the Mount of Beatitudes. Below them, in silver splendor, lay the rippling waters of the Sea of Galilee; all was calm; a spirit of peace and quietude overshadowed the worshipful throng. That which Jesus then spoke was not written with burnished swords of steel, but came forth as the gentle breeze of a cool and pleasant evening. There was no thunderous "Thou shalt not," only a soft spoken plea, "Here is the way; walk ye in it." It was a new day, a new order, a new way, a new gospel; the patterns of the future were being formed; from henceforth, through all generations, the Messiah and his disciples would teach correct principles and let all who heard govern themselves. Such is the perfect gospel standard.

And so now—as the Sermon on the Mount continues— Jesus, leaving the sweet bliss and serene blessedness of the Beatitudes, turns their thoughts to the harsh realities of the law of Moses; to the yoke that hung heavily on their bowed heads and aching shoulders; to these scrupulosities and performances by which they were bound. This yoke, with all its burdensome rituals and restrictions, was about to be removed by their Redeemer and Deliverer. The set time for him to fulfill the law and make an end to all its curtailing provisions was not far distant. His chosen Twelve in particular, and all his newly won disciples in general, must condition their minds to reject the old and receive the new, to turn their hearts from Moses, who bore record of the Messiah, to Jesus, who was the Messiah.

"Think not that I am come to destroy the law, or the prophets," Jesus said. For nearly fifteen hundred years all the faithful in Israel—and all the souls they had won from their Gentile neighbors and oftimes overlords—had bowed their backs and harnessed their strength as they struggled to keep the law of Moses the man of God. For all these years the law and the prophets had testified of a coming Messiah; the performances of the law were types and shadows of his ministry and mission; the words of the prophets were inspired utterances that bore the same witness. Now the Messiah had come, and soon he would—according to the promises—atone for the sins of the world and thus fulfill the law.

Nothing was to be lost; no act of the past would be shunted aside or deemed useless. The law had been the most glorious system of worship on earth during the period of its ascendancy. But now it was to be replaced; the schoolmaster's work was done, and the students of righteousness, yet in the elementary grades, were about to enter the gospel university where the fulness of revealed truth awaited their study.

"I am not come to destroy, but to fulfill," Jesus continued. "For verily I say unto you, Heaven and earth must pass away, but one jot or one tittle shall in no wise pass from the law, until all be fulfilled."

Even his disciples must continue to keep the law for the present. Sacrifices were still the order of the day. And he, with his disciples, would yet keep that final Passover feast when the sacrament of the Lord's Supper would be instituted; together they would then eat the paschal lamb, in similitude of the sacrifice of the Lamb of God; and they would do it during the last moments of the law's legal continuance; they would do it while the true Lamb of God was en route to Golgotha to be sacrificed. But for now, though true believers were beginning to receive the higher principles of the higher law, the law itself was still in force.

"Whosoever, therefore, shall break one of these least commandments, and shall teach men so to do, he shall in no wise be saved in the kingdom of heaven; but whosoever shall do and teach these commandments of the law until it be fulfilled, the same shall be called great, and shall be saved in the kingdom of heaven."

Then came this sobering indictment against their Jewish leaders: "For I say unto you, That except your righteousness shall exceed the righteousness of the scribes and Pharisees, ye shall in no case enter into the kingdom of heaven." What an awesome responsibility is assumed by self-styled ministers who teach the traditions of their fathers rather than the pure principles of revealed religion, and who thereby teach people to break "one of these least commandments," as it were!

When Jesus gave the Sermon in Bountiful to the Nephites, the law had been fulfilled. Gethsemane and the cross were past; the blood of the last authorized paschal lamb had been spilt in similitude of his eternal sacrifice; sacrifices by the shedding of blood were no longer required or accepted. "For verily I say unto you, one jot nor one tittle hath not passed away from the law," Jesus then said, "but in me it hath all been fulfilled."

> And behold, I have given you the law and the commandments of my Father, that ye shall believe in me, and that ye shall repent of your sins, and come unto me with a broken heart and a contrite spirit. Behold, ye have the commandments before you, and the law is fulfilled.
>
> Therefore come unto me and be ye saved; for verily I say unto you, that except ye shall keep my commandments, which I have commanded you at this time, ye shall in no case enter into the kingdom of heaven. . . .

Therefore those things which were of old time, which were under the law, in me are all fulfilled.

Old things are done away, and all things have become new.[2]

He Contrasts the Law of Moses and the Law of Christ
(*Matthew 5:21-47; JST, Matthew 5:23-26, 29, 31-34, 42-43, 50; 3 Nephi 12:21-37, 48; Luke 6:27-30, 32-35; 12:58-59; JST, Luke 6:27-30, 33*)

Jesus now sets a pattern for all other preachers of righteousness. He illustrates his profound and sobering concept relative to the law of Moses, and he states additional gospel concepts that grow out of his illustrations. These all are twelve in number.

1. *Murder and anger.*

Moses' law—more properly Jehovah's law given through Moses—forbade murder. "Thou shalt not kill; and whosoever shall kill, shall be in danger of the judgment of God." The same prohibition applies under the gospel law, but this higher law, in addition, raises a higher standard. It strikes at the cause of murder, which is anger. The man whose fired bullet misses its human target is as guilty as the marksman whose bullet brings death to the intended victim. It is the feeling one has in his heart that counts, not the eventuality that occurs. "Whosoever hateth his brother is a murderer: and ye know that no murderer hath eternal life abiding in him." (1 Jn. 3:15.) And so Jesus says: "But I say unto you that whosoever is angry with his brother, shall be in danger of his judgment."

Let us envision at this point, if we may, what Jesus is doing here and in all the illustrations that follow. He is saying: 'Jehovah of old—through Moses—said such and such; but now I say unto you something more or something different.' He is placing himself on a par with the God of Israel; he is saying: 'God Almighty did or said thus and so, but I, Jesus, add to, amend, alter, delete from, and change the word of God.' It is blasphemy, pure and simple, for a mortal so to

135

speak; but, no, in this case it is an affirmation of Messiah-ship, and Jesus is guiltless in his affirmations, for he is Jehovah; and if Jehovah edits Jehovah, so be it—who has a better right!

2. *Profanity.*

Further: "Whosoever shall say to his brother, Raca, or Rabcah, shall be in danger of the council; and whosoever shall say to his brother, Thou fool, shall be in danger of hellfire." That is, profane and vulgar epithets and expressions—for such, in the Jewish culture, were the nature of the words here recited—when hurled at our fellowmen lead to damnation. The fires of Gehenna burn in the hearts of those whose minds think and speak evilly against their brethren. Among the abominations that the Lord hates is listed "an heart that deviseth wicked imaginations." (Prov. 6:16-19.) Men curse themselves when they think and speak ill of their brethren. Profane, vulgar, contemptuous, and unholy expressions degrade their author more than they taint the soul of the hearer.

3. *Reconciliation between brethren.*

We must do all in our power to assuage the hurt feelings of our brethren if we ourselves are to stand blameless before the Lord. "If ye shall come unto me, or shall desire to come unto me," Jesus says, "or if thou bring thy gift to the altar, and there rememberest that thy brother hath aught against thee, Leave thou thy gift before the altar, and go thy way unto thy brother, and first be reconciled to thy brother, and then come and offer thy gift." That is, if we choose to come unto Christ and to be one with him in his fold; if we bring our gifts to his holy altar, that our wealth and means may be used to further his work on earth; and if we then remember that others have aught against us, our obligation, more important than the gifts we bestow, is to heal the wounded feelings of our brethren. Jesus speaks here not of our anger or ill feeling toward others, but of their ill feelings, for whatever cause, against us. No matter that we are the one who has been wronged. The gospel standard calls for us to search out those whose anger is kindled against us and to do all in our power to douse the fires of hate and animosity. "Go thy way unto thy brother, and first be reconciled to thy brother," he said to the Nephites, "and then come unto me with full purpose of heart, and I will receive you."

4. *Avoiding legal entanglements.*

With particular reference to the Twelve and others engaged in missionary work, in ministerial service, and in building up the kingdom, Jesus said: "Agree with thine adversary quickly, whiles thou art in the way with him; lest at any time the adversary deliver thee to the judge, and the judge deliver thee to the officer, and thou be cast into prison. Verily I say unto thee, Thou shalt by no means come out thence, till thou hast paid the uttermost farthing." It was more important, in the social and political circumstances then prevailing, for the Lord's servants to suffer legal wrongs than that their ministries be hindered or halted by legal processes.

5. *Adultery.*

Mosaic fiat decreed: "Thou shalt not commit adultery." Jesus, who himself had given the decree to "them of old time," now says: "But I say unto you, That whosoever looketh on a woman to lust after her hath committed adultery with her already in his heart." His is now a higher law; it is not the immoral act alone that the gospel condemns—it is also the lewd and lustful desires that lead to its commission. "He that looketh on a woman to lust after her, or if any shall commit adultery in their hearts, they shall not have the Spirit, but shall deny the faith and shall fear." (D&C 63:16.)

6. *Casting sins away.*

Jesus has spoken of sins of the heart and of the mind and of the mouth. Anger is as murder; profanity leads to hell; ill feelings against our brethren canker the soul; lewdness, evil thoughts—adultery committed in the heart—are as the very act itself. Gospel standards govern what is in the hearts of men as well as the deeds they do. In this setting, he then says:

> Behold, I give unto you a commandment, that ye suffer none of these things to enter into your heart;
>
> For it is better that ye should deny yourselves of these things, wherein ye will take up your cross, than that ye should be cast into hell.

Based on this principle, the Master Teacher uses two parabolic illustrations that dramatize the severity—even harshness—of action that should be taken to rid ourselves of the sins involved and of all sin. "Wherefore," that is, in the light of the principles just enunciated, "if thy right eye offend thee, pluck it out and cast it from thee; for it is profitable for thee that one of thy members should perish, and not that thy whole body should be cast into hell. Or if thy right hand offend thee, cut it off and cast it from thee; for it is profitable for thee that one of thy members should perish, and not that thy whole body should be cast into hell." These statements about the eye and the hand were not included in the recorded account of the Sermon in Bountiful.

The severity of such a course—plucking out an eye or severing a hand—staggers reality. Scarcely is there an affliction calling for such a drastic operation. No suffering invalid parts with an eye or a hand unless life itself is at stake. And so, having selected with care the most drastic of all remedies, Jesus reveals his true meaning:

> And now this I speak, a parable concerning your sins; wherefore, cast them from you, that ye may not be hewn down and cast into the fire.

Have there ever been such teachings as this to show the need to cast away our sins, to cast them away lest we die spiritually, to cast them away lest our eternal souls be themselves cast into fire?

7. *Divorce.*

Under the law of Moses, divorce came easily; but recently freed from Egyptian slavery, the chosen race had yet to attain the social, cultural, and spiritual stability that exalts marriage to its proper place in the eternal scheme of things. Men were empowered to divorce their wives for any unseemly thing. "It hath been said, Whosoever shall put away his wife, let him give her a writing of divorcement."

No such low and base standard is acceptable under gospel law. Thus Jesus summarized his perfect marriage order by saying: "But I say unto you, That whosoever shall put away his wife, saving for the cause of fornication, causeth her to commit adultery: and whosoever shall marry her that is divorced committeth adultery." Divorce is totally foreign to celestial standards, a verity that Jesus will one day expound in more detail to the people of Jewry. For now, as far as the record reveals, he merely specifies the high law that his people should live, but that is beyond our capability even today. If husbands and wives lived the law as the Lord would have them live it, they would neither do nor say the things that would even permit the fleeting thought of divorce to enter the mind of their eternal companions. Though we today have the gospel, we have yet to grow into that high state of marital association where marrying a divorced person constitutes adultery. The Lord has not yet given us the high standard he here named as that which ultimately will replace the Mosaic practice of writing a bill of divorcement.

8. *Gospel oaths.*

Here again we come to a standard of conduct that— geared to the needs of various cultures and conditions—has varied, with divine approval, from one age to the next. Abraham and the ancients, who lived by gospel standards, were permitted to take oaths—to swear in the Lord's name, thus certifying that they would act or speak in a named way. Such a certification guaranteed their words because the oath made God their partner, and God cannot lie or fail. The words they then spoke became the Lord's words and were accepted as true; and the deeds they vowed by an oath to do became the Lord's performances, and they must be done at the peril of one's life, for God has all power and he cannot fail in any particular to do that which he is bound to do.

Today it is the practice among Christian people to swear with an oath to tell the truth, the whole truth, and nothing but the truth in certain judicial proceedings. Under the Mosaic law the taking of oaths was so common and covered such a variety of circumstances that, in practice, little verity attended statements that were not made with an oath. "If a man vow a vow unto the Lord, or swear an oath to bind his soul with a bond; he shall not break his word, he shall do according to all that proceedeth out of his mouth." (Num. 30:2.) And so Jesus, rejecting the old and proclaiming the new, said: "And again it is written, thou shalt not forswear thyself, but shalt perform unto the Lord thine oaths; But I say unto you, Swear not at all; neither by heaven; for it is God's throne: Nor by the earth; for it is his footstool: neither by Jerusalem; for it is the city of the great King. Neither shalt thou swear by thy head, because thou canst not make one hair white or black. But let your communication be Yea, yea; Nay, nay; for whatsoever cometh of more than these is evil."

Under the perfect law of Christ every man's word is his bond, and all spoken statements are as true as though an oath attended each spoken word.

9. Retaliation.

Retaliation—with the inevitable bitterness and smallness of soul that attends it—cannot do other than keep hatred alive in the souls of men. If a man gouge out the eye of his neighbor, what benefit accrues to the wounded person if he retaliate by gouging out the eye of the offender? Has he enlarged his own soul, or has he permitted it to shrivel to the same smallness as the soul of his attacker? "Ye have heard that it hath been said, An eye for an eye, and a tooth for a tooth," Jesus said, using words, found in the law of Moses, that summarized both the letter and the spirit of those ancient rules. "But I say unto you, That ye resist not evil," he continued, "but whosoever shall smite thee on thy right cheek, turn to him the other also." Luke preserves for us the more complete account and meaning of Jesus' saying on this point: "And unto him who smiteth thee on the cheek, offer also the other; or, in other words, it is better to offer the other, than to revile again. And him who taketh away thy cloak, forbid not to take thy coat also. For it is better that thou suffer thine enemy to take these things, than to contend with him. Verily I say unto you, Your heavenly Father who seeth in secret, shall bring that wicked one into judgment."

"Contention leads to bitterness and smallness of soul; persons who contend with each other shrivel up spiritually and are in danger of losing their salvation. So important is it to avoid this evil that Jesus expects his saints to suffer oppression and wrong rather than lose their inner peace and serenity through contention. 'He that hath the spirit of contention is not of me,' he told the Nephites, 'but is of the devil, who is the father of contention, and he stirreth up the hearts of men to contend with anger, one with another. (3 Ne. 11:29.)' " (*Commentary* 1:228.)

10. *Persecution by legal process.*

To his apostles and ministers—those whose talents and strength must be devoted, without hindrance, to the preaching of the gospel and the building up of the kingdom—Jesus had this special counsel: "And if any man will sue thee at the law, and take away thy coat, let him have it; and if he sue thee again, let him have thy cloak also. And whosoever shall compel thee to go a mile, go with him a mile; and whosoever shall compel thee to go with him twain, thou shalt go with him twain. Give to him that asketh of thee, and from him that would borrow of thee turn not thou away."

Nothing is so important as the spread of truth and the establishment of the cause of righteousness. The petty legal processes of that day must not be permitted to impede the setting up of the new kingdom.

11. *The law of love.*

Ye have heard that it hath been said, Thou shalt love thy neighbour, and hate thine enemy.

But I say unto you, Love your enemies, bless them that curse you, do good to them that hate you, and pray for them which despitefully use you, and persecute you;

That ye may be the children of your Father which is in heaven: for he maketh his sun to rise on the evil and on the good, and sendeth rain on the just and on the unjust.

For if ye love them which love you, what reward have ye? do not even the publicans the same?

And if ye salute your brethren only, what do ye more than others? do not even the publicans so?

Of olden time, and in ages past, Israel's enemies had been God's enemies, and the Gentile nations were kept away at sword's point; had it not been so, the chosen people would have been swallowed up by the world. Their world was one of force and violence in which whole nations were forced to believe what their rulers decreed or be destroyed from off the face of the earth. This tight grip on the minds of men has now been loosened, and now the gospel is to go to the world—all men everywhere are to hear the word. Israel must love the Gentiles, for they are to be adopted into the family of Jehovah.

All men will be judged by what is in their own hearts. If their souls are full of hatred and cursings, such characteristics shall be restored to them in the resurrection. Loving one's enemies and blessing one's cursers perfects the soul. Such perfection is the object of the gospel, and of it Jesus now chooses to speak.

12. *Perfection.*

As a climax to all his sayings contrasting the old Mosaic order with the new gospel law, and by way of commandment to all those who would forsake the old and cleave unto the new, Jesus proclaimed to the Jews:

Ye are therefore commanded to be perfect, even as your Father who is in heaven is perfect.

To his Nephite brethren—to whom he spoke after his resurrection, after he had risen in immortal glory with a celestial body, after he had received all power in heaven and on earth—his proclamation was couched in these words:

Therefore I would that ye should be perfect even as I, or your Father who is in heaven is perfect.

Perfection—a relative degree of perfection in this life, and eternal perfection, the kind possessed by the Father, in the life to come—these are gained by full obedience to the fulness of gospel law. This is the doctrine of exaltation, the doctrine that as God now is, man may become; this is the doctrine that mortals have power to become like Deity in power, might, and dominion; in wisdom, knowledge, and truth; in love, charity, mercy, integrity, and in all holy attributes. "Ye shall be even as I am, and I am even as the Father; and the Father and I are one," Jesus said to certain faithful Nephite disciples. (3 Ne. 28:10.)

If the newly called saints overcome anger; if they are reconciled with their brethren; if they rise above lewd and lascivious thoughts and commit no adultery in their hearts; if they cast away their sins, as though severing an offending hand; if their every spoken word is true as though sworn with an oath; if they do not retaliate when others offend them; if they turn the other cheek and resist not evil impositions; if they love their enemies, bless those who curse them, and pray for those who despitefully use them and persecute them—if they do all these things, they will become perfect even as their Eternal Father is perfect. And perfection comes not by the law of Moses, but by the gospel. "If therefore perfection were by the Levitical priesthood, (for under it the people received the law,) what further need was there that another priest should rise after the order of Melchisedec, and not be called after the order of Aaron?" (Heb. 7:11), Paul asks. But—thanks be to God— "another priest," Jesus the Son of God, arose; and ministering in all the glory of the gospel, he is now fulfilling the old law and inviting men to believe and obey the new law.

At this point he is somewhat less than halfway through the Sermon on the Mount. Now he turns from contrasting the old and the new to an out-and-out proclamation of new and glorious standards.

NOTES

1. These words were spoken by the Lord to the Nephites after his resurrection, and hence after the law of Moses was fulfilled, a situation that did not prevail when he discoursed on the same subject near Capernaum in his Jewish Sermon on the Mount.

2. As it was with the Nephites, so it is with all who have received the word of truth in the same measure to which it came to them: 'Except all such keep the gospel commandments, which are thus offered to them, they shall in no case enter into the kingdom of heaven.' Salvation for the dead is for those only who would have received and lived the gospel with all their hearts had the principles been offered to them while they dwelt in mortality.

Chapter 43

JESUS DISCOURSES ON GOSPEL STANDARDS

Good and upright is the Lord:
therefore will he teach sinners in the way.
The meek will he guide in judgment:
and the meek will he teach his way.
And all the paths of the Lord
are mercy and truth
unto such as keep his covenant
and his testimonies. (Ps. 25:8-10.)

Jesus Saith: 'Care for the Poor'
(3 Nephi 13:1-4; Matthew 6:1-4; JST, Matthew 6:1, 3)

A mighty sermon is in progress; Jesus is speaking by the power of the Holy Ghost; we are hearing wondrous words—words of light and truth and revelation. Our minds are open, our hearts are receptive, and our souls are afire with the spirit of everlasting life that attends each spoken thought. He is now counseling us to walk as becometh saints and to do the things that his disciples in all ages have always done. His next subsermon is: 'Care for the worthy poor; give alms in righteousness; impart of your substance to those in need; give generously because you love the Lord and your fellowmen.'

"Verily, verily, I say that I would that ye should do alms

unto the poor," he says. It is right; it is good; it is the will of the Master—we should care for the worthy poor among us. As long as greed and selfishness find place among us mortals, there will also be poor among us. And it is the will of the Lord that the poor among his people receive their just wants and needs. "It is my purpose to provide for my saints," he says, "for all things are mine. But it must needs be done in mine own way; and behold this is the way that I, the Lord, have decreed to provide for my saints, that the poor shall be exalted, in that the rich are made low. For the earth is full, and there is enough and to spare. . . . Therefore, if any man shall take of the abundance which I have made, and impart not his portion, according to the law of my gospel, unto the poor and the needy, he shall, with the wicked, lift up his eyes in hell, being in torment." (D&C 104:15-18.)[1]

"But take heed that ye do not your alms before men to be seen of them; otherwise ye have no reward of your Father who is in heaven." Poverty or wealth are too often the happenstance of climate or geography or war. Some men are born to wealth, others to slavery. Today's rich may be tomorrow's paupers. And alms should not be given to exalt the giver, but to save the recipient. "Therefore when thou doest thine alms, do not sound a trumpet before thee, as the hypocrites do in the synagogues and in the streets, that they may have glory of men. Verily I say unto you, They have their reward. But when thou doest alms, let it be unto thee as thy left hand not knowing what thy right hand doeth; That thine alms may be in secret: and thy Father which seeth in secret himself shall reward thee openly."

Jesus Teaches Men How to Pray
(Matthew 6:5-15; JST, Matthew 6:7, 10-14, 16; 3 Nephi 13:5-15; Mark 11:25-26; Luke 11:1-8; JST, Luke 11:4-5)

Prayer and works of charity go hand in hand. Amulek, in a moving sermon, calls upon men to pray unto the Lord for temporal and spiritual blessings; to pray in secret and in public; to pray vocally and in their hearts. Then he says: "After ye have done all these things, if ye turn away the needy, and the naked, and visit not the sick and afflicted, and impart of your substance, if ye have, to those who stand in need—I say unto you, if ye do not any of these things, behold, your prayer is vain, and availeth you nothing, and ye are as hypocrites who do deny the faith. Therefore, if ye do not remember to be charitable, ye are as dross, which the refiners do cast out." (Alma 34:17-29.)

Jesus, in his Sermon on the Mount, turns from almsgiving to prayer. Again, it is the will of the Lord that his people should pray. They are to pray to the Father, in the name of the Son, by the power of the Spirit; they are to thank the Lord for all they have received and to importune before his throne for all that in wisdom should be theirs. Jesus does not now give them the whole law of prayer, but he does chart for them a course which, if pursued, will save them from the prayer failures of the Pharisees and lead them to an eventual full understanding of the true order of prayer.

"And when thou prayest, thou shalt not be as the hypocrites are: for they love to pray standing in the synagogues and in the corners of the streets, that they may be seen of men. Verily I say unto you, They have their reward." Devout Jews, at set times, faced Jerusalem, covered their heads, cast their eyes downward, and ostentatiously went through the ritual of prayer. If the hour of prayer found them in the streets, so much the better, for all men would see their devoutness! To attract attention by saying one's own prayers aloud in the synagogue was not uncommon. Such were among the practices of the day.

"But thou"—who hast come into the fold of Christ, and who thereby know better than to follow these mocking imitations of true prayer—"when thou prayest, enter into thy closet, and when thou hast shut thy door, pray to thy Father which is in secret; and thy Father which seeth in secret shall reward thee openly." And further: "When ye pray, use not vain repetitions, as the hypocrites do; for they think that they shall be heard for their much speaking." The repetitious chants, the thoughtless "Hail Mary's," and the memorized "Our Father's" of modern Catholicism, the repeated mouthings of the poetic phrases of the prayer book—vain repetitions!—these are included in what Jesus here condemns. Prayers that ascend beyond the ceiling, to be heard before the Throne in the sidereal heavens, must be uttered "with all the energy of heart," as Mormon's colloquial expression puts it. (Moro. 7:48.)

"Be not ye therefore like unto them: for your Father knoweth what things ye have need of, before ye ask him." How then shall the saints pray? "After this manner therefore pray ye," Jesus says:

> *Our Father who art in heaven, Hallowed be thy name.*
>
> *Thy kingdom come. Thy will be done on earth, as it is done in heaven.*
>
> *Give us this day, our daily bread.*
>
> *And forgive us our trespasses, as we forgive those who trespass against us.*
>
> *And suffer us not to be led into temptation, but deliver us from evil.*
>
> *For thine is the kingdom, and the power, and the glory, forever and ever, Amen.*

Jesus did not say: 'This is the prayer to use; memorize it; say it by rote,' but he gave a pattern, a model, a type. 'Pray after this manner; in such simple words as these; in this general way; without ostentation. Call upon your Eternal Father, and ask him for your needs, both great and small.' And how wondrous are the words he used!

Our Father who art in heaven. God is our Father, the father of our spirits; we are his children, his offspring, literally. We lived in his presence, dwelt in his courts, and have seen his face. We were as well acquainted with him then as we are with our mortal fathers now. He is a holy man, has a body of flesh and bones, and dwells in a heavenly abode. When we approach his throne in prayer, we think—not alone that he is the Almighty, by whose word the earth, the sidereal heavens, and the universe came into being, but that he is a gracious and loving Father whose chief interest and concern is his family, and that he wants all his children to love and serve him and to become like him. Perfect prayer manifests our personal relationship to him who hears and answers the petitions of the faithful.

Hallowed be thy name. 'We approach thee in awe—reverentially—in the spirit of worship and thanksgiving, and we praise thy holy name. Thou art glorious beyond anything we can envision; all that is good we ascribe unto thee, and we desire to consecrate our life and being unto thee, for thou hast made us, and we are thine.'

Thy kingdom come. Thy will be done on earth, as it is in heaven. Thy kingdom: the earthly kingdom of God which is the Church. *Thy kingdom:* the millennial kingdom, the kingdom of heaven, which shall be when there is a new heaven and a new earth whereon dwelleth righteousness. These are the kingdoms for which we pray. After Jesus' resurrection and before his ascension, the newly ordained apostles, who by that time will be seasoned and tempered as few men have ever been, will ask him: "Lord, wilt thou at this time restore again the kingdom to Israel?" (Acts 1:6.) And even in our day, the faithful continue to pray: "May the kingdom of God go forth, that the kingdom of heaven may come, that thou, O God, mayest be glorified in heaven so on earth, that thine enemies may be subdued; for thine is the honor, power and glory, forever and ever." (D&C 65:6.)

'Thy kingdom come! Let it be, O Lord, for in that glorious millennial day; in that day when Zion shall cover the earth, when all Israel shall be gathered home from their long dispersion, when every corruptible thing shall have been consumed, when the vineyard shall have been burned and few men left—then shall thy will be done on earth as it is in heaven. May we, O Lord, prepare for that day by living as though it were here.'

Give us this day our daily bread. 'But our concerns are not alone for the promised day of triumph and glory when thy people shall prevail in all the earth. We need food, clothing, and shelter, health of body, and strength of mind.' Our daily wants must be supplied, and he who notes the sparrow's fall will also provide manna for his people from day to day. He calls upon us to sow and reap and harvest and bake and eat. The concerns of daily life, however trivial, are the concerns of Omnipotence, and we are to rely upon him in faith for all things.

And forgive us our trespasses, as we forgive those who trespass against us. Or, as it is otherwise rendered—less perfectly, we feel—"Forgive us our debts, as we forgive our debtors"; or, yet again: "Forgive us our sins; for we also forgive every one that is indebted to us." "For if ye forgive men their trespasses, who trespass against you, your heavenly Father will also forgive you; but if ye forgive not men their trespasses, neither will your heavenly Father forgive you your trespasses." When he judges whose judgment is just, he will, as it is written, "recompense unto every man according to his work, and measure to every man according to the measure which he has measured to his fellow man." (D&C 1:10.) We judge ourselves; forgive and be forgiven; sow mercy and reap the same, for every seed brings forth after his own kind. "Ye ought to forgive one another; for he that forgiveth not his brother his trespasses standeth condemned before the Lord; for there remaineth in him the greater sin." (D&C 64:1-14.)[2]

And suffer us not to be led into temptation, but deliver us from evil. "Lead us not into temptation." The Lord does not lead us into temptation, except in the sense that he has placed us here in a probationary estate where temptation is the order of the day. We are here in mortality to be tried and tested; to see if we will keep the commandments; to overcome the world. We are here to learn how to bridle our passions and control every lustful and evil desire. None of us want to be tested beyond our capacity to resist; we want to be delivered from evil, to flee from the presence of sin, and to go where goodness and righteousness are. The trials of life are difficult enough without any of us placing ourselves in a position where sin and evil are made attractive. Foolish indeed is that man who, intending to remain morally clean, yet exposes his mind to pornographic things that in their nature invite lustful thoughts and deeds into his life.

For thine is the kingdom, and the power, and the glory, forever and ever. All things are the Lord's. His is the kingdom—both the earthly kingdom, which is the Church, and that glorious realm of celestial rest prepared for his saints. His is the power—nothing is too hard for the Lord; he is omnipotent; he it is who will change this earth into a heaven, and he it is who will raise lowly mortals to that eternal exaltation which makes of man a god. His is the glory—that is, the dominion, the exaltation, and the endless kingdoms; and also, the light and truth and infinite wisdom and knowledge he possesses.

How glorious it is to address such a holy and exalted person by the greatest of all titles, Father, and to be privileged to have audience with him on our own invitation, anytime we pray in faith with all the strength and energy of our souls!

The Lord's Prayer, as we have come to call these expressive words, spoken by Jesus as part of the Sermon on the Mount (as we are aware from Matthew and 3 Nephi) was also recorded by Luke—apparently, however, as given by Jesus on a different occasion. To his account, Luke appends these instructive words of Jesus: "And he said unto them, Your heavenly Father will not fail to give unto you whatsoever ye ask of him. And he spake a parable, saying, Which of you shall have a friend, and shall go unto him at midnight, and say unto him, Friend, lend me three loaves; For a friend of mine has come to me in his journey, and I have nothing to set before him; And he from within shall answer and say, Trouble me not: the door is now shut, and my children are with me in bed; I cannot rise and give thee. I say unto you, Though he will not rise and give him because he is his friend, yet because of his importunity, he will rise and give him as many as he needeth."

"Lay Up for Yourselves Treasures in Heaven"
(Matthew 6:16-24; JST, Matthew 6:22; Luke 11:33-36; 12:33-34; JST, Luke 11:37; 12:36; 3 Nephi 13:16-24)

Jesus now says a few well-chosen words about fasting, about laying up treasures in heaven, and about seeking spiritual light.

In all ages the Lord has called upon his people to fast and pray and seek him with all their strength and power. Fasting—the abstaining from food and drink for a designated period—gives a man a sense of his utter dependence upon the Lord so that he is in a better frame of mind to get in tune with the Spirit. Moses and Jesus both fasted for forty days as they sought that oneness with the Father out of which great spiritual strength comes. As with almost all else, however, fasting among the Jews no longer served its true purpose; it had become degenerate, self-serving, and ostentatious. Jesus expected his new followers to fast—not as the Pharisees, but in a true spirit of worship and self-effacement.

"When ye fast," he said, thus endorsing fasting as such, and thus counseling his disciples that they should so do, "be not, as the hypocrites, of a sad countenance: for they disfigure their faces, that they may appear unto men to fast. Verily I say unto you, They have their reward." Their fathers—rebellious in spirit, reproachful of prophetic counsel—had fasted "for strife and debate, and to smite with the fist of wickedness," and to make—ostentatiously—their voice "heard on high." (Isa. 58:1-4.) "But thou, when thou fastest," Jesus instructed, "anoint thine head, and wash thy face; That thou appear not unto men to fast, but unto the Father which is in secret: and thy Father, which seeth in secret, shall reward thee openly."

"While yet on earth men may lay up treasures in heaven.

These treasures, earned here and now in mortality, are in effect deposited to our eternal bank account in heaven where eventually they will be reinherited again in immortality. Treasures in heaven are the character, perfections, and attributes which men acquire by obedience to law. Thus, those who gain such attributes of godliness as knowledge, faith, justice, judgment, mercy, and truth, will find these same attributes restored to them again in immortality. 'Whatever principle of intelligence we attain unto in this life, it will rise with us in the resurrection.' (D&C 130:18.) The greatest treasure it is possible to inherit in heaven consists in gaining the continuation of the family unit in the highest heaven of the celestial world." (*Commentary* 1:239-40; Alma 41:13-15; D&C 130:18.)

> *Lay not up for yourselves treasures upon earth, where moth and rust doth corrupt, and where thieves break through and steal:*
>
> *But lay up for yourselves treasures in heaven, where neither moth nor rust doth corrupt, and where thieves do not break through and steal:*
>
> *For where your treasure is, there will your heart be also.*

Christ is the light; the gospel is the light; the plan of salvation is the light; "that which is of God is light; and he that receiveth light, and continueth in God, receiveth more light; and that light groweth brighter and brighter until the perfect day." As the light of the sun enters the body through our natural eyes, so the light of heaven—the light of the Spirit which illuminates our souls—enters through our spiritual eyes. "The light of the body is the eye," Jesus says; "if therefore thine eye be single to the glory of God, thy whole body shall be full of light."

"But if thine eye be evil"—if we choose darkness rather than light—"And that which doth not edify is not of God, and is darkness" (D&C 50:23-24)—"thy whole body shall be full of darkness. If therefore the light that is in thee be darkness, how great is that darkness!"

153

"How great is that darkness!" If the saints of God cease to serve with an eye single to the glory of God; if their spiritual eyes are dimmed by sin; if their eyes, being evil, admit carnality and heresy and false doctrine into their souls; if the light that once was theirs turns to darkness, "how great is that darkness!"

Later, in Judea, teaching there what the Galileans have already heard, Jesus will express kindred concepts in these words:

> No man, when he hath lighted a candle, putteth it in a secret place, neither under a bushel, but on a candlestick, that they which come in may see the light.

"A light that is hidden, whose guiding rays are covered by a bushel, is of no value to one stumbling in darkness. Similarly, the true saints must let the gospel light shine forth from them to all men, lest the saints, [like] the hidden candle, fail to fulfill their purpose in life. Jesus in effect is saying: 'No man accepts the gospel and then buries its light by continuing to walk in darkness; rather, he holds the light up before men so that they, emulating his good works, may also come to the Father.' " (*Commentary* 1:240.)

> The light of the body is the eye: therefore when thine eye is single, thy whole body also is full of light; but when thine eye is evil, thy body also is full of darkness. Take heed therefore that the light which is in thee be not darkness. If thy whole body therefore be full of light, having no part dark, the whole shall be full of light, as when the bright shining of a candle doth give thee light.

"Through the natural eyes men see the light which guides them in their physical existence, through their spiritual eyes, the spiritual light which leads to eternal life. As long as the natural eyes are unimpaired, men can see and be guided by the light of day; and as long as the spiritual eyes are single to the glory of God—that is, as long as they are undimmed by sin and are focused solely on righteousness—men can view and understand the things of the Spirit. But if apostasy enters and the spiritual light turns to darkness, 'how great is that darkness!' " (*Commentary* 1:240.)

Also in Judea, in connection with one's treasure being where his heart is, Jesus will say:

> *Sell that ye have and give alms; provide not for yourselves bags which wax old, but rather provide a treasure in the heavens, that faileth not; where no thief approacheth, neither moth corrupteth.*

Truly treasures in heaven are to be preferred to those stored in purses that wear out and from which earthly treasures will be lost!

> *No man can serve two masters: for either he will hate the one, and love the other; or else he will hold to the one, and despise the other. Ye cannot serve God and Mammon.*

Light and darkness cannot dwell together. It cannot be both day and night at the same time; water cannot be both sweet and salty at the same hour. No man can serve God, who is the author of light and righteousness, while he is in the employ of Lucifer, who is the author of darkness and sin. Mammon is an Aramaic word for riches. 'Ye cannot serve God and love riches and worldliness at the same time.'

The Lord Supplies the Needs of His Twelve Ministers
(*3 Nephi 13:25-34; Matthew 6:25-34; JST, Matthew 6:25-30, 34, 36-39; Luke 12:22-32; JST, Luke 12:26, 30-34*)

Now Jesus turns to the Twelve. He has something to say specifically to them about their ministerial labors. They are to forsake worldly pursuits—their fishing boats, the customs house, their fields and vineyards, all temporal enterprises—and use all of their time, talents, and means for the building up of the earthly kingdom and the establishment of the cause of Christianity. Others also, the seventies among them, will tread a like path in due course. The Lord's missionaries and ministers engage in such important labors that no worldly pursuit can be permitted to interfere; nothing pertaining to this world can be allowed to dilute and divide the energy and strength of the Lord's servants.

Other members of the Church are expected—nay, obligated; it is a command; they must do it—to provide for their own. Work, industry, frugality—sowing, reaping, and eating our bread by the sweat of our faces—such is the royal order of life. From the beginning men have been commanded to labor in seed time and harvest and to lay up in store against times of winter and famine. Cain reaped in the fields and Abel tended his flocks; Abraham, Isaac, and Jacob had their flocks and herds, their fields and gardens and vineyards. This is a temporal world, and men who dwell thereon are appointed to deal with temporal concerns. The gospel law requires men to care for their own needs and those of their families. And, "if any provide not for his own, and specially for those of his own house, he hath denied the faith, and is worse than an infidel." (1 Tim. 5:8.)

But for selected ones who are called to spread the truth and minister for the salvation of their fellows, it is otherwise; they may be called to go forth without purse or scrip, to forsake houses and lands and orchards, to do whatever circumstances require, and to rely upon the Lord for food and drink and raiment and a place to lay their head—all to the end that the Lord's work may spread and be established among all men.

In the Nephite account we read that "Jesus . . . looked upon the twelve whom he had chosen, and said unto them: Remember the words which I have spoken. For behold, ye are they whom I have chosen to minister unto this people. Therefore I say unto you"—the command was to them, not to the whole congregation—"take no thought for your life, what ye shall eat, or what ye shall drink; nor yet for your body, what ye shall put on."

In Matthew's account the instructions are more extended and express. To the Twelve who were with him in his personal ministry, Jesus said: "I say unto you, Go ye into the world, and care not for the world; for the world will hate you, and will persecute you, and will turn you out of their synagogues. Nevertheless, ye shall go forth from house to house, teaching the people; and I will go before you. And your heavenly Father will provide for you, whatsoever things ye need for food, what ye shall eat; and for raiment, what ye shall wear or put on. Therefore I say unto you, Take no thought for your life," and so on.

We hear now the eloquent reasoning of the Master Teacher. "Is not the life more than meat, and the body than raiment?" he asks. Shall we concern ourselves with life itself—the life of the body and the life of the soul—or merely with the food we eat and the rags or robes we chance to use as covering raiment? Then, using words that are eloquent in their simplicity, and drawing his illustrations from the beauties of nature that surround them, Jesus continues:

Behold the fowls of the air, for they sow not, neither do they reap, nor gather into barns; yet your heavenly Father feedeth them. Are ye not much better than they? How much more will he not feed you?

Wherefore take no thought for these things, but keep my commandments wherewith I have commanded you.

For which of you by taking thought can add one cubit unto his stature?

And why take ye thought for raiment? Consider the lilies of the field, how they grow; they toil not, neither do they spin.

And yet I say unto you, that even Solomon, in all his glory, was not arrayed like one of these.

Therefore, if God so clothe the grass of the field, which today is, and tomorrow is cast into the oven, how much more will he not provide for you, if ye are not of little faith?

Therefore take no thought, saying, What shall we eat? or, What shall we drink? or, Wherewithal shall we be clothed?

The leading servants and chief underlings of the kings of the earth dwell in palaces, command fortresses, and are waited upon by lesser servants. Robes and rich food and soft beds and lewd entertainment abound for them. Herod Antipas and his courtiers lived such a life. But not so with the great King. His disciples, dressed often in rags, eating the

157

rough food of the poor, sleeping in guest chambers, or even with the beasts of burden when there was no room in the inn—his chief disciples, his apostles, were to travel and live as he himself did.

None but the Lord would dare call upon chosen followers to live such a life and pursue such a course, and none but he could assure them that their essential needs would be met. The contrast between the courtiers of earthly kings and the disciples of the Eternal King is dramatic. The gospel standard is high and soul developing. It is no wonder that the newly called and as yet untested apostles were troubled at the prospects of the future. For their comfort and assurance, Jesus said: "Why is it that ye murmur among yourselves, saying, We cannot obey thy words because ye have not all these things, and seek to excuse yourselves, saying that, After all these things do the Gentiles seek. Behold, I say unto you that your heavenly Father knoweth that ye have need of all these things." Then came that great and wondrous declaration:

Wherefore, seek not the things of this world but seek ye first to build up the kingdom of God, and to establish his righteousness, and all these things shall be added unto you.

It is common among us to quote the less perfect translation of this statement, which says, "Seek ye first the kingdom of God, and his righteousness," rather than the inspired rendition, "Seek ye first to build up the kingdom of God, and to establish his righteousness." Both statements are true; both are profound; both present a standard and a concept around which the saints should rally; and the Nephite account does in fact preserve the first of the two, which is, of course, the ultimate objective of true believers. To seek the kingdom of God and his righteousness, in the ultimate and eternal sense, is to seek the celestial kingdom and the state of righteousness in which God dwells. The process by which this ultimate goal is attained is to devote oneself to building up the earthly kingdom, which is the Church, and to establish the Cause of Righteousness on earth. Having so taught, and as a summary for this mid-portion of the Sermon on the Mount, our Lord said: "Take, therefore, no thought for the morrow; for the morrow shall take thought for the things of itself. Sufficient unto the day shall be the evil thereof."

NOTES

1. "Blessed are the poor who are pure in heart, whose hearts are broken, and whose spirits are contrite, for they shall see the kingdom of God coming in power and great glory unto their deliverance; for the fatness of the earth shall be theirs. For behold, the Lord shall come, and his recompense shall be with him, and he shall reward every man, and the poor shall rejoice; And their generations shall inherit the earth from generation to generation, forever and ever." (D&C 56:18-20.)

2. This revelation also says: "I, the Lord, will forgive whom I will forgive, but of you it is required to forgive all men. And ye ought to say in your hearts—let God judge between me and thee, and reward thee according to thy deeds."

Chapter 44

JESUS TEACHES DOCTRINE TO HIS SAINTS

The Lord hath anointed me to preach
good tidings unto the meek.
(Isa. 61:1.)

The Lord . . . hath anointed me to preach
the gospel to the poor. (Luke 4:18.)

He Saith: 'Judge Righteous Judgments'
(Matthew 7:1-5; JST, Matthew 7:1-8; Luke 6:37-38, 41-42;
3 Nephi 14:1-5)

In sweet and sublime simplicity, with an eloquence and
power possessed by none other, the One sent to preach good
tidings to the meek, to preach the gospel to the poor,
continues to pour forth the inspired wisdom of his Sermon
on the Mount. He has just finished the special counsel ap-
plicable only to those special witnesses and their associates
whose commission it is to preach to the world and to build
up the kingdom—the instruction relative to forsaking all
earthly interests and devoting themselves exclusively to the
service of the ministry. Now he has a message for all his
people, apostles and disciples alike. All must live the law to
gain the blessing; all must do good and work righteousness;
all must acquire for themselves, here and now, the attributes

160

of godliness, if they are to possess them in eternity; all must keep the commandments to be saved in his Father's kingdom.

Matthew introduces his account of this portion of the Sermon on the Mount by saying, "Now these are the words which Jesus taught his disciples that they should say unto the people. Judge not unrighteously, that ye be not judged; but judge righteous judgment. For with what judgment ye shall judge, ye shall be judged; and with what measure ye mete, it shall be measured to you again." The Nephite record says that when Jesus had spoken to the Twelve the message on missionary service, "he turned again to the multitude," to whom he said: "Verily, verily, I say unto you, Judge not, that ye be not judged," and so on. Luke's account includes this provision: "Condemn not, and ye shall not be condemned: forgive, and ye shall be forgiven: Give, and it shall be given unto you; good measure, pressed down, and shaken together, and running over, shall men give into your bosom."

These words, thus, are a message for his saints, for all the people, for those who choose him as the way, the truth, and the life. The sense and meaning of each rendition is expressive of the divine will: 'Condemn not, that ye be not condemned; judge wisely and righteously, so that ye shall be judged in like manner;[1] and the Lord shall recompense to every man according to his work, and measure to him "according to the measure which he has measured to his fellow man." (D&C 1:10.)'

Our Lord continues to speak: "And again, ye shall say unto them"—that is, Ye, my disciples, shall "say unto the people"—"Why is it that thou beholdest the mote that is in thy brother's eye, but considerest not the beam that is in thine own eye? Or how wilt thou say to thy brother, Let me pull out the mote out of thine eye; and canst not behold a beam in thine own eye?"

It was ever thus. Even the members of the kingdom, striving as they are to perfect their lives; even those who know the truth and who are seeking to live by the high standards of the gospel; even these chosen ones can see the motes—the small splinters, the tiny dry twigs or stalks, the lesser faults—in the doings of their brethren in the Church; but they cannot see the beams—the great roof-beams, the large pieces of timber that hold up the house—which are part of their own doings.

> Once I said unto another,
> In thine eye there is a mote,
> If thou art a friend, a brother,
> Hold, and let me pull it out.
> But I could not see it fairly,
> For my sight was very dim,
> When I came to search more clearly
> In mine eye there was a beam.
>
> If I love my brother dearer,
> And his mote I would erase,
> Then the light should shine the clearer,
> For the eye's a tender place.
> Others I have oft reproved,
> For an object like a mote,
> Now I wish this beam removed,
> Oh, that tears would wash it out![2]

At this point in the Jewish sermon, but not in the one delivered to the Nephites, Jesus rebukes in scathing terms the false ministers who then led the people astray. "And Jesus said unto his disciples," Matthew records, "Beholdest thou the scribes, and the Pharisees, and the priests, and the Levites? They teach in their synagogues, but do not observe the law, nor the commandments; and all have gone out of the way, and are under sin. Go thou and say unto them, Why teach ye men the law and the commandments, when ye yourselves are the children of corruption? Say unto them, Ye hypocrites,"—and here he extends the law of the mote and the beam to all men— "first cast out the beam out of thine own eye; and then shalt thou see clearly to cast out the mote out of thy brother's eye."

'Ye teach that Moses forbade adultery, but ye yourselves are adulterers. Ye teach that men should honor their parents, but ye have dishonored your own fathers by your disobedience. Ye teach that men must repent and gain a remission of their sins, and yet ye yourselves are full of corruption. Ye teach that the Messiah shall come to redeem his people, and yet the one who now ministers among you with Messianic power ye reject.'

He Saith: 'Seek to Know the Truth'
(Matthew 7:6-14; JST, Matthew 7:9-12, 14-17, 22; 3 Nephi 14:6-14; Luke 6:31)

Jesus personally is not destined to do all the teaching that must be done; he alone will not take the message of salvation to every person; he can be in only one place at one time; while he speaks to this congregation, assembled above Capernaum on the Mount of Beatitudes, there are other congregations—throughout Palestine, Asia, the realm of the Roman Caesars, and the whole world—that could be assembled to hear the word of truth. Others must be called and trained and sent forth to proclaim the everlasting word. And so Jesus continues to tell his disciples what they shall say as they carry his message to the hosts who shall never see his mortal face or hear his blessed voice.

"Go ye into the world," he directs, "saying unto all, Repent, for the kingdom of heaven has come nigh unto you."

'Go! No longer sit at ease in your homes and in your synagogues! Arise; gird up your loins, and go! The gospel must be preached everywhere; the whole earth must hear the message; the voice of truth must echo and re-echo in every ear; every heart must be penetrated; there are none to escape. The voice of the Lord is unto all men. Say: The kingdom of heaven is at hand; the gospel of salvation is here; the Church of Jesus Christ is now on earth; it is the kingdom of God on earth; and we are legal administrators who teach by the power of the Holy Ghost, and who perform the ordinances of salvation so they will be binding on earth and sealed everlastingly in the heavens. Repent, and believe the gospel. Live its laws and be saved.'

And the mysteries of the kingdom ye shall keep within yourselves; for it is not meet to give that which is holy unto the dogs; neither cast ye your pearls unto swine, lest they trample them under their feet.

For the world cannot receive that which ye, yourselves, are not able to bear; wherefore ye shall not give your pearls unto them, lest they turn again and rend you.

Any gospel truth, however easy and simple, that is not understood, or that is beyond the present spiritual capacity of a given person to understand, is to him a mystery. Faith, repentance, and baptism are mysteries to the unbelieving Gentiles. But the mysteries of the kingdom, of which Jesus here speaks, are quite another thing. This phrase has a special meaning; it refers to the deep and hidden things of the gospel—to the calculus, as it were, which can only be comprehended after the student has become proficient in arithmetic, algebra, and geometry; it refers to the temple ordinances; to the gifts of the Spirit; to those things which can be known only by the power of the Holy Ghost.

The saints are to keep the deep and more mysterious doctrines to themselves and not offer to the world more than people are able to bear. Until the newborn babe in Christ is weaned, he cannot eat meat; the milk of the world must suffice. Gospel pearls in the hands of Gentile swine enable those hoofed and snouted beasts, wallowing in the filth and swill of their rebellion and disbelief, to rend the saints with their evil fangs. Thus: "It is given unto many to know the mysteries of God; nevertheless they are laid under a strict command that they shall not impart only according to the portion of his word which he doth grant unto the children of men, according to the heed and diligence which they give unto him." (Alma 12:9.)[3]

How will the world know of the truth and divinity of the gospel message when it is taught by the disciples? When the command comes to 'repent and believe the gospel,' how can the hearers come to know they must believe and obey at the peril of their salvation? Jesus continues to counsel:

Say unto them, Ask of God; ask, and it shall be given you; seek, and ye shall find; knock, and it shall be opened unto you. For every one that asketh, receiveth; and he that seeketh, findeth; and unto him that knocketh, it shall be opened.

It is the Lord's work that is involved; it is his gospel; he will bear record of its truth and divinity. He is no respecter of persons; he will give the Holy Ghost to those who hunger and thirst after righteousness, for, as Nephi said, "the Holy Ghost . . . is the gift of God unto all those who diligently seek him, as well in times of old as in the time that he should manifest himself unto the children of men."[4] Truth seekers must turn to the Lord for a final and conclusive answer on religious matters. Every person who hears the gospel preached by a legal administrator sent from God; every person who desires to know which of all the churches is right and which he should join; every person who is really concerned with the well-being of his eternal soul—every such person stands exactly where Joseph Smith stood at the beginning of this dispensation: He must ask of God, who giveth to all men liberally and upbraideth not.[5]

The preaching of the gospel, however, to those already mired in their own theological mud—no matter when or to whom or under what circumstances—always brings the same response; the reaction to the new message is as predictable as is the rising of the morning sun. Those who already think they possess the light of heaven; those who believe they are engaged in the Lord's service; those who have a form of godliness that satisfies their instinctive desires to worship—such will always say: 'We already have the truths of salvation; why should we give heed to this new nonsense which you preach?' Aware—partly by instinct and partly, no doubt, by the experiences already gained in discussing Jesus and his doctrines with others—that such a reaction would be forthcoming, "his disciples said unto him: They will say unto us, We ourselves are righteous, and need not that any man should teach us. God, we know, heard Moses and some of the prophets; but us he will not hear. And they will say, We have the law for our salvation, and that is sufficient for us."[6]

Jesus has already identified the door through which men must enter to gain a testimony of the new order that is now replacing the old Mosaic system. It is: Ask of God in faith and he will reveal the truth of it unto you by the power of the Holy Ghost. And so to answer the expressed anxieties of his disciples, he simply brings them back again to the basic reality involved: There is only one way to know the truth about God and his laws, and that is to receive personal revelation. "Then Jesus answered, and said unto his disciples, Thus shall ye say unto them:

> *What man among you, having a son, and he shall be standing out, and shall say, Father, open thy house that I may come in and sup with thee, will not say, Come in, my son; for mine is thine, and thine is mine?*
>
> *Or what man is there among you, who, if his son ask bread, will give him a stone?*
>
> *Or if he ask a fish, will he give him a serpent?*
>
> *If ye then, being evil, know how to give good gifts unto your children, how much more shall your Father who is in heaven give good things to them that ask him?*

To all this there is a conclusion to be reached, a grand climax to hear, a summit of inspired logic yet to shine forth. None but the one whose sermon we are hearing anew could have said it so well:

> *Therefore* [that is, in the light of all that he has just said] *all things whatsoever ye would that men should do to*

you, do ye even so to them: for this is the law and the prophets.

The Golden Rule, as we have come to call it; the law of Moses and the teachings of the prophets—all summarized in one sentence! Truly, never man spake as this Man!

And all this being so—the gospel being taught; the kingdom being once again established; the door being open for all who will to enter; the disciples being instructed in the part they are to play—Jesus now proclaims:

Repent, therefore, and enter ye in at the strait gate; for wide is the gate, and broad is the way that leadeth to destruction, and many there be who go in thereat. Because strait is the gate, and narrow is the way, which leadeth unto life, and few there be that find it.

Enter in at the strait gate of baptism; find yourself on the strait and narrow path leading to the celestial kingdom. Enter in at the strait gate of celestial marriage; find yourself on the strait and narrow path leading to eternal life in the highest heaven of the celestial world. The broad gate is always open, and all the influences of the world urge and entice men to enter and go downward to darkness; the narrow gate is open only to those who desire righteousness and who seek the Lord and his goodness. It is written:

Behold, the way for man is narrow,
But it lieth in a straight course before him,
And the keeper of the gate is the Holy One of Israel;
And he employeth no servant there;
And there is none other way save it be by the gate;
For he cannot be deceived,
For the Lord God is his name.

And whoso knocketh, to him will he open;
And the wise, and the learned, and they that are rich,
Who are puffed up because of their learning, and their
    wisdom, and their riches—
Yea, they are they whom he despiseth;

And save they shall cast these things away,
And consider themselves fools before God,
And come down in the depths of humility,
He will not open unto them.

But the things of the wise and the prudent
Shall be hid from them forever—
Yea, that happiness which is prepared for the saints.[7]

Jesus Speaks of Prophets, Good Works, and Salvation
(Matthew 7:15-29; 8:1; JST, Matthew 7:30-31, 33, 36-37; 3 Nephi 14:15-27; Luke 6:43-44, 46-49)

Now Jesus speaks some sharp and cutting words about the false prophets who are everywhere to be found in his day. But moments ago he pointed to the scribes, the Pharisees, the priests, and the Levites and said: "Ye yourselves are the children of corruption." They are apostate; they have all "gone out of the way"; they all are "under sin"; and neither do they "observe the law, nor the commandments." And the disciples, also but moments ago, have quoted these same blind guides of an erring race as saying: "God, we know, heard Moses and some of the prophets; but us he will not hear." Now Jesus excoriates these same teachers as, with reference to them—and in principle, also, to all future blind guides and erring religious teachers—he tells the people: "Beware of false prophets, which come to you in sheep's clothing, but inwardly they are ravening wolves."

False prophets—the curse and scourge of the world! How awful and awesome and evil it is when one pretends and professes to speak for God in leading men to salvation, but in fact has a message that is false, a doctrine that is not true, and a prophecy that will not come to pass. And how little do the Jewish people of Jesus' day know—or does the world today know—who among them are the false prophets. But then, false prophets are of the world; they follow the

168

practices of the world; they teach what the carnal mind desires to hear; they are loved by the world.

Moses, in whom the Jews trusted, and whose name was reverenced in all their synagogues, was the one who said: "Would God that all the Lord's people were prophets, and that the Lord would put his spirit upon them!" (Num. 11:29.) Paul would soon say: "Ye may all prophesy," and, "covet to prophesy." (1 Cor. 14:31, 39.) And John the Beloved would in a not-distant day hear from angelic lips the gracious words: "The testimony of Jesus is the spirit of prophecy." (Rev. 19:10.)

A true prophet is one who has the testimony of Jesus; one who knows by personal revelation that Jesus Christ is the Son of the living God, and that he was to be—or has been—crucified for the sins of the world; one to whom God speaks and who recognizes the still small voice of the Spirit. A true prophet is one who holds the holy priesthood; who is a legal administrator; who has power and authority from God to represent him on earth. A true prophet is a teacher of righteousness to whom the truths of the gospel have been revealed and who presents them to his fellowmen so they can become heirs of salvation in the highest heaven. A true prophet is a witness, a living witness, one who knows, and one who testifies. Such a one, if need be, foretells the future and reveals to men what the Lord reveals to him.

A false prophet is the opposite of all this. He does not know by personal revelation of the divine Sonship of the Prophet who was like unto Moses. He does not enjoy the gift of the Holy Ghost or hold the holy priesthood, and he is not a legal administrator who has power to bind and seal on earth and in heaven. He is not a teacher of true doctrine; he may believe any of an infinite variety of false doctrines, but he does not teach, in purity and perfection, the fulness of the everlasting gospel. Because he does not receive revelation or enjoy the gifts of the Spirit, he believes these things have ceased. He thinks: 'God, I know, heard Moses and some of the prophets; but me he will not hear.' Because he teaches false doctrines, he does not lead men to salvation, and in cases not a few he becomes a ravening wolf in sheep's clothing.[8]

To denounce these ravening wolves among the scribes and Pharisees who, parading before the people as prophets, yet tore and gashed and mutilated the souls of men with their false teachings; to excoriate the hypocritical practices of the priests and Levites, as they performed their sacrificial rites in similitude of a future Messiah who had in fact come and been rejected by them; to acclaim as false that which is evil—to do all this is not to denounce or reject that which is true and good. All Israel knew there had been true prophets in days of old. All Israel knew that some then living were claiming prophetic stature. All Israel knew—this above all— that the Lord God of their fathers had, by the mouth of Moses, the man of God, promised to raise up a prophet like unto Israel's great lawgiver, and that the prophet so called forth would be the Messiah.

The Jews themselves had sent priests and Levites to John to ask, "Art thou that prophet?" (John 1:21.) And many people, among them the man who was blind from birth, said of Jesus, "He is a prophet." (John 9:17.) None among them questioned that there had been and were and would be true prophets. They knew that God always had spoken and always would speak by the mouths of men called by him to the prophetic office. The issue then was—and now is—how to identify the true prophets; how to know who among the professing prophets represent the Lord and who have no such divine commission; how to tell the true from the false.

"Ye shall know them by their fruits," Jesus said. By their fruits—their words, their acts, the wonders that they do— these things shall separate true prophets and teachers from false ones. Do they receive revelations and see visions? Does the Holy Ghost speak by their mouth? Are they legal administrators who have power to bind and seal on earth and in heaven? Is their doctine true and sound and in harmony with all that is found in Holy Writ? Do they enjoy the gifts of the Spirit, so that the sick are healed under their hands? And does the Lord God give his Holy Spirit to attest the truth of their words and to approve the acts that they do? Without true prophets there is no salvation; false prophets lead people astray; men choose, at the peril of their salvation, the prophets whom they follow.

"Do men gather grapes of thorns, or figs of thistles?" Jesus asks. Matthew records no answer to the query, only the application: "Even so every good tree bringeth forth good fruit; but a corrupt tree bringeth forth evil fruit. A good tree cannot bring forth evil fruit, neither can a corrupt tree bring forth good fruit." Luke's account, however, quotes Jesus as saying:

> For a good tree bringeth not forth corrupt fruit; neither doth a corrupt tree bring forth good fruit. For every tree is known by his own fruit. For of thorns men do not gather figs, nor of a bramble bush gather they grapes.

Or, in other words, as Moroni wrote, quoting the words of his father, Mormon:

> A man being evil cannot do that which is good; neither will he give a good gift.
>
> For behold, a bitter fountain cannot bring forth good water; neither can a good fountain bring forth bitter water; wherefore, a man being a servant of the devil cannot follow Christ; and if he follow Christ he cannot be a servant of the devil. (Moro. 7:10-11.)

By way of conclusion to this part of his sermon, Jesus continued: "Every tree that bringeth not forth good fruit is hewn down, and cast into the fire. *Wherefore by their fruits ye shall know them.*"

Our Lord's mighty sermon is drawing to its close. He is about to lay the capstone on the structure of doctrine and counsel and exhortation which his gracious words have built, and that capstone is: Keep the commandments so as to be able to withstand the trials and tests that are ahead.

"Verily I say unto you, it is not every one that saith unto me, Lord, Lord, that shall enter into the kingdom of heaven," he says, "but he that doeth the will of my Father who is in heaven." Lip service alone does not save; it is not confessing that Jesus is the Lord, without more, that opens heaven's door; belief without works has no saving power. Keep the commandments; do the will of the Father; work and labor and struggle and strive—then expect salvation. Baptism alone does not save; celestial marriage alone does not exalt; church membership without more does not assure an inheritance in celestial glory. "After ye have gotten into this straight and narrow path, I would ask if all is done?" Nephi queries, and his answer is, "Nay." Rather: "Ye must press forward with a steadfastness in Christ, having a perfect brightness of hope, and a love of God and of all men. Wherefore, if ye shall press forward, feasting upon the word of Christ, and endure to the end, behold, thus saith the Father: Ye shall have eternal life." (2 Ne. 31:19-20.)

"For the day soon cometh, that men shall come before me to judgment, to be judged according to their works." 'I am the Judge; I am the Messiah; look unto me and live; I shall sit in judgment upon the world.' And, "Many will say to me in that day, Lord, Lord, have we not prophesied in thy name? and in thy name have cast out devils? and in thy name done many wonderful works?" To whom is he speaking? Is it not to those who have been baptized; those who have gained the testimony of Jesus, which is the spirit of prophecy; those who have received the holy priesthood and have cast out devils and worked miracles?

Two answers of equivalent meaning are recorded to his question; both are answers that will be given to those saints who have not endured to the end, who have not kept the commandments, and who have not pressed forward with a steadfastness in Christ after baptism. In one, the account says: "And then will I profess unto them, I never knew you: depart from me, ye that work iniquity." In the other account the words are: "And then will I say, Ye never knew me; depart from me ye that work iniquity."

'I never knew you, and you never knew me! Your discipleship was limited; you were not perfect members of my kingdom. Your heart was not so centered in me as to cause you to endure to the end; and so for a time and a season you were faithful; you even worked miracles in my name; but in the end it shall be as though I never knew you.'

And why call ye me, Lord, Lord, and do not the things which I say?

'If ye believe that I am he of whom the prophets testified; if ye accept me as the Promised Messiah; if I am the Son of God and ye call me Lord, then keep my commandments; endure to the end; worship the Father in my name, and ye shall be saved.' "Whosoever cometh to me, and heareth my sayings, and doeth them"—that is, he who is my disciple, he who believes my gospel and joins my church—"I will shew you to whom he is like:

He is like a man which built an house, and digged deep, and laid the foundation on a rock: and when the flood arose, the stream beat vehemently upon that house, and could not shake it: for it was founded upon a rock.

But he that heareth, and doeth not, is like a man that without a foundation built an house upon the earth; against which the stream did beat vehemently, and immediately it fell; and the ruin of that house was great.

Blessed are all they who receive the word with joy; who build their house of salvation upon him who is the Eternal Rock; and who then endure to the end—for they shall be saved with an everlasting salvation.

Blessed are all they who call Jesus, Lord, Lord; who have in their hearts the prophetic insight that men call the testimony of Jesus; and who are valiant in testimony all their days—for they shall wear the victor's crown.

Blessed are all they who keep the commandments; who are true and faithful to every trust; and who do ever those things which please Him whose we are—for they shall dwell everlastingly with him in celestial rest.

And so endeth the Sermon on the Mount, the Sermon on the Plain, the Sermon in Bountiful—the sermon like none other ever delivered. As for the people who heard him, they "were astonished at his doctrine; For he taught them as one having authority from God, and not as having authority from the scribes."

And so Jesus, as "great multitudes followed him," "was come down from the mountain," to be elsewhere and otherwise about his Father's business. The Lord be praised that we know as much as we do about what he said and did in his day!

NOTES

1. Mormon, who had the Nephite Sermon in Bountiful before him when he wrote, leaves us this analysis of properly judging all things: "Take heed, my beloved brethren, that ye do not judge that which is evil to be of God, or that which is good and of God to be of the devil. For behold, my brethren, it is given unto you to judge, that ye may know good from evil; and the way to judge is as plain, that ye may know with a perfect knowledge, as the daylight is from the dark night. For behold, the Spirit of Christ is given to every man, that he may know good from evil; wherefore, I show unto you the way to judge; for every thing which inviteth to do good, and to persuade to believe in Christ, is sent forth by the power and gift of Christ; wherefore ye may know with a perfect knowledge it is of God. . . . And now, my brethren, seeing that ye know the light by which ye may judge, which light is the light of Christ, see that ye do not judge wrongfully; for with that same judgment which ye judge ye shall also be judged." (Moro. 7:14-18.)

2. These are two of the verses of Eliza R. Snow's great Mormon hymn, "Truth Reflects Upon Our Senses," *Hymns*, no. 188.

3. This same truth, in principle, is found in latter-day revelation in these words: "Thou shalt declare glad tidings"—that is, present the message of the restoration to the world— "yea, publish it upon the mountains, and upon every high place, and among every people that thou shalt be permitted to see. . . . And of tenets [those doctrines which are over and above and deeper than the ones contained in the basic message itself] thou shalt not talk, but thou shalt declare repentance and faith on the Savior, and remission of sins by baptism, and by fire, yea, even the Holy Ghost." (D&C 19:29-31.)

4. In addition to the words quoted, Nephi also says: "For he that diligently seeketh shall find; and the mysteries of God shall be unfolded unto them, by the power of the Holy Ghost, as well in these times as in times of old, and as well in times of old as in times to come; wherefore, the course of the Lord is one eternal round." (1 Ne. 10:17-19.)

5. It was of James's words—"If any of you lack wisdom, let him ask of God, that giveth to all men liberally, and upbraideth not; and it shall be given"—that Joseph Smith said: "Never did any passage of scripture come with more power to the heart of man than this did at this time to mine." He pondered upon it again and again, until, guided by the Spirit, he was led to offer the prayer which rent the heavens and opened the dispensation of the fulness of times. (JS-H 1:10-20.)

6. "How similarly the spiritually closed mind operates in all ages! These Jewish attempts, to justify adherence to a false religion, sound as though they had been made by the ministers of modern Christendom. 'We ourselves are righteous, and what can these Mormon Elders teach us. True it is that God spoke to prophets of old, but revelation has ceased; there is no modern communion with heaven. We have the Bible and are Christians, and that is sufficient for us.' But Jesus' counsel is: 'Tell them to humble themselves, repent of their sins, and pray to the Father in mighty prayer so they may learn where the truth really lies.' " (*Commentary* 1:249.)

7. 2 Ne. 9:41-43.

8. Two statements from the Prophet Joseph Smith give prophetic sanction to the views on prophets here presented. First: "When a man goes about prophesying, and commands men to obey his teachings, he must either be a true or false prophet. False prophets always arise to oppose the true prophets and they will prophesy so very near the truth that they will deceive almost the very chosen ones." (*Teachings*, p. 365.) Second: "If any person should ask me if I were a prophet, I should not deny it, as that would give me the lie; for, according to John, the testimony of Jesus is the spirit of prophecy; therefore, if I profess to be a witness or teacher, and have not the spirit of prophecy, which is the testimony of Jesus, I must be a false witness; but if I be a true teacher and witness, I must possess the spirit of prophecy, and that constitutes a prophet; and any man who says he is a teacher or a preacher of righteousness, and denies the spirit of prophecy, is a liar, and the truth is not in him; and by this key false teachers and imposters may be detected." (*Teachings*, p. 269.)

Chapter 45

JESUS MINISTERS AS ONE HAVING AUTHORITY

Across the sea, along the shore,
In numbers ever more and more,
From lonely hut and busy town,
The valley through, the mountain down,
What was it ye went out to see,
Ye silly folk of Galilee?
The reed that in the wind doth shake?
The weed that washes in the lake? . . .

A Teacher? Rather seek the feet
Of those who sit in Moses' seat.
Go, humbly seek, and bow to them
Far off in great Jerusalem. . . .
What is it came ye here to note?
A young Man preaching in a boat.

A Prophet! Boys and women weak!
   Declare—and cease to rave—
Whence is it He hath learnt to speak?
   Say, who His doctrine gave?
A Prophet? Prophet wherefore He
   Of all in Israel's tribes?—

*He teacheth with authority
And not as do the scribes.*[1]

He Speaks as One Having Authority
(Matthew 7:28-29; JST, Matthew 7:36-37)

We are now in a high state of spiritual exhilaration, even exultation. Gracious and God-given words echo and re-echo through every fiber of our being. We walk down the gentle slopes, covered with grass and flowers and shrubs, as we go from the high plateau on the Mount of Beatitudes to the busy getting and giving of Capernaum and its lake-near environs. We are basking in the light and love and beauty of the Sermon on the Mount. We ponder every spoken word; each phrase sinks into our heart as though by fire, and our bosom burns with the truth and reality of it all. Our souls could not be more stirred had we stood with Moses on Sinai as the smoke and fire ascended, as the thunders rolled, and as the Holy Mount quaked with Jehovah's presence.

Never man spake as we have just heard the Lord Jesus speak. "The people were astonished at his doctrine," Matthew says, "For he taught them as one having authority, and not as the scribes." Or, rather, as we have already seen, "He taught them as one having authority from God, and not as having authority from the scribes." His voice was the voice of the Incarnate Jehovah; his words, spoken by the power of the Holy Ghost, were the words of his Father. Others were authorized to preach and teach by the scribes; he had his "authority from God." He came in his Father's name, used his Father's voice, and exercised his Father's power. This we have seen him do in the Sermon on the Mount, which itself was the ordination sermon and charge for the Twelve special witnesses, whom he had chosen to testify of him in all the world.

It is better, no doubt, to have a false religion and to worship false gods than to have no religion and no worship at all. Neutrality is as nothing, and indifference is denigrating and damning. Those who are lukewarm—who are neither hot nor cold; who take no affirmative stand; who do not seek the blessings available through worship—will one day be spewed out of the divine mouth, as it were, and find their place in one of the lesser eternal realms. And this much we can say for the scribes: they were anything but lukewarm. They had a zeal for religion, a zeal for worship, a zeal for God, but it was a misplaced, a twisted, and a perverted zeal. But those who are zealous, even in false causes, are at least prospective zealots—as witness Saul of Tarsus—in true causes. Our concern here is the comparison between the teachings of the scribes, who spoke without divine approval, and the teachings of him who was the Divine Voice.

"The teaching of their Scribes was narrow, dogmatic, material; it was cold in manner, frivolous in matter, second-hand and iterative in its very essence; with no freshness in it, no force, no fire; servile to all authority, opposed to all independence; at once erudite and foolish, at once contemptuous and mean; never passing a hair's breadth beyond the carefully-watched boundary line of commentary and precedent; full of balanced inference and orthodox hesitancy, and impossible literalism; intricate with legal pettiness and labyrinthine system; elevating mere memory above genius, and repetition above originality; concerned only about Priests and Pharisees, in Temple and synagogue, or school, or Sanhedrin, and mostly occupied with things infinitely little. It was not indeed wholly devoid of moral significance, nor is it impossible to find here and there, among the *débris* of it, a worthy thought; but it was occupied a thousandfold more with Levitical minutia about mint, and anise, and cumin, and the length of fringes, and the breadth of phylacteries, and the washing of cups and platters, and the particular quarter of a second when new moons and Sabbath-days began." (Farrar, pp. 201-2.) Such are the well-chosen words that depict the teachings—to say nothing of the inner feelings and twisted religious instincts—of the scribes. Teachers—call them false prophets, if you will, for

Jesus so designated them in the great sermon just delivered—who are without authority, who are devoid of inspiration, and who do not and cannot in fact speak for the Almighty—such teachers turn, in the very nature of things, to learned commentary about what inspired teachers of other ages have spoken and which is preserved in the form of scripture.

Now, in contrast, let us summarize how the Master Teacher approached his podium. "This teaching of Jesus was wholly different in its character, and as much grander as the temple of the morning sky under which it was uttered was grander than stifling synagogues or crowded school. It was preached, as each occasion rose, on the hill-side, or by the lake, or on the roads, or in the house of the Pharisee, or at the banquet of the Publican; nor was it any sweeter or loftier when it was addressed in the Royal Portico to the Masters of Israel, than when its only hearers were the ignorant people whom the haughty Pharisees held to be accursed.

"And there was no reserve in its administration. It flowed forth as sweetly and as lavishly to single listeners as to enraptured crowds; and some of its very richest revelations were vouchsafed, neither to rulers nor to multitudes, but to the persecuted outcast of the Jewish synagogue, to the timid inquirer in the lonely midnight, and the frail woman by the noon-day well. And it dealt, not with scrupulous rites and ceremonial cleansings, but with the human soul, and human destiny, and human life—with Hope and Charity, and Faith. There were no definitions in it, or explanations, or 'scholastic systems,' or philosophic theorising, or implicated mazes of difficult and dubious discussion, but a swift intuitive insight into the very depths of the human heart—even a supreme and daring paradox that, without being fenced round with exceptions or limitations, appealed to the conscience with its irresistible simplicity, and with an absolute mastery stirred and dominated over the heart. Springing from the depths of holy emotions, it thrilled the being of every listener as with an electric flame. In a word, its authority was the authority of the Divine Incarnate; it was the Voice of God, speaking in the utterance of man; its austere purity was yet pervaded with tenderest sympathy, and its awful severity with an unutterable love. It is, to borrow the image of the wisest of the Latin Fathers, a great sea whose smiling surface breaks into refreshing ripples at the feet of our little ones, but into whose unfathomable depths the wisest may gaze with the shudder of amazement and the thrill of love. . . .

"How exquisitely and freshly simple is the actual language of Christ compared with all other teaching that has ever gained the ear of the world! There is no science in it, no art, no pomp of demonstration, no carefulness of toil, no trick of rhetoricians, no wisdom of the schools. Straight as an arrow to the mark His precepts pierce to the very depths of the soul and spirit. All is short, clear, precise, full of holiness, full of the common images of daily life.

"There is scarcely a scene or object familiar to the Galilee of that day, which Jesus did not use as a moral illustration of some glorious promise or moral law. He spoke of green fields, and springing flowers, and the budding of the vernal trees; of the red or lowering sky; of sunrise and sunset; of wind and rain; of night and storm; of clouds and lightning; of stream and river; of stars and lamps; of fire and salt; of quivering bulrushes and burning weeds; of rent garments and bursting wine-skins; of eggs and serpents; of pearls and pieces of money; of nets and fish. Wine and wheat, corn and oil, stewards and gardeners, labourers and employers, kings and shepherds, travellers and fathers of families, courtiers in soft clothing and brides in nuptial robes—all these are found in His discourses. He knew all life, and had gazed on it with a kindly as well as a kingly glance. He could sympathize with its joys no less than He could heal its sorrows, and the eyes that were so often suffused with tears as they saw the sufferings of earth's mourners beside the bed of death, had shone also with a kindlier glow as they watched the games of earth's happy little ones in the green fields and busy streets." (Farrar, pp. 202-5.)

Jesus Heals the Servant of a Gentile Centurion
(Luke 7:1-10; Matthew 8:5-13; JST, Matthew 8:9-10, 12)

This Man, who spake as none else before or since—whose words exceed in wisdom those even of Enoch, and Moses, and Isaiah, all of whom received their inspiration from him, but who expressed the thoughts after the manner of their language, and according to their own talents and abilities—this Man now goes forth to do deeds that no others, before or since, have ever assayed to do. His authority was not only to use the voice and speak the words of Him whose servant he was, but to use the power given him to heal the sick and raise the dead. His miracles will stand as an attesting seal, written in the souls of men, to the words that he spoke.

We are with him now in Capernaum, his own city. A Roman garrison is located here. One of its officers, a centurion of heathen-Gentile birth, who commands between fifty and a hundred men, has an esteemed servant who is "ready to die" of a paralytic seizure. This centurion, a soldier in the service of Herod Antipas, is no ordinary Gentile upon whom the curse of disbelief rests, or who revels in the carnal lusts by which soldiers sometimes entertain themselves. He may have been a "proselyte of righteousness," one adopted into the family of Abraham, one who chose to live as an Israelite and worship the Lord Jehovah. At least he was a friend of the Jews and had, out of his own munificence, built for them a synagogue in Capernaum. Hearing that Jesus was coming into their city, he besought the elders of the Jews to intercede on his behalf. "My servant lieth at home sick of the palsy, grievously tormented," he said. And the importuning Jews told Jesus "that he was worthy for whom he should do this: For he loveth our nation, and he hath built us a synagogue." Jesus said, "I will come and heal him."

181

Jesus and the Jewish elders—plus the select group upon whom his countenance shone—started their journey to the home of the centurion. We may suppose that this military commander knew of the nobleman, who also served Herod Antipas, and whose son in Capernaum had been healed by Jesus' word, spoken twenty miles away in Cana. In any event, when Jesus was "not far from the house, the centurion sent friends to him" who said: "Lord, trouble not thyself: for I am not worthy that thou shouldest enter under my roof: Wherefore, neither thought I myself worthy to come unto thee: but say in a word, and my servant shall be healed. For I also am a man set under authority, having under me soldiers, and I say unto one, Go, and he goeth; and to another, Come, and he cometh; and to my servant, Do this, and he doeth it."

"The centurion's reasoning—profound in logic, perfect in showing forth faith—was to this effect: If I, a mere officer in the Roman army, must obey my superiors, and also have power myself to send others forth at my command, then surely the Lord of all needs but speak and his will shall be done." (*Commentary* 1:258.)

Those who were with Jesus marveled at the message from the centurion, and Jesus said: "I have not found so great faith, no, not in Israel." Such a teaching moment as this seldom arises, and of it the Master Teacher makes the most.

> *Many shall come from the east and west, and shall sit down with Abraham, and Isaac, and Jacob, in the kingdom of heaven. But the children of the wicked one shall be cast out into outer darkness; there shall be weeping and gnashing of teeth.*

In just a moment, he who was not sent but to the lost sheep of the house of Israel; he who came to his kindred, that the word of truth might go first to the Jews and at a later date to the Gentiles; he who was the God of Israel—in just a moment he was going to heal the servant of a Gentile whose faith exceeded the faith of the members of the chosen race.

But before doing so he chose to shake the theological foundations upon which Israel's preferential status rested. Many—not a few; Gentile hosts; members of the hated, alien nations—many would find glory in heaven with the ancient patriarchs, while the literal seed, being the children of Satan, Jews who should have been the children of the kingdom, would be cast out. How little his Jewish hearers understood the meaning of that which Jehovah had of old time said to Abraham: "As many as receive this Gospel shall be called after thy name, and shall be accounted thy seed, and shall rise up and bless thee, as their father." (Abr. 2:10.)

Then came the miracle, which attested to the truth of his doctrine. The message for the centurion was: "Go thy way; and as thou hast believed, so be it done unto thee. And his servant was healed in the selfsame hour."

Jesus Raises a Widow's Son from Death
(Luke 7:11-17)

It is now the day after the healing of the centurion's servant in Capernaum. Jesus, his disciples, and a great multitude have traversed their weary way—a distance of twenty-five miles—to a little Galilean village of no particular note, a place called Nain. It is, as we have seen, Jesus' wont to visit the towns and villages of Galilee, of Judea, and of all Palestine to preach the gospel and offer salvation to his people. Aside from the fact there was a funeral in Nain today, the day has been no different from the ceaseless caravan of days that pass endlessly along in hundreds of the sleepy villages of Israel. But ere the sun sets this day, such a miracle will be wrought in Nain as no man on earth has before seen. A dead youth, one prepared for consignment to the tomb, shall live again; one word from the Lord of life and the dried blood will flow again through a newly enlivened heart, and the breath of life will inflate anew the collapsed lungs of a dead corpse. Where there was death, with all its decay and sorrow, there will be life, with all its

183

growth and joy. This is the day when the Prince of life will smite the angel of death with the breath of his lips, and that which was cold and stiff and lifeless will rise in warmth and vigor and all the strength and beauty of youth.

Two multitudes are about to meet: one sorrowing because the only son of his mother, a widow, has passed to the great beyond—sorrowing because such a promising Israelite, whose help was so much needed by a weeping mother, was about to be laid in a lifeless tomb; the other a joyful multitude—a group of believing, rejoicing disciples in whose bosoms the fires ignited on the Mount of Beatitudes still burned; a group who, but yesterday, had heard their Prophet-Leader command a centurion's servant to arise from his paralytic bed, and it was so.

In one group, where sorrow and sadness reign, the central figure is a weeping widow, trudging beside a funeral bier, as the cortege approaches the final corpse-prepared resting place for her only and beloved son. Her thoughts are filled with death and all its dreads. In her is fulfilled the ancient proverb: "Make thee mourning, as for an only son, most bitter lamentation." (Jer. 6:26.) The central figure in the other group—where joy abounds and words of life and light flow freely—is the one who has life in himself because God is his Father, and to whom what men call death is but the transfer of an eternal soul to another realm of life.

The sorrowing mother has suffered through the siege of sickness; every mortal means has been used to stay the grim reaper's hand. We cannot but think that she importuned in faith, before the Eternal Throne, for the life of her son, her only son; but death, in the end, has come off victorious. "The well-known blast of the horn has carried tidings, that once more the Angel of Death has done his dire behest. In passionate grief the mother has rent her upper garment. The last sad offices have been rendered to the dead. The body has been laid on the ground; hair and nails have been cut, and the body washed, anointed, and wrapped in the best the widow could procure." (Edersheim 1:554.) The funeral itself has now been held; its sermons are over; mourning women have been employed to chant "in weird strains the lament: 'Alas, the lion! alas, the hero!' or similar words," and "the funeral orator, if one was employed," is preceding "the bier, proclaiming the good deeds of the dead." The youth lies on the open bier; friends and neighbors take turns, as pall-bearers, in carrying the mortal remains, and behind the bier come the mourning and sympathizing townspeople. "Up from the city close by came this 'great multitude' that followed the dead, with lamentations, wild chants of mourning women, accompanied by flutes and the melancholy tinkle of cymbals, perhaps by trumpets, amidst expressions of general sympathy. Along the road from Endor streamed the great multitude which followed the 'Prince of Life.' Here they met: Life and Death." (Edersheim 1:555-57.)

"And when the Lord saw her, he had compassion on her, and said unto her, Weep not." He who came to bear the sorrows of many was himself sorrowful. He "touched the bier: and they that bare him stood still." No doubt the pallbearers recognized the Prophet of Nazareth of Galilee whose fame was everywhere; at least his commanding presence and saintly demeanor stayed the funeral march. His words were simple; his command could not be gainsaid. There was no struggle, no stretching of "himself upon the child three times," no pleading with the Lord, as when Elijah raised the son of the widow of Zarephath from death. (1 Kgs. 17.) There was no shutting of the door, no praying to the Lord, no lying upon the child, so as to "put his mouth upon his mouth, and his eyes upon his eyes, and his hands upon his hands," as when Elisha raised from death the son of the great woman of Shunem. (2 Kgs. 4.)

With Jesus it was not so. He said simply: "Young man, I say unto thee, Arise. And he that was dead sat up, and began to speak." Then Jesus graciously, in tender solicitude, "delivered him to his mother."

The living die and the dead live again—because He wills it. There was no importuning of God, nor was there need for

185

such. Jesus did it. Jehovah was there. His words were "I say unto thee, Arise." He was claiming divinity, Messiahship, eternal godhood—and proving his claim (there was no blasphemy here!) by raising the dead!

And is not this first known instance of calling mortals from death to life by Jesus but a type and a shadow—a heaven-sent similitude—of what this same Jesus shall do for all his people at an appointed time? Will he not say to all, 'Come forth from your graves; step out of your tombs; arise from your biers. Live again—this time in glorious immortality, never to suffer the pangs of death again'? And will he not then deliver the righteous into the arms of their mothers and fathers and loved ones?

As the marvel of what had this day happened in Nain dawned upon the throngs in whose presence the miracle was wrought, is it any wonder, as Luke recounts, that "there came a fear on all: and they glorified God, saying, That a great prophet is risen up among us; and, That God hath visited his people. And this rumour of him went forth throughout all Judea, and throughout all the region round about."

Yes, it went even into the dungeon at Machaerus, where John the Baptist suffered in imprisoned silence for the testimony of Jesus that was his. And of this imprisonment and the part it played in the teachings of Jesus we shall soon see.

NOTE

1. These sweet words are taken from a footnote in Farrar, p. 205, and are attributed by him to Arthur Hugh Clough.

Chapter 46

JESUS AND JOHN TESTIFY OF EACH OTHER

John: "Behold the Lamb of God,
which taketh away the sin of the world....
He must increase, but I must decrease....
He that believeth on the Son
hath everlasting life."
(John 1:29; 3:30, 36.)

Jesus: "Among those that are born
of women
there is not a greater prophet
than John the Baptist." (Luke 7:28.)

John Sends His Disciples to Jesus
(Luke 7:18-23; Matthew 11:2-6; JST, Matthew 11:3, 6)

Our last report on the life and ministry of the one sent to prepare the way for Him by whom salvation comes; our last account relative to the blessed Baptist, who immersed the Son of God in Jordan's waters; our last record told of his imprisonment by Herod Antipas in a dungeon at the impregnable fortress at Machaerus. That word was that Jesus—compassionate, concerned, sorrowful because of the suffering of his beloved associate—sent angels to console and minister to his kinsman. John is still in his dungeon cell suffering manfully, as did so many of his fellow prophets, for the sure knowledge that is his that salvation is in the mighty Messiah whose witness he is.

We know little of what went on in the walled and barred place where the Baptist languished, only that the prisons of that day were places of unbearable torture and evil and heartless imposition. John did have visitors, however; there were times and circumstances when news from the outside could be spoken in his ears. His disciples were yet solicitous for his well-being, and they told him of the teachings and miracles of the Messiah. Word came to him of the eyes that were opened, the ears that were unstopped, and the lepers that were cleansed. He was told that the only son of a widow from Nain—dead, prepared for burial, en route to the cemetery—had responded to a gentle command, "Young man, I say unto thee, Arise," and was now secure in the arms of a rejoicing mother.

Apparently some of the Baptist's disciples desired not only to minister to his needs in the prison, not only to bring him news of the religious movement that was sweeping the land, but also to look to him, rather than to Jesus, as the prophet whom they should follow. Conversion is a process that seldom occurs in an instant suddenly. Gospel grace dawns gradually upon most believers. These disciples knew that John, whom they revered, had seen the heavens open and the Spirit of God descend upon Jesus, and they knew that he had heard the heavenly voice acclaim, "This is my beloved Son, in whom I am well pleased." (Matt. 3:17.) They knew that the son of Zacharias had sent others of his disciples, John the Beloved and Andrew among them, into the fold of Jesus by testifying: "Behold the Lamb of God!" (John 1:36) as Jesus walked among them. They knew that John claimed to be an Elias only, and that from the beginning he had taught that one who came after would baptize them with fire and with the Holy Ghost. All of the Baptist's teachings, every word that he spoke, and every act he performed pointed men toward the Messiah in whom they must believe to gain salvation. Yet there were some who still had not as yet followed his counsel to forsake the lesser light and cleave unto the Light of the world.

What can John do more than he has done? What more can he say than to them he hath said? Clearly there is only one remaining hope. John's disciples must come under the spell of Jesus' voice; they must feel the sweet spirit that comes forth from him; they must see his works, hear him teach the gospel, hear his voice testify of his own divine Sonship. They have heard John; let them now hear Jesus. Is this Prophet of Galilee, noble and renowned as he is, the very one of whom Moses taught? Is he the Messiah who was promised? Let them see and hear and learn for themselves; and so, at John's direction, they go from Machaerus, which is in the south of Perea, near the Dead Sea, to an unnamed location in Galilee.

Finding Jesus and the throngs who hear his words and whose sick he heals, they identify themselves; "John Baptist hath sent us unto thee," they say. Then comes the great question, the question upon which their salvation rests, the question that all investigators must answer for themselves: "Art thou he of whom it is written in the prophets that he should come, or do we look for another?" 'Art thou the Son of God who shall atone for the sins of the world, as promised by all the holy prophets since the world began—including John who sent us—or is our Messiah yet to come in another day to another people? We have heard John's witness. We know he said of you, "He is God's own Son, the Beloved One, the very Lamb of God who shall be sacrificed for the sins of the world," but we would hear the witness from your lips. Art thou the Deliverer, the Savior, the Redeemer, as John says you are?'

The question has been asked; it is a fair and proper inquiry; the issue is before the whole multitude; and Jesus will answer it—answer it in a way that no mortal imposter could. He will show in word and in deed that he is indeed the One of whom they speak.

Jesus Testifies of Himself and of John
(*Luke 7:21-35; JST, Luke 7:24; Matthew 11:6-19; JST, Matthew 11:7, 13-16, 21*)

John's disciples have zeroed in to the heart and core of revealed religion. They have asked: 'Art thou the Son of God, as John says, or is salvation to be found elsewhere and to come through another?' If Jesus answers 'I am he,' to what extent will he enhance the belief of John's followers, who already have heard their own teacher testify, in like words, to the divine Sonship of the one whom he baptized at Bethabara? It is not a spoken answer that is needed here; it is, rather, an answer written in fire, an answer that causes Sinai to quake and smoke to ascend like a furnace; it is an answer written in the flesh and blood and sinews of diseased bodies now made whole. Such an answer the Son of God is prepared to give. The abrupt query of John's disciples is left unanswered for the time being as far as spoken words are concerned. Jesus lets them listen to his sermons and see his miracles. "And in that same hour he cured many of their infirmities and plagues, and of evil spirits; and unto many that were blind he gave sight."

What must they think of one who John says is the Messiah, who does such wonders? Was it ever so in Israel of old? Did even Moses and the greatest of the prophets heal whole multitudes? Who before has ever opened the eyes of a legion of blind persons, or cured the infirmities and plagues of a whole nation of people? Jesus has answered their question, not in words but in works. Now he confirms with his lips the things his hands have done; he confirms the conclusion they must already have reached in their hearts. "Go your way," he says, "and tell John what things ye have seen and heard; how that the blind see, the lame walk, the lepers are cleansed, the deaf hear, the dead are raised, to the poor the gospel is preached." 'Tell John that his witness is true; know also within yourselves that I am he of whom the prophets spoke. These miracles attest to the truth of my words and of John's testimony. Ye have heard me preach the gospel to the poor, as Isaiah promised. What think ye, am I not he? Return and tell John what you have seen, and buoy up his spirit, in the prison of his depression, with the assurance that you now believe him because ye have seen the works I do.'

And further: Blessed is John—who has been faithful and true all his days, and who has been, and now is, valiant in the testimony of Jesus—and blessed also are "whosoever shall not be offended in me." That is, 'You yourselves also will be blessed with the saints if ye believe my words and are not offended by the strong doctrine that I teach.'

With this, the two disciples—who we must believe were now fully converted—left to make their wearisome way back to the south of Perea where an evil Antipas held John as a prisoner in the cause of righteousness. And we cannot but feel that their return southward was attended with a spirit of rejoicing that had not manifested itself in the long journey to see Him of whom the meridian Elias so fervently testified.

After their departure, Jesus said to the multitude concerning John: "What went ye out into the wilderness to see? Was it a reed shaken with the wind?" 'Why did you assemble by the thousands in the deserts around Bethabara, and in the waste places near Aenon? Was it to hear an uncertain sound blown on a muted trumpet? Did John ever waver in his testimony? Did the winds of false doctrine, and the hurricanes of disbelief of your rulers, cause him to so much as sway like a reed before them?' "And they answered him, No."

"But what went ye out for to see? A man clothed in soft raiment? Behold, they which are gorgeously apparelled, and live delicately, are in kings' courts." 'Was John clothed in the princely garments of Antipas, and Philip, and Archelaus, the royal sons of the wretched man who sat on the throne of Israel in the day I made flesh my tabernacle, which sons thereafter reigned in their father's stead? Or did he come in the rough and prophetic garb of an Elijah, from the peasant home of poor Judean folk, to whom all the graces of a kingly court were foreign?'

"But what went ye out for to see? A prophet? Yea, I say unto you, and much more than a prophet." How they had flocked to John to learn his doctrine and hear his testimony! By the thousands and the tens of thousands they had left their homes and traveled to Bethabara and to Aenon, journeys that meant camping overnight in the crude caravanserais of the day, on which occasions there was ample time to ponder and discuss the thunderous challenges of the fiery Judean preacher from Hebron. All Jerusalem, as the hyperbolic account expresses it, had gone out to hear a voice crying in the wilderness, a voice that commanded them to repent, to be baptized for the remission of sins, and to await the day when one coming after should baptize them with fire and the Holy Ghost; a voice that introduced, with testimony, the Lamb of God of whom Moses and all the prophets had spoken. Why had they gone forth to hear a voice that smote their consciences and called for a complete revolution in their way of life? What power swept over a whole people, impelling them to seek out the rugged, Elijah-like prophet of the deserts? And if they all esteemed John as a prophet, how could they escape believing his prophetic witness of the One who now ministered among them?

And he was more than a prophet—"much more than a prophet." It is as though Jesus said: 'Ye yourselves know John was a prophet. Ye went out to hear his voice because it was a prophetic voice, one that spoke the mind and will of the Lord, and now I say unto you that John was a prophet and much more than a prophet!'

How can a man be more than a prophet? What is there that is greater than to be a personal representative on earth of the Lord and to speak his mind and will to all men? Jesus gives a partial answer by now saying of John: "This is he, of whom it is written, Behold, I send my messenger before thy face, which shall prepare thy way before thee."

We learned from Jesus as he sat on the Mount of Beatitudes, delivering his incomparable Sermon on the Mount, that we should beware of false prophets—of the scribes and Pharisees, of the priests and Levites, who professed to be teachers and leaders and prophets but who were in fact ravening wolves in sheep's clothing. Though they wore the mantle of religious leadership, their false teachings tore apart the spiritual well-being of their flocks. Implicit in Jesus' denunciation of false prophets was the standing counsel to cleave unto true prophets. Now he is acclaiming John as a true prophet, "Yea . . . much more than a prophet." John, as a witness of his living Lord, was indeed a prophet, and, in addition, he prepared the way before that very Lord, so that the greatest prophetic ministry ever to grace the earth would be manifest. He served as the Lord's messenger, carrying the message that the Lord himself—the Great Immanuel, the God-with-us of whom Isaiah spoke—was indeed with them.

For I say unto you, Among those that are born of women there is not a greater prophet than John the Baptist: but he that is least in the kingdom of God is greater than he.[1]

There is more than a touch of irony here. As to John, the people honored him as a prophet; but as to Jesus, there was no such unreserved acceptance, even though John testified of him. "Whom did Jesus have reference to as being the least?" Joseph Smith asked. "Jesus was looked upon as having the least claim in God's kingdom, and [seemingly, or at least in the minds of the unbelieving among them] was least entitled to their credulity as a prophet; as though He had said, 'He that is considered [by many of you, as] the least among you is greater than John—that is I myself.'" (*Teachings,* p. 276.) For that matter, if John is the equal or superior of all the prophets, how could anyone be greater than he, except that Prophet of whom Moses and the inspired witnesses of all the ages had spoken?

And from the days of John the Baptist until now the kingdom of heaven suffereth violence, and the violent take it by force.

But the days will come, when the violent shall have no

power; for all the prophets and the law prophesied that it should be thus until John. Yea as many as have prophesied have foretold of these days.

And if ye will receive it, verily, he was the Elias, who was for to come and prepare all things. He that hath ears to hear, let him hear.

From the hour John finished the days of his preparation in the wilderness; from the time he first cried repentance to a spiritually sick generation; from the moment he first baptized believing souls in the mighty Jordan—from then "until now," everywhere and in all parts of Palestine, "the kingdom of heaven suffereth violence." Mark it well: the kingdom of heaven set up by John, the kingdom of God on earth, the Church of Jesus Christ, "suffereth violence." And further: "The violent take it by force." There is persecution; there is bitterness. The hosts of hell oppose every investigator who comes near to the truth; the scribes and Pharisees, the priests and Levites—they being the false prophets of the day—marshal their forces. Violence is the result, violence that will mount in intensity until the Elias of preparation is beheaded in Machaerus and the Prophet whose way he prepared is crucified on Calvary. And even then it shall not cease. Violence, born of Beelzebub, ever was and ever will be manifest against the saints until the millennial day, "when the violent shall have no power."[2]

Jesus continues his witness about John: "And all the people that heard him [meaning John], and the publicans, justified God, being baptized with the baptism of John." What a mighty tide of conversion and baptism attended the ministry of the Baptist! The baptism of John—immersion in water by a legal administrator for the remission of sins, the ordinance that prepares men for the baptism of fire and of the Holy Ghost that comes after—this baptism, of which even the hated publicans partook, was ordained of God. All men must be baptized to gain salvation.

"But the Pharisees and lawyers rejected the counsel of God against themselves, being not baptized of him." The counsel of God! God counsels baptism, baptism in water, John's baptism. Some professors of religion do not; they say it is only an outward sign of an inward grace, and that all that matters is how one feels in his heart, or if not that, all that counts is the baptism of desire, or the baptism of the Spirit. But Jesus says that all men—the Pharisees and the lawyers of his day, the false ministers of religion of our day—all must choose whose counsel to take, the counsel that comes from God or that which comes from man.

Then, as a conclusion to this part of his teaching, Jesus asks: "Whereunto then shall I liken the men of this generation? and to what are they like?" He answers: "They are like unto children sitting in the marketplace, and calling one to another, and saying, We have piped unto you, and ye have not danced; we have mourned to you, and ye have not wept. For John the Baptist came neither eating bread nor drinking wine; and ye say, He hath a devil. The Son of man is come eating and drinking; and ye say, Behold a gluttonous man, and a winebibber, a friend of publicans and sinners! But wisdom is justified of all her children."

'What illustration can I choose to show how petty, peevish, and insincere are you unbelieving Jews? You are like fickle children playing games: when you hold a mock wedding, your playmates refuse to dance; when you change the game to a funeral procession, your playmates refuse to mourn. In like manner you are only playing at religion. As cross and capricious children you reject John because he came with the strictness of the Nazarites, and ye reject me because I display the warm human demeanor that makes for pleasant social intercourse.' (*Commentary* 1:263.)

We have now heard John, as an Elias of preparation, bear testimony of the Elias of restoration; and have heard Jesus, in turn, testify of the divine mission of his forerunner. Shortly we shall see John, now languishing in a vile prison, seal his testimony with his blood, preparatory to the receipt of that eternal life of which he is already assured.

195

NOTES

1. Joseph Smith gave three reasons why John was considered one of the greatest prophets: "First. He was entrusted with a divine mission of preparing the way before the face of the Lord. Whoever had such a trust committed to him before or since? No man.

"Secondly. He was entrusted with the important mission, and it was required at his hands, to baptize the Son of Man. Whoever had the honor of doing that? Whoever had so great a privilege and glory? Whoever led the Son of God into the waters of baptism, and had the privilege of beholding the Holy Ghost descend in the form of a dove, or rather in the *sign* of the dove, in witness of that administration? . . .

"Thirdly. John, at that time, was the only legal administrator in the affairs of the kingdom there was then on earth, and holding the keys of power. The Jews had to obey his instructions or be damned, by their own law; and Christ Himself fulfilled all righteousness in becoming obedient to the law which he had given to Moses on the mount, and thereby magnified it and made it honorable, instead of destroying it. The son of Zacharias wrested the keys, the kingdom, the power, the glory from the Jews, by the holy anointing and decree of heaven, and these three reasons constitute him the greatest prophet born of woman." (*Teachings,* pp. 275-76.)

2. In this connection, as I have written elsewhere: "Under the law of Moses a lower standard of personal conduct was required of members of the kingdom than became the case when the gospel fulness was restored. In the old kingdom violent and carnal men exercised undue influence, but in the new kingdom their power was diminished. But the millennium itself must arrive before 'the violent shall have no power.'" (*Commentary* 1:263.)

Chapter 47

JESUS FACES HIS PHARISAIC FOES

She sat and wept beside his feet; the weight
Of sin oppressed her heart; for all the blame,
And the poor malice of the worldly shame,
To her were past, extinct, and out of date;
Only the sin remained—the leprous *state*.
She would be melted by the heat of love,
By fires far fiercer than are blown to prove
And purge the silver ore adulterate.
She sat and wept, and with her untressed hair,
Still wiped the feet she was so blessed to touch;
And He wiped off the soiling of despair
From her sweet soul, because she loved so much.[1]

His Feet Anointed in Simon's House
(Luke 7:36-50)

It is now autumn, A.D. 28. Jesus has been traveling, teaching, testifying, and healing for nearly two years. Timewise most of his mortal ministry is accomplished, and in another year and a half, by April of A.D. 30, he will be lifted up upon the cross by sinful men—sinful scribes and Pharisees, sinful priests and Levites, who will use a Roman arm and a Roman cross, a Roman nail and a Roman spear, to do what they cannot do personally.

And we are now seeing a gradually rising tide of Pharisaic opposition that will roll forward, on waves of hatred and bitterness, until it becomes a mighty crescendo of tumult and thunderous denunciation, punctuated with shrill cries of, "Crucify him; crucify him; his blood be upon us and our children." Already we have seen him rejected by his own in Nazareth; we have heard the murmuring charges of blasphemy when he forgave and then healed the paralytic in Peter's home in Capernaum; we have gone with him to the second Passover in Jerusalem, seen him heal on the Sabbath the man who for thirty-eight years had taken no step on his own; and we have felt pity for those who thereafter sought to slay him because he worked a miracle on their holy day. Back in Galilee, again because he healed on the Sabbath, we have seen the Rabbis, scribes, and Sanhedrinists conspire with the Herodians as to how they might put him to death.

And through it all we have heard Jesus speak loving words to the penitent—as illustrated in the Beatitudes—and send forth harsh denunciations toward his foes and oppressors, as witness his declarations, just made, against those who had called the Son of Man a glutton and a winebibber because of his friendly social intercourse with the people, and a friend of publicans and sinners because his arms and heart were open to all who would hear his voice.

We cannot doubt that this rising tide of opposition was part of the divine plan. It was the preaching of the gospel and the performance of his miracles, strange as this latter may seem, that caused it to spring forth. There will even be Jewish opponents who will seek to slay Lazarus, after he rises from the dead, lest people seeing him alive believe in Christ.

Jesus may not have courted persecution and opposition as such, but the proclamation of a new gospel dispensation, proclaimed to those who fear for their craft, can have no other effect. Indeed, it would appear that "in the unfolding of His Mission to Man, the Christ progressively placed Himself in antagonism to the Jewish religious thought of his time, from out of which He had historically sprung. . . . From the first this antagonism was there in what He taught and did; and it appeared with increasing distinctness in proportion as He taught. We find it in the whole spirit and bearing of what he did and said—in the house at Capernaum, in the Synagogues, with the Gentile Centurion, at the gate of Nain, and especially here, in the history of the much forgiven woman who had much sinned." (Edersheim 1:562.)

And so now we join Jesus in the home of Simon the Pharisee to see what happens when the "much sinned" woman anoints his feet with her tears and with costly ointment brought in an alabaster box. We do not know the name of the city, who Simon was, or who the woman was; only that the banquet, the anointing, and the blessed words spoken by Jesus, all took place somewhere in Galilee. In Holy Writ a fragmentary account only is preserved for us. From it, in Luke's language, we learn that "one of the Pharisees desired him that he would eat with him. And he went into the Pharisee's house, and sat down to meat."

Jesus has often eaten with publicans and known sinners, for which he has, by sinning Pharisees, been condemned. Now he accepts the invitation of one who wears the mantle of religion, but who has not received a remission of his sins in the waters of baptism, and in whose presence a woman of ill repute will come to render to Jesus the obeisance and respect that his host chose not to bestow. It was the social custom of the day for leading Pharisees of a village or city to invite visiting Rabbis to break bread with them in their abodes. Some of Jesus' disciples would have been included by Simon in his invitation. Hospitality was a way of life among them, and it was honorable and proper to feed and shelter visiting teachers and travelers.

Guests entering Palestinian homes often removed their sandals, lest the pollutions of the street contaminate the mats and rugs on which family prayers were offered. At the dining table they reclined on couches with their feet outward from the table, and the dining hall was accessible to others than those bidden to partake of its appetite-satisfying bounties. All of this enabled "a woman in the city, which was a sinner," carrying "an alabaster box of ointment," to enter uninvited and to stand behind Jesus. According to the social customs of the day she could even speak to the guests without being bidden to depart by the master of the house. This, however, she did not do; rather, she "stood at his feet behind him weeping, and began to wash his feet with her tears, and did wipe them with the hairs of her head, and kissed his feet, and anointed them with the ointment."

All of the usual amenities of the day had been ignored by the day's host, as Jesus will soon remind him. But what the host should have done, however reluctantly, the unbidden spectator—and she a woman—had now done with a full heart and in a spirit of penitence and thanksgiving. Why did she do it? What would impel a woman whose life had been stained with sin—stained? perhaps drenched and buried in sin, for her past life could not have been other than one of gross immorality—what would impel such a person to come uninvited, face the Sinless One, and, as her tears bedewed his feet, wipe them with her tresses and seal the washing thus made with an anointing of costly ointment? She first washed the feet of Jesus with her tears, then anointed them with oil. Why? And was all this done by an evil sinner? No!—not by any means. All this was the work and worship of a devout and faithful woman who had been a sinner but who was now cleansed; who was now free from the crushing burden of many offenses; who now walked in a newness of life because of him whose feet she now kissed and upon whom she now bestowed all the reverent and awe-inspired love that her whole soul had power to possess.

This we must know if we are to envision what really transpired on this inspiring occasion in the home of Simon the Pharisee. Here is a woman who once was a sinner but now is clean. Jesus is not going to forgive her sins—he has already done so; it happened when she believed and was baptized in his name; it happened when she repented with full purpose of heart and pledged her life and every breath she thereafter drew to the Cause of Righteousness. We are dealing with a convert who has come to pour out, in the spirit of thanksgiving and rejoicing, the gratitude of her soul to him who has freed her, freed her in times past, from the chains of bondage and hell.

None of this is known to Simon. He is in his sins, being unbaptized; and like Nicodemus, the master in Israel who knew not that men can be born again, Simon is, in his present state, spiritually incapable of conceiving that a woman whose soul once was scarlet is now as white as snow.

Simon thus "spake within himself"; that is, he thought to himself—and as the ancient proverb says: "Guard well thy thoughts, for thoughts are heard in heaven"—Simon thought to himself: "This man, if he were a prophet, would have known who and what manner of woman this is that toucheth him: for she is a sinner." There is no sprouting faith here. Jesus is only "this man," not, as so many are saying, a mighty prophet and even the Messiah, who is called Christ, who is God's Son. Simon's thoughts toward his guest are no more respectful than were his deeds.[2]

"Jesus answering"—he is answering the unspoken thoughts—"said unto him, Simon, I have somewhat to say unto thee. And he saith, Master, say on." Jesus then said:

> *There was a certain creditor which had two debtors: the one owed five hundred pence, and the other fifty.*
>
> *And when they had nothing to pay, he frankly forgave them both. Tell me therefore, which of them will love him most?*

In this illustration, which can scarcely be classed as a parable, "Jesus entered into the Pharisees' own modes of reasoning. Of two debtors, one of whom owed ten times as much as the other, who would best love the creditor who had freely forgiven them? Though to both the debt might have been equally impossible of discharge, and both might love equally, yet a *Rabbi* would, according to his Jewish notions, say, that he would love most to whom most had been forgiven. If this was the undoubted outcome of Jewish theology—the so much for so much—let it be applied to the present case. If there were much benefit, there would be much love; if little benefit, little love. And conversely: in such case much love would argue much benefit; little love, small benefit." (Edersheim 1:567-68.) As anticipated, Simon answered, "I suppose," and in this beginning there seems to be a touch of supercilious aloofness, an indication that Simon had no idea of whom Jesus had spoken, "I suppose," he replies, "that he, to whom he forgave most."

Jesus said, "Thou hast rightly judged." The answer had been given; the scene was set. All at the dinner table were attentive; all were acutely aware of Simon's host-imposed failures, of the woman's worshipful act, and of the Divine Presence, whose gracious words always presented a heavenly message in the best way. And so, turning to the woman, but speaking to Simon, Jesus said:

> Simon, Seest thou this woman? I entered into thine house, thou gavest me no water for my feet: but she hath washed my feet with tears, and wiped them with the hairs of her head.

> Thou gavest me no kiss: but this woman since the time I came in hath not ceased to kiss my feet.

> My head with oil thou didst not anoint: but this woman hath anointed my feet with ointment.

How beautifully painted is the picture; how expertly chosen are the words. Simon—a Pharisee, a leader of the people and man of note, a pillar in the synagogue, who gloried in his supposed righteousness—Simon proffered none of the usual civilities and courtesies, however ritualistic and meaningless they often were; but this woman, unnamed and otherwise unknown, reputed to be a sinner to whom the services in the synagogue held no allure, who scarcely deserved any attention in such an august gathering, had poured out, from the depths of her soul, such gratitude and thanksgiving and worship as is seldom seen. Then came the crowning pronouncement:

Wherefore I say unto thee, Her sins, which are many, are forgiven, for she loved much: but to whom little is forgiven, the same loveth little.

Thus Simon received the word; he stood instructed and rebuked, but it was the woman to whom the blessing must come. To her Jesus said, "Thy sins are forgiven." Properly rendered, the two phrases, the first to Simon and the second to the woman, should read: "Forgiven have been her sins, the many," and "Thy sins have been forgiven, the many." (Edersheim 1:568-69.) That is to say, her sins were forgiven in times past, which Jesus now confirms, not her sins are now being forgiven by some special dispensation.[3]

To conclude the whole matter—while "they that sat at meat with him began to say within themselves, Who is this that forgiveth sins also?" for they, like Simon, knew not what was involved in the law of repentance and baptism and forgiveness—Jesus "said to the woman, Thy faith hath saved thee; go in peace," or, again, as it is more properly rendered, "Go into peace" (Edersheim 1:569), meaning continue in the peace that is yours because you have believed and obeyed the gospel law.

Jesus Continues to Travel and Preach with His Friends
(Luke 8:1-3; JST, Luke 8:1)

Throughout his whole ministry, Jesus traveled, preached, and healed. We are now with him in the autumn of A.D. 28 when he is making another tour of Galilee. An unnamed woman has but recently washed his feet with her tears, dried them with her tresses, and then anointed them with ointment—as she worshipped at his feet—while he sat, or rather reclined, at meat in the home of Simon the Pharisee. Now, in Galilee, he is visiting "every city and village, preaching and showing the glad tidings of the kingdom of God."

We repeat—and the concept must be ever before us, lest we slip into the sectarian concept that Jesus' ministry was one of teaching ethical verities only, that he was not, as a teacher, first and foremost one who taught doctrine, or that he was not a theologian of superlative capacity—we repeat that his teaching was "the glad tidings of the kingdom of God." In other words, he preached the gospel, as all the prophets preached it. He proclaimed the fatherhood of God, his own divine Sonship, the fall of Adam, and the resultant atoning sacrifice of a Savior of the world. His message was: 'Come unto Christ and be perfected in him; accept him as the Son of God; believe his words and live his law; repent of your sins and be baptized with the baptism of John, that, in due course, you may receive the baptism of fire and of the Holy Ghost.' Jesus taught the gospel; let us never forget it. Should we do so, we shall build on a foundation of sand, and when the rains of uncertainty fall and the winds of skepticism blow and the floods of persecution beat vehemently upon us, our house of partial faith, of partial knowledge, of partial understanding will fall.

With reference to this missionary journey, Luke specifies that Jesus took with him a large entourage. Apostles, disciples, and loyal followers were almost always with him as he taught and traveled. His work was not done in a corner, and always, by precept and by example, he was training others to do and be as he did and was. This time they included "the twelve who were ordained of him"—those chosen and foreordained witnesses who were now beginning to bear with him the burdens of the earthly kingdom, and who would carry a witness of his name to nations afar off, before their mortal ministries ended; he took with him the Twelve; also "certain women, which had been healed of evil spirits and infirmities"; also "Mary called Magdalene, out of whom went seven devils"; also "Joanna the wife of Chuza Herod's steward"; also Susanna; and also "many others." And all of these "ministered unto him of their substance," which is to say, he traveled without purse or scrip, as it were, relying on the goodness of God and the sustaining help of his believing friends for food and for clothing and for shelter. Jesus obeyed his own law that the laborer is worthy of his hire and that "they which preach the gospel should live of the gospel." (1 Cor. 9:14.)

And who shall say that it is anything less than a glorious privilege to feed and aid the Holy One of Israel in his mortal labors? Could those who had substance do other than rejoice at the privilege of sharing it—be it only a crust or a crumb— with him whose all things are, but who made himself subject to all of earth's ills and needs, that in due course he might rise above all things? And wherein is this different in principle from what the faithful always do when they share their substance with the servants of the Lord, or with their fellowmen, always knowing that whatsoever they do unto the least of the Lord's ministers, or to the least of his earthly brethren, they do unto him?

Would that we knew more—someday we will!—of the faithful ones who trod in the tracks of Jesus; who heard the truths of heaven from his divine lips; who saw the miracles he wrought; who learned from him how they, in turn, should carry the same message of salvation—the gospel message; "the glad tidings of the kingdom of God"—to yet others of earth's inhabitants. We have slivers of knowledge about each of the Twelve, which we have noted or will yet mention in other connections. Of Susanna we know nothing; of Joanna, the wife of Chuza Herod's steward, the record also is bare, although we speculate that she may have been the mother of the young man, the nobleman's son, who was healed by Jesus' word spoken in Cana while the youth was in Capernaum.

Of Mary, called Magdalene, we must make special mention. Her life was interwoven intimately with that of the Lord Jesus himself. She apparently came from Magdala, as the identifying appendage to her name signifies. At some unrecorded time she was healed by Jesus from severe physical and mental maladies, and from her body the Master—of the seen and the unseen—cast out seven devils. Hers was no ordinary illness, and we cannot do other than suppose that she underwent some great spiritual test—a personal Gethsemane, a personal temptation in the wilderness for forty days, as it were—which she overcame and rose above—all preparatory to the great mission and work she was destined to perform.

How often it is that the chosen and elect of God wrestle with physical, mental, and devilish infirmities as they cleanse and perfect their souls preparatory to the ministerial service they are called upon to render. A Moses with his stammering tongue, and a Paul with his thorn in the flesh, are called upon to rise above their flesh-born ills and be the teachers and witnesses they were destined to be. That Mary Magdalene passed whatever test a divine providence imposed upon her, we cannot doubt. And so we find her here, traveling with and ministering to the needs of the One who chose his intimates with perfect insight.

Hereafter we shall see her at the cross, a sword piercing her soul as it pierced that of another Mary, the Blessed Virgin, as they both witness the death struggles of the One who had life in himself. Then we shall find her at Joseph's tomb where Jesus' body is laid; and again, bringing spices and ointments to embalm his body; and again in the bare and open tomb whence his resurrected body has risen; and again, seeing the angelic shape and hearing the angelic words, "Why seek ye the living among the dead? He is not here, but is risen" (Luke 24:5-6); and yet again in the Garden, as the first mortal to see a resurrected personage, we shall see her with the Risen Lord, anxious to embrace him, and being restrained by his gentle command and explanation that he had not yet ascended to his Father. We suppose also that she was in the upper room with the other sorrowing worshippers when the Lord, whose body was one of flesh and bones, now appeared to his saints, that they might feel the nail marks in his hands and in his feet and thrust their hands into the gaping wound in his riven side. Can we do other than rank Mary Magdalene with the Blessed Virgin, with Mother Eve, and with Sarah, the wife of Abraham?[4]

As to the other "women, which had been healed of evil spirits and infirmities," and as to the "many others," even their names, for the present, are unknown. Those today who are kindred in spirit to them, who have like faith and like good works, may, of course, see their ancient counterparts in visions. And in that glorious day when all the faithful sit down in the kingdom of God, with Abraham, Isaac, and Jacob, and all the holy prophets, to go no more out, then all shall know and love each other, and, indeed, shall even remember the long association they had in preexistence—all in preparation for the probations of mortality, for the day when each, according to his assignment, would play his role in the eternal gospel drama, in the unfolding plan of the Almighty for the salvation of his children.

But for now let us continue our journey through Galilee with the Blessed Party, headed by the Blessed Personality, as the Blessed Teachings fall from his lips and the Blessed Acts of providence and goodness are wrought by his hands. Soon, with this select group of favored friends of our Friend, the Lord Jesus, we shall see him heal one whose affliction was imposed by an evil spirit inhabiting his body—because of which healing the tide of rising opposition will swell to new heights, and Jesus will come forth with new and strong doctrine.

NOTES

1. Hartley Coleridge, quoted, Farrar, p. 231.

2. "If 'this Man,' this strange, wandering, popular idol, with His strange, novel ways and words, Whom in politeness he must call 'Teacher,' Rabbi, *were* a Prophet, He would have known who the woman was, and, if He had known who she was, then would He never have allowed such approach." (Edersheim 1:567.)

3. "In effect Jesus is saying: 'Her sins were many, but she believed in me, has repented of her sins, was baptized by my disciples, and her sins were washed away in the waters of baptism. Now she has sought me out to exhibit the unbounded gratitude of one who was filthy, but is now clean. Her gratitude knows no bounds and her love is beyond measure, for she was forgiven of much. Had she been forgiven of but few sins, she would not have loved me so intensely.'" (*Commentary* 1:265.)

4. "She is not to be confused with the unnamed though repentant sinner who anointed Jesus' feet in the home of Simon. (Luke 7:36-50.) It is one of the basest slanders of all history to suppose that Mary of Magdala was a fallen woman and therefore to use the term *Magdalene* as an appellation descriptive of reformed prostitutes." (*Commentary* 1:266.)

Chapter 48

THE FAMILY OF JESUS AND THE FAMILY OF LUCIFER

If ye were Abraham's children,
ye would do the works of Abraham. . . .
If God were your Father,
ye would love me. . . .
Ye are of your father the devil.
(John 8:39, 42, 44.)

"He Casteth out Devils through Beelzebub"
(Matthew 12:22-30; JST, Matthew 12:20-23; Mark 3:22-27; JST, Mark 3:18-19; Luke 11:14-15; 17:23; JST, Luke 11:15, 18-19, 23)

Our group of penitent believers—the Twelve, Mary Magdalene, Joanna, Susanna, and many others, both men and women—are traveling, preaching, healing, basking in the light of the Lord, through every city and village of Galilee. We say that they, all of them, were engaged in ministerial service, for we cannot doubt that Jesus called on others to express themselves, and delegated power and authority to worthy associates, as rapidly as they were able to perform the assigned labors. He was building men and sanctifying women, and though the records speak only of what he did and said—as they should, he being the Son of God—yet others were in process of growing in the things of the Spirit so that after his departure they would be prepared

208

to step forth in dignity and with honor and carry on the work the Master had commenced.

They—our missionary group—come into Capernaum, the site of so many of Jesus' wondrous doings. Here there is brought to him "one possessed with a devil, blind, and dumb." This poor suffering soul, what manifold miseries weighed him down. He neither saw nor heard, and to top it all—an ill much greater than the physical imperfections—he was possessed by a devil, by one of the evil spirits who craved a body, even such a one as this, and even for such a moment of ill-gotten tenancy as was here allowed. Jesus healed him. He saw; he spoke; the devil departed. It was no ordinary miracle, for the affliction was of no common kind; it was of such magnitude as to deserve special recitation in Holy Writ. We cannot doubt that the man somehow had gained faith to make possible and bring to pass the marvelous deed; and we know that immediately thereafter, "all the people were amazed"—as well they might be—and that hosts said, as though in unison, "Is not this the son of David?" 'Is not this the Messiah who was to come? Is he not that Prophet of whom Moses spoke? Is he not the Son of God who is to redeem his people? And shall we not, therefore, follow him, and live his law?'[1]

Such a fame and a name has now fastened itself to this famous Galilean, that his steps are everywhere dogged with spies and enemies sent by the Sanhedrin to gain evidence against him. The rising tide of opposition is beating with increasing fury upon the Eternal Rock. And so, Mark says, "the scribes which came down from Jerusalem said, He hath Beelzebub, and by the prince of the devils casteth he out devils."

His miracle was a known reality. Blind eyes now saw; deaf ears now heard; the demon from hell had given up his stolen home. Jesus' act of mercy and healing was known to all. They were even hailing him as David's Son! Unless this and like miracles are explained away, the priestcrafts of the priests will be replaced by a new order; the scribes and

Pharisees must disabuse the public mind or lose their positions of power and influence over the people.

He casteth out devils by Beelzebub! That is the solution to their problem, and from their standpoint it is a good one. Since the miracle cannot be denied, the alternative is to say it was wrought by Satanic power, that Satan cast out Satan, that the prince of devils said to an underling in his kingdom, Depart hence. This would even explain the opened eyes and the unstopped ears, for if Jesus operated by evil power, then all that he did was morally wrong.

This Pharisaic approach to Jesus and his ministry; this Rabbinic way of turning light into darkness; this priest-ridden denial and denunciation not of the miracle itself, but of the power by which it was wrought—all this is a perfect illustration of how Lucifer, in all ages, fights the truth. The latter-day miracle of Mormonism—Oh, it is nothing, say the ministers, because there is a flaw, so they assume falsely, in the doctrine. Pay no attention to the fruits of the prophetically planted tree, say the divines of the day; what if the fruit is good, for we have found (as they falsely suppose) a theological flaw in their beliefs. And since anyone can debate doctrine, let's get the spirit of contention in every heart; let's get an argument going about dotted I's and crossed T's; then people will forget the great and eternal blessings that flow from the restored gospel.

And so with the Pharisees. How helpful, they reason, if we can get the people arguing about the source rather than the fact of Jesus' power. If we can make people think he works by Satan's power, then no matter whether he raises the dead or calls down manna from heaven, it will all be part of demoniac delusion from which men must flee.

So perfectly does this Satan-born, Lucifer-inspired, devil-directed attack of the Pharisees illustrate how the enemy of all righteousness fights the truth, so cunning and evil is the approach, that it is worth our while to dwell upon it with some particularity. "To *us* a single well-ascertained miracle would form irrefragable evidence of the claims of Christ; to *them* it would not," as Edersheim so persuasively reasons. "They could believe in the 'miracles,' and yet not in the Christ. To them the question would not be, as to us, whether they were miracles—but, By what power, or in what Name, He did these deeds? From our standpoint, their opposition to the Christ would—in view of His Miracles—seem not only wicked, but rationally inexplicable. But ours was not their point of view.

"And here, again, we perceive that it was enmity to the *Person* and *Teaching* of Jesus which led to the denial of His claims. The inquiry: By what power Jesus did these works? they met by the assertion, that it was through that of Satan, or the Chief of the Demons. They regarded Jesus, as not only temporarily, but permanently, possessed by a demon, that is, as the constant vehicle of Satanic influence. And this demon was, according to them, none other than Beelzebub, the prince of the devils. Thus, in their view, it was really Satan who acted in and through Him; and Jesus, instead of being recognised as the Son of God, was regarded as an incarnation of Satan; instead of being owned as the Messiah, was denounced and treated as the representative of the Kingdom of Darkness. All this, because the Kingdom which He came to open, and which He preached, was precisely the opposite of what they regarded as the Kingdom of God. Thus it was the essential contrariety of Rabbinism to the Gospel of Christ that lay at the foundation of their conduct towards the Person of Christ. We venture to assert, that this accounts for the whole after-history up to the Cross.

"Thus viewed, the history of Pharisaic opposition appears not only consistent, but is, so to speak, morally accounted for. Their guilt lay in treating that as Satanic agency which was of the Holy Ghost; and this, because they were of their father the Devil, and knew not, nor understood, nor yet loved the Light, their deeds being evil. They were not children of the light, but of that darkness which comprehended Him not Who was the Light. And now we can also understand the growth of active opposition to

Christ. Once arrived at the conclusion, that the miracles which Christ did were due to the power of Satan, and that He was the representative of the Evil One, their course was rationally and morally chosen. To regard every fresh manifestation of Christ's Power as only a fuller development of the power of Satan, and to oppose it with increasing determination and hostility, even to the Cross: such was henceforth the natural progress of this history." (Edersheim 1:574-75.)

Much as this reasoning may salve or sear the consciences of the Pharisaic practicers of priestcraft; much as it may make the ministers of our day feel that Mormonism is a monumental fraud; much as it may lay to rest, in the public mind, the rising dawn of a new day—yet it is weak, futile, and doomed to ultimate failure. The real issues are: What is the truth, where is the truth, and who has the truth. In Jesus' day, the true answers lay with him; in our day, they rest with those of us who are his latter-day servants. Jesus has heretofore taught that to find the truth about religion, men must gain personal revelation from God by the power of the Holy Ghost. Now he contents himself by saying that he cast out devils by the power of God and not the power of the devil, and his declaratory reasoning is irrefutable. "How can Satan cast out Satan?" he asks, and he says in answer:

> Every kingdom divided against itself is brought to desolation; and every city or house divided against itself shall not stand.

With this reasoning none can contend; even the scribes and Pharisees must agree—it is a simple summation of all secular history. Divided kingdoms fall, and the day comes when they are left desolate. And so, he continues:

> If Satan cast out Satan, he is divided against himself; how then shall his kingdom stand?

His conclusion is irrefutable. Such strength as Satan has is in the united power of his evil ways; if he divides his strength, what is left?

> And if I by Beelzebub cast out devils, by whom do your

children cast them out? therefore they shall be your judges.

This would be a sore point. Jesus was not alone in casting out devils. Others, by faith, had the same power: others of the house of Israel then ministered among them with power to control the demons in hell. What power did they use? This was no longer a personal matter, a matter dealing with him alone. He had made converts, and whole congregations had come into the kingdom. If so many others found the truth, why shouldn't these bickering scribes?

But if I cast out devils by the Spirit of God, then the kingdom of God is come unto you. For they also cast out devils by the Spirit of God, for unto them is given power over devils, that they may cast them out.

Jesus cast out devils. He did it by the power of God, for Satan cannot cast out Satan, and, therefore, he is divine; the kingdom has been set up; the true Church has been established among them. And—mark it well—the others who cast out devils had the same power. They too were members of the Church; they too held the holy priesthood; they were followers of the One who then spoke to them.

Or else how can one enter into a strong man's house, and spoil his goods, except he first bind the strong man? and then he will spoil his house.

The reasoning is good; the conclusion is true; the lesson is well taught. Christ has entered the worldly realm of Lucifer, has bound the strong man who reigns therein, has cast out his minions from their ill-gotten abodes, and will in due course spoil the whole house and send away into outer darkness those whose dwelling it is.

He that is not with me is against me: and he that gathereth not with me scattereth abroad.

'I am Christ; I cast out devils in my Father's name; I heal the sick by his power; salvation comes by me. Let none of you longer stand neutral. Either ye are with me, or ye are against me. Unless you come unto me, and espouse my cause, and keep my commandments, ye are against me. There is no middle ground.'

Jesus Speaks of Forgiveness and the Unpardonable Sin
(*Matthew 12:31-37, 43-45; JST, Matthew 12:26, 37-39; Mark 3:28-30; JST, Mark 3:21-25; Luke 6:45; 11:24-26; 12:8-10; JST, Luke 11:25-27; 12:10-12*)

Our Theologian-Friend—for such he is: the Chief Theologian, among all the professors of religion ever to dwell on planet earth—our Theologian-Friend is now about to preach some strong, even harsh doctrine. He stands accused—by scribal scripturalists and Pharisaic preachers—of being in league with Lucifer; of casting out devils and working miracles by the power of Beelzebub, the prince of devils. They have said he is not an incarnate God but an incarnate devil. In his response he has shown that a house divided against itself cannot stand and that Satan cannot cast out Satan lest he destroy himself.

To understand the doctrine Jesus is about to preach, we must let our eyes rest, first, upon the scene of spiritual anarchy created by his miracles, by the resultant charges laid against him, and by his response thereto. Some of his hearers believe his teachings to the full; among them are the Twelve, Mary Magdalene, and the others who traveled and consorted with him. Some of his hearers are defiant, rebellious, hateful; in their hearts is the spirit of murder, and they would fain destroy him if they could. This group is headed and guided and influenced by the scribal spies of the Great Sanhedrin which sits in Jerusalem itself. Yet others of his hearers choose to stand neutral; their spiritual strength does not align them with the ensign of righteousness that he has raised. They fear the Pharisees and have postponed a decision as to where and with whom they will pledge their allegiance. It is of them that Jesus has just said that those who are not for him are against him—there is no such thing as neutrality in the cause of truth and righteousness, either on earth or in heaven—and they who do not gather with him, by their indifference and indecision, scatter abroad. But further, amid the religious contention aroused by Jesus' ministry, there were some of his disciples who had begun to fear and who, under the pressure of public opinion, had spoken against him.

As Luke records, Jesus said: "Whosoever shall confess me before men, him shall the Son of man also confess before the angels of God: But he that denieth me before men shall be denied before the angels of God." Then comes this explanation as to why these words had been forthcoming: "Now his disciples knew that he said this, because they had spoken evil against him before the people; for they were afraid to confess him before men. And they reasoned among themselves, saying, He knoweth our hearts, and he speaketh to our condemnation, and we shall not be forgiven."

We can envision somewhat the anxiety and anguish that engulfed their souls. They had known and still knew of his divine Sonship, and yet—fearing men, unable to withstand the social and religious pressures of the day—they had joined with the dominant religious groups and spoken evilly of this Man of whom Moses wrote. Can traitors be forgiven? Could they again find grace in his sight? His answer to their thoughts of anguish and sorrow was Christ-like. "Whosoever shall speak a word against the Son of man, and repenteth, it shall be forgiven him," he said, "But unto him who blasphemeth against the Holy Ghost, it shall not be forgiven him." The scene is thus set; we are now ready to hear Jesus' profound doctrine. In Matthew's account it follows the proclamation that those who are not for him are against him. Jesus now says:

Wherefore I say unto you, All manner of sin and blasphemy shall be forgiven unto men who receive me and repent; but the blasphemy against the Holy Ghost, it shall not be forgiven unto men.

And whosoever speaketh a word against the Son of man, it shall be forgiven him: but whosoever speaketh against the Holy Ghost, it shall not be forgiven him, neither in this world, neither in the world to come.

There is an unpardonable sin, a sin for which there is no

forgiveness, neither in time nor in eternity. It is blasphemy against the Holy Ghost; it is to deny Christ, to come out in open rebellion, to make open war against the Son of Man—after gaining, by the power of the Holy Ghost, a sure and perfect knowledge of the truth and divinity of the Lord's work. It is to shed innocent blood, meaning to assent unto the death of Christ—to crucify him afresh, Paul says[2]—with a full and absolute knowledge that he is the Son of God. It is to wage open warfare, as does Lucifer, against the Lord and his Anointed, knowing that the course so pursued is evil. It is to deny—to say the sun does not shine while seeing its blazing light—it is to deny Christ after a sure and irrevocable testimony has been received by the power of the Holy Ghost. Hence, it is a scurrilous and evil declaration against the Holy Ghost, against the sole and only source of absolute and sure knowledge. It is blasphemy against the Holy Ghost.[3]

Let men without this sure knowledge speak even against Christ himself; let them commit all manner of sins and blasphemies, even murder, and yet when the penalties have been paid and a proper repentance granted, men shall come forth in immortality and gain an inheritance in whatever kingdom of glory they merit. Only the sons of perdition shall be cast out eternally to live and reign with Lucifer in hell forever. Such is the mercy and wonder of that eternal plan—the gospel of God, now named after Christ his Son—which a gracious God has provided for all his children.[4]

We cannot reconstruct the sequential order in which each spoken sentence fell from the lips of Jesus. Our synoptic friends, in recounting the same episodes, select different portions of the same discourse to emphasize the doctrine or teaching that seemed to them to be of greatest import. And as Jesus so often taught in the midst of surging and moving throngs, it is natural to assume that he repeated, summarized, paraphrased, and expanded his expressions as the needs of the moment required. We can only use our best judgment in lacing the varying comments of Matthew,

Mark, and Luke into one consecutive narrative. Apparently at this point, as Mark records it, the following colloquy occurred:

And then came certain men unto him, accusing him, saying, Why do ye receive sinners, seeing thou makest thyself the Son of God.

Need we remind ourselves at this late date, as we study and ponder the sayings and doings of the Master, that he always and everywhere, without hesitancy, fear, or the slightest degree of self-effacement, has acclaimed and taught that he was God's Almighty Son. This is one point upon which there has been and is to be no question, no doubt, no secrecy. If he sometimes speaks in figures, or similitudes, or parables, so be it; but the message is always the same. 'I am the Son of God; I am the Messiah. Believe and obey my words. I am he; I am the Great Jehovah.' The Jews of that day heard what he said and knew what the words meant; for them it was a matter of believing or disbelieving, as it is also today when the message of salvation is proclaimed to a wicked world.

But he answered them and said, Verily I say unto you, All sins which men have committed, when they repent, shall be forgiven them; for I came to preach repentance unto the sons of men.

Thus, again we hear him phrase a profound proclamation. He came to cry repentance; there is no other course leading to salvation. Repent and believe the gospel; such ever has been and ever will be the divine will. Of course he received sinners. Who else is it that needs repentance? How else can he fulfill his divine commission to present the message of salvation to his mortal brethren?

And blasphemies, wherewith soever they shall blaspheme, shall be forgiven them that come unto me, and do the works which they see me do.

Was it any different now than it had always been? Had not this same Jesus said to them of old, "As often as my people repent will I forgive them their trespasses against

217

me." (Mosiah 26:30.) Did the very disciples themselves falter in their devotion and speak evilly of him? Let them repent. Were there those among men whose hearts were touched by the heavenly light and who desired salvation? Let them repent. Were there rebels, ungodly wretches, and scribes and Pharisees who thirsted for his blood? Let them repent. Repentance is for all accountable persons. There is no other gate through which men may walk to place their feet on the strait and narrow path leading to eternal life.

> *But there is a sin which shall not be forgiven. He that shall blaspheme against the Holy Ghost, hath never forgiveness; but is in danger of being cut down out of the world. And they shall inherit eternal damnation.*
>
> *And this he said unto them because they said, He hath an unclean spirit.*

Again the message is given that forgiveness is for all except those who shall be damned eternally, those who blaspheme against the Holy Ghost, those who crucify Christ afresh, as it were, having a perfect knowledge, born of the Spirit, that he is the Son of God. And even those who said he had an unclean spirit and cast out devils by Beelzebub, the prince of devils, could repent and be forgiven, if they would.

Now we come to that portion of our Lord's discourse in which he excoriates his Pharisaic foes and in which he tells those who oppose him why they shall be judged and found wanting.

> *Either make the tree good, and his fruit good; or else make the tree corrupt, and his fruit corrupt: for the tree is known by his fruit.*

'Be consistent, you Pharisees; make the tree good or bad. If it is good to cast out devils, and I cast them out, then my work is good, for a tree is known by its fruits; but if I am evil, as you say, then it must be a wicked thing to heal those possessed of evil spirits, for a corrupt tree bringeth forth evil fruit.' (*Commentary* 1:275.)

> *O generation of vipers, how can ye, being evil, speak*

good things? for out of the abundance of the heart the mouth speaketh.

A good man out of the good treasure of the heart bringeth forth good things: and an evil man out of the evil treasure bringeth forth evil things.

A parallel passage in Luke, spoken in another setting, that of the Sermon on the Plain, preserves for us these similarly oriented words: "A good man out of the good treasure of his heart bringeth forth that which is good; and an evil man out of the evil treasure of his heart bringeth forth that which is evil: for of the abundance of the heart his mouth speaketh." Such words need no exposition, only the spoken or unspoken reaffirmation, 'Never man spake as this Man.' He continues:

But I say unto you, That every idle word that men shall speak, they shall give account thereof in the day of judgment. For by thy words thou shalt be justified, and by thy words thou shalt be condemned.

Must men work the works of wickedness to be damned? Are overt and evil acts a requisite? Are they needed to warrant one's being cast down to hell? Jesus is here preaching strong doctrine. Something less than evil acts will pull down curses upon the heads of the children of men. It suffices to think evil thoughts and to speak evil words; these alone identify what is in the heart of man and, without more, show the nature and kind of being he is.[5]

Then came some of the scribes and said unto him, Master, it is written that, Every sin shall be forgiven; but ye say, Whosoever speaketh against the Holy Ghost shall not be forgiven. And they asked him, saying, How can these things be?

He has already taught the doctrine involved; he has already explained how forgiveness and pardoning grace operate. They have heard him say he came to preach repentance so that all sins might be forgiven; the question they ask has already been answered. And yet there is an exception to the law of forgiveness: it is that those who blaspheme against the Holy Ghost shall be damned eternally; for them there shall be no remission of sins—they cannot repent and they cannot be forgiven. But this condemnation is reserved for those only who have walked in the light and who now choose to say the sun does not shine while they see it. By raising the question again the scribes are going to great lengths to find fault with Jesus and raise questions in the public mind about his teachings.

And he said unto them, When the unclean spirit is gone out of a man, he walketh through dry places, seeking rest and findeth none; but when a man speaketh against the Holy Ghost, then he saith, I will return into my house from whence I came out; and when he is come, he findeth him empty, swept and garnished; for the good spirit leaveth him unto himself.

When a man is baptized for the remission of sins; when evil and iniquity are burned out of him as though by fire, by the power of the Holy Ghost; when he becomes clean, and pure, and spotless before the Lord; when he has thus sanctified his soul—if he then sins against the Holy Ghost and loses the Spirit of the Lord as his companion, he is left in a fit condition to be swallowed up in every form of evil and iniquity. The house that was once swept and garnished, that was once a fit habitation for the Holy Spirit of God— that house is now vacant. The Spirit of the Lord will not dwell there longer, and the spirit of evil returns—returns to a vacant house, with a force and vigor exceeding anything of the past. As Jesus further says:

Then goeth the evil spirit, and taketh with him seven other spirits more wicked than himself; and they enter in and dwell there; and the last end of that man is worse than the first. Even so shall it be also unto this wicked genera-tion.

There were those among them, obviously, who, having chosen to follow the Son of Righteousness, were now turning back, turning to worldly things, turning to follow Lucifer, their father, because their deeds were evil.[6]

"An Evil Generation: They Seek a Sign"
(*Matthew 12:38-42; Luke 11:16, 29-32; JST, Luke 11:32-33*)

Our Lord has just wrought a wondrous miracle: one who was deaf and dumb and possessed with an evil spirit has been blessed with a threefold miracle. Now he sees and speaks and is free from the shackling bondage of the demon who controlled his every thought and word and movement. How glorious it is to see such a wonder in Israel; but oh, what a mixed reaction it receives! To all those who believe in him who did the deed, it is an added sign and witness that he is the Messiah, their Deliverer, Savior, Redeemer, and King. But to those whose craft is in danger; who have sealed their hearts and minds against the new gospel dispensation; who say, God heard Moses and some of the prophets, but us he will not hear—to these scribal sectarians, as it were, the mighty miracle shows only that Jesus himself is possessed with a devil, and that all he does is by the power of the prince of devils. This view they have expressed, poisoning the minds of all whom they can influence. And their view has been refuted—in power, logically and conclusively—by the one at whose door the charge was laid.

What course is now open to them, and how shall they react? How shall they divert attention from their present discomfiture and rouse further animosity against this Nazarene who has taken upon himself the blasphemous assumption that he is divine? They must raise a new issue, or at least what will seem to be a new point of controversy. And so, "certain of the scribes and of the Pharisees," "tempting him," say: "Master, we would seek a sign from thee." Or, as Luke records it, they "sought of him a sign from heaven."

A sign from heaven! What, in heaven's name, had they just received? "They had already seen signs in such number and variety as had never before in all history been poured out upon a people. In their streets, houses, and synagogues, the lame leaped, the blind saw, the dumb spoke, paralytics walked and carried their beds, all manner of diseases were cured, devils were cast out, the dead raised—all by the com-

221

mand of him whom they now tempted. Yet, in the face of all this, they now demanded something new and different, some heavenly portent which would prove that what they had already seen was from above and not from beneath." (*Commentary* 1:277.)

Were they looking for a cloud by day and a pillar of fire by night to surround the Twelve? Was Jesus to divide the waters of the Sea of Galilee—congealing them with a wall of water on the right hand and on the left—so they all could walk from Capernaum to the land of the Gadarenes on dry ground? Did they expect to see Mount Zion or Mount Moriah quake, while smoke ascended up on high as from a furnace? Were they expecting this new Teacher to call down fire from heaven and consume six hundred Roman centurions with the sixty legions in which they served? How little they knew about how the Lord of heaven operates among men! True signs they had seen; signs of the sort they sought cannot be given without interfering with the divine law of agency under which all men must live.

"But he answered and said unto them," as Matthew records, "An evil and adulterous generation seeketh after a sign," and as Luke has it, "This is an evil generation: they seek a sign." Then as both synoptists say, "There shall no sign be given to it, but the sign of the prophet Jonas: For as Jonas was three days and three nights in the whale's belly; so shall the Son of man be three days and three nights in the heart of the earth."

A sign from heaven! What part do signs play in the eternal scheme of things? Why do these scripturally wise detractors of the Holy One feel they can rouse further ill feelings against him by demanding a sign? Should he give some sign that he has not yet given? Is there some great heavenly portent that will prove he is the Son of God?

Jesus came, it is true, to give signs and to work miracles. It was part of his ministerial assignment, and in so doing he was acting in the power and authority of his Father. Signs are for the saints, not the world. Signs follow those that believe; they are not designed to convert the wicked and ungodly. Faith precedes the miracle. "I will show miracles, signs, and wonders, unto all those who believe on my name," the Lord says. "And whoso shall ask it in my name in faith, they shall cast out devils; they shall heal the sick; they shall cause the blind to receive their sight, and the deaf to hear, and the dumb to speak, and the lame to walk. . . . But without faith shall not anything be shown forth except desolations upon Babylon." (D&C 35:8-11.)

There shall also be other signs, signs in the heavens above and in the earth beneath, wondrous portents that identify and bear record of things that are happening among men that affect their eternal salvation. But these also are understood only by those who have the gift and power of the Holy Ghost; they are understood by the saints only. The sign of the star was given to announce the birth of the Star of Israel, but only those who had faith, those who were waiting for the Consolation of Israel—the wise men from the East and a cluster of faithful souls in Palestine and in the Americas—only these few knew what it meant.

Those who seek signs—either to create faith or to feed their egos—whether in or out of the Church, shall fail in their search for divine approval. "He that seeketh signs shall see signs, but not unto salvation. . . . Faith cometh not by signs, but signs follow those that believe. Yea, signs come by faith, not by the will of men, nor as they please, but by the will of God. Yea, signs come by faith, unto mighty works, for without faith no man pleaseth God; and with whom God is angry he is not well pleased; wherefore, unto such he showeth no signs, only in wrath unto their condemnation." (D&C 63:7-11.)

For the scribes and Pharisees of all generations; for the wicked and ungodly in every age; for those without faith, who walk in worldly paths, there is only one sign, one alone, to prove Christ's divinity, and that is the sign of the prophet Jonas. That sign is that Jesus was crucified, died, and rose again the third day in glorious immortality. It is that as

Jonah of old spent three days and three nights in the belly of a whale, so shall the Son of Man spend a like period in an earthly tomb. It is that as the whale vomited Jonah from the blackness of a living tomb, so Jesus comes forth in a newness of life from a grave that cannot hold him. It is that the Son of Man—the Son of God—burst the bands of death, became the firstfruits of them that sleep, and ever liveth in immortal glory. The resurrection proves that Jesus is the Messiah; it is the sign, given of God, to all men of the truth and divinity of his work.

What sign does Deity give that there is a God? To the saints there are many, but to the wicked and ungodly there is only one—the fact of creation. God is the Creator, and all things denote there is a God. How could there be a creation without a Creator? Truly, the creation bears witness of the Creator.

What sign does he give that Christ is the Son of God? Again, to the saints there are many, but to the scribes and Pharisees of the world there is only one—the fact of resurrection. Christ is the Redeemer, and his redemption from death establishes his divinity. How could there be a resurrection without a Redeemer? Truly, the resurrection bears witness of the Redeemer.

What sign does he give that the Holy Ghost is the witness and testator, the revealer of saving truth in all ages? Once again, where the saints are concerned the signs are many, but to worldly people—and the world cannot, without repentance, receive the Holy Ghost—there is only one sign. It is the gift of prophecy; it is the reality of prophetic insight; it is the fact that God reveals, beforehand, by the mouths of his holy prophets, all things that concern and affect the salvation of men on earth. The Holy Ghost is a revelator, and the fact of revelation and of prophecy and of spiritual gifts identifies him as the power and source whence they come. How could there be revelation without a revelator? The presence of the gifts of the Spirit bears witness of the third member of the Godhead.

Such are the signs—and there are none others—that God gives to the wicked and ungodly. If they believe and repent, if they are baptized and receive the Holy Ghost, if they walk uprightly before the Lord—then signs without end, miracles unceasing, wonders beyond mortal comprehension, all these flow unto them forever and ever. Such is the law that governs signs.

And so, heaping condemnation upon those then present, and speaking by way both of doctrine and of testimony, Jesus says:

For as Jonas was a sign unto the Ninevites, so shall also the Son of man be to this generation.

The queen of the south [the Queen of Sheba] shall rise up in the day of judgment with the men of this generation, and condemn them; for she came from the utmost parts of the earth, to hear the wisdom of Solomon; and, behold, a greater than Solomon is here.

The men of Nineve shall rise up in the day of judgment with this generation; and shall condemn it; for they repented at the preaching of Jonas; and, behold, a greater than Jonas is here.

We must not leave these stern and prophetic declarations of the Prophet of Nazareth—given to sinners about signs— without an acute awareness of the effect of adultery upon spirituality. Adultery so dulls the spiritual sensitivities of men that it becomes exceedingly hard for them to believe the truth when they hear it. Sexual immorality is second only to murder in the category of personal crimes. For those guilty of so gross an offense against God and his laws, the road back to cleanliness and purity is a steep and a rocky course. It can be traversed but the way is not easy.

Further: "Some sins cannot be separated; they are inseparably welded together. There never was a sign seeker who was not an adulterer, just as there never was an adulterer who was not also a liar. Once Lucifer gets a firm hold over one human weakness, he also applies his power to kindred weaknesses." (*Commentary* 1:277.)[7]

Who Belongs to the Family of Jesus?
(Matthew 12:46-50; JST, Matthew 12:44; Mark 3:31-35;
JST, Mark 3:26; Luke 8:19-21; 11:27-28; JST, Luke 8:19-20; 11:29)

Our attention now turns to the Blessed Virgin and her other sons and daughters, the offspring of Mary and Joseph. Mary and some of Jesus' half-brothers seek to converse with him, but are unable to do so because of the throngs. He is told: "Thy mother and thy brethren stand without, desiring to speak with thee."

It seems to us, from the inspired records now extant among us, that the Master Teacher always used each successive event in his life as an occasion to teach doctrine and testify of his own divinity. So commonplace an event as the presence of his mother and some of her children—with whom he grew to maturity in Nazareth; with whom he played and worked and associated in the Galilean hills of yesteryear—became an occasion for a formal and profound pronouncement. Jesus said:

Who is my mother? and who are my brethren?

And he stretched forth his hand toward his disciples, and said, Behold my mother and my brethren!

And he gave them charge concerning her, saying, I go my way, for my Father hath sent me. And whosoever shall do the will of my Father which is in heaven, the same is my brother, and sister, and mother.

Either at this point or at another time—how can we ever be sure?—"a certain woman of the company lifted up her voice, and said unto him, Blessed is the womb which bare thee, and the paps which thou hast sucked. And he said, Yea, and blessed are all they who hear the word of God, and keep it."

There are some things more important than familial inheritances. True, Mary was blessed because she bare God's Son, but all women can be blessed with blessed Mary if they keep the commandments of the blessed God. True, these children of Mary were Jesus' brothers and sisters, the fruit of the same womb in which his mortal body was created from the dust of the same earth, but all the disciples were also his brothers and sisters if they did the will of his Father who is in heaven.

The blessings of heaven are available—freely, without money and without price—to all men. All men cannot be born into this world as the sons of God, after the manner of the flesh, but all, through righteousness, can be adopted into the family of the Eternal God and become joint-heirs with Christ of the fulness of the glory and power of the Father. All people cannot be the literal seed of Mary, but all, through righteousness, can be adopted into the family of her Firstborn Son and become his brothers and sisters. Indeed, the very plan of salvation itself calls for a new birth, a birth to righteousness, by which all disciples, all saints, become the sons and daughters of Jesus Christ. They are born again; they become members of his family.

And all these blessings are available because Jesus was the Son of God. Even in announcing them, lest Mary or any of his blood-kindred feel too great an intimacy, or feel they should exercise control over the Firstborn of Mary, he speaks of his own Father as being in heaven, and pointedly says: "I go my way, for my Father hath sent me."

Who, then, are members of the family of Lucifer, and who of the family of the Lord Jesus? Are we not all the children of him whom we list to obey? Is it not, as Alma said: "If a man bringeth forth good works he hearkeneth unto the voice of the good shepherd, and he doth follow him; but whosoever bringeth forth evil works, the same becometh a child of the devil, for he hearkeneth unto his voice, and doth follow him." (Alma 5:41.)

NOTES

1. Our account here given is from Matthew and accords with Mark. Another almost identical miracle, out of which grew the same counsel and analysis as Matthew and Mark append to this healing, is found in Luke in a different setting. Whether they are the same or different miracles cannot be determined by us or by anyone. There are as many views as there are scholars. It may well be that almost identical miracles brought forth like reactions from different people and resulted in a repetition by Jesus of substantially the same instruction. Or it may be, as so many exegetes conclude, that the Gospel authors de-

liberately grouped certain happenings together because of their content and without reference to their chronological evolvement. As Edersheim expresses it, "The Gospels present not a 'Life of Christ,' but the history of the Kingdom of God in its progressive manifestation." (Edersheim 1:570.) Each author must choose for himself how to handle the endless problems of this sort, problems that are left to us because of the fragmentary nature of the biblical accounts. In this instance, we are considering all of the related sayings and doings as though they composed one episode. Such at least makes for a cohesive, rounded presentation of the whole matter.

2. "It is impossible for those who were once enlightened, and have tasted of the heavenly gift, and were made partakers of the Holy Ghost, And have tasted the good word of God, and the powers of the world to come, If they shall fall away, to renew them again unto repentance; seeing they crucify to themselves the Son of God afresh, and put him to an open shame." (Heb. 6:4-6.)

3. "The blasphemy against the Holy Ghost, which shall not be forgiven in the world nor out of the world, is in that ye commit murder wherein ye shed innocent blood, and assent unto my death, after ye have received my new and everlasting covenant, saith the Lord God; and he that abideth not this law can in nowise enter into my glory, but shall be damned, saith the Lord." (D&C 132:27.)

4. "There is a difference between gaining forgiveness of sins and gaining salvation in the celestial kingdom. All men who do not commit the unpardonable sin will gain eventual pardon; that is, they will be forgiven of their sins; but those so forgiven, having been judged according to their works, will then be sent either to a telestial, terrestrial, or celestial kingdom, as the case may be. As a matter of fact, those destined to inherit kingdoms of glory will not be resurrected until they have repented and gained forgiveness of their sins. The telestial kingdom will be inhabited by those who have been tormented and buffeted in hell until they have gained forgiveness and become worthy to attain a resurrection." (*Commentary* 1:274-75.)

5. "If our hearts have been hardened"—and what more accurately describes the hearts of the scribes and Pharisees with whom we are here dealing?—"yea, if we have hardened our hearts against the word, insomuch that it has not been found in us, then will our state be awful, for then we shall be condemned. For our words will condemn us, yea, all our works will condemn us; we shall not be found spotless; and our thoughts will also condemn us." (Alma 12:13-14.)

6. In answering the question of these captious scribes, Jesus is saying in effect: 'If you gain a perfect knowledge of me and my mission, it must come by revelation from the Holy Ghost; that Holy Spirit must speak to the spirit within you; and then you shall know, nothing doubting. But to receive this knowledge and revelation, you must cleanse and perfect your own soul; that is, your house must be clean, swept, and garnished. Then if you deny me by speaking against the Holy Ghost who gave you your revelation of the truth, that is if you come out in open rebellion against the perfect light you have received, the Holy Ghost will depart, leaving you to yourself. Your house will now be available for other tenancy, and so the evil spirits and influences you had once conquered will return to plague you. Having completely lost the preserving power of the Spirit, you will then be worse off than if you had never received the truth; and many in this generation shall be so condemned.' (*Commentary* 1:276.)

7. In this connection, also, the Prophet Joseph Smith said: "When I was preaching in Philadelphia, a Quaker called out for a sign. I told him to be still. After the sermon, he again asked for a sign. I told the congregation the man was an adulterer; that a wicked and adulterous generation seeketh after a sign; and that the Lord had said to me in a revelation, that any man who wanted a sign was an adulterous person. 'It is true,' cried one, 'for I caught him in the very act,' which the man afterwards confessed when he was baptized." (*Teachings*, p. 278.)

SECTION VI

THE CONTINUING GALILEAN MINISTRY

THE CONTINUING GALILEAN MINISTRY

The Lord hath anointed me to preach
good tidings unto the meek;
. . . to comfort all that mourn;
To appoint unto them that mourn in Zion,
to give unto them beauty for ashes,
the oil of joy for mourning,
the garment of praise for the spirit of heaviness;
that they might be called trees of righteousness,
the planting of the Lord,
that he might be glorified.
(Isa. 61:1-3.)

We now see Jesus going forth in the majesty and glory of his eternal Godhood—preaching, healing, and testifying.

We see him among his Galilean neighbors and friends, some of whom have great faith; others have souls darkened by sin and unbelief.

He speaks in parables, particularly to those who are not prepared to receive the word in plainness. They hear of a sower, of seed that grows by itself, of wheat and tares, of mustard seed and of leaven, of hidden treasure and a pearl of great price, and of the gospel net.

He stills a storm on the Sea of Galilee, heals a demoniac

among the Gadarenes, raises the daughter of Jairus from death, heals the woman with the issue of blood, and causes the blind to see and the dumb to speak.

And in spite of it all, he is again rejected at Nazareth.

Then he instructs the Twelve and sends them forth, endowed with power from on high.

In sorrow we see the beloved Baptist beheaded by order of evil Antipas.

Then Jesus feeds the five thousand in a solitary place near Bethsaida-Julias, walks on the sea, and continues his miracles in the land of Gennesaret.

And finally, as the crowning event of this part of his ministry, we hear the sermon on the bread of life and the discourse on cleanliness.

How truly—according to the promises—did he replace mourning with the oil of joy, ashes with beauty, and the spirit of heaviness with the garment of praise!

O that all who saw and heard and felt what he then did might have believed in him—"that they might be called trees of righteousness" and "the planting of the Lord"!

Chapter 49

JESUS TEACHES IN PARABLES

Give ear, O my people, to my law:
incline your ears to the words of my mouth.
I will open my mouth in a parable:
I will utter dark sayings of old:
Which we have heard and known,
and our fathers have told us.
(Ps. 78:1-3.)

Why Jesus Taught in Parables
*(Matthew 13:1-3, 9-17, 34-35; JST, Matthew 13:10-11, 13, 15-16;
Mark 4:1-2, 9-12, 21-25, 33-34; JST, Mark 4:9, 18-20, 26;
Luke 8:4, 8, 16-18; JST, Luke 8:18)*

Every schoolboy knows Jesus taught in parables, but there
is scarcely a learned theologian or an educated divine in all
the universities of academia who knows why he chose this
unique form of pedagogy. There are, of course, a great many
scripturists who are aware of why he *said* he used parables,
but their approach, almost without exception, is to explain
that he could not possibly have meant what he said in the
literal and true sense of the word, and therefore that he used
parables for such and such a reason of their own devising.

It is only fair to say that the scriptural exegetes who have
speculated and pontificated, in the religious literature of the
day, as to why our Lord used parables, and as to what those

parables mean, have not had the advantages of what latter-day revelation says on the matters at hand. Nonetheless, for whatever reason, the shimmering fantasies of the learned men, as they pertain to our Lord's use of parables, are of little worth to us.

In our continuing struggle to learn of him by whom salvation comes, we are about to encounter the beginning of the parables. We do not know if these are the first parables related by Jesus—it is, in fact, a little unreasonable to assume that no others have been related in the twenty months or so since his baptism—but at least these are the first major parables preserved for us in the scriptural record. And it was their use at this time that caused his disciples to ask: "Why speakest thou unto them in parables?"

As a necessary prelude to our analysis of the parables as they fall from the divine lips, we shall do well to have before us the social and historical circumstances that brought them forth, and also an understanding of their nature, use, and purpose in the gospel plan. The following items of history and principle will help us gain the perspective we need.

1. *Nature of parables.*

"Parables are short stories which point up and illustrate spiritual truths. Those spoken by Jesus deal with real events, or, if fictitious, are so consistent and probable that they may be viewed as the commonplace experiences of many people." (*Commentary* 1:283.)

"The essential feature of a parable is that of comparison or similitude, by which some ordinary, well-understood incident is used to illustrate a fact or principle not directly expressed in the story. . . . The narrative or incident upon which a parable is constructed may be an actual occurrence or fiction; but, if fictitious, the story must be consistent and probable, with no admixture of the unusual or miraculous. In this respect the parable differs from the fable, the latter being imaginative, exaggerated and improbable as to fact; moreover, the intent is unlike in the two, since the parable is designed to convey some great spiritual truth, while the so-

234

called moral of the fable is at best suggestive only of worldly achievement and personal advantage. Stories of trees, animals and inanimate things talking together or with men are wholly fanciful; they are fables or apologues whether the outcome be depicted as good or bad; to the parable these show contrast, not similarity. The avowed purpose of the fable is rather to amuse than to teach. The parable may embody a narrative as in the instances of the sower and the tares, or merely an isolated incident, as in those of the mustard seed and the leaven.

"Allegories are distinguished from parables by greater length and detail of the story, and by the intimate admixture of the narrative with the lesson it is designed to teach; these are kept distinctly separate in the parable. Myths are fictitious stories, sometimes with historic basis of fact, but without symbolism of spiritual worth. A proverb is a short, sententious saying, in the nature of a maxim, connoting a definite truth or suggestion by comparison. Proverbs and parables are closely related, and in the Bible the terms are sometimes used interchangeably." (Talmage, pp. 298-99.)

2. *Many doctrines are reserved for the faithful.*

Every gospel teacher—from the Chief Elder, who is Christ, to the least and lowest of his servants—must determine, in all teaching situations, what portion of eternal truth he will offer to his hearers of the moment. The gospel and its eternal truths are always the same: what was true two thousand years ago is true today; the truths that enabled Abraham to serve Jehovah and gain salvation are the same as those which enable us to serve Christ and gain a like reward. But not all people in all ages and under all circumstances are prepared to receive the fulness of all gospel truths. The Lord gives his word to men line upon line, precept upon precept, here a little and there a little, confirming their hope, building each new revelation upon the foundations of the past, giving his children only that portion of his word which they are able to bear.

When the elders of Israel go forth to proclaim the gospel

to the world, they are subject to two commandments that the spiritually untutored might assume are contradictory. In one of them the Lord says, "Teach the principles of my gospel, which are in the Bible and the Book of Mormon." (D&C 42:12.) Does this mean they are free to teach all they know about all of the doctrines found in the standard works? In another revelation, the Lord says: "Declare glad tidings, . . . And of tenets thou shalt not talk, but thou shalt declare repentance and faith on the Savior, and remission of sins by baptism and by fire, yea, even the Holy Ghost." (D&C 19:29-31.) The clear meaning, of course, is that the servants of the Lord go forth to teach what people are prepared to receive, nothing more. They are to declare glad tidings, to proclaim the message of the restoration, to teach the simple and easy doctrines, and to leave the mysteries alone. They are not to present lessons in calculus to students who must first learn arithmetic; they are not to reveal the mysteries of the kingdom until people believe the first principles; they are to give milk before meat.

Alma summarized the restrictions under which preachers of righteousness serve by saying: "It is given unto many to know the mysteries of God; nevertheless they are laid under a strict command that they shall not impart only according to the portion of his word which he doth grant unto the children of men, according to the heed and diligence which they give unto him." Such is the universal principle; it is not how much the teacher knows, but how much the student is prepared to receive. Strong and deep doctrine, spoken to rebellious people, drives them further away and widens the gulf between them and the saints of God.

Then Alma, in pointed and express language, describes, as it were, the scribes and Pharisees, on the one hand, and the faithful disciples who surrounded Jesus, on the other: "And therefore," he continues, "he that will harden his heart, the same receiveth the lesser portion of the word; and he that will not harden his heart, to him is given the greater portion of the word, until it is given unto him to know the mysteries of God until he know them in full. And they that will harden their hearts, to them is given the lesser portion of the word until they know nothing concerning his mysteries; and then they are taken captive by the devil, and led by his will down to destruction. Now this is what is meant by the chains of hell." (Alma 12:9-11.)

Even the true saints—the believing disciples, those who have accepted the gospel and received the gift of the Holy Ghost—are not prepared to receive all things. We have the fulness of the everlasting gospel, meaning we have every truth, power, priesthood, and key needed to enable us to gain the fulness of salvation in our Father's kingdom. But we do not have, and are not yet prepared to receive, the fulness of gospel truth.

This is perfectly illustrated by the fact that we do not have the sealed portion of the Book of Mormon. That treasurehouse of Holy Writ contains an account of the creation of the world, of the dealings of God with men in all ages, of the Second Coming of the Son of Man, and of the millennial era when the earth shall rest and Zion prosper to the full—all of which we are not prepared to receive. The doctrines revealed to the brother of Jared, and which are recorded in the sealed portion of the Book of Mormon, were had among the Jaredites; they were known to the Nephites during their Golden Era; certainly they were known and taught in Enoch's Zion; but when the Lehite people "dwindled in unbelief," Moroni was commanded to "hide them up." "They shall not go forth unto the Gentiles until the day that they shall repent of their iniquity, and become clean before the Lord," Moroni says.

We live in a preparatory day, a day in which we are preparing, it is hoped, to receive the further light and knowledge that a gracious God has in store for us. As Moroni records: "And in that day that they shall exercise faith in me, saith the Lord, even as the brother of Jared did, that they may become sanctified in me, then will I manifest unto them the things which the brother of Jared saw, even to the unfolding unto them all my revelations, saith Jesus Christ, the Son of God, the Father of the heavens and of the earth, and all things that in them are." (Ether 4:1-7.)

3. *Parables hide gospel doctrines from those whose hearts are hardened.*

By speaking in parables, Jesus is simply practicing what he has been preaching. In the Sermon on the Mount he told the Twelve they were to go forth into the world, preach the gospel, call upon men to repent, and invite them to join the Church. They were instructed, however, to keep the mysteries of the kingdom within themselves, and not to give that which was holy unto the dogs, or to cast their pearls before swine. Jesus told them that the world could not receive that which they themselves were scarcely able to bear, and that if they gave gospel pearls to the wicked and ungodly, such unbelieving and rebellious people would first reject the message, and then use the very truths they had heard to rend and destroy and wreak havoc among those whose faith was weak.

Now we find Jesus on the Galilean shore in the midst of a great congregation, gathered out of every city. Among them are the Twelve, many disciples who know he is the Messiah, and many others, influenced by the scribes and Pharisees, who reject him as an imposter and believe his miracles are wrought by an evil power. So great is the press of the people that he enters a ship, seats himself, and addresses the multitude standing on the shore. Many truths and much exhortation—as his custom is—fall from his lips, in addition to which, the record says, "He spake many things unto them in parables."

Later, being alone with the Twelve and certain other favored disciples, he is asked why he speaks in parables and what the parables mean. As to the choice of parables as a means of teaching, be it noted, the disciples did not ask, 'Why speakest thou unto *us* in parables?' but, "Why speakest thou unto *them*"—unto the scribes and Pharisees; unto the spies sent by the Sanhedrin to find fault with his every word;

unto those whose hearts were hardened against the word—
"Why speakest thou unto *them* in parables?" Jesus
answered:

> *Because it is given unto you to know the mysteries of*
> *the kingdom of heaven, but to them it is not given.*

These words are from Matthew. But, better still, as Mark
preserves the account, Jesus said:

> *Unto you it is given to know the mystery of the*
> *kingdom of God: but unto them that are without, all these*
> *things are done in parables.*

That is to say, parables are for nonmembers of the
Church, for those outside the kingdom, or, at best, as we
shall see, for those who are weak in the faith; who are not
prepared to receive the truth involved in plain words; from
whom the full truth must, as yet, remain hidden. To the
Twelve, Mary Magdalene, and the other faithful disciples,
both male and female, who traveled and ministered with
him, to all of the believing saints of his day—to them it was
given to know the doctrine; for them it need not be hidden
in a parable.

> *For whosoever receiveth, to him shall be given, and he*
> *shall have more abundance; But whosoever continueth not*
> *to receive, from him shall be taken away even that he hath.*
>
> *Therefore speak I to them in parables: because they*
> *seeing see not; and hearing they hear not, neither do they*
> *understand.*
>
> *And in them is fulfilled the prophecy of Esaias concern-*
> *ing them, which saith, By hearing, ye shall hear and shall*
> *not understand; and seeing, ye shall see and shall not per-*
> *ceive.*

4. *Parables reveal truths to those whose hearts are open*
and receptive.

With it all, parables are majestic teaching devices, and
they do reveal truth, and they do add light and understanding to those who already have the gift of understanding, as
well as to those who are sincerely seeking truth.[1] The doctrines of salvation are presented in their most compelling

and convincing form when they are phrased in aptly chosen words, as when the Risen Lord ministered among the Nephites. Be it noted that he spake not unto them in parables; they were a people prepared for their King. The wicked and ungodly among them had been destroyed by the quakings and fires and whirlwinds and desolations in the Americas that attended the crucifixion, and those among the Nephites who remained were ready to receive the word of truth as it came in simplicity and plainness.

Yet parables, planted in the minds of truth seekers, help them remember the issues involved until such time as the full and plain knowledge parts the parabolic veil and stands revealed for all to see. And parables form a reservoir of knowledge about which even the saints can ponder and inquire as they seek to perfect and expand their limited views of gospel themes.

Continuing his denunciation of those to whom he must speak in parables because they are neither worthy nor qualified to hear the word in plainness, Jesus says:

For this people's heart is waxed gross, and their ears are dull of hearing, and their eyes they have closed; lest at any time they should see with their eyes, and hear with their ears, and should understand with their heart, and should be converted, and I should heal them.

Then Jesus makes the contrast and shows wherein his plain teachings and his parables, because these latter are also understood by his disciples, are of great worth unto those whose hearts are open.

But blessed are your eyes, for they see; and your ears, for they hear. And blessed are you because these things are come unto you, that you might understand them.

And verily, I say unto you, many righteous prophets have desired to see these days which you see, and have not seen them; and to hear that which you hear, and have not heard.

How blessed they were in that day to hear both the parables and the plain teachings! And yet how blessed are we to live in this day, a day when the word of God is again in the mouths of legal administrators, servants who now minister in the place and stead of him who filled his mission in Galilee and Judea and Perea and all Palestine!

5. *Parables are types and shadows of heavenly things.*

Pure doctrine is of heavenly origin. When it is revealed in plainness and simplicity, it lights the way to eternal life, as for instance the clear statement that men must repent and be baptized to gain salvation. But when for one reason or another it is unwise to set forth this or that truth in all its blazing grandeur, it may yet be appropriate to reveal a type or a shadow, a similitude, a dim and dawning light, something that points toward the doctrine in all its revealed splendor. So often such types and shadows and similitudes are parables. They bear record of eternal truths and point the attention of gospel students to the doctrines involved without specifying what the doctrines are or how they operate.

Thus parables are not sources to search to learn doctrine. They may serve as illustrations of gospel principles; they may dramatize, graphically and persuasively, some gospel truths; but it is not their purpose to reveal doctrine, or, standing alone, to guide men along the course leading to eternal life. Parables can only be understood, in their full and complete meaning, after one knows the doctrines about which they speak. For instance, in the course of revealing some things relative to unity, the Lord, in latter-day revelation, gives a very simple parable:

And let every man esteem his brother as himself, and practise virtue and holiness before me.

And again I say unto you, let every man esteem his brother as himself.

For what man among you having twelve sons, and is no respecter of them, and they serve him obediently, and he saith unto the one: Be thou clothed in robes and sit thou here; and to the other: Be thou clothed in rags and sit thou there—and looketh upon his sons and saith I am just?

*Behold, this I have given unto you as a parable, and it
is even as I am. I say unto you, be one; and if ye are not
one ye are not mine. (D&C 38:24-27.)*

Here, then, is a parable that illustrates something about
the Lord. What does it mean? Is he speaking of time or
eternity? Is it dealing with temporal or spiritual equality, or
both? Do all men enter this life, or the next, with equal en-
dowments? Does it have any reference to the twelve apostles,
or the twelve tribes or Israel? In what sense must the Lord's
people be one? And so on and so on. Parables are types and
shadows—something to ponder and analyze and pray about.
Indeed, this is one of their allures. They are a sort of religious puzzle awaiting solution, a sacred mystery waiting to
be uncovered.

"Perhaps no other mode of teaching was so common
among the Jews as that by Parables," Edersheim says. Their
parables, however, "were almost entirely illustrations of
what had been said or taught." Our Lord's parables were
also illustrations, but they were much more. They shed a
light of their own, or perhaps they shed the light of heaven
abroad. "All Parables bear reference to well-known scenes,
such as those of daily life; or to events, either real, or such as
every one would expect in given circumstances, or as would
be in accordance with prevailing notions.

"Such pictures, familiar to the popular mind"—especially in the case of Jesus' parables—"are in the Parable [it-
self] connected with corresponding spiritual realities. . . .
There is that which distinguishes the Parable from the mere
illustration. The latter conveys no more than—perhaps not
so much as—that which was to be illustrated; while the
Parable conveys this and a great deal beyond it to those, who
can follow up its shadows to the light by which they have
been cast. In truth, Parables are the outlined shadows—
large, perhaps, and dim—as the light of heavenly things falls
on well-known scenes, which correspond to, and have their
higher counterpart in spiritual realities. . . . Things in earth

and heaven are kindred, and the one may become to us Parables of the other." (Edersheim 1:580-82.)

6. *Parabolic teaching is often an act of mercy.*

We are now aware that parables present only that portion of the Lord's word which he in his wisdom feels to convey to us at any given time. In many cases this very act of limiting the amount of truth offered to men is itself an act of mercy. "For of him unto whom much is given much is required; and he who sins against the greater light shall receive the greater condemnation." (D&C 82:3.) To offer truths to wicked and ungodly creatures, which they will most assuredly reject, is to do more than cast pearls before swine. It is to make possible a greater condemnation upon those who reject the greater light.

"There is plainly shown an element of mercy in the parabolic mode of instruction adopted by our Lord under the conditions prevailing at the time. Had He always taught in explicit declaration, such as required no interpretation, many among His hearers would have come under condemnation, inasmuch as they were too weak in faith and unprepared in heart to break the bonds of traditionalism and the prejudice engendered by sin, so as to accept and obey the saving word. Their inability to comprehend the requirements of the gospel would in righteous measure give Mercy some claim upon them, while had they rejected the truth with full understanding, stern Justice would surely demand their condemnation." (Talmage, pp. 296-97.)

7. *Parables open the door to added light and knowledge.*

We now, as a prelude to our study of the parables as such, have considered their nature and character. We have reminded ourselves that the Lord gives to men only that portion of his word which they are prepared, spiritually, to receive, and we have seen how parables hide the doctrines of salvation from those whose eyes are not open to spiritual realities. We have also set forth how these wondrously phrased and perfectly presented parabolic utterances of

Jesus do in fact reveal great spiritual truths to those whose hearts are open and whose souls hunger and thirst for the things of the Spirit, and we have even come to know that inspired parables are types and shadows of heavenly things, and that by them the light of heaven is cast earthward for the eternal betterment and blessing of all those upon whom its rays shine. And we have noted that it is an act of divine mercy to withhold from shriveled and spiritually sick souls the full light of heaven, lest its assured rejection further condemn the unreceptive and disbelieving among men.

There remains for us one added verity to consider, and it is, perhaps, the greatest and most important use to which parables are put. Jesus came to preach the gospel and bear the sins of all those who would believe his words and live his laws. He came to proclaim the acceptable year of the Lord, to bring good tidings to the meek, to open the prison doors of darkness and unbelief, and to let the light of heaven dwell in the hearts of men on earth. He came to give every man as much of the truth of heaven as each man's earthbound soul would permit him to receive.

If the righteousness that Jesus thus rained upon men fell on seams of rock and dunes of sand, it was sloughed off as of no worth; if it fell in the pleasant valley of the Jordan or within the gates of Eden, then it caused grain to grow and fruit to ripen and cattle to drink and live. Peter, James, and John were prepared—spiritually, intellectually, morally—to drink the downpouring of divine light in the form of pure doctrine, for they walked in the valley of the Jordan and sought for the gate of Eden. But when the heaven-sent and life-giving truths fell upon the scribal spies from the Sanhedrin, they brought forth no more fruit than would a desert cloudburst in a weary wasteland of rock and sand and sulphur.

And yet, perchance, there would be a day when even the desert would blossom as the rose; when springs of living water would burst forth in the rocky and sandy souls of those who now disbelieve the truth and reject the Purveyor.

To them parables are a reminder of half-seen truths yet to be learned; they contain a few rays of spiritual light, hidden by the clouds of unbelief, which rays at any moment might burst through the misty veil to let light into human souls. They contain drops of truth, trickling down from eternal springs, from which eternal sources all are invited to come and drink and never thirst more.

Parables are a call to investigate the truth; to learn more; to inquire into the spiritual realities, which, through them, are but dimly viewed. Parables start truth seekers out in the direction of further light and knowledge and understanding; they invite men to ponder such truths as they are able to bear in the hope of learning more. Parables are a call to come unto Christ, to believe his doctrines, to live his laws, and to be saved in his kingdom. They teach arithmetic to those who have the capacity to learn calculus in due course. They are the mild milk of the word that prepares our spiritual digestive processes to feast upon the doctrinal meat of the kingdom.

And so, Jesus, having delivered the parable of the sower, without more ado says: "He that hath ears to hear, let him hear." That is to say: 'If you are capable of understanding this parable, then do so. Study, pray, ponder; seek enlightenment; atune yourself to the whisperings of the Spirit, until its full meaning and significance dawns upon you. In this way you will learn more of me and my gospel.'

Even the Twelve, however, felt the need for further guidance, which they then asked for and received. And after Jesus himself had interpreted—partially, at least—the parable of the sower, he said:

No man, when he hath lighted a candle, covereth it with a vessel, or putteth it under a bed; but setteth it on a candlestick, that they which enter in may see the light.

'I have given you this parable so that you may learn its meaning. It is as a candle set to give light in a house. I gave it so that you might learn more of my gospel; otherwise I would have hidden the candle under a vessel or a bed.' Or:

'No man who is a true minister, when he brings gospel light, covereth it with mystery and confusion (as is the case, for instance, with the sectarian creeds describing God), but he holds forth as much light before men as they are able to bear.' (*Commentary* 1:291.)

> *For there is nothing hid which shall not be manifested; neither was anything kept secret, but that it should in due time come abroad.*

'For no parable, no teaching, no mystery, no hidden thing, is to be kept from the knowledge of the faithful; eventually all things shall be revealed, and the righteous shall know them.' (*Commentary* 1:291.)[2] Then again, Jesus repeated: "If any man have ears to hear, let him hear," which is his plea to all to learn the meaning of his parables. But there is yet more to come. Jesus continues:

> *Take heed what ye hear; for with what measure ye mete, it shall be measured to you; and unto you that continue to receive, shall more be given; for he that receiveth, to him shall be given; but he that continueth not to receive, from him shall be taken even that which he hath.*

'But take heed how ye hear and accept gospel truth, for you shall be rewarded with new revelation only if you are prepared to receive it. The measure of attention you give to the truths already revealed will dictate how much new truth shall be meted to you. If you continue to receive light and truth, and abide in them, eventually you shall be perfected in the truth and know all things. But if you do not continue to receive gospel light, and to walk in that light, from you shall be taken even that light which you once had, and you shall walk in darkness.' (*Commentary* 1:291-92.)

And so, with all these principles and this exhortation before us, we are now ready to taste the sweetness of the first series of major parables recorded by our New Testament friends.

NOTES

1. Farrar, completely carried away in the witchery—the charm and fascination—of his

own words, calls our Lord's parabolic teaching "a method of instruction so rare, so stimulating, so full of interest—a method which, in its unapproachable beauty and finish, stands unrivalled in the annals of human speech." (Farrar, p. 246.) Doubtless our friend Farrar, being a devout man and a true believer, according to the limits of knowledge then available to him, has now, in the realms ahead, been privileged to read 3 Nephi in the Book of Mormon and discover the true "unapproachable beauty . . . of human speech," as it is there found in the plain words, devoid of parabolic covering, of the One who excelled all others in all things.

2. In this same connection, Nephi said: "There is nothing which is secret save it shall be revealed; there is no work of darkness save it shall be made manifest in the light; and there is nothing which is sealed upon the earth save it shall be loosed." (2 Ne. 30:17.)

Chapter 50

PARABLES SPOKEN BY JESUS

Hear this, all ye people;
give ear, all ye inhabitants of the world:
Both low and high, rich and poor, together.
My mouth shall speak of wisdom;
and the meditation of my heart shall be
of understanding. I will incline mine ear
to a parable. (Ps. 49:1-4.)

Parable of the Sower
(Matthew 13:3-9, 18-23; JST, Matthew 13:5, 19, 21; Mark 4:3-9, 13-20;
JST, Mark 4:15-17; Luke 8:5-8, 11-15; JST, Luke 8:12-13, 15)

"Behold, a sower went forth to sow"—to sow seeds of eternal truth in the souls of men; to sow the wonder-working word of Him whose name is Wonderful; to sow the seeds of eternal life in the hearts of men. And how beautiful upon the mountains are the feet of them who preach the gospel of peace, who say unto Zion: Thy God reigneth!

"A sower went out to sow his seed," and the seed he sows is "the word of the kingdom." Even now the Divine Sower, the Messenger of Salvation, is scattering his Father's word among them in soil of all sorts.

"The word of the kingdom"!—again we declare it: He is preaching the gospel; the plan of salvation; faith, repentance, and baptism; the receipt of the Holy Ghost; the ever-

248

lasting word. He is speaking of a kingdom; a kingdom of God on earth; a church to be presided over by apostles and prophets; an organized body—surely the Lord's house is a house of order—that administers salvation to all who enter its strait door and mingle with its saintly citizens, the citizens of the kingdom. And how beautiful upon the mountains are the feet of the Lord who is the Author of Salvation, who himself preaches the gospel of peace, and who says unto Zion: I am thy God; come unto me.

But let the sower be Christ—who it is in this instance—or let it be any of the lesser sowers whom he calls to labor in his fields, the principle is the same. The seed is the word of God, the gospel of salvation. Jesus preaches it and he directs his servants so to do. And the seed is the same whether sown by the owner of the field or by the servants whom he employs. And as to whether the seed sprouts and grows and ripens and is harvested, such depends not upon the seed, but upon the soil. The seed is good, all the seed, whether sown by the Divine Sower or by those whom he sends to spread "the word of the kingdom."[1]

Thus, this parable of the sower, as we are wont to call it, might more aptly be considered as the parable of the four kinds of soil. The growth of the seed depends upon the nature of the soil; it depends upon the hearts and minds and souls of the hearers of the word. "The imagery of it was derived, as usual, from the objects immediately before His eyes—the sown fields of Gennesareth; the springing corn in them; the hard-trodden paths which ran through them, on which no corn could grow; the innumerable birds which fluttered over them ready to feed upon the grain; the weak and withering struggle for life on the stony places; the tangling growth of luxuriant thistles in neglected corners; the deep loam of the general soil, on which already the golden ears stood thick and strong, giving promise of a sixty and hundred-fold return as they rippled under the balmy wind." (Farrar, pp. 244-45.) We know the seed is good; let us then look to the soil in which it is sown.

1. *The soil by the wayside.*

"And as he sowed, some fell by the way side; and it was trodden down, and the fowls of the air devoured it." Such was the parabolic story; the interpretation, given later by Jesus to the disciples only, was: "Those by the way side are they that hear; then cometh the devil, and taketh away the word out of their hearts, lest they should believe and be saved."

How sad are the prospects for those by the wayside; those whose souls are so hardened by false doctrines and evil deeds that the seed of the word cannot even sprout and begin to grow in their hearts. These are the scribes and Pharisees of society, the ministers of false religions, and the wicked and ungodly who love darkness rather than light because their deeds are evil. They were the ones in Jesus' day who bound themselves with the formalisms of Mosaic worship and refused to let the light of a new dispensation enter their hearts. They are the religionists in our day who close their ears to new revelation and choose to believe such doctrines as that men are saved by grace alone, without more, thus leaving them free to walk in worldliness and still, as they suppose, gain salvation. They are the wicked and ungodly in general, the liars and sorcerers and adulterers, the people who feed their souls on pornographic words and pictures. They are worldly people who are carnal, sensual, and devilish by nature, and who choose so to remain. Repentance is always open to all men, but those by the wayside choose to retain their hardened and rebellious natures.[2]

2. *The soil in stony places.*

The parable: "Some fell upon stony places, where they had not much earth; and forthwith they sprung up; and when the sun was up, they were scorched, because they had no deepness of earth; and because they had no root, they withered away."

The interpretation: "But he that received the seed into stony places, the same is he that heareth the word and readily with joy receiveth it, yet he hath not root in himself, and endureth but for a while; for when tribulation or persecution ariseth because of the word, by and by he is offended." Luke's account includes the expression that "they . . . for a while believe, and in a time of temptation fall away."

These are they who believe the word; they know the Book of Mormon is true, as it were; there is no question in their minds that Joseph Smith is a prophet; they have the testimony of Jesus in their souls; and they rejoice in the light from heaven that has come into their lives. But they do not press forward with a steadfastness in Christ; they do not continue to learn the doctrines of salvation; they do not pay their tithes and offerings and serve in the Church. They do not endure to the end. Persecution arises; trials and tribulations block their path; their temptations are greater than they can bear. Because their roots are not deeply embedded in gospel soil, the new plant withers. It cannot stand the scorching rays of the sun.

Luke says "it lacked moisture." The sacrifices required of the saints were too great. Though the word, at the first, seemed as a pearl of great price, other considerations waylaid the gospel pilgrims, and the labors expected of them no longer seemed worth the effort. They withered and died spiritually, and the fruit of eternal life never ripened in their lives.

3. *The soil where thorns grow.*

The parable: "And some fell among thorns, and the thorns grew up, and choked it, and it yielded no fruit."

The interpretation: "And these are they who receive the word among thorns; such as hear the word, and the cares of this world, and the deceitfulness of riches, and the lusts of other things entering in, choke the word, and it becometh unfruitful." Luke's account adds the "pleasures of this life" as one of the things that choke the seeds so they "bring no fruit to perfection."

They hear and receive the word among thorns! The seed is good and the soil is good, but they choose to let thorns and

251

thistles continue to grow along with the seeds of righteousness. They seek to serve both God and mammon at one and the same time. The plan of salvation calls for men to overcome this world and prepare for a better one which is to be, but the cares of this world lead them astray. The gospel calls for men to seek the riches of eternity and to let the wealth of this world take a place of secondary importance, but the deceitfulness of riches—the false sense of superiority they give—leads men in worldly rather than godly paths. The good word of God calls for men to bridle their passions, forsake all that is evil, and cleave unto all that is good, but the lusts of the flesh remaining in the hearts of believing men cannot do other than lead them on a downward course.

True saints seek, not the pleasures of this life—the things that money and power and learning confer—but the eternal joys born of the Spirit. The Lord wants no part-time saints. His people cannot have one foot in the kingdom and the other in the world and expect to survive spiritually. The Church and its interests must always take precedence in their lives; otherwise the thorns will choke the precious gospel plant; it will die and in due course be burned with the thorns.

4. *The good soil.*

The parable: "And other fell on good ground, and did yield fruit that sprang up and increased; and brought forth, some thirty, and some sixty, and some an hundred."

The interpretation: "But he that received seed into the good ground, is he that heareth the word and understandeth and endureth; which also beareth fruit, and bringeth forth, some an hundredfold, some sixty, and some thirty." In the Joseph Smith Translation, Luke has a variant reading: "But that which fell on the good ground are they, who receive the word in an honest and good heart, having heard the word, keep what they hear, and bring forth fruit with patience."

Hear, understand, endure, bring forth fruit; receive the word in an honest and good heart, keep the commandments, and bring forth fruit with patience. Such is the will of the

PARABLES SPOKEN BY JESUS

Lord. "If the seed falls on productive, fertile soil, and if it is thereafter nurtured and cared for, it bringeth forth a harvest. But even here crops of equal value are not harvested by all the saints. There are many degrees of receptive belief; there are many gradations of effective cultivation. All men, the saints included, shall be judged according to their works; those who keep the whole gospel law shall bring forth an hundred fold and inherit the fulness of the Father's kingdom. Others shall gain lesser rewards in the mansions which are prepared." (*Commentary* 1:289.)

Parable of the Seed Growing by Itself
(Mark 4:26-29)

In his first recorded parable, that of the sower, we heard Jesus speak of sowing the seed of the gospel kingdom in all sorts of soil. Seed sown on hard and beaten paths was trodden under foot, or eaten by the fowls of heaven; it was seed that neither sprouted nor took root nor grew. Seed sown on stony ground found growth for a moment in the scanty covering of soil, but the sprouting plants withered and died when persecutions and tribulations and temptations beset the new converts. Seed sown amid the thorns and thistles of worldliness, after an initial growth, was smothered and choked by the cares and riches and lusts of the world so that it brought forth no fruit unto perfection. Only the seed sown in good soil, and which was nurtured and dunged and cultivated, brought forth abundantly the fruit of eternal life. In this parable of the sower, Jesus himself, in particular, and all of his servants, in general, were the sowers of the seed.

Now he speaks a second parable that grows out of the first. It is concerned with the seed sown in good soil, the seed that brings forth fruit, the seed that is reaped and gathered unto eternal life. And it is addressed to his servants, those sent forth by him to sow his seeds; in it he counsels them as to how they should act when they sow their seeds of salvation in the hearts of men.

"And he said, So is the kingdom of God, as if a man

should cast seed into the ground; And should sleep, and rise night and day, and the seed should spring and grow up, he knoweth not how."

'My earthly kingdom; the church that I have established among men; that organization which is the church and kingdom of God on earth; the very organization among men which administers the gospel and offers salvation to all who believe and obey—this very kingdom of God—grows in this manner: My servants first cast seed into good soil; they preach the gospel to the honest in heart. Then they leave the event in the hands of that Lord whose seed it is; they go about their other business, or go elsewhere to preach the word. It is as though night and day pass; the sun sends forth his rays by day and the mists of the night water the seed; then it sprouts and grows. My servants know not how the conversion is brought to pass, only that the seed sown in good soil somehow brings souls into the kingdom.'

"For the earth bringeth forth fruit of herself; first the blade, then the ear, after that the full corn in the ear. But when the fruit is brought forth, immediately he putteth in the sickle, because the harvest is come."

Seeds sown in the soil of the earth and seeds sown in the souls of men, both spring forth by a power greater than that of the sower. Paul may plant and Apollos water, but it is God who giveth the increase. The life is in the seed, be it the corn sown in the soil or the word sown in the soul. As the earth brings forth, first the blade, then the ear, and finally the corn fully ripened for the harvest, so the good seed grows in the good soil of goodly souls, preparing them for the day when the servants of the Lord shall thrust in their sickles and reap, thus laying up in store saved souls for the Lord of the harvest.

Parable of the Wheat and the Tares
(Matthew 13:24-30, 36-43; JST, Matthew 13:29, 39-44; D&C 86:1-7)

Jesus has now put forth one parable concerning the sower who sowed the seeds of eternal truth in diverse kinds of soil, and another concerning the seed of truth itself as it grows, miraculously and unaided by human hands, in the souls of the honest in heart. In each instance, we at least, and certainly even his Jewish hearers to some extent, can discern his meaning and intent. It is not as though he had told us in plain words, as his wont was among the Nephites, what profound truths he was then dispensing. But he has left us, in language of unexcelled excellence, parabolic illustrations upon which we can ponder and about which we can pray, until their full and glorious meanings burst through the storm clouds of darkness that hold back the radiance of the sun.

Having given us this much experience in the manner of presentation, in the use, and in the interpretation of his parables, Jesus now presents us with one of his more complex and difficult parabolic utterances. It is the parable of the wheat and the tares, one that required a special interpretation for the apostles of old, and one that required a latter-day revelation to enable us to bring its deep and hidden meanings to light. And mayhap, even yet, we await further spiritual enlightenment before its full significance is spread before us.

In this literary gem, preserved for us by our friend Matthew only, we learn how the Son of Man and his servants sowed good seed throughout the world; how Lucifer and his servants over-sowed the wheat fields with tares; how and why the wheat and the tares were permitted to grow together until the day of burning; and how the wicked will then be thrust into a furnace of fire, while the righteous shall shine forth in celestial splendor in the kingdom of the Father. The parable ends with the challenge: "Who hath ears to hear, let him hear." Let us then attune our ears to the wondrous words now spoken by Him at whose feet we rejoice to sit and whose teachings we so desire to savor. We shall view the parable and its interpretation point by point.

The parable: "The kingdom of heaven is likened unto a man which sowed good seed in his field."

The interpretation: "He that soweth the good seed is the Son of man; The field is the world; the good seed are the children of the kingdom."

The latter-day interpretation: "Verily, thus saith the Lord unto you my servants, concerning the parable of the wheat and of the tares: Behold, verily I say, the field was the world, and the apostles were the sowers of the seed."

The Church of Jesus Christ, the earthly organization through which salvation is offered to men; the kingdom of God on earth that prepares men for an inheritance in the kingdom of God in heaven; the organization that is in effect the kingdom of heaven on earth; this blessed and holy congregation of true believers—it is likened unto the Son of Man, and his holy apostles, and all his righteous servants who went forth into the world, preached the gospel, and made converts.

The whole world—not just Galilee and Judea and all of Canaan—the whole world is the field in which converts are made. The gospel and the Church and the kingdom and the blessings and the glory of it all, these are offered to all men. The seeds that are sown in all the world are the children of the kingdom. The sowers are not planting truths in human soil as in the parable of the sower; they are not dropping doctrinal gems in the hearts of men and then awaiting that Divine Providence which brings forth the blade and the ear and the ripened corn as in the parable of the seed growing by itself. Here the seeds sown are people; they are converts to the truth; they are members of the Church; they are the children of the earthly and heirs of the heavenly kingdom; and they are scattered upon all the face of the earth. They are here and there and everywhere, for the whole world is the field, and the apostles and they who ministered at their direction were commanded to go into all the world and preach the gospel to every creature. The words used are the same as in the other parables, but the symbolism and meaning and message are different.

The parable: "But while men slept, his enemy came and sowed tares among the wheat, and went his way."

The interpretation: "The tares are the children of the wicked one; The enemy that sowed them is the devil."

The latter-day interpretation: "And after they [the apostles and their fellow ministers of old] have fallen asleep the great persecutor of the church, the apostate, the whore, even Babylon, that maketh all nations to drink of her cup, in whose hearts the enemy, even Satan, sitteth to reign—behold he soweth the tares; wherefore, the tares choke the wheat and drive the church into the wilderness."

Satan sows tares in the field of the Lord; or, rather, he over-sows or sows on top of the wheat. And as the seeds sown by the Son of Man and his servants are the children of the kingdom, the true saints of God, so the seeds sown by Satan—the tares—are the children of the devil. They are followers of that wicked one; they are carnal and sensual people who choose a false system of religion because it permits them to gratify their passions and live after the manner of the world.

Be it noted that the tares—as far as this parable is concerned—are sown after the day of Jesus and his meridian ministers. The great apostasy came after the apostles had "fallen asleep." When there were no longer apostles and prophets to guide the Church, the saints were tossed to and fro and carried about with every wind of doctrine. The tares choked the wheat; the children of the kingdom were led astray; and the Church was driven into the wilderness.[3]

The parable: "But when the blade was sprung up, and brought forth fruit, then appeared the tares also. So the servants of the householder came and said unto him, Sir, didst not thou sow good seed in thy field? from whence then hath it tares? He said unto them, An enemy hath done this. The servants said unto him, Wilt thou then that we go and gather them up?"

The latter-day interpretation: "But behold, in the last

days, even now while the Lord is beginning to bring forth the word, and the blade is springing up and is yet tender—Behold, verily I say unto you, the angels are crying unto the Lord day and night, who are ready and waiting to be sent forth to reap down the fields."

This is a multi-dispensation parable. It had its beginning when Jesus and the apostles sowed the children of the kingdom in the nations of the earth. In and after their day tares—the children of Satan—were planted in the earthly field, and the tares choked out the wheat. Then the seed was sown again; the children of the kingdom again were found in the field; the blade sprang up amid the tares; and the servants of the Lord, as in former days, would have destroyed the tares, and even the angels cried out for the hastening of the harvest.[4]

The parable: "But he said, Nay; lest while ye gather up the tares, ye root up also the wheat with them. Let both grow together until the harvest: and in the time of harvest I will say to the reapers, Gather ye together first the wheat into my barn; and the tares are bound in bundles to be burned."

The interpretation: "The harvest is the end of the world, or the destruction of the wicked. The reapers are the angels, or the messengers sent of heaven. As, therefore, the tares are gathered and burned in the fire, so shall it be in the end of this world, or the destruction of the wicked. For in that day, before the Son of man shall come, he shall send forth his angels and messengers of heaven. And they shall gather out of his kingdom all things which offend, and them which do iniquity, and shall cast them out among the wicked; and there shall be wailing and gnashing of teeth. For the world shall be burned with fire. Then shall the righteous shine forth as the sun, in the kingdom of their Father."

The latter-day interpretation: "But the Lord saith unto them, pluck not up the tares while the blade is yet tender (for verily your faith is weak), lest you destroy the wheat also. Therefore let the wheat and the tares grow together until the harvest is fully ripe; then ye shall first gather out the wheat from among the tares, and after the gathering of the wheat, behold and lo, the tares are bound in bundles, and the field remaineth to be burned."

The scope and sweep of the message here revealed is as broad as the earth and as enduring as the ages. The wheat is now being gathered out from among the tares. Israel is being gathered into the sheepfold of the Good Shepherd. Messengers from heaven—Peter, James, and John; Moses, Elijah, and Elias; and all the angelic host who have restored priesthoods, conferred keys, and given powers to men—have joined hands with mortals on earth to gather the elect and to seal up the law and bind up the testimony against those who are to be burned when the Son of Man comes. Soon the harvest will be fully ripe; the wheat will be stored in the Lord's barns; the tares will be bound in bundles; and the burning will commence.[5]

Parable of the Mustard Seed
(Matthew 13:31-32; Mark 4:30-32; Luke 13:18-19)

Though each of the parables stands by itself to teach a designated portion of eternal truth, it takes them all together to place in perspective those truths with which they deal. In the parable of the sower, the good word of God was sown in divers soils and only a portion of the seed grew and brought forth fruit. In the parable of the wheat and the tares even that portion which grew was choked by thorns; the kingdom was destroyed for a time; and only the latter-day sowing anew of the saving seeds enabled the growth of that wheat which would be gathered into barns before the burning of the bundles of tares. In each of these parables there is an element of sorrow and sadness; evil triumphs in many hearts; multitudes reject the gospel seed; and other multitudes who had the truth changed themselves from the wheat of the kingdom to the tares of the devil, and the field was burned. But now, in the parable of the mustard seed, we shall see how the kingdom of God on earth shall grow and increase, how it shall be displayed for all to see, and how success shall attend its labors.

"The kingdom of heaven," Jesus said, "is like to a grain of mustard seed, which a man took, and sowed in his field: Which indeed is the least of all seeds: but when it is grown, it is the greatest among herbs, and becometh a tree, so that the birds of the air come and lodge in the branches thereof."

One of the great beauties of parables is that they may have many meanings and applications all of which are true and proper. Their full significance is and can be known only to those who have an over-all knowledge of the dealings of Deity with men, and who also are enlightened by the power of the same Spirit that guided the one who gave the parables. "Parables must have been utterly unintelligible to all who did not see in the humble, despised, Nazarene, and in His teachings, the Kingdom. But to those whose eyes, ears and hearts had been opened, they would carry most needed instruction and most precious comfort and assurance." (Edersheim 1:592.)

To the more enlightened among his Jewish hearers, Jesus' words in this parable would have given some concept at least of the great truths he sought to convey. Two of his expressions—that of "mustard seed" and, as Luke expresses it, "a great tree"—were well known and had clear meaning. Their use and application in the case at hand is, of course, quite another matter.

As to the first: "The expression, 'small as a mustard-seed,' had become proverbial, and was used, not only by our Lord, but frequently by the Rabbis, to indicate the smallest amount, such as the least drop of blood, the least defilement, or the smallest remnant of sun-glow in the sky. 'But when it is grown, it is greater than the garden-herbs.' Indeed, it looks no longer like a garden-herb or shrub, but 'becomes,' or rather, appears like, 'a tree'—as St. Luke puts it, 'a great tree,' of course, not in comparison with other trees, but with garden-shrubs."

As to the second: "A tree, whose wide-spreading branches afforded lodgment to the birds of heaven, was a familiar Old Testament figure for a mighty kingdom that gave shelter to the nations. [Ezek. 31; Dan. 4.] Indeed, it is specifically used as an illustration of the Messianic Kingdom. [Ezek. 17:23.]" (Edersheim 1:592-93.)

To those in sectarian Christendom who have sufficient interest in scriptural study to seek for an interpretation of this parable, some such conclusion as this is generally reached: It contrasts the small and rising beginning of Christianity in Jesus' day with the worldwide dominion now enjoyed by those who suppose they are followers of the Nazarene. They assume, falsely, "that the Kingdom of Heaven, planted in the field of the world as the smallest seed, in the most humble and unpromising manner, would grow till it far outstripped all other similar plants, and gave shelter to all nations under heaven." (Edersheim 1:593.)[6]

The most complete and best application and meaning, however, is preserved for us in the language of Joseph Smith. After quoting the words of the parable, he says: "Now we can discover plainly that this figure is given to represent the Church as it shall come forth in the last days. Behold, the Kingdom of Heaven is likened unto it. Now, what is like unto it?

"Let us take the Book of Mormon, which a man took and hid in his field, securing it by his faith, to spring up in the last days, or in due time; let us behold it coming forth out of the ground, which is indeed accounted the least of all seeds, but behold it branching forth, yea, even towering, with lofty branches, and God-like majesty, until it, like the mustard seed, becomes the greatest of all herbs. And it is truth, and it has sprouted and come forth out of the earth, and righteousness begins to look down from heaven, and God is sending down His powers, gifts and angels, to lodge in the branches thereof.

"The Kingdom of Heaven is like unto a mustard seed.

261

Behold, then is not this the Kingdom of Heaven that is raising its head in the last days in the majesty of God, even the Church of the Latter-day Saints." (*Teachings,* pp. 98-99.)

Parable of the Leaven
(Matthew 13:33; Luke 13:20-21)

Yet another portion of the eternal picture portrayed in parables is seen in the parable of the leaven. The mustard seed became a tree that displayed the kingdom of heaven on earth before the world, but the leaven worked silently, without observation, unknown to many among men, to establish the plans and purposes of Divine Providence. Jesus said simply: "The kingdom of heaven is like unto leaven, which a woman took, and hid in three measures of meal, till the whole was leavened."

In this parable of the leaven we see the glory and triumph of the kingdom in the hearts of men. The Messianic kingdom comes not in martial splendor; there are no rolling drums and tramping feet; the Son of David does not march before his armies; trumpets do not herald his coming, and standard bearers raise no visible ensign to the nations. The new kingdom, like leaven, is hidden in the hearts of men. The leaven of life, the leaven of righteousness, the leaven of the word of God—the yeast of eternal truth—is "kneaded" into the souls of men. Then its spreading, penetrating, life-giving effect enlarges the soul and "raises" sinners into saints.

Legal administrators teach the gospel and testify of its divinity; their testimonies, hidden in the hearts and minds of men, begin the soul-enlarging process of conversion. Lumps of lifeless dough live, and after being baked in the ovens of life become as desirable to the taste as the manna once rained from heaven upon the Lord's people.[7]

Parable of the Hidden Treasure
(Matthew 13:44; JST, Matthew 13:46)

After giving the parable of the leaven, Jesus sent the

multitude away, went with his disciples into a house in Capernaum, and at the request of the disciples interpreted the parable of the wheat and the tares.[8] Then he gave three more parables to the disciples alone. The first of these is the parable of the hidden treasure. "Again, the kingdom of heaven is like unto a treasure hid in a field," Jesus said. "And when a man hath found a treasure which is hid, he secureth it, and, straightway, for joy thereof, goeth and selleth all that he hath, and buyeth that field."

"By seeming accident a man sometimes discovers the gospel treasure. Unaware of the saving grace of our Lord, devoid of true religious understanding, overburdened with the cares of the world, hardened by sin, walking in an ungodly and carnal course—he suddenly stumbles onto Christ and the pure Christianity found in his true Church. Immediately all else seems as dross. Temporal wealth becomes but glittering tinsel as compared to the eternal riches of Christ. Then worldly things are forsaken; then no sacrifice is too great for the new convert, as he seeks a valid title to the treasures of the kingdom." (*Commentary* 1:300.)[9]

A woman comes out of Sychar to draw water from Jacob's well and finds one there who gives her living water. Gentile nations, composed of people who have never heard of Christ and are devoid of any desire to gain the cleansing power of his blood, meet Paul and Silas and find a great treasure. Hosts of earth's pilgrims, traveling and wandering they know not where, with no knowledge of Joseph Smith and the restoration, chance to meet a Mormon missionary or move into a Mormon community, and suddenly the riches of eternity are opened to their view.

And so it is with the kingdom of heaven, with the only true and living church upon the face of the whole earth: Though it operates openly among men, though its gospel gifts and goodly fruits are seen on every hand, yet it is hidden from those whose hearts are not yet attuned to the Infinite; it is hidden until, of a sudden, the finder, scarcely having supposed that so great a treasure would be hidden in so unlikely a spot, makes a great discovery. The treasure is recognized for what it is, and it is available for the taking. Immediately the finder sells all that he hath—he cannot buy it for a lesser price; there is no fixed amount on a price tag; he cannot haggle and offer anything less than all he has; it is not for sale on a bargain counter; its purchase calls for the sacrifice of all things—and so the finder, be he rich or poor, sells all that he hath; he forsakes the world and its wealth; he turns from the worldliness of the past and walks in paths of righteousness; and he buyeth the field and possesseth the treasure. It is his. He found it.

Parable of the Pearl of Great Price
(Matthew 13:45-46)

"Again, the kingdom of heaven is like unto a merchant man, seeking goodly pearls: Who, when he had found one pearl of great price, went and sold all that he had, and bought it."

Now Jesus has somewhat more to say about how the struggling pilgrims of earth, far removed from their heavenly home, come to find the gospel, the most precious possession of life. The treasure hidden in the field is found by chance. Honest-hearted souls find themselves in contact with true ministers and the truths that from them flow, and they sell all that they have to purchase the newly discovered gospel of salvation.

But here Jesus speaks of earnest and devout investigators; of truth seekers who desire to better their circumstances; of people who consciously follow the dictates of their consciences; of those who follow the promptings and heed the whisperings of that Spirit, the light of Christ, which enlighteneth every man born into the world. These are those who know there is more to life than to eat, drink, and be merry. They are trying to cast off carnality and live by godly standards. They may be philanthropists or artists; they may serve on committees and join groups who work for freedom, social betterment, and the preservation of human rights; they study the Bible, seek truth, and join uplifting organizations, including various of the churches of the day. They are seeking goodly pearls.

After long and diligent search; after going from one level of light to heights of greater illumination; perhaps after joining one church or another in search of the peace that passeth understanding; after seeking truth with an open heart—after, shall we not say it, after reading and pondering and praying about the Book of Mormon; after investigating the prophetic claims of Joseph Smith and his successors—at the end of a long search, lo, the pearl of great price is found. It is the everlasting gospel. It is the Church and kingdom of God on earth. It is all that men can desire; its blessings are peace in this life and eternal life in the world to come.

Do investigators then sell all that they have to buy such a pearl? They can do nothing less. And the Lord, whose pearl it is, asks their all. As with those who find the hidden treasure, there is no haggling, no bargaining, no agreeing to come into the Church with this or that reservation, no offering of less than one's whole soul and all that the truth seekers have and are. What matters it if all the pearls of the past are sold, if all the causes and organizations, however "goodly," go by the board? The newly found pearl, the kingdom of heaven, will use all the talents and strength and abilities of those who give their all to gain it.[10]

Parable of the Gospel Net
(Matthew 13:47-53; JST, Matthew 13:50-51, 53)

The parable: "Again, the kingdom of heaven is like unto a net, that was cast into the sea, and gathered of every kind: Which, when it was full, they drew to shore, and sat down, and gathered the good into vessels, but cast the bad away."

The interpretation: "So shall it be at the end of the world. And the world is the children of the wicked. The angels shall come forth, and sever the wicked from the just, and shall cast them out into the world to be burned. There shall be wailing and gnashing of teeth."

What an awesome and ominous picture this is! The gospel net is cast into the sea; the fishers of men seek to draw all men into the kingdom. The catch is great, but it includes fish of all kinds, some of which are gathered in vessels to be saved, and others are cast away to be burned along with the wicked who were never caught in the gospel net. The net here meant is a draw net or a seine, which may be as much as half a mile in length; it is leaded below so it will sweep the bottom of the sea, while corks keep the top floating near the surface. As it is swept along the beach it gathers in fish of every sort without reference to their ultimate use or worth.

So it is with those who join the Church—they are oftimes as diverse and varied as men can be. "Rich and poor, bond and free, Jew and Gentile, learned and ignorant, sincere and hypocritical, stable and wavering—men of all races, cultures, and backgrounds accept the gospel and seek its blessings." (*Commentary* 1:302.) Some are repentant and worthy and will be put in vessels; others are swept along by the tides of social pressure. Some are drawn in by the tight net of business necessity and economic advantage; yet others join with the saints to inherit property, marry selected persons, or gain political preferment. And all such shall be cast away with the wicked to be burned. There are many reasons for coming into the earthly kingdom of heaven; salvation is a personal matter, and only those who meet the divine standards will find eternal place and lot with the saints.

> Though in the outward Church below
> Both wheat and tares together grow,
> Ere long will Jesus weed the crop
> And pluck the tares in anger up.[11]

The wheat and the tares together grow! Such, we have seen, was the parable telling of the present intermixture of the righteous and the wicked in the earthly kingdom, meaning more particularly the world. Now, in the parable of the draw net, we see that same condition within the Church and kingdom itself. And try as we may—men being weak and mortal and fallible; sins being hidden and devious and unknown—until the Son of Man comes, the kingdom will not be wholly cleansed.

Those in the Church are not perfect, and more than church membership is needed to save and exalt. Baptism alone is not enough: thereafter the newly born babes in Christ must grow to a spiritual maturity; they "must press forward with a steadfastness in Christ, having a perfect brightness of hope, and a love of God and of all men"; they must feast "upon the word of Christ, and endure to the end." (2 Ne. 31:20.) Those caught in the gospel net have power to become the sons of God; after baptism they must "work out" their "salvation with fear and trembling" before the Lord. (Philip. 2:12.)[12]

As of this moment, there are tares among the wheat. "In a great house"—and God's house is his church, his earthly kingdom—"there are not only vessels of gold and of silver, but also of wood and of earth; and some to honour, and some to dishonour." (2 Tim. 2:20.) For truly, "they are not all Israel, which are of Israel." (Rom. 9:6.) "If a man therefore purge himself from these"—his sins, the sins committed after baptism, the burdens of iniquity that rest upon him, though he was drawn in by the great gospel net—"he shall be a vessel unto honour, sanctified, and meet for the master's use, and prepared unto every good work." (2 Tim. 2:21.) This, then, is the conclusion—and also the moral—of the parable: "Let every one that nameth the name of Christ depart from iniquity." (2 Tim. 2:19.)

Such is the parable of the gospel net.[13] Following its recitation, and as he ended, for the moment, his preachments by parables, Jesus asked his disciples, "Have ye understood all these things? They say unto him, Yea, Lord." It is a mark of true discipleship to understand all scripture, the parables included; indeed, only those enlightened by the power of the Holy Ghost gain the full meaning and intent of the written word, for scripture is both given and understood by the same holy power, the power that comes from the Lord through his Spirit.[14]

Then Jesus said unto them: "Every scribe well instructed in the things of the kingdom of heaven, is like unto a householder; a man, therefore, which bringeth forth out of his treasure that which is new and old."

They—the Twelve, all the disciples, both male and female—knew the meanings of the parables, the deep, hidden, glorious meanings of these gems of literary elucidation and of gospel knowledge. Ergo: They must teach and testify of these very things. As a householder who displays his treasures—both the old and the new; that which hath value because of its antiquity, and that which is of great worth because it is new and can be used—as a householder displays his treasures, so the disciples must bring forth out of the storehouses of their souls the eternal truths of the gospel and teach them to their fellowmen. "It becometh every man who hath been warned to warn his neighbor." (D&C 88:81.)[15]

Truly, this Man, who spake as none other had ever done, fulfilled that "which was spoken by the prophet, saying, I will open my mouth in parables; I will utter things which have been kept secret from the foundation of the world." (Matt. 13:35.)

NOTES

1. "According to Jewish authorities there was twofold sowing, as the seed was either cast by the hand or by means of cattle. In the latter case, a sack with holes was filled with corn and laid on the back of the animal, so that, as it moved onwards, the seed was thickly scattered. Thus it might well be, that it would fall indiscriminately on beaten roadway, on stony places but thinly covered with soil, or where the thorns had not been cleared away, or undergrowth from the thorn-hedge crept into the field, as well as on good ground." (Edersheim 1:586-87.)

2. In commenting about this parable, Joseph Smith said: "Men who have no principle of righteousness in themselves, and whose hearts are full of iniquity, and [who] have no desire for the principles of truth, do not understand the word of truth when they hear it. The devil taketh away the word of truth out of their hearts, because there is no desire for righteousness in them." (Teachings, p. 96.)

3. "According to the common view, these tares represent what is botanically known as the 'bearded Darnel,' a poisonous rye-grass, very common in the East, 'entirely like wheat until the ear appears,' or else (according to some), the 'creeping wheat' or 'couch-grass,' of which the roots creep underground and become intertwined with those of the wheat. But

the Parable gains in meaning if we bear in mind that, according to ancient Jewish (and, indeed, modern Eastern) ideas, the Tares were *not* of different seed, but only a degenerate kind of wheat. Whether in legend or symbol, Rabbinism has it that even the ground had been guilty of fornication before the judgment of the flood, so that when wheat was sown tares sprang up. The Jewish hearers of Jesus would, therefore, think of these tares as [a] degenerate kind of wheat, originally sprung at the time of the Flood, through the corruptness of the earth, but now, alas! so common in their fields; wholly undistinguishable from the wheat, till the fruit appeared: noxious, poisonous, and requiring to be separated from the wheat, if the latter was not to become useless." (Edersheim 1:589.)

This view that the tares were a "degenerate kind of wheat" symbolically accords with the revealed interpretation of the parable that the tares are children of the wicked one who arose to replace the children of the kingdom. All men are of the same race; those who do good and work righteousness become children of the kingdom, and those who choose to do the works of him who is evil become the children of the devil.

4. "We learn by this parable," Joseph Smith wrote, "not only the setting up of the Kingdom in the days of the Savior, which is represented by the good seed, which produced fruit, but also the corruptions of the Church, which are represented by the tares, which were sown by the enemy, which His disciples would fain have plucked up, or cleansed the Church of, if their views had been favored by the Savior. But He, knowing all things, says, Not so. As much as to say, your views are not correct, the Church is in its infancy, and if you take this rash step, you will destroy the wheat, or the Church, with the tares; therefore it is better to let them grow together until the harvest, or the end of the world, which means the destruction of the wicked, which is not yet fulfilled." (*Teachings,* pp. 97-98.)

5. "The harvest and the end of the world have an allusion directly to the human family in the last days. . . . As, therefore, the tares are gathered and burned in the fire, so shall it be in the end of the world; that is, as the servants of God go forth warning the nations, both priests and people, and as they harden their hearts and reject the light of truth, these first being delivered over to the buffetings of Satan, and the law and the testimony being closed up, as it was in the case of the Jews, they are left in darkness, and delivered over unto the day of burning; thus being bound up by their creeds, and their bands being made strong by their priests, [they] are prepared for the fulfilment of the saying of the Savior—'The Son of Man shall send forth His angels, and they shall gather out of His Kingdom all things that offend, and them which do iniquity; and shall cast them into a furnace of fire, there shall be wailing and gnashing of teeth.' We understand that the work of gathering together of the wheat into barns, or garners, is to take place while the tares are being bound over, and [incident to] preparing for the day of burning: [and] that after the day of burnings, the righteous shall shine forth like the sun, in the Kingdom of their Father." (*Teachings,* p. 101.)

It should be clear that "in giving the parable of the wheat and the tares, Jesus was actually summarizing the doctrines of the apostasy, the restoration of the gospel in the latter-days, the growth and development of the latter-day kingdom, the millennial cleansing of the earth, the glorious advent of the Son of Man, and the ultimate celestial exaltation of the faithful." (*Commentary* 1:297.)

6. "The evident falsity of this interpretation is seen from the fact that the original, pure Christianity practiced by the primitive saints never did more than sprout its head above ground; within a relatively short time the original plant was trodden down, destroyed, and replaced by those noxious and thorny plants which make up the present churches of so-called Christendom. It is only in the dispensation of the fulness of times that the true Christian tree is to grow until it becomes 'a great tree'; it is only in this final age that the true gospel message is to roll forth until the knowledge of God covers the earth as the waters cover the sea. (D&C 65; Isa. 11.)" (*Commentary* 1:298.)

7. An application of this parable to the latter-day kingdom is given by the Prophet in these words: "It may be understood that the Church of the Latter-day Saints has taken its rise from a little leaven that was put into three witnesses. Behold, how much this is like the parable! It is fast leavening the lump, and will soon leaven the whole." (*Teachings,* p. 100.)

8. Whether our Lord gave all of the parables in the thirteenth chapter of Matthew in immediate consecutive order is a matter of some uncertainty. Two of them, the parable of

the mustard seed and the parable of the leaven, are recorded by Luke in a different setting. It may be that Matthew grouped them all together for convenience in presentation, or, what is yet more probable, that Jesus repeated the same parables on numerous occasions to different congregations. There is no reason to suppose that a parable once given should never be spoken again; if the message was worth the attention of one congregation, so it would be of another. We should, however, no matter what view we take of the time and circumstances of their delivery, know assuredly that the message they contain and the doctrines they allude to are what is important to us.

9. This parable has also an allusion to the gathering of Israel in the last days. "The Saints work after this pattern," the Prophet said, after quoting the parable. "See the Church of the Latter-day Saints, selling all that they have, and gathering themselves together unto a place that they may purchase for an inheritance, that they may be together and bear each other's afflictions in the day of calamity." (Teachings, p. 101.)

10. "Seekers after truth may acquire much that is good and desirable, and not find the greatest truth of all, the truth that shall save them. Yet, if they seek persistently and with right intent, if they are really in quest of pearls and not of imitations, they shall find. Men who by search and research discover the truths of the kingdom of heaven may have to abandon many of their cherished traditions, and even their theories of imperfect philosophy and 'science falsely so called,' if they would possess themselves of the pearl of great price." (Talmage, pp. 293-94.)

11. Hymns, no. 102.

12. "All who are caught in the gospel net are not saved in the celestial kingdom; church membership alone gives no unconditional assurance of eternal life. (2 Ne. 31:16-21.) Rather, there will be a day of judgment, a day of sorting and dividing, a day when the wicked shall be cast out of the Church, 'out into the world to be burned.' For those then living the Second Coming will be an initial day of burning, sorting, and judgment (Matt. 25:31-46; D&C 63:54); for all men of all ages the ultimate day of sorting and dividing will occur, after all men have been raised from the dead, at the final great day of judgment. (2 Ne. 9:15-16.)" (Commentary 1:302.)

13. Joseph Smith in applying this parable to latter-day conditions wrote: "Behold the seed of Joseph, spreading forth the Gospel net upon the face of the earth, gathering of every kind, that the good may be saved in vessels prepared for that purpose, and the angels will take care of the bad. So shall it be at the end of the world—the angels shall come forth and sever the wicked from among the just, and cast them into the furnace of fire, and there shall be wailing and gnashing of teeth." (Teachings, p. 102.)

14. With reference to the parables considered in this chapter, Joseph Smith said: "These things are so plain and so glorious, that every Saint in the last days must respond with a hearty Amen to them." (Teachings, p. 102.)

15. These treasures of truth, old yet ever new, are exemplified by "the Book of Mormon coming forth out of the treasure of the heart. Also the covenants given to the Latter-day Saints, also the translation of the Bible—thus bringing forth out of the heart things new and old." (Teachings, p. 102.)

Chapter 51

JESUS MINISTERS AMONG THE GADARENES

Master, the tempest is raging!
The billows are tossing high!
The sky is o'er shadowed with blackness.
No shelter or help is nigh.

Carest thou not that we perish?
How canst thou lie asleep
When each moment so madly is threatening
A grave in the angry deep?[1]

He Stills a Storm on the Sea of Galilee
(Mark 4:35-41; JST, Mark 4:30; Matthew 8:18-27; Luke 8:22-25;
9:57-62; JST, Luke 8:23)

Some six miles south and east of the shore of the ofttimes turbulent Galilean sea lay the prosperous city of Gadara where dwelt the Gadarenes (Gergesenes). Straight across the lake from Capernaum was Gergesa. Those who lived in these and other eastern areas must see the face and hear the voice of the Son of God. His work must not be done in a corner; every ear must hear his words, every eye must see his glory; all must have the privilege to believe, to follow, to obey, to be saved. We have no record of any visit by the Man from Nazareth to this area of the Decapolis except that which he now plans to make, but the miracle and wonder of his brief ministry among the rebellious of that area is such that neither they nor any who hear of it will ever be able to erase the memory.

It has been a long day. Jesus is weary. Great multitudes have pressed upon him, so much so that he delivered his public parables from a ship while the thronged congregation stood on the shore. Thereafter in a house in Capernaum he continued to preach in parables and otherwise to his disciples. Again on the seashore the multitude throngs about, hanging on every word, their souls crying out for the divine message.

It is now evening, and he says to his disciples, "Let us go over unto the other side of the lake." This decision apparently takes them by surprise, for it is only then that they "sent away the multitude." Then, as Mark says, "they took him even as he was in the ship," which seems to mean they departed without preparation in the way of food or clothing or traveling necessities. Whether their departure was a change in plans or the continuation of a course already fore-known in the mind of the Master we do not know; of this only we cannot doubt: Jesus, following the dictates of the Spirit, was continuing his foreordained ministry, and the coming events—the stilling that night of the Galilean storm, and the confrontation the next day with the legion of evil spirits—were among the most dramatic events of his ministry.

As Jesus and the elect few—certainly all or part of the Twelve among them; perhaps only the Twelve, because of space limitations—as these few hastened to push off from shore into the beckoning seclusion of the waters of Gennesaret, a sudden interruption halted their progress. Three men, apparently men of note and prominence, came forward to pledge their allegiance to the Master's cause and to offer their services in his behalf. Their individual offers and the divine responses invoked to each were so instructive as to warrant their inclusion in the writings of the synoptists. The proffers of service and our Lord's rejoinders were:

1. *The case of the vainglorious scribe.*

Swept along by the tide of popular acclaim, feeling the exhilaration that always attends a new and great and achieving movement, a certain scribe—a recognized religious leader, a prominent minister of the day, as it were—stepped forward to offer his services in the newly established church. "Master, I will follow thee whithersoever thou goest," he said.

From Jesus' response it seems clear that the offer was a self-serving plea for a position of preferment—a minister of the old dispensation seeking an equivalent rank in the new. "But in spite of the man's high position, in spite of his glowing promises, He who cared less than nothing for lip-service, and who preferred 'the modesty of fearful duty' to the 'rattling tongue of audacious eloquence,' coldly checked His would-be follower. He who had called the hated publican gave no encouragement to the reputable scribe. He did not reject the proffered service, but neither did He accept it. Perhaps 'in the man's flaring enthusiasm, He saw the smoke of egotistical self deceit.' He pointed out that His service was not one of wealth, or honour, or delight; not one in which any could hope for earthly gain." (Farrar, p. 248.)

In short, the Lord Jesus chooses his own ministers. All men who repent may enter his earthly kingdom and become heirs of the universal blessings thereby offered to all. Only those prepared by foreordination, chosen, as it were, from before the foundations of the world, are selected to lead and guide the destinies of the holy kingdom. And so, without denying church membership, but while withholding approval of the proffered ministerial assistance, Jesus said:

The foxes have holes, and the birds of the air have nests; but the Son of man hath not where to lay his head.

When and while men serve on full-time missions—as Jesus himself did for the more than three years here involved—all worldly matters slip away into relative insignificance. The Lord's ministers deny themselves of houses and lands and families and friends—of whatsoever need be—to carry on that work which excels in importance all other. There is no record that the scribe who sought to call himself to the ministry took any further steps to achieve his initially sought purpose.

2. *The case of the reluctant disciple.*

In contrast to the scribe who sought for himself an ecclesiastical appointment in the new kingdom, we see now a disciple who was, in fact, called by Jesus to serve on a mission. "Follow me," came the divine word; 'teach my gospel; testify of me; build up my kingdom; forsake all for my name's sake.' This disciple—whose heart was known to Him who calls His own—had faith; he knew the worth of the pearl of great price; but he also had worldly interests that seemed important to him. "Lord, suffer me first to go and bury my father," he implored. Back came the divine word:

> Let the dead bury their dead: but go thou and preach the kingdom of God.

'I have called you; forsake the things of this world and seek for those of a better. What is the life or death of family or friends to those who are taking life and salvation to a dying world? Let those who are spiritually dead bury those in whose bodies the breath of life no longer dwells. Go thou; preach the gospel of the kingdom; proclaim faith, repentance, baptism, and the gift of the Holy Ghost. Bring souls unto me, and you shall have rest with them in the kingdom of my Father.'

3. *The case of the delaying disciple.*

Yet another disciple—willing to serve, but concerned with the time and place of his call; willing to go on a mission and preach the gospel, but questioning the field of his present assignment—said: "Lord, I will follow thee; but let me first go bid them farewell, which are at home at my house." 'I will go, but let it be on my terms and conditions, not those of the Church.' To him Jesus gave the reply that has become proverbial for all time:

> No man, having put his hand to the plough, and looking back, is fit for the kingdom of God.[2]

But now, at last, they set sail, traveling eastward across those blessed waters which are so much a part of the lives of the Holy One and his holy apostles. Yet even now, they are not alone; so great is his fame, so popular his appeal, and so compelling his presence, that many seek to follow him onto the turbulent waters and into the descending dusk. "There were also with him other little ships," Mark says. What happened to them as the events of the evening rose to their fearsome yet triumphant climax we know not. Perhaps they returned to a safe harbor and a secure anchor as the impending storm rose in violence over the surging waters; perhaps they too were buffeted by the violent winds, as their fearsome passengers dreaded the seeming death that lay ahead in the angry deep; and perhaps those who sailed in these lesser crafts also marveled and worshipped when the awesome decree went forth, "Peace, be still," and the violent waters of Gennesaret became calm.

In Galilee, of great and wondrous fame, is found the Sea of Galilee—the lake of Gennesaret, the sea of Tiberias—an inland mere of fresh, fish-filled water. Into it on the north flows the newborn Jordan; out of it on the south drains the mature and mighty river in which both John and Jesus baptized, and which meanders downward through a rich and fertile valley to the Dead Sea. This lake of Galilee, which Jesus so much loved and from whose life-giving waters the sons of Jonas and the sons of Zebedee, and many others of the disciples, made their living, is some thirteen miles long and seven miles wide. It is 695 feet below sea level and lies at the base, on the east and west, of rugged hills and mountains cut by canyons and gorges down which tempestuous winds and atmospheric downdraughts blow, making the otherwise calm waters subject to sudden and violent storms.

Such an atmospheric assault came forth in the lowering dusk of this memorable evening as Jesus and his intimates set forth toward Perea and the eastern shore. Whether the storm arose wholly without warning or the experienced sailors who governed the craft saw signs of the tempest ahead and yet launched their ship forth because the passenger whose will they sought to do had so commanded, we cannot tell. Nor does it matter, though we prefer to believe they set forth knowing that peril lay ahead because He willed it.

In any event, it is clear that the storm itself was unusually fierce. "There arose a great tempest in the sea," Matthew says, "insomuch that the ship was covered with the waves." Mark says: "There arose a great storm of wind, and the waves beat into the ship, so that it was now full"; and Luke adds that "they were filled with fear, and were in danger."

Through it all, we see the Mortal Messiah seeking the physical refreshment his tired body so much needs at the moment. "Jesus is asleep, for very weariness and hunger, in the stern of the ship, His head on that low wooden bench, while the heavens darken, the wild wind swoops down those mountain-gorges, howling with hungry rage over the trembling sea; the waves rise and toss, and lash and break over the ship, and beat into it, and the white foam washes at His feet. His Humanity here appears as true as when He lay cradled in the manger; His Divinity, as when the sages from the East laid their offerings at His Feet." (Edersheim 1:600.)

None fear floods and storm-lashed seas more than those who work with water and know its onrushing power and the utter helplessness of mortal strength before its overpowering waves. Is it any wonder that Jesus was awakened from what must have been a deep sleep with cries of, "Master, carest thou not that we perish?" as Mark records; "Master, master, we perish," as Luke has it; and, "Lord, save us: we perish," as Matthew records—all of which expressions must have been part of the earnest and fear-filled importunings of that dread moment.

Jesus, now awake, before he arises from the wooden bench whereon he lay, says to those who sought his help: "Why are ye fearful, O ye of little faith?" After the storm is quelled, he will say to them again: "Where is your faith?" From this we need not suppose they were without faith. Their very importunings bore witness of their assurance that this man, whom they followed as the Messiah, could do whatever must be done to prevent disaster. Their lack of faith—as with all of us—was one of degree; had they believed with that fervor that might have been the case, they of themselves could have stilled the storm, without arousing their weary Lord from his needed rest.

But after this, "he arose, and rebuked the winds and the sea; and there was a great calm." The raging waters and the roaring winds ceased; the mighty waves became calm ripples. "Peace, be still," he said, and all was calm and serene. "When 'He was awakened' by the voice of His disciples, 'He rebuked the wind and the sea,' as Jehovah had of old ["He rebuked the Red sea also, and it was dried up"—Ps. 109]— just as He had 'rebuked' the fever, and the paroxysm of the demonised. For, all are His creatures, even when lashed to frenzy of the 'hostile power.' And the sea He commanded as if it were a sentient being: 'Be silent! Be silenced!' And immediately the wind was bound, the panting waves throbbed into stillness, and a great calm of rest fell upon the Lake. For, when Christ sleepeth, there is storm; when He waketh, great peace." (Edersheim 1:602.)

And they being afraid wondered, saying one to another, What manner of man is this! for he commandeth even the winds and water, and they obey him.

What manner of man, indeed! Heretofore he has cleansed lepers, cast out devils, and even given life to a cold corpse. Now the very elements obey his word. And yet it is not the miracles of themselves that cause the world to wonder; rather, it is the miracles coupled with the repeated personal witness that he is the Son of God, their Savior and Redeemer.

Others have performed miracles, always, however, in his name and by his authority; others have even controlled the elements, as he through them has willed it. Moses stretched forth his rod and the waters of the Red Sea parted. Whatever turbulence throbbed through their restless waves ceased at his word; the laws of gravity ceased to triumph and the very waters congealed, forming a wall on the right hand and on the left, between which the chosen seed then trod on dry ground. Enoch moved mountains and changed rivers from their courses. Elijah and Elisha smote the waters of Jordan with a holy mantle, and they divided hither and thither, leaving dry ground for their path. Unto the servants of the Lord "is given power to command the waters." (D&C 61:27.) It is not the miracle per se; it is the fact that Jesus, who performed the miracle, said he was God's Son—leaving the *deed* as proof of his *words*.[3]

We cannot leave our brief consideration of this stupendous miracle, however, without at least opening the door to the symbolic uses to which it may be put. For instance, manifestly it teaches that the Lord Jesus is ever near his friends and will preserve them in perilous circumstances, even if their safety calls for control of the elements.

Also, the sea—a raging, restless sea—is a symbol of a sinful and wicked world. The beasts seen by Daniel in vision and used as types of worldly kingdoms came up out of the sea, a sea upon which the four winds of heaven strove. (Dan. 7.) And the Lord said to Isaiah: "The wicked are like the troubled sea, when it cannot rest, whose waters cast up mire and dirt. There is no peace, saith my God, to the wicked" (Isa. 57:20-21)—leaving us to conclude that when Christ calms the seas of life, peace enters the hearts of men.

Further, there are those also who have likened the Church itself to a ship, steered and sailed by apostles and prophets through the waves of the world, which rage and toss, violently and with force, against the tempested bark, and yet never prevail. The divine ship never sinks; its faithful passengers never drown in the angry deep, because Christ sails his own ship. He may seem to be asleep on a bench with a pillow under his head, but he is there. And when in times of great peril he is aroused by the pleas of his servants, once again he rebukes the winds and the waters; he delivers those who have faith in his name; he speaks peace to troubled souls; his voice is heard again, "Peace, be still."

Jesus Heals a Demoniac among the Gadarenes
(Mark 5:1-20; JST, Mark 5:6, 11, 13-15, 17; Luke 8:26-39; JST, Luke 8:27, 31-33, 35, 37; Matthew 8:28-34; JST, Matthew 8:29-30)

Scarcely a ripple marred the calm surface of the lake of Gennesaret as the Jewish ship anchored near Gerasa (Gergesa) on the Perean side of the sea. Striving winds and raging billows and crashing waves—all part of the now-stilled storm—no longer beat upon the ship and the rock-strewn shore. He whose voice had spoken to matter unorganized and caused the earth to come rolling into existence; he who had gathered the waters into one place, calling the dry land *earth* and the gathering together of the waters *sea*—had spoken peace to the Galilean tempest, and all was calm. The elements were at rest.

Whether it was a late hour of the day of parables or an early hour of the day after, we do not know—only that the storm of the journey had been stilled and earth's elements were at peace. Jesus and his fellow preachers set foot on Perean soil and almost immediately they were confronted with a spiritual storm, a tempest of devilish opposition and human torment, that far overshadowed the recently silenced winds and quelled waves of their inland mere. They were met by a man out of the tombs who for a long time had been possessed by devils. He dwelt in no house, wore no clothing, and was "exceeding fierce," so much so "that no man might pass by that way." In his maddened and raging state "no man could bind him, no, not with chains: Because that he had been often bound with fetters and chains, and the chains had been plucked asunder by him, and the fetters broken in pieces: neither could any man tame him. And always, night and day, he was in the mountains, and in the tombs, crying, and cutting himself with stones."[4]

This poor, shrieking, tormented creature—his body bruised and gashed and naked—impelled by some power or instinct beyond human ken, seeing Jesus afar off, ran to meet him. There they stood—the Prince of Peace who had spoken peace to the winds and the waves, and the maddened maniac whose every act was subject to the will of the demons from hell—there they stood, good and evil facing each other, the one about to act, the other to be acted upon. Then, on his own motion, Jesus spoke the word that would restore lost harmony to the suffering demoniac, that would quell and allay the strife within him, a strife more perilous than the pounding waves of the sea. "Come out of the man, thou unclean spirit," he said.

But there was no immediate obedience. Other purposes were yet to unfold. Rather, the suffering Gadarene fell down, worshipped Jesus, and, his voice framing the words placed on the tongue by the evil power, acclaimed: "What have I to do with thee, Jesus, thou Son of the most high God?" There was no divine knowledge in the demented man; he neither knew nor in his present state cared whether Jesus was the Messiah. But the devils from the deep knew—and do know—that he is God's Son. Their memory of preexistence remains; they remember the day when, at his word, they fell as lightning from heaven. "The devils also believe, and tremble." (James 2:19.) Then from the mouth of the man came the blasphemous words of many devils, spoken as though there was but one: "I adjure thee by God, that thou torment me not." And also, this time speaking in the plural: "Art thou come hither to torment us before the time?" The devils, who know Jesus is the Lord, know also that their destiny is one of eternal torment, one in which they are cast out forever from the divine presence and from every ray of hope and light and betterment.

Jesus asked the man: "What is thy name?" or rather, "he commanded him saying, Declare thy name," and demons within him answered by his mouth: "My name is Legion: for we are many." Or: "He said, Legion: because many devils were entered into him." The poor soul was in complete subjection to the demoniac will; their words were his words, and his voice was their voice.

Knowing they had no choice but to come out of the man—for Jesus had so commanded—the devils "besought him much that he would not send them away out of the country." Apparently they were assigned to tempt those in that area and feared the wrath of Lucifer if they failed to bend to his will. Also, "they besought him that he would not command them to go out into the deep," meaning the eternal abyss, the abysmal pit of eternal torment, which shall be their eventual everlasting inheritance. "And he said unto them, Come out of the man."

Now there was, "a good way off," a great herd of swine, about two thousand in number, "feeding on the mountain." As Matthew records it, the demons said: "If thou cast us out, suffer us to go away into the herd of swine," and Jesus said, "Go." In Mark's account, the devils besought him, saying: "Send us into the swine, that we may enter into them. And forthwith Jesus gave them leave." Luke's conclusion is that "he suffered them" so to do.

Some cavilers exhibit a mocking concern as to whether Jesus commanded or merely permitted the devils to enter the swine, as though it made the slightest difference. They pretend to find in his act, whatever it was, an unwarranted destruction of the property of others. Surely it was an unethical if not an immoral act, they contend. If such it is assumed to be, so be it. But, realistically, who is to say that He who sends hail to beat down the ears of ripened corn, or storms to sink fish-filled boats, may not also send devils into swine to sweep them in a maddened surge to a watery grave?

But be that as it may be. "Then went the devils out of the man, and entered into the swine: and the herd ran violently down a steep place into the lake, and were choked." As to the locale, Edersheim tells us: "About a quarter of an hour to the south of Gersa [Gerasa] is a steep bluff, which descends abruptly on a narrow ledge of shore. A terrified herd running down this cliff could not have recovered its foothold, and must inevitably have been hurled into the

281

Lake beneath. Again, the whole country around is burrowed with limestone caverns and rock-chambers for the dead, such as those which were the dwelling of the demonised." (Edersheim 1:607.)

Why did the demons desire to enter the bodies of the swine? Or, for that matter, how came they to take up tenancy in the body of the man? We cannot tell and do not know how it is that evil spirits—few or many—gain entrance into the bodies of mortal men. We do know that all things are governed by law, and that Satan is precluded from taking possession of the bodies of the prophets and other righteous people. Were it not so, the work of God would be thwarted—always and in all instances—for Lucifer leads the armies of hell against all men, and more especially against those who are instrumental in furthering the Lord's work.

There must be circumstances of depression and sin and physical weakness that, within the restrictions of divine control, permit evil spirits to enter human bodies. We do know their curse is to be denied tabernacles, and we surmise that the desire for such tenancy is so great that they, when permitted, even enter the bodies of beasts.

And it may be, in this instance, that the devils, ejected from their ill-gotten home by a power they could not resist, sought to thwart His work by the next-best expedient available to them—that of destroying the livelihood of many people, so they would rise up in anger against Him who destroyed their craft. And, in fact, this is what happened.

When they who fed the swine saw what was done, " they fled, and went and told it in the city and in the country." The word was noised about in Gerasa and Gadara and the whole countryside. All the people were stirred up to a high point of wonder and amazement. The owners of the swine, those who knew the healed demoniac, and all who heard of the wondrous happenings hastened "to see what was done." They "came to Jesus, and found the man, out of whom the devils were departed, sitting at the feet of Jesus, clothed, and in his right mind: and they were afraid."

Our evangelist friends tell us only what happened and the few spoken words that tie the whole miraculous series of events together. Hours must have elapsed before the word reached the inhabitants of the area, and yet other hours before the multitudes assembled near the sea to hear and see for themselves. It may even be that more than one day was involved. No doubt the assembling hosts came in groups, both large and small, and arrived at different times.

Jesus and those who were with him would not have done other than teach them the gospel of the kingdom. Such was the message they were proclaiming in every city and place where a single listening ear would hearken to their words. The accounts do tell us that after the people assembled to the place where Jesus and the healed man sat, the feeders and keepers of the swine recited again, for all to hear, how he that was possessed of the devils was healed and also concerning the swine. Nor can we suppose that Jesus and the disciples remained silent. Never was there a time when Jesus was not the center of all eyes, when his words did not ring with clarity in nearby ears. Never was there a teaching situation that he did not utilize to proclaim his gospel to every creature. We cannot doubt that the Gadarenes, on that day or those days, as the case may be, heard the word of truth from him who is the Truth.

But when all had been done that he came to do, when those who walked in darkness had seen a great light, when the doctrine had been taught and the testimony borne—with the healed demoniac there as a living witness of the truth of it all—then was Jesus rejected by the Gadarenes. "Then the whole multitude of the country of the Gadarenes round about besought him to depart from them; for they were taken with great fear."

" 'And they were afraid'—more afraid of that Holy Presence than of the previous furies of the possessed. The man indeed was saved; but what of that, considering that some of their two thousand unclean beasts had perished! Their precious swine were evidently in danger; the greed and gluttony of every apostate Jew and low-bred Gentile in the place were clearly imperilled by receiving such a one as they saw that Jesus was. With disgraceful and urgent unanimity they entreated and implored Him to leave their coasts. Both heathens and Jews had recognised already the great truth that God sometimes answers bad prayers in His deepest anger. Jesus Himself had taught His disciples not to give that which was holy to the dogs, neither to cast their pearls before swine, 'lest they trample them under their feet, and then turn again and rend you.' He had gone across the lake for quiet and rest, desiring, though among lesser multitudes, to extend to these semi-heathens also the blessings of the kingdom of God. But they loved their sins and their swine, and with a perfect energy of deliberate preference for all that was base and mean, rejected such blessings, and entreated Him to go away. Sadly, but at once, He turned and left them. Gergesa was no place for Him; better the lonely hill-tops to the north of it; better the crowded strand on the other side." (Farrar, p. 259.)

But Jesus and his associates did not depart without leaving a witness. The healed man desired to attach himself to the missionary group and go over the lake to Capernaum. To him, however, Jesus said: "Go home to thy friends, and tell them how great things the Lord hath done for thee, and hath had compassion on thee." Of his subsequent missionary service we know only that "he departed, and began to publish in Decapolis, how great things Jesus had done for him; and all that heard him did marvel."

We cannot doubt that the purposes of the Gadarene ministry were fulfilled—in the stilling of the storm as they journeyed thitherward; in the healing of the possessed demoniac near Gerasa; in the teaching and testifying that grew out of the miracle; and in the continuing witness of the one by whose mouth Satan once spoke but out of which now came a witness of Christ that no man could refute.[5]

NOTES

1. *Hymns*, no. 106.

2. " 'No man having joined the Church of Jesus Christ is fit for salvation in the celestial kingdom unless he endures to the end in keeping the commandments.' " (*Commentary* 1:305.)

3. In answer to those who argue that no miracle was involved during this darksome night on Gennesaret, Canon Farrar records these choicely chosen words: "If we believe that God rules; if we believe that Christ rose; if we have reason to hold, among the deepest convictions of our being, the certainty that God has not delegated His sovereignty or His providence to the final, unintelligent, pitiless, inevitable working of material forces; if we see on every page of the Evangelists the quiet simplicity of truthful and faithful witnesses; if we see in every year of succeeding history, and in every experience of individual life, a confirmation of the testimony which they delivered—then we shall neither clutch at rationalistic interpretations, nor be much troubled if others adopt them. He who believes, he who *knows*, the efficacy of prayer, in what other men may regard as the inevitable certainties or blindly-directed accidents of life—he who has felt how the voice of a Saviour, heard across the long generations, can calm wilder storms than ever buffeted into fury the bosom of the inland Lake—he who sees in the person of his Redeemer a fact more stupendous and more majestic than all those observed sequences which men endow with an imaginary omnipotence, and worship under the name of Law—to him, at least, there will be neither difficulty nor hesitation in supposing that Christ, on board that half-wrecked fishing boat, did utter His mandate, and that the wind and the sea obeyed; that His word was indeed more potent among the cosmic forces than miles of agitated water, or leagues of rushing wind." (Farrar, pp. 252-53.)

4. Matthew speaks of two demoniacs; Mark and Luke mention only one. Elder Talmage presents the usual sectarian explanation of this discrepancy by saying: "It is possible that one of the afflicted pair was in a condition so much worse than that of his companion that to him is accorded greater prominence in the narrative; or, one may have run away while the other remained." (Talmage, p. 310.) From the Inspired Version, however, we know there was only one; Matthew's account is corrected to conform to the accounts of Mark and Luke. If Elder Talmage had had access to this more perfect biblical account, his expressions relative to this and a number of other matters would have been different.

5. Taken as a whole, as I have written elsewhere, our accounts of the healing of the Gadarene demoniac teach the following truths:

"(1) That evil spirits, actual beings from Lucifer's realm, gain literal entrance into mortal bodies;

"(2) That they then have such power over those bodies as to control the physical acts performed, even to the framing of the very words spoken by the mouth of those so possessed;

"(3) That persons possessed by evil spirits are subjected to the severest mental and physical sufferings and to the basest sort of degradation—all symbolical of the eternal torment to be imposed upon those who fall under Satan's control in the world to come;

"(4) That devils remember Jesus from pre-existence, recognize him as the One who was then foreordained to be the Redeemer, and know that he came into mortality as the Son of God;

"(5) That the desire to gain bodies is so great among Lucifer's minions as to cause them, not only to steal the mortal tabernacles of men, but to enter the bodies of animals;

"(6) That the devils know their eventual destiny is to be cast out into an eternal hell from whence there is no return;

"(7) That rebellious and worldly people are not converted to the truth by observing miracles; and

"(8) That those cleansed from evil spirits can then be used on the Lord's errand to testify of his grace and goodness so that receptive persons may be led to believe in him." (*Commentary* 1:311.)

Chapter 52

A CONTINUING MINISTRY OF MIRACLES

Jesus is the Christ, the Eternal God; . . .
he manifesteth himself unto all those
who believe in him,
. . . working mighty miracles, signs, and
wonders,
among the children of men according to
their faith.
(2 Ne. 26:12-13.)

Faith Precedes the Miracle

"It is by faith that miracles are wrought; . . . if these things have ceased, then has faith ceased also." (Moro. 7:37-38.) "If there be no faith among the children of men God can do no miracle among them." (Ether 12:12.)

"And who shall say that Jesus Christ did not many mighty miracles? . . . And the reason why he ceaseth to do miracles among the children of men is because that they dwindle in unbelief, and depart from the right way, and know not the God in whom they should trust." (Morm. 9:18-20.)

Miracles are the fruit of faith. Signs follow those who believe. If there is faith, there will be miracles; if there are no miracles, there is no faith. The two are inseparably intertwined with each other; they cannot be separated, and there cannot be one without the other. Faith and miracles go together, always and everlastingly. And faith precedes the miracle.

Faith is power, the power of God, the power by which the worlds were made. Where there is faith there is power, and where a people do not have power to heal the sick and perform miracles, they have no faith.

Faith is an eternal principle, an eternal law; it is built into the universe itself as a governing, controlling force; it is ordained of God and shall endure forever. It takes no special divine decree to cause the effects of the law of gravity to be manifest everywhere on earth at all times. The law has been established and the effects that flow from it are everlastingly the same. So it is with faith. He who has given a law unto all things has established faith as the power and force by which he and his shall operate in righteousness forever. No special divine decree is needed to utilize the power of faith; it is like gravity: anytime any person in any age conforms to the law involved, the ordained results will attend.

In this connection, be it also noted that among the gifts of the Spirit—where healings are involved—there are two gifts: one is faith to heal, the other, faith to be healed. Manifestly Jesus had faith to perform miracles under any and all circumstances and for whomsoever he chose; that his acts always conformed to holy and just principles is implicit in the very nature of things. We are aware that at times he performed miracles on his own motion and for his own purposes, as in the casting out of the legion of devils from the Gadarene demoniac and in the stilling of the storm on the lake of Gennesaret. But as we are about to see, except in special and unusual circumstances—and these were numerous in the life of Jesus—healing miracles are and should be performed as a result of the faith of the one receiving the divine blessing.

It is, of course, beyond our present purview to speak in

extenso about faith and the signs and miracles that are its companions; such would be a volume by itself.[1] But to envision why and how Jesus operated as he is about to do in his Galilean ministry, we must be reminded of at least the foregoing basic concepts.

Jesus Raises the Daughter of Jairus from Death
(Mark 5:21-24, 35-43; JST, Mark 5:27-28; Luke 8:40-42, 49-56; JST, Luke 8:51; Matthew 9:1, 18-19, 23-26; JST, Matthew 9:24-25)

After his Gadarene ministry, Jesus sailed some seven miles westward across the now calm Galilean waters to Capernaum and its environs. Great throngs awaited him on the shore—reverential, respectful, worshipful—hungering for more of the heavenly manna that he dispensed so freely. Perhaps those who set sail in the many small ships that followed him into the storm-darkened night had been with him near Gerasa—seeing what was done to the demoniac and hearing what was said to the Gadarenes—so that they now, returning ahead of him, had alerted the Galileans of his coming. But however the people learned of his return, as the isles shall wait for his law, so they upon whom his countenance now shone also waited for his word.

Among those on the shore—all hungering and thirsting after righteousness; all anxious to feed their souls with more of the heavenly bread that fell from his lips; all rejoicing in the parables of the past and the miracles that had been wrought among them—among these were two who needed special help, two upon whom his countenance was about to shine as it did on but few people in Palestine. One was Jairus, a ruler of the synagogue in Capernaum, whose twelve-year-old daughter lay even then at death's door; the other, an unnamed woman suffering from an incurable feminine malady, an issue of blood that none could heal.

Jesus' miracles varied according to the needs and circumstances of those on whose behalf they were wrought. He performed the same gracious acts in one way on one occasion, in other ways at subsequent times—all to the end that those involved might be led along the path to eternal life in his Father's kingdom. He has just spoken peace to a Galilean tempest and called a legion of devils out of a wracked and tormented body, acting in each case on his own authority, taking no steps to build up the faith of the beneficiaries of his goodness. Each of these miracles manifest the absolute power inherent in him; sometimes Jesus healed the sick because he had faith to heal and not because they had faith to be healed.

But now in the case of Jairus's daughter and the woman with the issue of blood, we are about to see healings because those who sought the blessing had faith to be healed. And in each instance we shall see the Blessed One—bearing in himself, as it were, the sicknesses and infirmities of his brethren—we shall see him, with tender solicitude, encourage and increase the faith of those who seek his goodness; we shall see him strengthen their faith lest by any chance they fail to obtain the blessings they seek.

One of the first to meet Jesus as he came ashore was Jairus, "a ruler of the synagogue" in Capernaum. We know Jesus had preached often and wrought miracles in that very house of worship, and we know that such preaching was done at the solicitation of the Jewish elders who held local synagogue rule. Thus Jesus and Jairus knew and respected each other; this devout Jew had heard Jesus preach, had believed his words, and had rejoiced in the knowledge of other miracles. Is it too much to suppose he was present on that glorious Capernaum Sabbath when Jesus cast the evil spirit from the man in the synagogue of that city?

But whatever their prior association, Jairus had faith in Christ, and coming this day, "he fell down at Jesus' feet" "and worshipped him." "My little daughter lieth at the point of death," he said. "I pray thee, come and lay thy hands on her, that she may be healed; and she shall live."

Can anyone doubt the faith of Jairus? Or that he knew and understood the ordinance of administration to the sick?

"Come and lay thy hands on her," he pled, "and she shall live"! "Is any sick among you? let him call for the elders of the church; and let them pray over him, anointing him with oil in the name of the Lord: And the prayer of faith shall save the sick, and the Lord shall raise him up." (James 5:14-15.) "And the elders of the church, two or more, shall be called, and shall pray for and lay their hands upon them in my name." (D&C 42:44.)

Jesus' miracles were wrought in divers ways, with or without oil, with or without the laying on of hands, always as occasion required; but the request of Jairus that he come and conform to the ritual he had ordained in his Church, and which he had followed on selected occasions in the past, was the logical and proper request for him to make. The ordinance of laying on of hands, in divers spiritual connections, was common among the Jews, as it had been in all dispensations that went before.

Jesus' heart was touched, and he purposed within himself that Jairus's faith should not go unrewarded. "And Jesus went with him; and much people followed him, and thronged him." And it was in the midst of this pressing, surging multitude that the woman with the issue of blood slipped forward in secret to but touch the hem of his garment, an episode that delayed their progress toward the home of Jairus and of which we shall speak more particularly hereafter.

As Jesus ceased speaking to the woman and the reason for their delay vanished, "there came from the ruler of the synagogue's house certain which said, Thy daughter is dead: why troublest thou the Master any further?" Receiving this word, what would be more natural than for Jairus to thank Jesus for coming thus far, and excuse himself to return home to comfort his wife and arrange for the funeral.

Jesus, however, overheard the message. Immediately, before any thought of doubt or fear or resignation to the will of a seeming divine providence could arise, he said: "Be not afraid, only believe." "Fear not: believe only, and she shall be made whole." 'She is dead; no matter, I am the Lord also of the dead; if thou canst but believe, she shall live again.' This miracle is to be wrought, as healings generally are, because of the faith of the family members, not because Jesus had absolute power within himself and could, if he chose, speak to the winds or the devils and have them obey.

That Jairus's faith remained firm, perhaps even increased, we cannot doubt, for Jesus—taking only Peter, James, and John with him—continued to Jairus's home, to do that which only one having the power of God can do. Indeed, it is not too much to suppose that Jairus knew of the raising of the widow's son from death at Nain. Word of such wondrous deeds spread like wildfire through the whole country; such deeds of mercy were not done in a corner, and each one fed the faith of others who needed and desired like blessings.

Arriving at the place where the dead daughter now lay, Jesus with her parents and the three chief apostles entered the home "and found it occupied by the hired mourners and flute-players, who, as they beat their breasts, with mercenary clamour, insulted the dumbness of sincere sorrow, and the patient majesty of death." (Farrar, p. 272.) To this wailing chorus of mourners—some bowed in true grief, others chanting and shrieking their false sorrows as the actors they were paid to be—Jesus said: "Why make ye this ado, and weep? the damsel is not dead, but sleepeth."

"Not dead, but sleepeth"! That she was dead they well knew, "and they laughed him to scorn." Yet how much more refined and consoling it is to say "Lazarus sleepeth," though for days the processes of decomposition have been at work in the former home of his spirit. "True, she was dead as men view death, for her spirit had left her body. Yet in the kindly perspective of eternity, the dead are merely as those who are asleep; for a moment the body, without life, is unconscious to its surroundings; but soon—as when the sleeping soul, following a night of repose, gains consciousness with the rising sun—the body will awaken to a new life of resurrected immortality. How comforting to know that the dead are only sleeping and that those who rest in the Lord shall awake to everlasting life." (*Commentary* 1:316.)

Then Jesus put forth the shrieking wailers with their mourning minstrelsy, "took the damsel by the hand"—she was a maid of about twelve years of age—"and said unto her, *Talitha cumi.*" "Damsel, I say unto thee, arise." 'Little maid, arise!' Then "her spirit came again"; the living, intelligent, sentient part of the human personality received a new mortal life; the spirit daughter of the Eternal Father entered again the body created from the dust of the earth. The maid arose; she walked; and Jesus "commanded to give her meat."

After the miracle, Jesus gave the parents certain instructions that are difficult for us to understand. "And her parents were astonished," Luke says, as well they should have been, "but he charged them that they should tell no man." Mark's account says "he charged them straitly that no man should know it." Matthew makes no mention of the restrictive counsel, but says only: "And the fame hereof went abroad into all that land."

We cannot suppose for a moment that Jesus was trying to keep this miracle secret. This wondrous deed that turned death into life; that bore record of the divinity of the One who even now was forecasting his own future victory over the grave; that could be performed only in righteousness and only by the power of God—this mighty miracle should, as Matthew says, send his fame into all the land.

Indeed, the parents could not enshroud in secrecy that which was already public knowledge; everyone in the whole area would soon know, because of the way Jesus himself had handled the successive events, that the little maid who once was dead now lived. Her death had been announced openly to the multitude as Jesus ended his conversation with the woman whom he healed of the issue of blood. Jesus himself had replied, openly and before the multitude, that notwithstanding her death she would "be made whole." All the people would soon know that she now lived, and would be expected to wonder how and by what means life had come to her again. The hired mourners, whose earnings had been aborted by the act of divine mercy, all knew of her death and would soon know that she now lived. The thing was not done in the dark; multitudes did and would know what the Master had wrought. Why then this charge of secrecy?

Perhaps, as is so often the case, the fragmentary accounts of our evangelist friends do not convey the full tenor and purport of the charge given by Jesus to the parents. We know, for instance, as a matter of standard gospel counsel, that those who enjoy the gifts of the Spirit and who possess the signs which always follow those who believe are commanded not to boast of these spiritual blessings. In our day, after naming the miraculous signs that always attend those who have faith, those who believe the very truths taught by Jesus anciently, the Lord says: "But a commandment I give unto them, that they shall not boast themselves of these things, neither speak them before the world; for these things are given unto you for your profit and for salvation." (D&C 84:73.) On another occasion the Lord in our day directed, "Talk not of judgments, neither boast of faith nor of mighty works." (D&C 105:24.)

Perhaps the charge to "tell no man" meant they were not to tell the account in a boastful way, lest a spirit of pride—a spirit of self-adopted superiority—should come into their souls. There were times when Jesus told the recipients of his healing power to go forth and testify of the goodness of God unto them, and other times when he limited the extent and detail of their witness. Without knowing the people and all the attendant circumstances, we cannot sit in judgment and determine why he gave differing directions to different people.

Jesus Heals the Woman with an Issue of Blood
(*Mark 5:25-34; Luke 8:43-48; Matthew 9:20-22*)

We come now to the staunching of the flow of feminine

blood of an unnamed woman to whom legend has given the name Veronica. Of her we know only that she was a woman of great faith—probably already a baptized member of the Church—who "had an issue of blood twelve years, And had suffered many things of many physicians, and had spent all that she had, and was nothing bettered, but rather grew worse."

Too ashamed even to mention the nature of her affliction, yet knowing Jesus had power to heal, she pressed near him as he and Jairus walked together and said within herself: "If I may but touch his garment, I shall be whole." Too timid, too shy to claim audience before him or to ask him to center his divine attention on such a lowly one as she esteemed herself to be, yet she sought just to be near him, just to feel his presence, just to touch the hem of the sacred garments he wore. Then she would be healed, and he need not so much as slacken his stride as he went with the ruler of the synagogue to raise to life the maid whose whole span of life measured the same as the years of her disease.

That there was no healing power in the hem of Jesus' garment, nor in any of the physical things he possessed, nor in any relic from any source, however saintly, goes without saying. It is axiomatic. But on the other hand, anything that enables a person to draw near unto the Lord and to center his affection and trust in him may properly be used to increase faith and to gain the blessings that come in no other way. Even the Urim and Thummim itself, carried in the breastplate of the ancient high priests in Israel, was but an instrument that enabled them to center their faith in Jehovah and receive, by revelation, his mind and will. And so it was, to a lesser extent, with the fringes and tassels on the borders of the garments of the Rabbis in Jesus' day.

From the beginning the garments of the saints have enjoyed a special and sacred place in true worship. They cover that nakedness which when exposed leads to lewd and lascivious conduct. They stand as a symbol of modesty and decency and are a constant reminder to true believers of the restraints and controls placed by a divine providence upon their acts. Adam and Eve made for themselves aprons of fig leaves to cover their nakedness and preserve their modesty. The Lord himself made coats of skins to cover the bodies of our first parents, that they, being clothed and wholesome before him, might attain those feelings which foster reverence and worship.

And the Lord Jehovah commanded Moses to direct the children of Israel, through all their generations, to "make them fringes [tassels] in the borders [corners] of their garments, . . . and that they put upon the fringe of the borders a ribband of blue." Why and of what moment was such a dress code? We can see how the dress standards given to Adam and Eve taught modesty and placed the new mortals in a frame of mind to live and worship by proper standards. Immodest, ornate, and worldly dress is an invitation to unclean thoughts and immoral acts, which are foreign to that conduct and worship desired by Him whose we are. But why such minutely prescribed dress requirements as these given to ancient Israel? Jehovah gives the answer: "It shall be unto you for a fringe, that ye may look upon it, and remember all the commandments of the Lord, and do them; and that ye seek not after your own heart and your own eyes, after which ye use to go a whoring." That is: 'Your garments, your clothing, shall be a shield and a protection to you. They shall cover your nakedness and keep from you the lusts of the eyes and the lusts of the flesh, and the special adornments on them shall remind you continually to walk as becometh saints.' All this is to be, Jehovah decreed, "That ye may remember, and do all my commandments, and be holy unto your God." (Num. 15:37-41.)

Now we see Jehovah, as Jesus, ministering personally among the people, and—we cannot doubt—dressed in the manner in which he himself had of olden times decreed that faithful Israelites should dress.[2] And now we see Veronica— if so she may be called—looking upon the fringes of his garments; remembering the ancient covenant that by so doing she was agreeing to keep the commandments; and feeling within herself that if she but touched the sacred fringes on the garments of him whom she accepted as God's Son, surely she would be healed. That such a desire should enter her heart was, under all the circumstances, both natural and proper. It was a sign—not of belief in magic or relics or any special power in the clothing itself, but of faith in him who wore the garments and who had designed them in such a way as to remind his people of their covenant to keep his commandments.

And so, she "came behind him, and touched the border of his garment: and immediately her issue of blood stanched." She was healed; she felt it in her body; her organs began to function according to the original plan and purposes of the great Creator; the hemorrhaging fountain of affliction no longer flowed. Overcome with emotion and gratitude she slipped back into the throng without a word.

"And Jesus, immediately knowing in himself that virtue had gone out of him, turned him about in the press, and said, Who touched my clothes?" There were immediate denials on the part of the disciples. Peter said, "Master, the multitude throng thee and press thee, and sayest thou, Who touched me?"[3]

This question—"Who touched me?"—was asked not to gain information, but to encourage the timid suppliant to identify herself and to bear testimony of the healing power that had come into her life. And she, seeing her act was not hidden from him by whose power she was now made whole, came forward—trembling, fearful, grateful—fell at his feet, and declared to him and to all "for what cause she had touched him, and how she was healed immediately." Jesus confirmed how and in what manner and by what means she had been blessed. "Daughter, thy faith hath made thee whole," he said, "go in peace, and be whole of thy plague."[4]

And so it is in the surging throngs of life. Many who are spiritually sick; who have had an issue of sorrow and sin, lo these many years; who spend their substance on the things of this world—many such are within arm's length of the Lord and need only to reach out and take hold of his church to find his healing power.

Jesus Causes the Blind to See and the Dumb to Speak
(*Matthew 9:27-34; JST, Matthew 9:36*)

Jesus now journeys from Jairus's home to the house in Capernaum where he abides when in that part of Galilee. He is followed by two blind men who plead for sight. "Thou son of David, have mercy on us" is the plea of the sightless ones. Jesus makes no response; he has no apparent intention of causing the light of the sun to break through the seal that physical imperfection has placed upon eyes that see nothing but everlasting night. At least any act on his part must result from a clear and firm faith in the hearts of those who seek his healing goodness.

Up to this point in his mortal ministry, there is no recorded instance of Jesus opening blind eyes. Lame men have leaped, lepers have been cleansed, and dead bodies have been reanimated as mortal houses for eternal spirits, but there is not as yet a specific account of sightless eyes seeing. We suppose the fault is with the scriptural accounts that have come down to us, for the opening of blind eyes is singled out in the Messianic prophecies as among the great wonders he shall work. The Book of Mormon Messianic assurance is that Jesus would work mighty miracles, heal the sick, raise the dead, cause the lame to walk, "the blind to receive their sight," and the deaf to hear, and that he would cure all manner of diseases. (Mosiah 3:5.) The biblical promise, as given by Isaiah in a passage of wondrous beauty, and which applies to his coming as a mortal and in millennial glory, is found in these words: "Your God will come. . . . Then the eyes of the blind shall be opened, and the ears of the deaf shall be unstopped. Then shall the lame man leap as an hart, and the tongue of the dumb sing." (Isa. 35:4-6.)

In the cases now before us, the two blind persons, having within themselves faith to be healed, follow Jesus into the house, continuing to importune for his healing power. "Believe ye that I am able to do this?" he asks them. Their answer is "Yea." "Then touched he their eyes, saying, According to your faith be it unto you. And their eyes were opened."[5]

"And straitly he charged them, saying, Keep my commandments, and see ye tell no man in this place, that no man know it." "Healed persons are obligated to repay Deity for his beneficent goodness to them, insofar as they can, by devoted service in his cause. They have no right to turn again to evil practices or former false beliefs. Such would make a mockery of the sacred power exercised in their behalf. Jesus was not going about healing people and leaving them free to continue in the ungodly practices and beliefs of the Jews. After being made whole by the Master Physician, the healed persons were obligated to keep the commandments, to join the Church of Jesus Christ, if they had not already done so, and to endure in righteousness to the end so that an eventual celestial inheritance would be assured." (*Commentary* 1:321.)

The command of secrecy was of a limited nature. They were told to "tell no man in this place," which we assume means in Capernaum. Matthew tells us that they "spread abroad his fame in all that country," which apparently means a much larger area than Capernaum. How strictly the healed persons kept the charge of secrecy we do not know. Nor can we tell why it was imposed. Perhaps Capernaum proper was such a wicked city that to testify of more miracles in that place would have been casting pearls before swine, giving the unbelievers among them occasion to turn again and rend the Great Healer.

Apparently, however, the two healed persons did not keep the charge of secrecy as fully at least as Jesus desired. Of this somewhat human reaction Farrar phrases these words of rebuke and condemnation: "There are some who have admired their disobedience, and have attributed it to the enthusiasm of gratitude and admiration," he says. Those to whom he here refers are Catholic apologists who applaud rather than condemn the men for their breach of confidence. "But was it not rather the enthusiasm of a blatant wonder, the vulgarity of a chattering boast?" he asks. Then he sets forth this reasoning: "Did not the holy fire of devotion which a hallowed silence must have kept alive upon the altar of their hearts die away in the mere blaze of empty rumour? Did not He know best? Would not obedience have been better than sacrifice, and to hearken than the fat of rams? Yes. It is possible to deceive ourselves; it is possible to offer to Christ a *seeming* service which disobeys His inmost precepts—to *grieve* Him, under the guise of honouring Him, by vain repetitions, and empty genuflexions, and bitter intolerance, and irreverent familiarity, and the hollow simulacrum of a dead devotion. Better, far better, to serve Him by doing the things He said than by a seeming zeal, often false in exact proportion to its obtrusiveness, for the glory of His name. These disobedient babblers, who talked so much of Him, did but offer Him the dishonouring service of a double heart; their violation of His commandment served only to hinder His usefulness, to trouble His spirit, and to precipitate His death." (Farrar, p. 273.)

As these two men left the house, glorying in their newly found sight, others "brought to him a dumb man possessed with a devil." He cast out the devil; the dumb spake; the multitudes marveled, saying, "It was never so seen in Israel." But the Pharisees continued their chant of hatred and evil by renewing the charge, "He casteth out devils through the prince of devils."

We read of no restriction being placed on this man as far as telling about his healing was concerned. But the Pharisaic reaction to it shows how knowledge of his miracles could interfere with Jesus' continuing ministry.

Jesus Is Again Rejected at Nazareth
(Mark 6:1-6; Matthew 13:54-58)

A year has passed since Jesus, preaching in the synagogue in Nazareth, announced that he came to fulfill Isaiah's great Messianic prophecies. Then it was that those of his own town "wondered at the gracious words which proceeded out of his mouth"; asked, "Is not this Joseph's son?"; were told, "No prophet is accepted in his own country"; and, being condemned for their unbelief, rose in anger, thrust him from their city, and attempted to cast him headlong from the brow of a hill. (See chapter 34, herein.)

Now, in part at least, and with even less excuse for such a rebellious course, the Nazarenes are about to reject again the one person who could save and redeem them. Leaving Capernaum with his disciples, he returns to Nazareth and on the Sabbath day once more teaches in their synagogue. What he said we do not know, but as with the previous preachment, the people were astonished; they marveled at his gracious words, so much so that they began to ask: "From whence hath this man these things."

Further, they now knew of his miracles and the wonders that his hands had done throughout all the land. Word had reached them of the blind eyes that now saw; of the lepers whose flesh was made whole; of the Gadarene demoniac out of whom a legion of devils had been cast; of the stilling of the storm on the lake of Galilee; of the raising of the widow's son in Nain and Jairus's daughter in Capernaum, both of whose spirits had gone on to another sphere while their bodies lay cold and dead and decomposing. His fame was everywhere, and the reason for it was known to all. And so his Nazarene neighbors asked: "And what wisdom is this which is given unto him, that even such mighty works are wrought by his hands?" And further: "Is not this the carpenter, the son of Mary, the brother of James, and Joses, and of Juda, and Simon? and are not his sisters here with us?"

"And they were offended at him." Why? Why should

anyone take offense because someone else goes about doing good? Why should men seek to slay a man because he raises the dead or stills a storm? Why should their spirits be stirred up within them because he preaches the Sermon on the Mount or gives forth with an endless flow of gracious words? These Nazarenes were witnesses against themselves. They heard his words and knew of his works, and yet they rejected him. It was not reason but emotion that motivated them. They were offended because their deeds were evil.

And so Jesus, who "marveled because of their unbelief," said unto them: "A prophet is not without honour, but in his own country, and among his own kin, and in his own house." His sisters still lived in Nazareth, married, we suppose, to Nazarenes; his mother and brothers had moved to Capernaum after the wedding feast at Cana; and of this whole body of kinfolk, only the Virgin Mother, as of this time, believed and knew of his divine mission.

And so, "he did not many mighty works there because of their unbelief," Matthew tells us. Mark is even more express: "He could there do no mighty work, save that he laid his hands upon a few sick folk, and healed them."

Truly, he who came with healing in his wings, to bear the sorrows and sickness of the people, limited his wonder-working miracles to those who by faith merited the inestimable blessings involved. And now Jesus—we cannot believe that it is other than in sadness—is leaving Nazareth for the last time. His own received him not. There is to be a brief moment for other ears to hear, and other eyes to see, and other hearts to be touched. He must continue to preach elsewhere, and he must send others forth to represent him, as he is now about to do.

NOTES

1. For a brief, initial analysis of the law of faith, reference may be made to *Mormon Doctrine*, 2nd ed., pp. 261-67.

2. The mode and manner of dress among the Jews of Jesus' day was itself a symbol of their religion and their way of life. Rabbis and leaders in particular took great pains to dress properly. We cannot doubt that Jesus and the apostles followed the standards of ex-

cellence in dress that then prevailed. This means that each of them—Jesus included—wore five standard articles of clothing. These were: (1) *Headgear,* which consisted either of a *Sudar,* or turban, or a *Maaphoreth,* "which seems to have served as a covering for the head, and to have descended over the back of the neck and shoulders, somewhat like the Indian pugaree." (2) *Sandals.* (3) *An inner garment.* Of that worn by Jesus, Edersheim says: "The *Chaluq,* or more probably, the *Kittuna,* which formed his inner garment, must have been close-fitting, and descended to His feet, since it was not only so worn by teachers, but was regarded as absolutely necessary for any one who would publicly read or 'Targum' the Scriptures, or exercise any function in the Synagogue. As we know, it 'was without seam, woven from the top throughout;' and this closely accords with the texture of these garments." (4) *A girdle.* This was used to fasten the inner garment around the middle. (5) *An outer garment.* The square outer garment, or *Tallith,* was the one that carried "the customary fringes of four long white threads with one of hyacinth knotted together on each of the four corners." As we are aware, "the quaternion of soldiers who crucified Christ made division of the riches of His poverty, taking each one part of His dress, while for the fifth, which, if divided, would have been rent to pieces, they cast lots." (Edersheim 1:624-25.)

3. "Giving blessings and performing priesthood ordinances is often the most physically taxing labor which the Lord's true ministers ever perform. There is nothing perfunctory or casual about the performance of these holy ordinances; great physical exertion and intense mental concentration are part of the struggle to get that spirit of revelation so essential in an inspired blessing or other performance." (*Commentary* 1:319.)

Joseph Smith, under date of March 14, 1843, wrote in his journal: "Elder Jedediah M. Grant enquired of me the cause of my turning pale and losing strength last night while blessing children. I told him that I saw that Lucifer would exert his influence to destroy the children that I was blessing, and I strove with all the faith and spirit that I had to seal upon them a blessing that would secure their lives upon the earth; and so much virtue went out of me into the children, that I became weak, from which I have not yet recovered; and I referred to the case of the woman touching the hem of the garment of Jesus. The virtue referred to is the spirit of life; and a man who exercises great faith in administering to the sick, blessing little children, or confirming, is liable to become weakened." (*Teachings,* pp. 280-81.)

4. "Doubtless she dreaded His anger, for the law expressly ordained that the touch of one afflicted as she was, caused ceremonial uncleanness till the evening. But His touch had cleansed her, not hers polluted Him." (Farrar, p. 271.)

5. "Frequently in opening the eyes of the blind, Jesus, as here, coupled his spoken command with some physical act. On this and other occasions he touched the sightless eyes. (Matt. 20:30-34.) In healing the man in Jerusalem who was blind from birth, he anointed the man's eyes with clay made with spittle and then had the man wash in the pool of Siloam. (John 9:6-7.) The blind man of Bethsaida was healed by application of saliva to his eyes. (Mark 8:22-26.) Similarly, in healing a deaf man with a speech impediment, Jesus both touched the man's tongue and put his own fingers into the man's ears. (Mark 7:32-37.)

"None of these unusual and dissimilar acts are essential to the exercise of healing power. Healing miracles are performed by the power of faith and in the authority of the priesthood. By doing these physical acts, however, the Master's apparent purpose was to strengthen the faith of the blind or deaf person, persons who were denied the ability to gain increased assurance and resultant faith by seeing his countenance or hearing his words." (*Commentary* 1:320.)

Chapter 53

JESUS SENDETH FORTH THE TWELVE

The twelve traveling councilors
are called to be the Twelve Apostles,
or special witnesses of the name
of Christ in all the world, . . .
to officiate in the name of the Lord,
. . . to build up the church,
and regulate all the affairs of the same
in all nations. (D&C 107:23, 33.)

Jesus Reaps a Plenteous Harvest
(Matthew 9:35-38; Mark 6:6)

Again as always; now as afore; in season and out of season; from the rising of the sun until men slumber in the darkness of the night—everlastingly—Jesus is found, in one city and village after another, "preaching the gospel of the kingdom."

He has just left Nazareth—for the last time, as we suppose—having there been rejected again by his own. The light of his countenance shall not again shine upon those among whom he grew to maturity. To them he is Joseph's son and Mary's son; he is the brother of James and Joses and Simon and Judas, none of whom believe he is the Prophet of whom Moses spoke. To the Nazarenes he is a carpenter, the son of a carpenter, whose sisters yet dwell among them, and who themselves—his own flesh, those conceived in the same womb that bare him—think no differently of him than they do of their other brothers.

And so Jesus, accompanied by his disciples, is touring and preaching again in "all the cities and villages" of Galilee. He teaches in their synagogues and preaches on their streets. His message: the gospel—the gospel of his Father; the eternal plan of salvation ordained in the heavens above before the foundations of the world; the gospel that he has made his own and that now bears his name. He is telling men what they must do to be saved in his Father's kingdom. His message: 'Come unto me and be perfected in me; accept me as the Son of God and live my law; repent; be baptized in my name for the remission of your sins; receive the promise of the companionship of the Holy Spirit; and press forward all your days in doing good and working righteousness.'

His is "the gospel of the kingdom"—none other—the gospel that admits men, here and now, into the kingdom of God on earth, which is the Church, and which prepares them for an inheritance in the celestial kingdom of heaven hereafter. And as he preaches, he heals "every sickness and every disease among the people," meaning that those who accept him and believe his gospel are healed, and those who—as in Nazareth—reject him, among them he can do no mighty works. Signs follow those who believe. Jesus is making converts, and the sick and the decrepit and the diseased among them are being healed of their afflictions.

Success attends his labors; multitudes hang on his every word; there is more ministerial service to be performed than one man can do. He can preach in only one village at a time; there are others who need to be healed, others who cry out for the cleansing of their spirits and the healing of their bodies, others than those to whom he can minister personally. "When he saw the multitudes, he was moved with compassion on them, because they fainted, and were scattered abroad, as sheep having no shepherd."

This, in part at least, is the day seen by the prophets of old. Had not Jehovah said by the mouth of Ezekiel: "Woe be to the shepherds of Israel"—to the priests and Levites, to the scribes and Pharisees, to those who should have been guides and lights and teachers of the people—"Woe be to the shepherds of Israel that do feed themselves! should not the shepherds feed the flocks?" Had not Jehovah said of those who should have cared for his flock: "The diseased have ye not strengthened, neither have ye healed that which was sick, neither have ye bound up that which was broken, neither have ye brought again that which was driven away, neither have ye sought that which was lost."

Did not Jehovah promise by the mouth of Ezekiel: "Behold, I, even I, will both search my sheep, and seek them out. . . . I will feed my flock, and I will cause them to lie down, saith the Lord God. I will seek that which was lost, and bring again that which was driven away, and will bind up that which was broken, and will strengthen that which was sick. . . . And I will make with them a covenant of peace. . . . And ye my flock, the flock of my pasture, are men, and I am your God, saith the Lord God." (Ezek. 34:2, 4, 11, 15-16, 25, 31.)

Had not Jehovah said by the mouth of Jeremiah: "Woe be unto the pastors that destroy and scatter the sheep of my pasture! saith the Lord. . . . Ye have scattered my flock, and driven them away, and have not visited them. . . . And I will gather the remnant of my flock. . . . And I will set up shepherds over them which shall feed them: and they shall fear no more, nor be dismayed, neither shall they be lacking, saith the Lord. Behold, the days come, saith the Lord, that I will raise unto David a righteous Branch." (Jer. 23:1-6.)

True, these divine prophecies shall see their most glorious fulfillment when Jehovah returns, continuing ever as the Branch of David, to bring again Israel into his fold in the last days, but even now he whom Jeremiah called "The Lord Our Righteousness," as he dwells in mortality among them, is reaching forth his arm to gather in his lost sheep. He is, for their day and generation, offering them the blessings of his earthly kingdom, to say nothing of the blessings of his Father's heavenly kingdom. He is setting up shepherds over them, that tender and loving care may be extended to all.

And so, viewing with compassion his fainting, scattered, diseased, and afflicted sheep, the Chief Shepherd—changing the figure from one of sheep and shepherds to one of fields and harvests—the Lord of the earthly harvest says: "The harvest truly is plenteous, but the labourers are few; Pray ye therefore the Lord of the harvest, that he will send forth labourers into his harvest."

Others than he must now labor in the vineyards of the Lord that more souls may be prepared for the eternal harvest that lies ahead. More converts must be made, and they must be fellowshipped with the earthly saints. Others than he must nourish the newborn babes in Christ who have joined his church and become members of his kingdom; others than he must keep them "continually watchful unto prayer, relying alone upon the merits of Christ," as Moroni expresses it. (Moro. 6:4.) Others than he must counsel those who are now numbered among the Church of God to add to their faith virtue, "and to virtue knowledge; And to knowledge temperance; and to temperance patience; and to patience godliness; And to godliness brotherly kindness; and to brotherly kindness charity"—all to the end that an entrance might be "ministered" unto them "abundantly into the everlasting kingdom" in heaven, as Peter expresses it. (2 Pet. 1:1-11.) Others than he must counsel them to build on the foundation of faith and repentance and baptism and "go on unto perfection," as Paul expresses it. (Heb. 6:1-3.) And the first to be so chosen are the Twelve Apostles of the Lamb.

Apostles Sent Forth to Labor in the Vineyard
(Matthew 10:1, 5-15; JST, Matthew 10:12; Mark 6:7-13; Luke 9:1-6)

Those chosen ones, the holy apostles—foreordained from before the foundations of the earth to be with Jesus in his mortal ministry; called anew by him as he traveled and taught in the land of their inheritance; ordained to the holy apostleship on a mountain near Capernaum—these special witnesses of the goodness and grace of the Son of God are now to be sent forth on missions.

That these chosen ones are prepared for the labors and sacrifices and persecutions that lie ahead we cannot doubt. Indeed we cannot conceive how any of the shepherds of Israel, any of the laborers in the vineyard of the Lord, could have been better prepared. Aside from their spiritual talents, acquired in ages past in the presence of God, they had all been the intimate associates—the students and disciples—of the Son of God for months or years, as the case may be. It may be that all of them walked and talked, and ate, slept and lived with him from the earliest days of his mortal ministry. It is logical so to assume. From the scanty snatches of historical data preserved for us from that day, however, we know at least the following:

John the Beloved, Andrew, Simon, Philip, and Nathanael—five of the Twelve—in February of A.D. 27, two years before, came to know, and so testified, that he was the Messiah. They, at that time, gladly put on the mantle of discipleship and began to walk in his paths, learn his ways, and minister on his errands. They were with him when he turned water into wine in Cana; when he attended the first Passover of his ministry, cleansed the temple, and wrought many miracles; when, for nine months, he traveled and preached and healed in Judea; when he ministered and taught in Samaria and then in Galilee. They were with him when he healed the nobleman's son and they heard his great

Messianic sermon in the synagogue in Nazareth when his own people sought to kill him. They received the priesthood, performed baptisms, and were themselves preachers of righteousness. And although they are not identified by name, the other seven of the Twelve may have been participants in all or most of these earthly acts of the Divine One.

During January or February of A.D. 28, Jesus called Peter and Andrew, and James and John to special ministerial service. He made them fishers of men; they were with him on that glorious Sabbath in Capernaum when he healed multitudes (including Peter's mother-in-law) and preached much; they accompanied him as he traveled and preached throughout Galilee, as others of the future Twelve may have done also. Jesus healed lepers, forgave sins, raised paralytic persons to health—all in their presence.

In March of A.D. 28, Matthew was called to forsake his post as a publican tax collector and to follow Jesus. Miracles and teachings continued. And in the early summer of that year the Twelve were chosen and ordained. They all may have been with him all along—mingling among the reverent and worshipful disciples who rejoiced in his doctrines and gloried in his deeds—but certainly they were all with him henceforth. They saw the centurion's servant healed and the widow's son raised from death. They saw the blind and the dumb healed, heard his parables, and wondered and feared when he spoke peace to the tempestuous waves on Galilee. They knew of the Gadarene out of whom went a legion of devils, of the woman with the issue of blood, and of Jairus's daughter. Miracles seen by their eyes, doctrines heard by their ears, spiritual experiences felt in their souls—these were a way of life with the Twelve. They themselves had taught and ministered and prayed and labored. They were now prepared to go forth, two by two, and magnify their callings as apostles of the Lord Jesus Christ.

True ministers—those whose words and deeds have divine approval—are always endowed with power from on high. They always hold the holy priesthood, which is the power and authority of God, delegated to man on earth, to act in all things for the salvation of men. They never call themselves; they do not and cannot endow themselves with divine authority. They must be called of God. Even Christ "glorified not himself to be made an high priest" (Heb. 5:5); even he was called and given power and sent forth by his Father.[1] Those who are called of God thus become his servants, his agents, his ambassadors. They are sent forth to do what he wants done and to represent him. Their words are his words and their acts his acts; when they serve within the field and scope of their authorization, it is as though the Lord himself had said or done whatever is involved.

And so Jesus "called his twelve disciples together, and gave them power and authority"—power and authority to preach the everlasting gospel; to proclaim the saving truths; to perform the ordinances of salvation—all so that men might be saved in his Father's kingdom. And in the very nature of things—it could not be otherwise—he "gave them power and authority over all devils, and to cure diseases." They had this power "to heal all manner of sickness and all manner of disease" because signs always follow faith; miracles always attend the preaching of the gospel; no man since the world was has had faith without having something along with it; and so, if any believed their words—and they taught the same gospel that He himself preached—there must be signs following. The sick must be healed; the dead must be raised; devils must be cast out; otherwise the power of God unto salvation, which is the gospel, would not be present. And so Jesus said to them, "Heal the sick, cleanse the lepers, raise the dead, cast out devils: freely ye have received, freely give."[2]

To whom shall they preach? To all men? No. There will be a day when they will be sent to all men everywhere, for the message of salvation shall go to every nation, and kindred, and tongue, and people. All are the children of the Father; he loves them all, and he seeks to save them all. But there is an order of priority. Every man is to hear the gospel in his time and in his own season; some are entitled to hear it first, others at a later date. "Go," then, "to the lost sheep of the house of Israel." It is their right and privilege, as the seed of Abraham, to step ahead of the aliens who know not God. "Go not into the way of the Gentiles, and into any city of the Samaritans enter ye not." Their day lies ahead; in due course the blessings of salvation shall be offered to them, but first, let the chosen seed open their hearts, if they will.[3]

What shall they preach? "Preach the kingdom of God." Say: "The kingdom of heaven is at hand." That is: 'Preach the gospel of the kingdom; proclaim that salvation comes by me; command all Israel to repent and be baptized; exhort them to keep the commandments and perfect their lives; say what ye have heard me say. I am the light; do that which ye have seen me do.'[4]

How are they to be sustained in their ministries? And how will their temporal needs be supplied? Those to whom they are sent will care for them, providing food, clothing, and shelter as their circumstances warrant. They are to rely on the Father; he will not let them go hungry or naked or without a place to lay their heads. They are to take neither gold nor silver nor brass in their purses. They are to carry no baskets of provisions—scrip, as such were called—nor bread to eat, nor "two coats apiece." The workman, they were told, was "worthy of his meat."[5] They were denied the luxury of leather shoes and were not to carry staves; rather, their feet were to be shod with sandals, and they might carry a single staff. Their dress was to be simple and their needs few, leaving them free to devote all their time and strength to the preaching of the word.

Do all of the Jews, all of those who are of Israel, have an equal right to hear the gospel? Are the Twelve to divide their time equally among the people? No. Even among the lost sheep of the house of Israel some have preference over others. "And into whatsoever city or town ye shall enter, inquire who in it is worthy; and there abide till ye go thence."

Just as Israel is to hear the message before it goes to the Gentiles, so those in Israel who are worthy, who desire righteousness, who are living according to the best light and knowledge they have—these are favored above their fellows; the gospel is to be taught to them first. Jesus is not sending his disciples out to find harlots and whoremongers and thieves and robbers—although any of these may repent and be saved—but he is sending them to find the honest in heart, the upright among men, those whose prior living has made them worthy to hear an apostolic voice. Such are the ones in whose homes the Twelve shall abide and where they shall leave their blessings.

"And when ye come into a house, salute it." Greet those who dwell therein with good will; honor them in all they have done that is good; offer to teach them the doctrines of salvation; account them worthy to receive the glad tidings that salvation can be theirs if they will believe and obey. Salute them in love and with an open heart, and seek to bring them into the kingdom of God on earth.[6]

"And if the house be worthy, let your peace come upon it: but if it be not worthy, let your peace return to you." 'If those in the house are worthy; if they are seeking light and truth and knowledge; if they desire righteousness and are willing to repent and forsake the world—then make with them a covenant of peace (as Jehovah promised through Ezekiel); make with them the gospel covenant, which is the covenant of peace. Assure them that through the glad tidings of great joy—the tidings of peace on earth, good will to men—they shall gain peace in this life and eternal life in the world to come. Let thy peace, which is my peace, which is gospel peace—the peace that passeth understanding—rest upon them. But if they are not worthy, if they do not believe and obey, the offer of eternal peace will have no efficacy; your peace will return to you, and you shall go hence and seek other houses where perchance your peace may rest forever.'

"And whosoever shall not receive you, nor hear your

words, when ye depart out of that house, or city, shake off the dust of your feet. Verily I say unto you, It shall be more tolerable for the land of Sodom and Gomorrha in the day of judgment, than for that city."

It is an awesome and a fearful thing to reject the word of truth. When Jesus speaks and men receive not his gracious words, they are damned for their disbelief. When his servants speak and men reject the same truths, they also are damned. When legal administrators preach the gospel by the power of the Holy Ghost, their teachings are binding on earth and in heaven. Those who believe and obey are saved; those who believe not and who keep not the commandments are damned. Believers are sealed up unto eternal salvation; unbelievers are sealed up unto eternal damnation. As we hear Jesus instruct the Twelve, it is as though we are hearing again the fiery words of that John who came before to prepare the way: "He that believeth on the Son hath everlasting life: and he that believeth not the Son shall not see life; but the wrath of God abideth on him." (John 3:36.)

In our day, as the Lord again sends laborers into his vineyards, as he again sends his servants to speak peace to the worthy and to condemn the ungodly, we hear him say: "They who go forth, bearing these tidings unto the inhabitants of the earth, to them is power given to seal both on earth and in heaven, the unbelieving and rebellious; Yea, verily, to seal them up unto the day when the wrath of God shall be poured out upon the wicked without measure—Unto the day when the Lord shall come to recompense unto every man according to his work, and measure to every man according to the measure which he has measured to his fellow man." (D&C 1:8-10.)

It is today as it was anciently. We preach the same gospel, we hold the same priesthood, and we are subject to the same divine direction. "In whatsoever place ye shall enter," the Lord tells us, "and they receive you not in my name, ye shall leave a cursing instead of a blessing, by casting off the dust of your feet against them as a testimony, and

312

cleansing your feet by the wayside." (D&C 24:15.) It is as though those who reject the message are not worthy to receive even the dust that cleaves to an apostolic sandal.

And again: "Let all those take their journey, as I have commanded them," the Lord says, "going from house to house, and from village to village, and from city to city. And in whatsoever house ye enter, and they receive you, leave your blessing upon that house. And in whatsoever house ye enter, and they receive you not, ye shall depart speedily from that house, and shake off the dust of your feet as a testimony against them. And you shall be filled with joy and gladness; and know this, that in the day of judgment you shall be judges of that house, and condemn them; And it shall be more tolerable for the heathen in the day of judgment, than for that house; therefore, gird up your loins and be faithful, and ye shall overcome all things, and be lifted up at the last day." (D&C 75:18-22.)[7]

Having been properly instructed, the apostles, as Luke tells us, "went through the towns, preaching the gospel, and healing everywhere." Mark tells us "they went out, and preached that men should repent. And they cast out many devils, and anointed with oil many that were sick, and healed them."

As it had been and was with their Master, so it was and would be with those whom he had chosen. They preached the gospel; they cried repentance; they anointed with oil; they healed the sick. Then as now the gospel was true, and among true believers signs followed. The Lord be praised.

NOTES

1. "We believe that a man must be called of God, by prophecy, and by the laying on of hands, by those who are in authority, to preach the Gospel and administer in the ordinances thereof." (A of F 5.)

2. "Salvation is free." (2 Ne. 2:4.) "Come, my brethren, every one that thirsteth, come ye to the waters; and he that hath no money, come buy and eat; yea, come buy wine and milk without money and without price." (2 Ne. 9:50; Isa. 55:1.)

3. "In the providences of the Lord, the gospel, in the meridian of time, was offered first to the house of Israel and thereafter to the Gentiles. Jesus himself ministered primarily among his own kindred of the chosen seed. 'I am not sent but unto the lost sheep of the house of Israel,' he said. (Matt. 15:24.) Missionaries sent forth during Jesus' mortal

ministry were commanded to confine their labors to their wayward kindred of Jacob's lineage. Later, after our Lord's resurrection, they were to receive the commandment to carry the message of salvation to all men. (Mark 16:14-20.)" (*Commentary* 1:325.)

4. What does it mean to say "The kingdom of heaven is at hand?" It means: "The Church of Jesus Christ is here; it has been organized and established; it is the kingdom of God on earth; enter into it through the waters of baptism, and be ye saved." (*Commentary* 1:325.) Identically the same message is carried by the elders in this day: "Ye shall go forth baptizing with water, saying: Repent ye, repent ye, for the kingdom of heaven is at hand." (D&C 42:7; 33:9-11; 39:19-20.)

5. Hospitality was a way of life among the Jews. By way of modern analogy it is reported: "When travelling in the East no one need ever scruple to go into the best house of any Arab village to which he comes, and he will always be received with profuse and gratuitous hospitality. From the moment we entered any house, it was regarded as our own. There is not an Arab you meet who will not empty for you the last drop in his waterskin, or share with you his last piece of black bread. The Rabbis said that Paradise was the reward of willing hospitality." (Farrar, n. 3, p. 276.)

Similar but not wholly identical divine direction was given to missionaries in the early days of this dispensation. "Thou shalt take no purse nor scrip, neither staves, neither two coats," the Lord said, "for the church shall give unto thee in the very hour what thou needest for food and for raiment, and for shoes and for money, and for scrip." (D&C 24:18.) Also: "It is expedient that I give unto you this commandment, that ye become even as my friends in days when I was with them, traveling to preach the gospel in my power; For I suffered them not to have purse or scrip, neither two coats. Therefore, let no man among you, for this commandment is unto all the faithful who are called of God in the church unto the ministry, from this hour take purse or scrip, that goeth forth to proclaim this gospel of the kingdom." (D&C 84:77-78, 86.)

6. Gospel salutations not only lead people to receive the gospel, but they also cement the fellowship and good will that does and should exist among the Lord's saints. For those who have come into the kingdom and who are worthy of the blessings of the gospel, the revealed salutation is: "I salute you in the name of the Lord Jesus Christ, in token or remembrance of the everlasting covenant, in which covenant I receive you to fellowship, in a determination that is fixed, immovable, and unchangeable, to be your friend and brother through the grace of God in the bonds of love, to walk in all the commandments of God blameless, in thanksgiving, forever and ever. Amen. And he that is found unworthy of this salutation shall not have any place among you; for ye shall not suffer that mine house shall be polluted by him." (D&C 88:133-134.)

7. Related concepts are revealed in these words: "He that receiveth you not, go away from him alone by yourselves, and cleanse your feet even with water, pure water, whether in heat or in cold, and bear testimony of it unto your Father which is in heaven, and return not again unto that man. And in whatsoever village or city ye enter, do likewise. Nevertheless, search diligently and spare not; and wo unto that house, or that village or city that rejecteth you, or your words, or your testimony concerning me. Wo, I say again, unto that house, or that village or city that rejecteth you, or your words, or your testimony of me; For I, the Almighty, have laid my hands upon the nations, to scourge them for their wickedness." (D&C 84:92-96.)

Chapter 54

JESUS INSTRUCTS THE TWELVE

He is a chosen vessel unto me,
to bear my name before the Gentiles,
and kings, and the children of Israel:
For I will shew him how great things he must suffer
for my name's sake. (Acts 9:15-16.)[1]

I think that God hath set forth
us the apostles last, as it were appointed to death:
for we are made a spectacle unto the world,
and to angels, and to men. . . .
Even unto this present hour we both hunger,
and thirst, and are naked,
and are buffeted, and have no certain
dwellingplace;
And labour, working with our own hands:
being reviled, we bless; being
persecuted, we suffer it:
Being defamed, we intreat: we are made
as the filth of the world,
and are the offscouring of all things
unto this day. (1 Cor. 4:9-13.)[2]

Apostles and Saints Face Persecutions and Trials
(Matthew 10:16-23; JST, Matthew 10:14, 19-20; Luke 12:11-12;
JST, Luke 12:13)

Most of what Jesus said by way of commandment and instruction to the apostles, as he sent them forth on missions, was prophetic and eternal in nature. It applied not to the brief period—probably not more than three months—during which they traveled, two by two, through the cities and villages of Palestine, but to their lifelong ministries and to their successors in the apostolic office, including those who hold the same keys and powers today. Matthew preserves the most extended account of our Lord's words on this occasion, though some of what he recounts is recorded by Mark and Luke in other connections. That Jesus may have said some of the same things in different settings is of no moment one way or the other. For clarity and ease of presentation we shall consider the same expressions, wherever made, as though they were part of Matthew's one continuing account.

Behold, I send you forth as sheep in the midst of wolves: be ye therefore wise as serpents [be ye therefore wise servants], and harmless as doves.

Jesus is not saying, 'Wolves shall come among you; wolves shall enter the flock; wolves shall rend the sheep; therefore, be wise in all you do.' What he does say is: 'Without are wolves—ravening, murderous, hunger-maddened wolves—and I send the sheep and the lambs of my flock out among them; ye are to leave the safety of the sheepcote and go out into the world where, except for my preserving care, ye shall be rent and destroyed. Therefore, be wise servants; give no unneeded offense; be to all to whom ye are sent as harmless as doves.' Neither the saints nor the apostles court persecution or martyrdom; rather, they do all they can, in honor, to avoid these Satan-spawned evils. Ordinarily the work progresses more rapidly and ascends to greater heights when peace and fair-mindedness prevail than when all the vomit and bitterness of hell are gushing forth upon the helpless sheep.[3]

But beware of men: for they will deliver you up to the councils, and they will scourge you in their synagogues; And ye shall be brought before governors and kings for my sake, for a testimony against them and the Gentiles.

Queries: Persecution—the heritage of the faithful—whence does it come? Who wields the sword that slays the saints, and who hurls the spear that pierces the side of Him who hangs on the cross?

Answers: It is a joint undertaking; a confederacy of evil powers unite to do the deeds; all participants play their parts as actors on an evil stage. Satan is the ultimate author; priests and ministers of false religions stir up the basest of men, who in turn wield the sword, and the legal processes of both church and state combine to justify, approve, and authorize the insane madness that fights the truth.

Persecution is an essential part of the creeds of all false religions. There is an eternal law—a law as eternal as heaven and earth and the universe—that truth will prevail. Left to itself true religion—though it may be delayed or hindered in its progress—must and will prevail. The only effective weapon of false religions—and it yields only momentary success—is to persecute true believers.

'Hence, ye apostles, ye missionaries, ye ambassadors of Christ, beware of evil men. They will deliver you to the council, to the local Sanhedrins, to the Jewish elders and priests, who will sit in judgment on your new wine, which cannot be contained in old bottles. They will scourge you in the synagogues to the chanting accompaniment of a psalm. And further, ye shall be brought before Felix and Festus and Herod, and even before Caesar himself; ye shall be hailed before the judgment bars of men, and then shall ye bear a testimony which shall stand as a witness against them before the eternal bar of the Great Jehovah.'

Yes, strange as it may seem, persecution is a religious rite; and whereas the Jews scourged their heretics in their synagogues, to the accompaniment of psalmic music, today's ministers of false religions heap revilings and persecutions

317

upon the saints to the accompaniment of chants that say: "Delusion, false prophets, wife-stealers, non-Christians," or whatever else Satan puts in their minds. Such was the mad mania that confronted the apostles anciently, and such is the reborn dementia which opposes them today.

But when they deliver you up, take no thought how or what ye shall speak: for it shall be given you in that same hour what ye shall speak. For it is not ye that speak, but the Spirit of your Father which speaketh in you.

Or, as Luke has it: "The Holy Ghost shall teach you in the same hour what ye ought to say." This is a power that none but the saints of God possess. They alone have the gift of the Holy Ghost, which is the right to the constant companionship of that member of the Godhead based on faithfulness. No man of himself could possibly know what to say, either by way of doctrine or of testimony, when hailed before earthly tribunals or when standing in the congregations of the wicked, for no man knows the hearts of men. But God, who knows all things, promises, by the power of his Spirit, to put words into the mouths of his servants. "Neither take ye thought beforehand what ye shall say," is his word, "but treasure up in your minds continually the words of life, and it shall be given you in the very hour that portion that shall be meted unto every man." (D&C 84:85.) Peter and John before the Sanhedrin, after the healing of the man lame from his mother's womb, and Paul before Agrippa, testifying that Jesus rose from the dead, are but illustrations of the power of speech given to the Lord's servants when the need for divine help requires it.

And the brother shall deliver up the brother to death, and the father the child: and the children shall rise up against their parents, and cause them to be put to death.

O the depravity and wickedness and moral degeneracy that is practiced in the name of religion! Lucifer would slay, if he could, every righteous person—none of the true saints would be left in mortality—and when depraved fanatics submit themselves to the will of the devil, they willingly de-liver up unto death even their own family members.

And ye shall be hated of all the world for my name's sake; but he that endureth to the end shall be saved.

Though hated by all men; though the whole world op-pose them; though every power of earth and hell combine to do them ill[4]—yet the apostles (and all the saints) must endure in righteousness all their days to merit celestial salva-tion. They must "press forward with a steadfastness in Christ, having a perfect brightness of hope, and a love of God and of all men, . . . feasting upon the word of Christ" (2 Ne. 31:20-21), doing good and working righteousness, if they are to gain eternal life. "I will prove you in all things," the Lord says to his saints, "whether you will abide in my covenant, even unto death, that you may be found worthy. For if ye will not abide in my covenant ye are not worthy of me." (D&C 98:14-15.)

But when they persecute you in one city, flee ye into another; for verily, I say unto you, Ye shall not have gone over the cities of Israel, till the Son of man be come.

'Flee from persecution; do not court martyrdom; seek to live and spread the gospel; it is better to live for me than to die for me. There is work to be done; there are souls to be saved; you cannot carry forward my work on earth if you are dead. And so great is the labor, my servants will not have gone over the cities where scattered Israel is to be found till I come in my glory to gather the remainder of mine elect from the four winds, from one end of heaven to the other.'

Teach the Gospel Boldly and in Plainness
(Matthew 10:24-33; JST, Matthew 10:26; Luke 6:40; 12:1-7)

How will the people react to the teachings of the apostles? They are going forth to preach the gospel of the kingdom even as Jesus preaches it. They are going forth to heal the sick, cleanse the lepers, raise the dead, and cast out devils, even as Jesus does. They are to be his alter egos, to stand in his place and stead, to say what he would say and to do what he would do. How, then, will the people react to their words and deeds? Obviously they will respond as though Jesus himself were there. Already many have rejected Jesus; these same persons, and others of like mind and similar spiritual depravity, will now reject those who speak and heal in Jesus' stead. And so he counsels the Twelve, and, in principle, all of his followers:

> *The disciple is not above his master, nor the servant above his lord. It is enough for the disciple that he be as his master, and the servant as his lord. If they have called the master of the house Beelzebub, how much more shall they call them of his household?*

'Ye know how I have been received. The scribes and Pharisees reject my doctrine and disallow my testimony; they say I cast out devils and perform miracles by the power of the prince of devils; they have even called me Satan himself; and as it is with me, so shall it be with my disciples.' But that those who bear the ignominy shall also wear the crown, he affirmed by saying, as Luke has it: "The disciple is not above his master: but every one that is perfect shall be as his master." 'I am perfect; suffer and do as I suffer and do, and ye shall be perfect.' "And ye shall be even as I am, and I am even as the Father; and the Father and I are one." (3 Ne. 28:10.)

How then shall the disciples feel about the persecutions and evil speaking of those who serve another master? "Fear them not," Jesus says. Also: "Beware ye of the leaven of the Pharisees, which is hypocrisy," as Luke records in introducing the same thoughts, apparently repeated in a different setting, but having essentially the same meaning as when first spoken to the Twelve. 'Fear them not; go about your business; preach the gospel; do the things I sent you to do; let not opposition impede the work. Proclaim the gospel for all to hear.'[5]

> *For there is nothing covered, that shall not be revealed;*

neither hid, that shall not be known. Therefore whatsoever ye have spoken in darkness shall be heard in the light; and that which ye have spoken in the ear in closets shall be proclaimed upon the housetops.

'You have learned the doctrines of salvation from me as we have walked alone between the villages of Galilee; we have conversed together in the deserts and on the mountains. What you have heard in darkness, you must now speak in the light; that which was hidden from the world is now to go to them. Go forth; proclaim my word in every ear.' "For verily the voice of the Lord is unto all men, and there is none to escape; and there is no eye that shall not see, neither ear that shall not hear; neither heart that shall not be penetrated." (D&C 1:2.)

And I say unto you my friends, Be not afraid of them that kill the body, and after that have no more that they can do.

"And whoso layeth down his life in my cause, for my name's sake, shall find it again, even life eternal." (D&C 98:13.) Why then should the disciples fear death?

But I will forewarn you whom ye shall fear: Fear him, which after he hath killed hath power to cast into hell: yea, I say unto you, Fear him.

'Fear the Lord; fear him who holds the keys of death and hell; fear to do evil, lest you lose your souls.' "Fear him which is able to destroy both soul and body in hell." [6]

Are not five sparrows sold for two farthings, and not one of them is forgotten before God? But even the very hairs of your head are all numbered. Fear not therefore: ye are of more value than many sparrows.

Based on all this—on the prophetic counsel that persecution awaits his ministers; on the pronouncement that the disciples shall be treated even as their Master; on the solemn exhortation to preach the gospel, and the yet more solemn warning to be faithful in life and in death—based on these teachings, Jesus now says:

Whosoever therefore shall confess me before men, him

will I confess also before my Father which is in heaven. But whosoever shall deny me before men, him will I also deny before my Father which is in heaven.

God is his Father! Again and again he says it, and our salvation depends upon gaining for ourselves a sure testimony that such is the case. "Whosoever shall confess that Jesus is the Son of God, God dwelleth in him, and he in God." (1 Jn. 4:15.) "If thou shalt confess with thy mouth the Lord Jesus, and shalt believe in thine heart that God hath raised him from the dead, thou shalt be saved." (Rom. 10:9.)

What Happens When the Gospel Is Preached?
(Matthew 10:34-42; 11:1; JST, Matthew 10:34; Mark 9:41; Luke 12:49-53; JST, Luke 12:58)

Does the gospel bring peace on earth and good will among men? Such is its design and intent; such was the assurance in the anthem of praise sung by the angelic choir to acclaim the birth of the Prince of Peace; and such is the inborn longing and hope of the saints of all the ages. But the reality is far removed from the ideal. The gospel both saves and damns; it brings peace to the penitent and sorrow to sinners. And when the righteous and the wicked all mingle together in one social milieu, the preaching of the gospel spawns anarchy and contention and warfare. The enemies of God and the opponents of true doctrine do not take kindly to the gospel of the kingdom, to the building up of the kingdom of God on earth. When the apostles preach the gospel, what will the effect be on a weary and wicked world? Jesus answers:

Think not that I am come to send peace on earth: I came not to send peace, but a sword.

Suppose ye that I am come to give peace on earth? I tell you, Nay; but rather division.

The gospel divides men. Those who believe and obey go in one direction; the unbelieving and rebellious choose an opposite course. From among the unbelievers come the persecutors, and the persecutors wield the sword against the

322

saints. They have wielded it against our Lord; they will yet thrust its cutting edge into the flesh of the apostles; and many of the saints shall seal their testimonies with their own blood. Such is the effect, among the wicked and ungodly, of the preaching of the gospel.

> *For they are not well pleased with the Lord's doings; therefore I am come to send fire on the earth; and what is it to you, if I will that it be already kindled?*
>
> *But I have a baptism to be baptized with; and how am I straitened till it be accomplished!*

'I am come to send the flames of turmoil and persecution, the burning agony of family discord, wherever my gospel is preached in the world; and, lo, this fire is already kindled on every hand. But do not be perturbed, for even I have a baptism of blood and death to be baptized with, for my own familiar friend shall lift up his hand against me, one of my own official church family shall betray me; and what a burdensome pressure and responsibility rests upon me until I have accomplished this very mission and ordeal for which I came into the world.'[7] As to the effect, even in the intimacy of the family circle, of the preaching of the gospel, Jesus says:

> *For I am come to set a man at variance against his father, and the daughter against her mother, and the daughter in law against her mother in law.*
>
> *And a man's foes shall be they of his own household.*
>
> *He that loveth father or mother more than me is not worthy of me: and he that loveth son or daughter more than me is not worthy of me.*

How severe the tests of life sometimes are! Mortals come here to be tried and tested, "to see if they will do all things whatsoever the Lord their God shall command them." (Abr. 3:25.) And if such necessitates a choice between father and mother, or son and daughter, and the saving power of the gospel of the Lord Jesus Christ, then so be it. But one thing is needful, and that is, to save our souls. No one is justified in maintaining family peace and unity if by so doing he must forsake the gospel and its saving truths.

And he that taketh not his cross, and followeth after me, is not worthy of me.

'I shall carry my cross to the place of crucifixion, where I shall die in pain and agony, die as earth's Chief Martyr. He that is not willing to take his own cross and, following me, carry it to a martyr's death on Calvary, is not worthy of me and of that eternal life which my Father has prepared for all the faithful.'

He who seeketh to save his life shall lose it: and he who loseth his life for my sake shall find it.

'He that saves himself from persecution and death by denying me and my gospel shall lose eternal life, while he who lays down his life for me and my gospel shall have eternal life.'

He that receiveth you receiveth me, and he that receiveth me receiveth him that sent me.

How great the importance to rivet these eternal truths in the hearts of men! No one ever receives and accepts the Lord Jesus Christ without also receiving and accepting the apostles and prophets who bear witness of him. Christ and his prophets are one; they rise or fall together. No one in Jesus' day could believe he was the Son of the Father without also believing in the Father of the Son; no one could believe he was the Messiah without also believing Peter, James, and John were his apostles, his friends, his witnesses. Jesus and his apostolic witnesses can no more be separated than can the Father and the Son. To believe in one is to believe in the other. This is the law of agency, every agent of the Lord standing in His place and stead, representing Him, saying and doing what He wants said and done.

In a passage of transcendent beauty, the Lord Jesus, in modern times, says to his servants, his agents, those whom he has chosen and called to minister in his name and for and on his behalf in this dispensation: "Behold, I send you out to reprove the world of all their unrighteous deeds, and to teach them of a judgment which is to come. And whoso receiveth you, there I will be also, for I will go before your face. I will be on your right hand and on your left, and my Spirit shall be in your hearts, and mine angels round about you, to bear you up. Whoso receiveth you receiveth me; and the same will feed you, and clothe you, and give you money. And he who feeds you, or clothes you, or gives you money, shall in nowise lose his reward. And he that doeth not these things is not my disciple; by this you may know my disciples." (D&C 84:87-91.)

He that receiveth a prophet in the name of a prophet shall receive a prophet's reward; and he that receiveth a righteous man in the name of a righteous man shall receive a righteous man's reward.

And whosoever shall give to drink unto one of these little ones a cup of cold water only in the name of a disciple, verily I say unto you, he shall in no wise lose his reward.

How sound and glorious this is! Receive a prophet for what he is and gain a prophet's reward. What is the reward received by prophets? That it is eternal life, the greatest of all the gifts of God, none will doubt. Thus, by accepting a true prophet men gain eternal life. Full acceptance presupposes obedience to whatever prophetic counsel and direction is forthcoming. The same reasoning applies to receiving a righteous man and gaining a righteous man's reward, which reward is exaltation in the highest heaven of the celestial world. And even those who perform but the slightest service for the Lord's anointed, or for the little ones of his earthly kingdom—doing so because those served are the chosen of Jehovah—shall be rewarded for their goodness.

And so endeth the instructions to the Twelve. Having so spoken, Jesus "departed thence to teach and to preach in their cities," and the traveling witnesses of his name went forth to teach and testify in the way he had commanded them.

NOTES

1. These are the words of the Risen Lord, spoken with reference to Paul.

2. These words were written by Paul and are descriptive of himself and the others of the Twelve in his day.

3. There is an old tradition, dating back almost to apostolic times, that Peter, at this point, asked: "But how then if the wolves should tear the lambs?" To this Jesus is said to have answered: "Let not the lambs fear the wolves when the lambs are once dead, and do you fear not those who can kill you and do nothing to you, but fear Him who after you are dead hath power upon soul and body to cast them into the Gehenna of fire." (Farrar, p. 277.)

4. As to the hatred of the world for the saints, the Roman historian Tacitus says that Nero "inflicted the most cruel punishments upon a sect of people who were holden in abhorrence for their crimes, and called by the vulgar 'Christians.' The founder of that name was Christ, who suffered death in the reign of Tiberius, under his procurator Pontius Pilate. . . This pernicious superstition, thus checked for a while, broke out again; and spread not only over Judea where the evil originated, but through Rome also, whither everything bad upon earth finds its way and is practised. . . . A vast multitude were apprehended who were convicted, not so much of the crime of burning Rome, as of hatred to mankind. . . . They were criminals, deserving the severest punishments." (Cited. *Dummelow*, p. 662.)

5. "Those who preach the gospel are to do so boldly, without timidity or trepidation, not fearing the face of man, but with the courage of their convictions and in the fervor of their testimonies. 'Use boldness, but not overbearance,' Alma said. (Alma 38:10-12.) Truths learned in the day of preparation and schooling are to be broadcast from the housetops." (*Commentary* 1:333.)

6. The destruction of the soul in hell is a figurative expression. It is a spiritual death; it is to die as pertaining to the things of the Spirit and to be cast into outer darkness until the full penalty has been paid for sin. See *Mormon Doctrine*, 2nd ed., pp. 756-59, and related passages.

7. This interpreting paraphrasing of Jesus' words is my own, taken from *Commentary* 1:335-36.

Chapter 55

HEROD BEHEADS THE BLESSED JOHN

It is great sin to swear unto a sin;
But greater sin to keep a sinful oath.
Who can be bound by any solemn vow
To do a murderous deed?[1]

This Man Called John

We must now turn our attention to the ministry, mission, and martyrdom of the blessed Baptist—to him who prepared the way before the Blessed One; who served as an excelling Elias in time's meridian; and who is about to seal his testimony with his own blood. And when Jesus hears of the death of his kinsman—they were second cousins—and learns that a martyr's blood now stains a dungeon cell at Machaerus, it will have a marked effect on his own ministry.

Many things might be said of John Ben Zacharias—of this son of Zacharias and Elisabeth; of this man whose birthright it was to sit in Aaron's seat, the priestly ruler in Israel; of this man who did in fact seal up the old dispensation and usher in the new.

John Ben Zacharias—here is a man who sat in council with the Gods before ever the foundations of this earth were laid; who was a friend of Michael and Gabriel and Raphael; who made covenant with Abraham, and was an associate of

Isaiah and Nephi and Joseph Smith in that seraphic sphere where the sons of God awaited their mortal probations.

John Ben Zacharias—here is a man who was seen in vision by Lehi and Nephi and Isaiah, each of whom foresaw his ministry, and even foretold the very words he would speak: as the voice of one crying in the wilderness; as the baptizer of the One upon whom the Holy Spirit would descend bodily, in calmness and serenity, like a dove; as the witness of the divine sonship of the Lamb of God who taketh away the sins of the world.

John Ben Zacharias—here is a man whose birth was announced by that angelic ministrant who stands next to Michael in the holy hierarchy of the eternal worlds; whose mother was the aged Elisabeth, who, like Sarah, was past the childbearing years; and whose father, a pure Levite, would also suffer a martyr's death.

John Ben Zacharias—here is a man who was born in the hill country of Judea; who grew up in the desert areas of Hebron; who came from the deserts and wildernesses of Palestine, wearing the prophetic garb made of camel's hair, to proclaim repentance and to prepare the way before One who should come after.

This man called John; this holy and valiant Levite; this Elias; this forerunner; this voice crying in the wilderness; this one than whom there has not been a greater prophet—this man called John came to prepare the way before the Son of God.

He was filled with the Holy Ghost from his mother's womb and, in fact, bore his first mortal testimony of Jesus the Lord while he was yet in the womb of an aged mother.

He was ordained by an angel of God—Gabriel, we presume—when but eight days old, and given power to overthrow the kingdom of the Jews, and to make straight the way before the Lord.

He was himself baptized while yet in his childhood—it could not have been other than at eight years of age—and when he ministered and taught at Bethabara and Aenon and elsewhere, he in turn baptized many for the remission of their sins.

He held the Aaronic Priesthood—receiving it no doubt from his father—and was the last legal administrator of the Mosaic dispensation and the first divinely called and legally recognized agent of Jehovah in the newly-set-up Christian era.

He assembled great congregations of true believers—all Jerusalem came out to hear his prophetic words, and many heeded his call to repentance—but all who came to him were encouraged and invited—nay, commanded—to follow the One who came after who would baptize with fire and with the Holy Ghost.

His great cry—"Behold the Lamb of God, which taketh away the sin of the world" (John 1:29)—and his doctrinal testimony—"He that believeth on the Son hath everlasting life: and he that believeth not the Son shall not see life; but the wrath of God abideth on him" (John 3:36)—these were his crowning and oft-repeated declarations. There is no preaching to compare with sound doctrine mingled with pure testimony.

When this chosen and beloved prophet—John Ben Zacharias of the seed of Aaron—was imprisoned by that evil miscreant Antipas, then Jesus sent angels to his dungeon-bound kinsman to minister comfort and hope and eternal assurance. And we cannot doubt that this strait and severe prophet—who is akin to Adam and Abraham and Moses in faith and prophetic power—that this desert Elias not only entertained angels, as it is the right of one holding the Aaronic Priesthood so to do, but that he also beheld the visions of eternity and knew the things of God in a measure and to a degree seldom vouchsafed to mortal men.

This man called John stood, as no other has ever done, at the crossroads of history. He closed the door on the past and opened the door of the future. He proclaimed Jehovah's *amen*—the divine *so-be-it*; the heaven-sent *it is over and done*, as it were—as pertaining to the rituals and performances and ordinances of Moses, the greatest of Israel's prophets; and he opened the door to the simplicity and beauty of the fulness of the everlasting gospel.

How great is that prophet who can say to Moses: 'Thou man of God—thou mighty one like unto whom there was not again among the ancients such a prophet—Moses, thou man of God, be silent. No longer does thy law apply; no longer are your ordinances valid; sacrifices shall now cease; no longer shall those who sit in Aaron's seat make an atonement for the sins of repentant Israel. The law of Moses is now swallowed up by the law of Christ.'

How great is that prophet who can say to the Son of God: 'I am thy forerunner, thy Elias; my voice announces you to all who shall come after. By my priesthood I shall immerse you in baptism, and my act in so doing shall be binding on earth and in heaven. I am the friend of the Bridegroom. Great congregations shall come unto thee and be saved because of me.'

Praise be to God for the life and ministry of the blessed Baptist, of John the son of Zacharias—a ministry that is about to be ended with Herod's axe, so that John, dying before Christ, may serve as his forerunner among the departed dead and then rise with him in glorious immortality in the first resurrection to reign everlastingly in that heavenly kingdom where Gods and angels dwell.

Antipas Holds an Evil Feast
(Mark 6:21-29; JST, Mark 6:22; Matthew 14:6-12)

Herod the Great, a polygamist having ten wives and numerous progeny—many of whom he murdered, and all of whose descendants inherited his evil, voluptuous, and ruthless ways—left one son whose deeds of infamy have attained a fame and a name of almost as great ill-repute as that of his dissolute father. This was Herod Antipas, the sycophant who, under Rome, ruled in Galilee. Herod the Great sought the life of Christ and ended up, in mad dementia, slaughtering the Innocents of Bethlehem, a crime so unspeakably evil and so unutterably irresponsible as to send eternal shudders through all Christendom; and yet so numerous were his murders and so great was the river of blood shed by him that the slaughter of Rachel's children in the coasts of Bethlehem scarcely merits a mention in secular sources. Herod Antipas took the life of Christ's forerunner under circumstances showing forth such weakness of character and such submission to lecherous passion that once again all Christendom is repelled at the horror and evil of it all.

"Herod Antipas, to whom, on the death of Herod the Great, had fallen the tetrarchy of Galilee, was about as weak and miserable a prince as ever disgraced the throne of an afflicted country. Cruel, crafty, voluptuous, like his father, he was also, unlike him, weak in war and vacillating in peace. In him, as in so many characters which stand conspicuous on the stage of history, infidelity and superstition went hand in hand. But the morbid terrors of a guilty conscience did not save him from the criminal extravagances of a violent will. He was a man in whom were mingled the worst features of the Roman, the Oriental, and the Greek." (Farrar, p. 295.)

Our present concern is with Herod Antipas and two other sons of Herod the Great: Aristobulus and Herod Philip, not the tetrarch, but one of the royal family who lived as a private citizen in Rome. Aristobulus had a daughter, Herodias, who married her uncle, Herod Philip, and they in turn had a grown daughter name Salome. Herod Antipas was married to a daughter of Aretas, Emir of Arabia.

On a visit to Rome, Herod Antipas became entangled with Herodias, his brother Philip's wife, and she left Philip to marry Antipas, taking Salome with her. Thus Herod Antipas married his sister-in-law, who was also his niece; and as a result, the daughter of Aretas left Antipas and returned to her father, who later waged a victorious war against his quondam son-in-law.

It was this incestuous and illegal marriage that caused John the Baptist to say to Herod Antipas: "It is not lawful for thee to have her." It was this firm pronouncement that caused the Baptist to gain the undying enmity of Herodias and of Salome, and it was this same declaration that caused Herod to arrest John and imprison him in the dungeons of Machaerus. "And when he would have put him to death, he feared the multitude, because they counted him as a prophet." (Matt. 14:4-5.)

Among the wicked and ungodly, riotous living is the norm; their aim in life is to eat, drink, and be merry, and that which sates one's appetite and gratifies one's passions is to be desired above all. "All that is in the world, the lust of the flesh, and the lust of the eyes, and the pride of life" (1 Jn. 2:16)—these are the things their souls desire. It is one of the signs of the times that those who know not God and seek not his face will be eating and drinking—eating as gluttons and drinking as drunkards—until the Son of Man comes.

And nowhere are the gluttons more greedy nor the drunkards more sottish than among the degraded royalty of imperial courts. The Caesars in Rome hold great banquets for the great and mighty among them. They swill up delicacies with swinish gluttony, take an emetic, vomit up their guzzlings, and commence to gorge themselves anew. Belshazzar appoints a great feast for a thousand of his lords. They and their wives and concubines drink wine from the golden vessels taken from the holy Temple of Jerusalem, and in the midst of it all, the handwriting on the wall spells out the doom of their kingdom. Herod Antipas, aping the debauchery of Rome—a debauchery that will soon revel in orgies of immorality and in gladiatorial combats between human combatants—Herod Antipas appoints a feast day to honor himself. The scriptural account says simply:

> But when Herod's birthday was come, he made a supper for his lords, high captains, and the chief priest of Galilee.

And therein is set forth one of the signs of those times. The topers and gluttons who came together to eat and drink at Herod's board and to do honor to the tetrarch were his own rulers, the captains of his Roman mercenaries, and—mark it well—"the chief priest of Galilee." The leading Levites—Aaron's sons—were linking arms with their alien overlords. It was as when the Pharisees took counsel with the Herodians as to how they might destroy Jesus, because he healed a man with a withered hand on the Sabbath. And it is a far cry from the day of divine vengeance when fire came down from heaven and devoured Nadab and Abihu, Aaron's sons, because they offered strange fires, upon the altar, before the Lord. But perhaps even this which is to occur at Herod's feast is as handwriting on the wall foretelling his destruction, or as fire from heaven that will ultimately consume him, and his house, and Herodias, and Salome, and all who ally themselves with such as these.

Such feasts as this were not complete without entertainment, without something to feed the lusts and arouse the passions of those now gorged with food and half drunken with wine. Dancers, especially dancing women, were in great demand. Taking into account the sensuous nature of the Herods, the mean and vulgar demeanor of the military men, the adultery-centered proclivities of the chief priests; having in mind the depraved and vulgar displays Herod would have seen at Caesar's banquets; knowing of the perversions and sexual excesses found in all Oriental courts, and the loose and low moral standard of all the Gentiles and many of the Jews; being aware of all this, and more—over which a decent propriety must draw a curtain of silence—we have no difficulty envisioning the type of banquet entertainment that was presented at these kingly feasts.

As to how, in this instance, Salome became the featured dancer before Herod and his lords, we know not, but suppose that an evil Herodian craftily planned the sensuous spectacle, with an evil Salome both agreeing and taking delight in the prospect of exposing her body to the gawking eyes of her stepfather and his voluptuous friends. In any event, "when the banquet was over, when the guests were full of meat and flushed with wine, Salome herself, the daughter of Herodias, then in the prime of her lustrous beauty," danced—lewdly, lasciviously, seductively—before "those dissolute and half-intoxicated revellers." Then Herod, "in the delirium of his drunken approval, swore to this degraded girl, in the presence of his guests, that he would give her anything for which she asked, even to the half of his kingdom." (Farrar, p. 300.)[2]

Hearing this, the lewd daughter of an adulterous mother hastened to her maternal parent for further instructions. "What shall I ask?" she queried. The crafty and conniving Herodias, to whom adultery and murder were but the normal accompaniments of her depraved and godless course, replied: "The head of John the Baptist."

Then went Salome "straightway with haste unto the king." Immediately with haste! "What a touch is that! and how apt a pupil did the wicked mother find in her wicked daughter!" Then stood Salome before Antipas and all his lords, and said: "I will that thou give me by and by in a charger the head of John the Baptist." "Her indecent haste, her hideous petition, show that she shared the furies of her race." They show also how those enmeshed in immoral and lascivious living find it easy, perhaps natural, to make murder and every debasing crime a part of their way of life. 'Bring me here, now, as soon as the headsman's axe can fall, upon one of the golden dishes that grace thy table, the gory head of that Jew who dares to say it is not lawful for thee to have my mother as thy wife.'

Herod is stunned; he is plunged into sudden grief; his fawning friends are appalled. "It was a bitter termination of his birthday feast. Fear, policy, remorse, superstition, even whatever poor spark of better feeling remained unquenched under the dense white ashes of a heart consumed by evil passions, all made him shrink in disgust from this sudden execution. He must have felt that he had been duped out of his own will by the cunning stratagem of his unrelenting paramour."

Yet sin begets sin; pride builds upon pride; and he who

is guilty of one offense cannot escape the commission of another, lest he be punished or held up to disrepute for the first. As with Pilate, who gave the order to crucify One whom he knew to be innocent, lest it be reported in Rome that the procurator was not Caesar's friend, so with Antipas, who feared to lose face with his nobles should he break his intemperate oath.

"If a single touch of manliness had been left in him he would have repudiated the request as one which did not fall either under the letter or spirit of his oath, since the life of one cannot be made the gift to another; or he would have boldly declared that if such was her choice, his oath was more honoured by being broken than by being kept. But a despicable pride and fear of man prevailed over his better impulses. More afraid of the criticisms of his guests than of the future torment of such conscience as was left him, he immediately sent an executioner to the prison, and so at the bidding of a dissolute coward, and to please the loathly fancies of a shameless girl, the axe fell, and the head of the noblest of the prophets was shorn away."

Thus came the murder, for how else can it be named? And then was brought the head of one who had now sealed his testimony with his own blood, one whose earth-sealed lips would now cry out in a better realm for that vengeance which a just God lays upon those who make martyrs of his prophets. Placed "on one of the golden dishes which graced the board," the marred visage of the man of God would forever haunt the souls of his murderers.

According to tradition, Herodias celebrated her victory by ordering "the headless trunk to be flung out over the battlements for dogs and vultures to devour." "And his disciples came, and took up the body, and buried it, and went and told Jesus."

The forerunner's work on earth was done. What rejoicing there must have been that day in paradise as he mingled with the spirits of just men made perfect, proclaiming to them that He by whom salvation comes would soon minister among them, would open their prison doors—for the separation of their spirits from their bodies seemed as a prison to them—and would bring forth his saints in glorious immortality.

"Precious in the sight of the Lord is the death of his saints." (Ps. 116:15.) Jehovah reigneth, and all things are going forward according to his plans and purposes.

Jesus Hears of John's Death
(Luke 9:7-9; Mark 6:14-16; Matthew 14:1-2, 13)

As a mortal among mortals, Jesus learned of John's death from the Baptist's disciples who, with loving care, had taken up "his corpse, and laid it in a tomb." Had necessity required, he would have learned the sad fate—a fate both sad and glorious, for he that layeth down his life for Christ and his cause shall gain eternal life—had necessity required, Jesus would have known by the power of the Spirit that his forerunner had died a martyr's death. We know of no reason, in this instance, however, why he should have received by revelation that knowledge which other mortals would learn from their fellow mortals.

As our friend Farrar has it, there was at this time "an atmosphere already darkened by the storm-clouds of gathering opposition," and in this atmosphere, "like the first note of a death-knell tolling ruin, there broke the intelligence of a dreadful martyrdom. The heaven-enkindled and shining lamp has suddenly been quenched in blood. The great Forerunner—he who was greatest of those born of women—the Prophet, and more than a prophet, had been foully murdered."

After noting that it was at about this time that the apostles reported their missions, Farrar says: "Another piece of intelligence reached Jesus; it was that the murderous tetrarch was inquiring about Him; wished to see Him; perhaps would send and demand His presence when he returned to his new palace, the Golden House of his new capital at Tiberias. For the mission of the Twelve had tended more than ever to spread a rumour of Him among the people, and speculation respecting Him was rife. All admitted that He had some high claim to attention. Some thought that He was Elijah, some Jeremiah, others one of the Prophets; but Herod had the most singular solution to the problem.

"It is said that when Theodoric had ordered the murder of Symmachus, he was haunted and finally maddened by the phantom of the old man's distorted features glaring at him from a dish on the table; nor can it have been otherwise with Herod Antipas. Into his banquet hall had been brought the head of one whom, in the depth of his inmost being, he felt to have been holy and just; and he had seen, with the solemn agony of death still resting on them, the stern features on which he had often gazed with awe. Did no reproach issue from those dead lips yet louder and more terrible than they had spoken in life? Were the accents which had uttered, 'It is not lawful for thee to have her,' frozen into silence, or did they seem to issue with supernatural energy from the blood-less lips?

"If we mistake not, that dissevered head was rarely thenceforth absent from Herod's haunted imagination from that day forward till he lay upon his dying bed. And now, when but a brief time afterwards, he heard of the fame of another Prophet—of a Prophet transcendently mightier, and one who wrought miracles, which John had *never* done—his guilty conscience shivered with superstitious dread, and to his intimates he began to whisper with horror, '*This is John the Baptist whom I beheaded: he is risen from the dead,* and therefore these mighty works are wrought by him.' Had John sprung thus suddenly to life again to inflict a signal vengeance? Would he come to the strong towers of Machærus at the head of a multitude in wild revolt? or glide through the gilded halls of Tiberias, terrible, at midnight, with ghostly tread? 'Hast thou found me, O mine enemy?'"

And so it was that Jesus, aware of Herod's hallucinations and not at this time courting persecution or premature arrest, "departed thence by ship into a desert place apart," where the feeding of the five thousand took place.

And as to John, his body returned to the dust whence it came; his spirit continued to speak among the spirits of the dead—awaiting the day when body and spirit, inseparably connected, would rise with Christ in immortal glory, even then to continue his labors in the work of the Holy One whose eternal witness he is.

And, further, as to John: acting under the direction of Peter, James, and John, his apostolic superiors, he came to Joseph Smith and Oliver Cowdery, on the fifteenth day of May, 1829, on the banks of the Susquehanna River in western New York, and there conferred upon them the ancient Levitical order in which he had ministered while in mortality.

> *Upon you my fellow servants,*
> *In the name of Messiah*
> *I confer the Priesthood of Aaron,*
> *Which holds the keys of the ministering of angels,*
> *And of the gospel of repentance,*
> *And of baptism by immersion for the remission of sins;*
> *And this shall never be taken again from the earth,*
> *Until the sons of Levi do offer again*
> *An offering unto the Lord in righteousness. (D&C 13.)*

And so once again there are those on earth who can sit in Aaron's seat; who, being subject to those who sit in Moses' seat, can prepare the way for that which—in the eternal providences of Him in whose hand is all power—is about to come to pass.

And again we say: Jehovah reigneth; blessed be his great and holy name, both now and forever. Amen.

NOTES

1. Shakespeare, *Henry VI,* Part II, act 5, sc. 1.
2. These words, and those hereafter quoted in this chapter, aside from the scriptural quotations themselves, are taken from chapter 28 of Farrar, pp. 294-305. Though containing the usual speculative conclusions, from the standpoint of literary craftsmanship, this is

one of Farrar's best essays. I have not hesitated to quote selected literary gems and to paraphrase others, as is also the case, occasionally, throughout this work, with particular reference to the writings of Edersheim and Farrar, two of the best sectarian authors. Short of receiving personal revelation on all points, no one author can think of all the meanings or set forth every nuance of thought on all points. Further, it seems a waste of literary talent not to preserve some of the thoughts and modes of expression that those of old, who wrote on the same subjects, were led by the spirit of truth to record. Those who are acquainted with the original sources—be they the two authors mentioned, or Josephus, Tacitus, or whosoever—will know that all authors have followed this practice. Elder Talmage does so in his scholarly work. It is also the course followed by the authors of the scriptures themselves, as when John the Apostle quotes and paraphrases, without identifying his original source, a prior account of John the Baptist, as is set forth in the first chapter of the Gospel of John.

Chapter 56

JESUS FEEDS THE FIVE THOUSAND

And it came to pass that he brake bread again
and blessed it, and gave
to the disciples to eat.
And when they had eaten
he commanded them
that they should break bread,
and give unto the multitude.
And when they had given unto the multitude
he also gave them wine to drink,
and commanded them that they should give
unto the multitude.
Now, there had been no bread,
neither wine, brought by the disciples,
neither by the multitude;
But he truly gave unto them bread to eat,
and also wine to drink.
And he said unto them:
He that eateth this bread eateth of my body
to his soul; and he that drinketh of this wine
drinketh of my blood to his soul;
and his soul shall never hunger nor thirst,
but shall be filled. (3 Ne. 20:3-8.)

He Prepares a Table in the Wilderness
(Luke 9:10-11; JST, Luke 9:10; Matthew 14:13; Mark 6:30-32; JST, Mark 6:32-33)

Jesus now plans to feed five thousand men, "beside women and children," with five small barley loaves and two sardine-like fish. The spartan banquet—if such it may be called when contrasted with the gluttonous feasts at Machaerus—is to be held in a solitary meadow near Bethsaida-Julias to the north and east of the Sea of Galilee. As to the multiplying of the loaves and fishes, John tells us that Jesus "himself knew what he would do" beforehand (John 6:6), and that this foreknowledge applied also to the preparation for the desert feast we cannot doubt.

And so, before the miraculous banquet can be served, the table in the desert must be prepared. The question, "Can God furnish a table in the wilderness?" must be answered anew, as it was in the day of Moses when Jehovah served quail to all Israel. (Ps. 78:13-20.) Before the multiplying of the loaves and fishes, Jesus and his disciples must go to the expanse of "green grass" where the companies of fifty and of a hundred will sit; the guests must be invited; they must be famishing for want of food, with none available to them; the pressing need for divine intervention must be present; there must be a young lad there with five loaves and two fishes; Jesus must have taught and healed so that the miracle will bear witness of his doctrine and of his divinity; and then—all being in readiness—the wonder will occur.

It should not be thought a thing unreasonable among them that the Son of God would exercise his creative power to give meat to hungering men. Indeed, their tradition was that when the Messiah came he would—as Moses had done—give them bread from heaven, provide them water to drink, feed them flesh according to their needs. Others before had fed Israel miraculously when their needs were great. Should it not happen again?

Had not Moses, the servant of Jehovah—when they, lusting for the fleshpots of Egypt, said, "Why came we forth out of Egypt?"—had not he given all Israel, some three million of them, flesh for thirty days, until it came out of their nostrils and became loathsome unto them? (Num. 11:18-23, 31-33.) Had not Jehovah rained bread from heaven upon them, six days a week, for forty years, as they dwelt in the wilderness? (Ex. 16.)

Was not Elijah fed by the ravens as he hid himself by the brook Cherith? Did not the fowls of heaven bring him "bread and flesh in the morning, and bread and flesh in the evening," lest he die of the famine? And did he not say to the widow of Zarephath, "The barrel of meal shall not waste, neither shall the cruse of oil fail, until the day that the Lord sendeth rain upon the earth," and it was so? (1 Kgs. 17:1-16.)

And Elisha, upon whom the mantle of Elijah fell, did he not bring oil and bread and corn into being from the very elements, as it were? What of the widow whose husband had been a prophet and whose two sons were to be taken as bondmen by a creditor? Did not Elisha cause them to pour oil from one small vessel until many great vessels were full, so they might sell the great store of oil thus created and have sufficient means to meet their needs? And does not the scripture say of Elisha:

> And there came a man from Baalshalisha, and brought the man of God bread of the firstfruits, twenty loaves of barley, and full ears of corn in the husk thereof. And he said, Give unto the people, that they may eat.
>
> And his servitor said, What, should I set this before an hundred men? He said again, Give the people, that they may eat: for thus saith the Lord, They shall eat, and shall leave thereof.
>
> So he set it before them, and they did eat, and left thereof, according to the word of the Lord. (2 Kgs. 4:1-7, 42-44.)

Why, then, should it be thought a thing unreasonable among them that the Son of God himself should give them a simple peasant-type meal of barley loaves and fish? Had he not, for that matter, as they all knew, turned water into wine at Cana? Others acting in Jehovah's name had fed Jehovah's people in days of old. Why not Jehovah himself do now what his servants of old had done? Was not that which was done by the Messianic messengers of old but a type and a shadow of what would be when the Messiah, whose witnesses they were, came among men in power and glory, to save and redeem, both temporally and spiritually?

And so now, Jesus and his disciples leave Capernaum to go to Bethsaida-Julias; the preparations for the desert feeding of the hungry multitudes are going forward in a normal and natural way. There are, it would seem, at least five good and sufficient reasons why Jesus and his fellow itinerant preachers should make this journey. They are:

1. *Both he and the Twelve are greatly in need of physical rest.* They have all been teaching and healing and traveling, almost with greater zeal than their strength permits. The Twelve have just returned from their missions and have told Jesus "all things, both what they had done, and what they had taught." They too had been preaching the gospel of the kingdom, casting out devils, healing the sick, perhaps even raising the dead, for such was included in the promises made to them. And so Jesus said unto them: "Come ye yourselves apart into a solitary place, and rest a while; for there were many coming and going, and they had no leisure, not so much as to eat. And they departed into a solitary place by ship, privately."

2. *Their departure will have a much-needed quieting effect upon the people.* Galilee is in turmoil because of the murder of the Baptist, whom the people revered as a prophet. It is not expedient for great multitudes to assemble around Jesus and the Twelve, lest the Herodians esteem these teachers and witnesses to be political agitators deserving the same arrest and imprisonment suffered by John. Josephus tells us that the seeming political agitations of John were the excuse used for his arrest. This must not now happen to Jesus or any of the Twelve. And at this time there might be a political

uprising among the people if Jesus and his associates longer remain with them. They are considered as leaders by many, and the people are seeking a standard round which to rally.

3. *It seemed wise for Jesus and the Twelve to withdraw from the domains and power of Herod.* Capernaum in Galilee was part of the tetrarchy of Antipas. Bethsaida-Julias, though near the eastern border of Galilee, was subject to the more peaceful Philip. As we have seen, Herod Antipas, demented and maddened by the weight of sin, hearing of Jesus' miracles and fame, assumed he was John the Baptist risen from the dead and had sent forth word that "he desired to see him." The climate was ripe for further political persecution, and Jesus and his followers would do well to go away for a slight season while things cooled down.

4. *The feeding of the hungering thousands could only take place in a solitary place,* in the deserts and hills where no food was available; otherwise the need for divine intervention would not be compelling. *And Jesus must work this miracle, not alone to fulfill the Messianic tradition had among them, but to bear witness in a way none others can that he is indeed the One of whom Moses and the prophets spoke.* Those of old who had fed the hungering by divine power had all done it in Jehovah's name. Jesus must go forth and say he is the Son of God, the Promised Messiah, and then work the miracle; then exercise divine power; then multiply the loaves and fishes—a thing he could not do if he were a deceiver.

5. And, finally, as we shall hereafter see in some detail, *the multitude must be fed, at the appointed place, so that Jesus, back again in Capernaum, can preach his incomparable sermon on the bread of life.* The feeding of the multitude is but prelude to the doctrine he is about to teach. Men are not saved because miracles are wrought in their presence; salvation comes only to those who believe the doctrines of salvation and who then act in harmony with them. The teaching that is to grow out of the miracle is greater than the miracle itself, and the teaching cannot come, with anywhere near the desired effect, without the miracle.

Jesus Teaches, Heals, and Feeds the Multitude
(John 6:1-15; JST, John 6:12-13; Mark 6:33-46; JST, Mark 6:36, 39;
Matthew 14:14-23; Luke 9:11-17; JST, Luke 9:10-13)

This miracle, with its attendant circumstances, is recounted by all four of the Evangelists. Each preserves his own views as to what transpired on this never-to-be-forgotten day, and all of the accounts taken together enable us to paint a vivid picture of the only scenes of this kind ever to transpire among men. The Man whose words we love and whose deeds we revere first taught his scattered sheep; then he healed those who were lame and maimed among them; after this, he fed them all with earthly manna; then he went off by himself to commune alone with his Father; and finally, he walked on the ridges of the waves as a tempestuous wind whipped the Galilean sea into a frothy and frenzied maelstrom.

John tells us the Feast of the Passover "was nigh," and Mark specifies that the multitudes sat on "green grass." It was spring—early April of A.D. 29—and great throngs of Galileans had left their fields and shops to travel to Jerusalem to worship the Lord and covenant anew to follow the God of their fathers. Thousands of pilgrims were free to dally in Capernaum or hasten to a solitary site near Bethsaida-Julias, where the voice of their own Galilean Prophet might be heard. Perhaps he would heal their sick as he had done elsewhere. Was he, in fact, the Messiah as both he and his confederates so often said? Public interest ran high, and the Eternal Paschal Lamb meant to teach the traveling throngs who were en route to sacrifice their own paschal offerings in Jerusalem.

Jesus and the Twelve took ship. From Capernaum to their east coast destination was six miles by water; it would be somewhat farther on land. "And he took them, and went aside privately into a solitary place belonging to the city called Bethsaida," Luke says. After disembarking, "Jesus went up into a mountain, and there he sat with his disciples," John adds.

Their departure was seen by the people, who followed on foot, out of all the cities; word of his destination went from mouth to mouth; a great congregation awaited him across from the Jordan and on the east of the lake. These all assembled in a green valley. John says that "a great multitude followed him, because they saw his miracles which he did on them that were diseased."

Perhaps Jesus and his party gained some rest, at least some respite from the crowds, as they crossed the sea and as they sat on the mountain. But when Jesus saw the multitudes, he "was moved with compassion toward them, because they were as sheep not having a shepherd; and he began to teach them many things." So says Mark. Luke says he "spake unto them of the kingdom of God."

Jesus was doing what he had done before. It was his age-old pattern; as he always did, he preached the gospel, summarized the plan of salvation, told the people in whom they must believe and what they must do to be saved. He told them who he was and who the Twelve were. How important it is to know this, and how often it is repeated by the inspired authors!

As he said at the first Passover of his ministry, 'Though men destroy this body, I shall rise again the third day'; as he said to Nicodemus, 'I am the Son of Man who came down from heaven; whosoever believeth in me shall not perish but have eternal life; I am the Only Begotten Son; through me all men may be saved'; as he said to the woman of Samaria at Jacob's Well, 'I that speak unto thee am the Messias'; as he said in the synagogue in Nazareth, 'I am he of whom Isaiah spake; in me are the Messianic prophecies fulfilled; I am the Messiah'; as he said in healing one sick of the palsy, 'I Jesus, who am God, forgive you of your sins'; as he said at the second Passover, after healing the impotent man at the pool of Bethesda, 'I am the Son of God; my Father and I are equal; the Father hath committed all judgment into my hands; he that believeth on me hath everlasting life; even the dead shall hear my voice; all men must honor me even as they honor the Father'—as he said day in and day out, everywhere and everlastingly, always, in season and out of season, early and late, to men, women, and children, to every living soul, so he said again to the multitude near Bethsaida-Julias: 'I am the Son of God; salvation comes by me; believe my words and live my law, and I will give you a place in my Father's kingdom.'

Again we say: How important it is to know this! Jesus preached the gospel first and healed afterwards; the healings came to those who believed his words and accepted him as God's Son. However much this runs counter to the speculative views of the divines, it yet remains as a basic reality that must be understood if we are to come anywhere near a true view of him who, though mortal for a season, is Lord of all everlastingly.

And so Jesus first preached the gospel to the multitudes who came to hear his word. Then, as Luke says, he "healed them that had need of healing," or as Matthew recounts, he "was moved with compassion toward them, and he healed their sick."

Sometime during the day, Jesus said to Philip, one of the Twelve: "Whence shall we buy bread, that these may eat?" That Jesus had no intention of buying bread but was simply testing Philip—and through him all of the Twelve—is clear from John's comment: "And this he said to prove him: for he himself knew what he would do." Philip answered: "Two hundred pennyworth of bread is not sufficient for them, that every one of them may take a little." That sum, obviously, was more than the disciples had in their common purse.

His conversation with Philip caused the apostles to discuss the matter among themselves, and to wonder what should be done. At some point in time, "One of his disciples, Andrew, Simon Peter's brother, saith unto him, There is a lad here, which hath five barley loaves, and two small fishes; but what are they among so many?" And Philip's words are but a far-off echo of a servitor in another day who said: "What, should I set this"—this meal of twenty barley loaves and a few ears of corn in the husk—"before an hundred men?" And Jesus' coming response was but an echo of Elisha's word: "Give the people, that they may eat: for thus saith the Lord, They shall eat, and shall leave thereof." (2 Kgs. 4:43-44.)

Finally, following full discussion among themselves, and after their faith had been tested—and found wanting—"when the day began to wear away, then came the twelve, and said unto him, Send the multitude away, that they may go into the towns and country round about, and lodge, and get victuals; for we are here in a solitary place."

This, then, was their answer; and this was the perfect teaching moment, the time for divine intervention. Jesus said: "They need not depart; give ye them to eat." They said: "Shall we go and buy two hundred penny-worth of bread, and give them to eat?" Jesus said: "How many loaves have ye? go and see." The answer came: "We have but five loaves and two fishes; and except we should go and buy meat, we can provide no more food for all this multitude."

"And he commanded them to make all sit down by companies upon the green grass. And they sat down in ranks, by hundreds, and by fifties. And when he had taken the five loaves and the two fishes, he looked up to heaven, and blessed, and brake the loaves, and gave them to his disciples to set before them; and the two fishes divided he among them all. And they did all eat, and were filled."

"When they had eaten and were satisfied, he said unto his disciples, Gather up the fragments that remain, that nothing be lost. Therefore they gathered them together, and filled twelve baskets with the fragments of the five barley loaves, which remained over and above unto them that had eaten."

Thus was the miracle wrought; so was the deed done; and such are the attendant circumstances. The concordant testimony of four independent witnesses appends a solemn certitude to the wonder that has happened. Needless to say, the creative power thus exercised by him who for the moment is as a mortal is in fact the power of God.

As the reality of what was done this day in a green lowland place not far from Bethsaida-Julias (literally, the *house of fishing,* or, as we might say, *Fisher-town*) dawns upon us; as we ponder the wonder of it all, bread and fish springing instantly into being, from the very elements, because he willed it—as we marvel at such a miracle, we ask: Why and for what purpose was it done? What message are we to receive from this miracle of two millenniums ago? To all of this, these thoughts readily occur:

1. *He did it*—and such an ordinary and prosaic reason it is!—*because men were hungry and there was no food available to them.* Unless men eat, they die; mortal meat is part of mortal life.

2. *He acted out of love and compassion for his fellowmen.* Though he would not turn stones into bread to appease his own hunger—a famishing, gnawing hunger born of forty days of fasting—yet for others, whose needs were less and whose hunger was but one day old, he would exercise his own divine power. As his Father makes the rains fall and the sun shine upon all his children, be they good or evil, so will the Son provide bread for those who have come to hear his words.

3. *But he will not glut their souls with the delicacies that grace Herod's board, nor will he sate their appetites with rich food.* They shall have barley bread, the foodstuff of the peasant and the poor. They shall spread upon this coarse product of the baker's oven a savory made of fish. John's account uses "a peculiar word for 'fish,' *opsarion,* which properly means what was eaten along with the bread, and specially refers to the small, and generally dried or pickled fish eaten with bread, like our 'sardines' or the 'caviar' of Russia, the pickled herrings of Holland and Germany, or a peculiar kind of small dried fish, eaten with the bones, in the North of Scotland." (Edersheim 1:682.)

4. In the course of the day, as various conversations led up to the climactic miracle, *he tested the faith of his disciples*—as he tests all of us hour by hour in the most ordinary affairs of our lives—and as we have seen, his chosen ones, in this case, failed to pass the test.

5. He dramatized his own saying, given in the Sermon on the Mount, that his missionaries, his servants, *those who go forth on his errand to teach his word, need take no thought for their temporal wants.* Such will be supplied by the Father. He who feeds the fowls of the air and clothes the lilies of the field will care for the needs of his own.

6. *The miracle came as a sign*—nay, not a sign only, but as a crowning proof—*of his Messiahship.* He first claimed to be the Son of God and then performed miracles, which he could not have done if he were a deceiver.

7. Would it be amiss, as some have done, to say *the miracle acclaimed him as the bread of the world;* as the source—unexhausted and inexhaustible—of all that sustains life; as the one in whom there is always enough and to spare; as the one who, now and always, will care for all the spiritual needs of all the hungering souls of all the ages?

8. *Does it not also testify that all that he does is organized and regulated?* His house is a house of order and not of confusion. The recipients of his goodness sat down in companies and in ranks; they were counted and numbered; there was no disorder, no commotion, no disturbance. None sought to come afore, and none resisted the command to be seated systematically. There was peace and serenity, and the Spirit of the Lord was present.

9. *Here also divine economy was in operation.* Though he could supply loaves and fishes that the world itself could not contain, yet the uneaten fragments, the crusts and crumbs, the slivers of uneaten fish—all these were picked up in baskets and saved, for waste is sin.

10. *Jesus offered a blessing on the food;* he gave thanks to a gracious God, who is the source of all good things, for that which was then supplied. And as he himself offered the

prayer, it means, according to the Jewish custom, that he himself also ate of the food.

11. *He manifest his own creative powers.* He did not call upon the Lord as did Elisha; he did not act in the name of another as had Elijah and Moses; but acting himself, in his own name, because he was God, he created loaves and fishes. If worlds come rolling into being at his word and by his creative power, then why not a few barley loaves and sufficient fish savory to go with them?

12. And, finally, *the supplying of bread from heaven, as it were, formed the basis for the not-far-distant sermon on the bread of life*—one of the greatest and most powerful sermons of his ministry, as we shall see.

No doubt other points could be made, and the attentive student can search out his own types and shadows and applications, as he should; but what is here given illustrates, at least, what can be learned from any of the glorious teaching situations concerning Jesus our Lord.

"The miracle produced a profound impression. It was exactly in accordance with the current expectation, and the multitude began to whisper to each other that this must undoubtedly be 'that Prophet which should come into the world'; the Shiloh of Jacob's blessing; the Star and the Sceptre of Balaam's vision; the Prophet like unto Moses to whom they were to hearken; perhaps the Elijah promised by the dying breath of ancient prophecy; perhaps the Jeremiah of their tradition, come back to reveal the hiding-place of the Ark, and the Urim, and the sacred fire." (Farrar, pp. 310-11.)

And since he was "that Prophet"—the very Messiah; their Deliverer; the one through whom all Israel might be saved—what then? To the expectant throng—had they not heard his wondrous words, seen his miracles, and been fed to the full?—to them it seemed as if the hour of Jewish triumph had come at long last. They must "make him a king"; nay, he was king already; rather, they must "take him by force" and require that he act in his kingly capacity. Let the Roman yoke fall; here at last was one who could defeat the armies of Antipas and more. Here was one who could strike the death blow against that wretched man, Caesar, who reveled in his orgies and lusts in his Gentile city.

That such misdirected zeal must not go unchecked was perfectly clear to the one around whom the swell of zealotry surged. His disciples must withdraw lest they partake of this false spirit, and the people must disperse to ponder, in less excitable circumstances, the true meaning and significance of the doings of that day. "And straightway Jesus constrained his disciples to get into a ship, and to go before him unto the other side." He was insistent that they depart immediately. They must leave the environs of Bethsaida-Julias and go to that Bethsaida which is the companion city to Capernaum, the two cities, but four miles apart, sharing a common Galilean harbor. With his disciples en route back it was easier for Jesus to send the multitude away.

Then "he went up into a mountain apart to pray." He must thank his Father for the marvels of that day, for he of himself did only that which his Father commanded. He must counsel again with the great God whose Son he was, lest he overstep any of the bounds or vary so much as a hair's breadth from the course decreed by the Father. He must receive that spiritual refreshment and guidance which even he needed to bear the growing burden that rested upon his divine shoulders. From the hallowed spot where he communed with the Eternal he soon returned—perhaps having been so directed by him to whom he prayed—to walk on the surging waves of that lake which was so much a part of his life.

Chapter 57

JESUS WALKS ON THE SEA OF GALILEE

The waters saw thee, O God,
the waters saw thee;
they were afraid: the depths also were troubled.
Thy way is in the sea,
and thy path in the great waters. (Ps. 77:16, 19.)

The waters were gathered together,
the floods stood upright as an heap,
and the depths were congealed in the heart
of the sea. (Ex. 15:8.)

Jehovah Rules the Waters

Working with waters has always been part of the prophetic way. By faith the worlds were made; by faith the elements are controlled; by faith the mountains move and the seas divide. And the waters of the world are always used to subserve the purposes of faithful men.

From that creative day when Jehovah, by his word, divided the waters above the firmament from those beneath the broad expanse of heaven; from that primeval day when he gathered the waters into one place, calling the dry land earth and the great waters seas; from that antediluvian day

353

when he caused the rains to fall and water the parched land, to give life to plants and herbs, to give drink for man and beast—from that day water has always been used for the benefit and blessing of created things.

Water, the liquid that falls from the clouds as rain; the unstable substance that flows in great rivers and small streams; the moisture that accumulates in ponds and lakes and seas; the element without which there cannot be life— the birth of man itself being brought to pass by water and blood and the spirit—water, wondrous water, was made for man. It was made to supply his needed fluids and to cleanse his body; to give life to animals and fowls and plants; to serve as a home for fish; to form vapors of steam, storms of snow, and glaciers of ice; to be handled and used and governed—all in the interests of God's crowning creation, the being whom he made in his own image.

Truly, water was made for man, made for him to use for his own purposes. His is the power to control and govern it. With it he irrigates his gardens and gives drink to his flocks and herds. From it he catches fish, and over it he sails. He freezes it into ice to refrigerate his products; he vaporizes it into steam to drive great locomotives; he uses its power to generate electricity. He swims in it, skis on its frozen crystals, and skates on its congealed surface. Its uses are as varied and broad as the earth itself.

And water is subject not alone to the natural laws that man must learn and to which he must conform, but it is subject also to the eternal law of faith, a law that in the eternal sense is also a natural law. And further, water is used by the Lord to further his own purposes—to give life to men; to cleanse them from their sins; to drown them in death when his judgments are poured out.

"I, the Lord, in the beginning blessed the waters"—so our revelations record in a passage whose full meaning has not yet been given—"but in the last days, by the mouth of my servant John, I cursed the waters." (D&C 61:14.)

Perhaps the cursing here involved will attain its dooming

destiny when the visions of the future that John saw become a reality. In one of these he saw that "a great mountain burning with fire was cast into the sea; and the third part of the sea became blood; And the third part of the creatures which were in the sea, and had life, died; and the third part of the ships were destroyed." (Rev. 8:8-9.) In another he saw that one of the angels who carry "the vials of the wrath of God, . . . poured out his vial upon the sea; and it became as the blood of a dead man; and every living soul died in the sea. And the third angel poured out his vial upon the rivers and fountains of waters; and they became blood." (Rev. 16:1-4.) And perhaps we are seeing even now a little trickling prelude of what John foretold as we struggle to maintain the natural purity of our rivers and seas into which great floods of contaminating chemicals and stinking refuse are poured as men seek to rid themselves of the rubbish and garbage of our so-called civilization.

"And, as I, the Lord, in the beginning cursed the land," our revelation continues, "even so in the last days have I blessed it, in its time, for the use of my saints, that they may partake the fatness thereof." (D&C 61:17.) That this blessing upon the land will attain its glorious fulfillment in the nearing millennial era is, of course, perfectly clear. In the meantime the first sprouting forth of the blessings that can grow from the soil are beginning to burst upon us as we learn better how to use the good earth from which we are fed.

But our concern, with reference to the miracle we are about to witness, is to know that Jehovah rules the waters, and that what he does to and with them—whether it be by his own voice or by the voice of his servants, it is the same.

Thus we see Jesus arranging for the immersion of Adam and his seed in water, that they may all come forth, born again, born anew from a second watery womb. We see baptism in water established as an eternal ordinance, with the waters in which it was performed in ancient Israel being called "the waters of Judah." (1 Ne. 20:1.) We see the saints, in all dispensations, in holy and sacred ordinances, sprinkled with water that they become clean from the carnality and evil of the world. We see men drink the sacramental wine and water in witness of the new covenant that God hath made with his people. And we hear a divine voice assure all men that whosoever so much as gives a cup of cold water to a prophet or righteous man—because he wears the prophetic mantle or walks in the paths of righteousness—shall in nowise lose his reward.

We see Enoch go forth and say to the mountains, 'Be thou removed,' and to the rivers, 'Turn thou into another course,' and it is so. We see a great land come up out of the depth of the sea to which the enemies of the people of God flee in the days of Enoch.

We see Jehovah, by the mouth of his servant Noah, sending in the floods until the valleys and hills and every high mountain are immersed in the surging torrents. It is the baptism of the earth. We see the earth divided in the days of Peleg—was it perchance by his mouth as he spoke Jehovah's word?—so that the dry lands that once were in one place become continents and islands surrounded by seas of water.

We see Moses, the man of God—by his own voice, which was the voice of Jehovah—stretch out his hand upon the waters of Egypt so they all turn to blood, including the waters that are in the Nile and in all the streams and rivers and ponds, and in all the pots and vessels. We see the fish die, smell the stench of the rivers, and know there is nothing for the Egyptians to drink.

We see Moses stretch forth his hand over the Red Sea and divide it so that all Israel, numbering in the millions, "went into the midst of the sea upon the dry ground: and the waters were a wall unto them on the right hand, and on their left." We learn that "the floods stood upright as an heap, and the depths were congealed in the heart of the sea." (Ex. 14:19-31; 15:8.) And we see the pursuing armies of Pharaoh drowned in the depths of the sea as the congealing power is withdrawn and the floods surge forth in all their unchecked fury.

When Israel thirsts for water in their desert wilderness, we see Moses, at Meribah, smite the rock with his rod, so that rivers of fresh water gush forth, that all Israel and their beasts die not for want of water.

When Israel, under Joshua, march to the flooding banks of Jordan, as soon as the soles of the feet of them that bare the ark are dipped in the brim of the water, lo—as Joshua by his own mouth decreed—we see the waters stand up as a heap and all Israel pass over on dry ground.

When the Lord sent a famine in Israel, it was by the mouth of Elijah that he sealed the heavens for three years and six months, that it rained not; and it was by his word that the dews of heaven and the moisture of the clouds came again.

At the time of the translation of Elijah, when he was taken up into heaven in a chariot of fire without tasting death, we see, first, Elijah, and then Elisha—by their own mouths—smite the waters of Jordan with a mantle, so that they divide hither and thither, permitting the prophetic feet to go over on dry ground.

We see a faithful man in Israel felling a beam with a borrowed axe; the head comes off and falls into the water. Then at the word of the prophet Elisha—mark it well—"the iron did swim," and the axe head is recovered. (2 Kgs. 6:1-7.) Solid iron swims in water as though it were a cork because Jehovah and his prophets, by faith, have power over the waters.

And we shall yet see, for these things are in the future, the Son of Man at his coming—perhaps by the mouths of his servants the prophets—"command the great deep, and it shall be driven back into the north countries, and the islands shall become one land; . . . and the earth shall be like as it was in the days before it was divided." (D&C 133:23-24.) And then, after his coming, upon those nations that go not up year after year to Jerusalem to keep the Feast of Tabernacles, "even upon them shall be no rain." (Zech. 14:16-19.) The Lord will use the elements to punish the people in the millennial day even as he speaks in this day by "the voice of thunderings, and the voice of lightnings, and the voice of tempests, and the voice of the waves of the sea heaving themselves beyond their bounds." (D&C 88:90.)

We have spoken thus about the waters of the world—and there is much more that could be acclaimed—to show how the Lord uses them at will to bless and to curse, that it might not seem a thing incredible to now see two men walk upon the waters of Gennesaret. Jesus and Peter are about to defy the gravitational forces of nature and make the rolling waves and surging foam their footpath. Few miracles seem to excite such wonder and interest as does this one. And it is indeed such a miracle as is not elsewhere inscribed in the hearts of the saints, nor found in the records of the Lord's people, but it is one that accords with the manner and way in which Jesus—whether as Jehovah, or as a mortal, or as the Risen God—deals with the faithful. And it is one that we might expect of him who turns water into wine, who stills storms, and who has power over the elements.

"Be of Good Cheer; It Is I; Be Not Afraid"
(Matthew 14:24-33; Mark 6:47-52; JST, Mark 6:50; John 6:16-21)

From the mountaintop where he prayed—shall we not rather say, communed and conversed—with his Father, Jesus saw the peril and strugglings of his beloved friends as they sought the safety of the western shore of the Galilean lake. They were seabound because he had "constrained" them so to travel. Their preference had been to remain with him and bask in the glory of that wondrous multiplying of five barley loaves and two small fish into a banquet that fed five thousand men, plus women and children, and yet left twelve baskets of uneaten food. His awareness of their plight must have come by the power of the Spirit rather than the natural eye, for they were more than four—perhaps were five or six—miles away. It was still night, and a tempestuous wind, blowing out of a darkened sky, was whipping the waves into a surging fury.

358

These noble souls who stood at Jesus' side, who believed his words and loved his law, who wrought miracles in his name, and who one day would bear witness of that blessed name before kings and rulers and before nations scarce then known to them—these chosen ones had embarked for Bethsaida and Capernaum, twin cities on the western shore of Galilee that shared a common harbor. Their seaborn journey, though not wholly a willing one, was at least one of obedient conformity to the Master's word. They had sailed in the calm of deepening dusk, only to encounter a storm of the night as the wild winds blew down the canyons and ravines and across the inland sea. Matthew says their "ship was . . . tossed with waves: for the wind was contrary." Mark says Jesus "saw them toiling in rowing," doing all in their power to avoid a disastrous shipwreck. And John says it was "dark, . . . And the sea arose by reason of a great wind that blew." In some eight or ten hours they traveled less than four miles from the shore.

Their peril was great. Even strong men cannot resist indefinitely the battering waves and the rolling power of a storm at sea. It was now the fourth watch of the night, sometime between three and six A.M. Jesus had left them to struggle and toil till their strength was spent. Now he came to the rescue. He came to them "walking on the sea"; his feet pressed on the crests of the waves; his weight was borne by the foaming liquid beneath his feet; it was as though the watery waves were a stone-set street. The iron swam when Elisha spoke; the waters of the Red Sea congealed at a word from Moses; the storm-tossed Sea of Galilee was as a dusty Galilean lane because Jesus willed it. He walked on the water—literally, actually, and in reality.

But even now he yet tests their faith by walking "as if he would have passed by them." "They all saw him, and were troubled." "It is a spirit," they said—and well might they so suppose, for since the world began there was no account of a mortal man, weighted down with flesh and bones and apparel, treading lightly on the waves of the sea. "They cried out for fear," as might be expected, for an added and unknown peril—a spirit from the unseen world—a peril beyond the winds and the waves with which they were acquainted, seemed more than they could then bear.

In answer to their cries Jesus spoke: "Be of good cheer," he said; "it is I; be not afraid."

Peter answered: "Lord, if it be thou"—or, better, 'Since it be thou'—"bid me come unto thee on the water." A single word of response, spoken above the whistling wind and the noise of the boisterous waves beating against the ship, pierced the darkness and din of the storm: "Come." And come Peter did. He too walked on the water. Jesus and Peter were both supported by the liquid highway beneath them, a highway that surged and rolled as the wind-driven waves responded to the tempestuous forces that disturbed their calm.

"Over the vessel's side into the troubled waves he sprang, and while his eye was fixed on his Lord, the wind might toss his hair, and the spray might drench his robes, but all was well; but when, with wavering faith, he glanced from Him to the furious waves, and to the gulfy blackness underneath, then he began to sink, and in an accent of despair—how unlike his former confidence!—he faintly cried, 'Lord, save me!' Nor did Jesus fail. Instantly, with a smile of pity, He stretched out His hand, and grasped the hand of His drowning disciple, with the gentle rebuke, 'O thou of little faith, why didst thou doubt?' And so, his love satisfied, but His over-confidence rebuked, they climb—the Lord and His abashed Apostle—into the boat; and the wind lulled, and amid the ripple of the waves upon a moonlit shore, they were at the haven where they would be; and all—the crew as well as His disciples—were filled with deeper and deeper amazement, and some of them, addressing Him by a title which Nathanael alone [as far as the written record shows] had applied to Him before, exclaimed, 'Truly Thou art the Son of God.' " (Farrar, p. 313.)

Our synoptist authors tell us that when Jesus and Peter

entered the ship, "the wind ceased," leaving us to believe that once again he stilled a Galilean storm with a word. At this point Matthew says: "Then they that were in the ship came and worshipped him, saying, Of a truth thou art the Son of God." We are left to conclude that those so doing were the sailors or other passengers, for the apostles had long since had such a witness in their souls. To the extent the chosen disciples joined in this worship, it was but a reaffirmation of that which they already knew, even as it is common among us to affirm and reaffirm our knowledge of the divine sonship of this same Holy Being.

Mark, however, says "they were sore amazed in themselves beyond measure, and wondered. For they considered not the miracle of the loaves: for their heart was hardened." It would appear that this amazement and wonder may have been the feelings of the disciples as well as the others who sailed in the battered bark. Why, in the light of all that has transpired in their lives, would there be a lingering strain of doubt and uncertainty in any disciple's mind? "The answer is found in the fact that the chosen disciples had not yet received the gift of the Holy Ghost. Though they were all pillars of spiritual strength and righteousness, save Judas only, yet 'the things of God knoweth no man, but the Spirit of God.' (1 Cor. 2:11.) Until the natural man becomes a new creature of the Holy Ghost, until man is born again, until his stony heart is touched by the Spirit of the living God, he cannot, by any power of his own, stand sure and steadfast in the cause of truth." (*Commentary* 1:348-49.)

It is no more difficult to believe that Jesus or Peter or any faithful person could walk on a tempestuous sea than it is to believe in any other miracle. "If, believing in God," as Farrar puts it, "we believe in a Divine Providence over the lives of men—and, believing in that Divine Providence, believe in the miraculous—and, believing in the miraculous, accept as truth the resurrection of our Lord Jesus Christ—and, believing that resurrection, believe that He was indeed the Son of God—then, however deeply we may realise the beauty and the wonder and the power of natural laws, we realize yet more deeply the power of Him who holds those laws, and all which they have evolved, in the hollow of His hand; and to us the miraculous, when thus attested, will be in no way more stupendous than the natural, nor shall we find it an impossible conception that He who sent His Son to earth to die for us should have put all authority into His hand."

Continuing, Farrar gives this aptly expressed application of the miracle here recounted: "So then if, like Peter, we fix our eyes on Jesus, we too may walk triumphantly over the swelling waves of disbelief, and unterrified amid the rising winds of doubt; but if we turn away our eyes from Him in whom we have believed—if, as it is so easy to do, and as we are so much tempted to do, we look rather at the power and fury of those terrible and destructive elements than at Him who can help and save—then we too shall inevitably sink. Oh, if we feel, often and often, that the water-floods threaten to drown us, and the deep to swallow up the tossed vessel of our Church and Faith, may it again and again be granted us to hear amid the storm and the darkness, the voices prophesying war, those two sweetest of the Savior's utterances—

'Fear not. Only believe.'
'It is I. Be not afraid.' "[1]

Jesus Heals in the Land of Gennesaret
(Matthew 14:34-36; Mark 6:53-56)

Gennesaret, meaning garden of riches, was a small region in Galilee, located on the western shore of the lake near Capernaum. It was also a city, perhaps Tiberias, south of Capernaum and Magdala. Rich soil and plenteous harvests supported a large population scattered in many villages and cities. It was here, apparently because the storm had driven them southward from their intended landing in the Capernaum-Bethsaida area, that Jesus and his disciples disembarked after the miracle of the walking on the sea.[2]

Jesus and his party were well known, and almost immediately they were surrounded by believing and worshipful souls who sought to hear his words and feel his power. Messengers "ran through that whole region round about"; people everywhere heard of his presence; and believing multitudes hastened to him, carrying on pallets "those that were sick," and bringing to him "all that were diseased." It was a day of rejoicing and miracles. Those who were diseased and sick, so great was their faith, "besought him that they might only touch the hem of his garment," that their maladies might be cured.[3] And they were blessed according to their desires, for "as many as touched were made perfectly whole."

Through all their villages and cities and country it was the same; the sick were placed in the streets where they needed but to touch the border of his garment to have health and vigor and cleanliness and strength surge anew through their diseased bodies.[4] This day was a pleasing and blessed interlude between the storm of the night and the coming confrontation in the synagogue of Capernaum when hatred and opposition would spring forth even among many of those who had eaten the loaves and feasted on the fishes. And it is to the deep and profound teachings of that contentious scene that we shall next turn our attention—teachings that marked the turning point in the mortal ministry of the Mortal Messiah.

NOTES

1. Farrar, p. 314. "Why did Jesus walk on the water and then quell the storm?

"(1) To reach the boat, keep a planned rendevous with the apostles, and save them in their hour of despair and physical exhaustion.

"(2) To teach again by concrete means, under circumstances where no natural explanation could spiritualize the miracle away, that faith is a principle of power by which natural forces are controlled. (*Mormon Doctrine*, 2nd ed., pp. 261-267.)

"(3) To bear testimony that he was indeed the promised Messiah, the Son of God, the Incarnate Word, who though made flesh to fulfil the Father's purposes, yet had resident in him the powers of divinity. Here in the boat with weak mortals was he 'who hath gathered the wind in his fists, who hath bound the waters in a garment' (Prov. 30:4), he who 'spreadeth out the heavens, and treadeth upon the waves of the sea.' (Job 9:8.) And that the disciples knew him for what he was, and saw in this renewed manifestation of his power the proof of his eternal godhood, is evident from the fact that they then worshiped him and acclaimed, 'Of a truth thou art the Son of God.' (Matt. 14:33.)" (*Commentary* 1:347.)

2. "The boat which bore the disciples had drifted out of its course—probably owing to the wind—and touched land, not where they had intended, but at Gennesaret, where they moored it. There can be no question, that by this term is meant 'the plain of Gennesaret,' the richness and beauty of which *Josephus* and the Rabbis describe in such glowing language. To this day it bears marks of having been the most favoured spot in this favoured region." (Edersheim 2:5.)

3. "Perhaps they had knowledge of the woman who, plagued for twelve years with an issue of blood, had been healed by touching the hem of his garment (Mark 5:25-34); perhaps they considered the garment fringe as holy because of the divine command that garments be bordered in blue so that all Israel might 'look upon it, and remember all the commandments of the Lord, and do them' (Num. 15:37-41); or perhaps, overpowered in the divine presence, they sought even the slightest and least physical contact with him. But in any event, so great was their faith that all partook of his infinite goodness and were healed." (*Commentary* 1:350-51.)

4. Comparable scenes and events drawn from the subsequent apostolic ministries include these: *As to Peter,* "And by the hands of the apostles were many signs and wonders wrought among the people, . . . Insomuch that they brought forth the sick into the streets, and laid them on beds and couches, that at the least the shadow of Peter passing by might overshadow some of them." (Acts 5:12-15.) *As to Paul,* "And God wrought special miracles by the hands of Paul: So that from his body were brought unto the sick handkerchiefs or aprons, and the diseases departed from them, and the evil spirits went out of them." (Acts 19:11-12.)

Chapter 58

THE SERMON ON THE BREAD OF LIFE

And thou shalt remember all the way
which the Lord thy God led thee these forty years
in the wilderness, to humble thee,
and to prove thee, to know what was in thine heart,
whether thou wouldest keep
his commandments, or no.
And he humbled thee, and suffered thee to hunger,
and fed thee with manna,
which thou knewest not, neither did
thy fathers know; that he might make thee
know that man doth not live by bread only,
but by every word that proceedeth
out of the mouth of the Lord doth man live.
(Deut. 8:2-3.)

To him that overcometh will I give to eat
of the hidden manna. (Rev. 2:17.)

Manna Is for All Men

Jesus is about to speak of "the hidden manna" which
none but those who believe and obey shall ever taste. For
forty years Israel ate manna—bread from heaven—which all

men saw. This "manna was as coriander seed, and the colour thereof as the colour of bdellium." It fell as dew upon the camp of Israel, each night except the one preceding the Sabbath. The people gathered it in containers, ground it in mills, beat it in mortars, baked it in pans, and made cakes of bread. It tasted like fresh oil, was the staple diet of the people, and preserved them from famine and death. For twelve thousand days—six days a week, fifty-two weeks a year, for forty years—Israel ate manna to their hearts' content. "I will rain bread from heaven for you," Jehovah said; and rain it, he did, a rain of temporal food suited for the digestive processes of mortal people who must eat or die. (Ex. 16:4-36; Num. 11:4-9.)

And so Israel ate and lived—temporally. Among them, from time to time, were those who understood that their diet of heavensent bread came in similitude of a greater food, a "hidden manna," an unseen heavenly bread, of which men must eat if they are to be fed spiritually. As men die temporally for want of temporal bread, so they die spiritually for want of spiritual food.

Israel's daily diet of manna—and they collected enough on the sixth day to satisfy their needs on the Sabbath—was given not alone to feed their bellies, but to test them spiritually. It came to the people, to all of them, from the Lord—to prove them, to signify what was in their hearts, to establish whether they would keep the commandments or continue to walk after the manner of the Egyptians whose fleshpots they had forsaken to eat the manna of the wilderness. "Man does not live by bread only," Moses proclaimed. Let there be temporal bread lest there be temporal death. But man lives—spiritually and eternally—only when he feasts upon "hidden manna," when he lives "by every word that proceedeth out of the mouth of the Lord." (Deut. 8:2-3.)[1]

Jesus, not for twelve thousand consecutive days as did Jehovah to their fathers, but for one glorious meal, rained bread from heaven. He fed, not the millions in all the camps of ancient Israel, but a few, a mere five thousand men plus women and children, in an isolated place near Bethsaida-Julias. Yet in the miracle of the loaves and fishes was manifest the same gracious goodness shown forth upon all Israel anciently: (1) Food came to hungry mouths to satisfy their temporal needs; and (2) it was done to bear record of that heavenly bread, that hidden manna, that spiritual food, of which all men must eat if they are to gain eternal life. This meaning of the miracle is what Jesus is about to expound in a synagogue, in a wicked city, to Israelites whose rebellion and unbelief ranks with that of their fathers in Moses' day.

And as the Lord tested Israel by means of the ancient manna, so Jesus is about to test Jewish Israel by expounding the meaning of the miracle in which they had gained such a great initial feeling of rejoicing. He is going to see whether they will "keep his commandments, or no"; and as it was anciently, so shall it now be. A few will believe and obey; most of the people will seek only to glut their souls with the bread of the world, which sustains life among those who are carnal, sensual, and devilish. The things of the Spirit—spiritual food—is not for them, as they will soon attest.

Only yesterday on the green fields near Bethsaida-Julias, on the eastern side of the Lake of Gennesaret, Jesus the Messiah, doing what no mortal of himself had power to do, fed the multitude with temporal food. From the beginning of his ministry to that day his popular appeal had swept over the land as a flood. His doctrine and his deeds testified of his divinity. All men, save those whose hearts were bound by the chains of priestcraft, flocked to his standard and desired his help and blessings.

There was a tradition, taught by the Rabbis and firmly entrenched in the public mind, that when Messiah came, he would feed them with bread from heaven. "The miracle of the manna had become a subject of the proudest remembrances and the fondest legends of the nation. 'God,' says the Talmud, 'made manna to descend for them, in which were all manner of tastes. Every Israelite found in it what best pleased him. The young tasted bread, the old honey, and the children oil.' It had even become a fixed belief that the Messiah, when He came, would signalize His advent by a repetition of this stupendous miracle. 'As the first Saviour—the deliverer from Egyptian bondage,' said the Rabbis, 'caused manna to fall for Israel from heaven, so the second Saviour—the Messiah—will also cause manna to descend for them once more." (Geikie, pp. 516-17.)

Thus, when Jesus multiplied the five barley loaves and the two small fishes, it was as though the traditional sign had been given. The peak of his popular appeal had come. In their eyes he stood on the summit. He was the Messiah, they reasoned, and must reign as their king. They must take him by force, if need be, and install him as the Deliverer who would break the Gentile yoke, to say nothing of providing them with bread from heaven as it had been in the day of Moses. No doubt many of them had doubts and anxious moments as they reflected during the night on his utter refusal to receive the Messianic mantle proffered by them.

And so now in the synagogue in Capernaum—the synagogue built by the good centurion whose son was healed; the synagogue ruled by Jairus, whose daughter was raised from death; the synagogue upon whose "lintel has been discovered . . . the device of a pot of manna, ornamented with a flowing pattern of vine leaves and clusters of grapes" (Edersheim 2:29)—in this setting Jesus will teach them of the hidden manna of which the loaves and fishes were but a symbol. And here his popularity will plummet. This sermon will mark the parting of the ways between him and the people generally. Previous opposition centered primarily in the scribes and Pharisees, the Rabbis and rulers, the Sadducees and Herodians; now the generality of the people will harden their hearts against Him who refused to conform to their concept of a temporal ruler.

It is a day of sorrow and a day of crises. Indeed: "The dawn of that day broke on one of the saddest episodes of our Saviour's life. It was a day in the synagogue at Capernaum on which He deliberately scattered the mists and exhalations of such spurious popularity as the Miracle of the Loaves had gathered about His person and His work, and put not only His idle followers, but some even of His nearer disciples, to a test under which their love for Him entirely failed. That discourse in the synagogue forms a marked crisis in His career. It was followed by manifestations of surprised dislike which were as the first mutterings [among the people generally] of that storm of hatred and persecution which was henceforth to burst over His head." (Farrar, p. 315.)

Jesus Brings the Hidden Manna
(John 6:22-47; JST, John 6:26-27, 40, 44)

By preparing a table in the wilderness where a hungering host was fed as though manna had again been rained from heaven, Jesus did two things:

1. He set the stage, prepared the way, and provided the symbolism that would enable him to teach, under circumstances in which none could ever forget his words, that there was an eternal bread, a spiritual food, a hidden manna, which men must eat to gain eternal life; and

2. He fanned the flames of Messianic expectancy into a raging fire—here at last was the Coming One who would feed them as Moses (so they supposed) had fed their fathers. "A few, doubtless, had worthier thoughts, but, to the mass, the Messiah's kingdom was as gross as Mahomet's paradise. They were to be gathered together into the garden of Eden, to eat, and drink, and satisfy themselves all their days, with houses of precious stones, beds of silk, and rivers flowing with wine, and spicy oil for all. It was that He might gain all this for them that they had wished to set Him up as king." (Geikie, pp. 516-17.)

Thus, as we have seen, they had, in the swelling emotion of the moment, sought to place a kingly crown upon that head whose only earthly crown was to be one of thorns. Their failure so to do sowed the seeds of doubt and dismay in many minds. Following this failure to start the rebellion against Rome that in their view would have led to the triumph of the Jews over all others, they had seen the disciples depart for the western shore in the only available boat. With some reluctance the excited multitude, at Jesus' behest, had themselves dispersed to seek lodging in the nearby cities and villages. Jesus, as they knew, had remained with them on the eastern side of the then placid waters, waters that would soon be whipped into a storm-tossed fury by the tempestuous winds of the night. When the morning came Jesus was gone. Later other boats came from Tiberias, and in them many of the people found passage back to Capernaum; others, no doubt, walked back to their home locales or continued as pilgrims, bound toward Jerusalem and their annual Passover.

Those who returned by the other boats must have numbered among them the Galileans who were more particularly offended by Jesus' refusal to accept a crown from their self-seeking hands. When they found him—apparently already in the synagogue—with an abruptness bordering on discourtesy, certainly with a demeanor lacking in civility, they asked: "Rabbi, when camest thou hither?"

That Jesus had spent the night communing with his Father; that he had walked on the fearful waves which all but sank the boat wherein the disciples rowed and struggled to stay afloat; that a sudden calm attended his entrance into the storm-tossed ship; that the blessed party had landed in the area of Gennesaret where multitudes flocked together to hear his words and feel his love; that messengers had run through all the region round about so their sick and diseased might be carried and brought to his presence; that he had healed them all, even those who but touched the hem of his garment—none of these things were as yet known to the harsh interrogators who had followed him in small boats from the fields where the table in the wilderness had been set, and where he had told them plainly that he would not be a judge and a divider over them in the temporal sense. Nor did Jesus feel any need to account to them for his goings and comings and his words and deeds. Waving their impertinent query aside, he answered:

> *Verily, verily, I say unto you, Ye seek me, not because ye desire to keep my sayings, neither because ye saw the miracles, but because ye did eat of the loaves and were filled.*

> *Labor not for the meat which perisheth, but for that meat which endureth unto everlasting life, which the Son of Man hath power to give unto you; for him hath God the Father sealed.*

As jackals devour their prey and are no longer ravished by the pangs of hunger; as wolves drink in the blood and gulp down the torn flesh of sheep to sate their ravenous appetites; and as oxen in their stalls are satisfied by the fodder put before them, so those who now confront Jesus had filled their bellies at his table and now desired to repeat the process.

'Give us corn without sowing, harvests without reaping, bread without baking. No longer need we labor at our oars and struggle with our nets when two small fish, at the Messiah's touch, will feed thousands. The Deliverer is here; he will feed us as Moses fed our fathers. Give us loaves and fishes forever, and in thy beneficent goodness add raisins and oil and wine to our diet. Surely we shall now feast more sumptuously than Herod himself.'

For them the whole point of the miracle of the loaves was lost. Their need was to keep his sayings, to feast upon the words of Christ, to drink from the Eternal Fountain. Loaves and fishes perish, but there is a food which is eternal, "which endureth unto everlasting life." This is the food he is prepared to give them; it is the everlasting word, the word of truth, the gospel of salvation. As the woman of Samaria was invited to drink living water and never thirst more; so they were invited to eat living bread and never hunger more. This bread was available, without money and without price, from the Son of Man, "for him hath God the Father sealed." Or in other words: "Him hath God the Father marked out or authenticated as his only Son; that is, he is the One, chosen, appointed, and *openly approved* (by unnumbered signs and evidences) to give the spiritual meat which endureth to everlasting life, for he is the Son of that holy Man who is the Father." (*Commentary* 1:351.)[2]

That Jesus' words—profound and deep as we might at first blush assume them to be—were understood by his Jewish hearers is perfectly clear from their response. It was the practice of all the Rabbis to speak in metaphors, and all the people were extensively schooled in understanding their hidden sayings.[3] Jesus' words meant, to them, that there was some added "labor" to be performed, something more than all the rituals and performances of their Mosaic system, if they were to gain eternal blessings. "What shall we do, that we might work the works of God?" they asked. 'What do you require of us more than we are already doing?'

His answer came back with all the authority and finality of Jehovah, speaking amid the fires and thunder of Sinai; his answering words were driven into their hearts with all the power of logic and divine wisdom. They were at the heart and core and center of true worship. There was indeed something more they must do; God their Father required it of them; it was, in fact, the very foundation upon which all else rested. He said:

> *This is the work of God, that ye believe on him whom he hath sent.*

"Believe on the Lord Jesus Christ, and thou shalt be saved." (Acts 16:31.)

"If thou shalt confess with thy mouth the Lord Jesus, and shalt believe in thine heart that God hath raised him from the dead, thou shalt be saved." (Rom. 10:9.)

This is the work of God! "This is my work and my glory—to bring to pass the immortality and eternal life of man." (Moses 1:39.)

"Jesus Christ . . . hath abolished death, and hath brought

life and immortality to light through the gospel." (2 Tim. 1:10.)

'Believe in Christ; believe that I am he; believe my gospel; give heed to the doctrines I have taught from Dan to Beersheba; this is the will of God concerning you.'

They knew the meaning of his words, but, in spite of all that had happened, they did not believe in their hearts that he was the one who would break the bands of death and bring life and immortality to all men. If he were what he claimed to be, let him prove his divinity. "What sign shewest thou then, that we may see, and believe thee? what dost thou work?"[4] Let him expand the miracle of the loaves until it fulfilled their tradition of what the Messiah would do. What was one meal as compared to a continual diet of heavenly food? Their tradition was that their Messiah would bring again manna from heaven. "For, all that the first deliverer Moses had done, the second—Messiah—would also do. And here, over their Synagogue, was the pot of manna—symbol of what God had done, earnest of what the Messiah would do: that pot of manna, which was now among the things hidden, but which Elijah, when he came, would restore again!

"Here, then, was a real sign. In their view the events of yesterday must lead up to some such sign, if they had any real meaning. They had been told to believe on Him, as the One authenticated by God with the seal of truth, and Who would give them meat to eternal life. By what sign would Christ corroborate His assertion, that they might see and believe? What work would He do to vindicate His claim?" (Edersheim 2:29-30.)

"Our fathers did eat manna in the desert; as it is written, He gave them bread from heaven to eat," they said. (John 6:31.) "To understand the reasoning of the Jews, implied but not fully expressed, as also the answer of Jesus, it is necessary to bear in mind . . . that it was the oft and most anciently expressed opinion that, although God had given them this bread out of heaven, yet it was given through the merits of Moses, and ceased with his death." (Edersheim 2:30.)

Up to this point in this discussion, the name of Moses has not been used either by Jesus or the Jews—only a reference to the manna that came from God that all concerned knew to have been in the days of Moses. Jesus, however, aware of their tradition that the manna had come "through the merits of Moses," now affirms:

Verily, verily, I say unto you, Moses gave you not that bread from heaven; but my Father giveth you the true bread from heaven.

'Think not that Moses, through any merit of his own, gave manna to Israel; it was I, Jehovah, who so blessed my people. But now the Father himself, who is Lord above all, gives you the Eternal Bread.'

For the bread of God is he which cometh down from heaven, and giveth life unto the world.

Again we must be aware of the Jewish tradition. It was that though their fathers had eaten manna, such was a figure of something greater. In their view: "The real bread from heaven was the Law." (Edersheim 2:30.) And so again those in conversation with Jesus could not have done other than suppose he was offering them something in addition to what they already had, something in addition to the law of Moses with all its rituals and performances. If such newly offered bread was to give "life unto the world"—and be it remembered that he is the life and the light of men, and that it is his gospel which brings life and immortality to light—if the offered bread was to bring life, surely they wanted such a reward. And so they said: "Lord, evermore give us this bread." Then came the great pronouncement:

I am the bread of life: he that cometh to me shall never hunger; and he that believeth on me shall never thirst.

Salvation is in Christ; in one way or another the message goes forth. He is the bread that men must eat. They must feast upon his word. Those who do so shall be filled with the Holy Ghost.

But I said unto you, That ye also have seen me, and believe not.

O that they had believed in him! O that all men today might believe in him—believe in him as he is revealed and made known by the apostles and prophets whom he has sent forth to testify of his goodness and grace for this present day! And all who do believe shall receive the rewards of which he now speaks:

All that the Father giveth me shall come to me; and him that cometh to me I will in no wise cast out.

For I came down from heaven, not to do mine own will, but the will of him that sent me.

And this is the Father's will which hath sent me, that of all which he hath given me I should lose nothing, but should raise it up again at the last day.

And this is the will of him that sent me, that every one which seeth the Son, and believeth on him, may have everlasting life: and I will raise him up in the resurrection of the just.

Thus does Jesus bear testimony of his own divine Sonship and of that salvation which comes because of his atoning sacrifice. He is the Son of God. He came to do the will of the Father. All those who are given him by the Father shall be saved. All who believe in him shall have eternal life. He will raise them up in the resurrection of the just.

The testimony he bears is true; the witness he gives cannot be denied; the doctrine he teaches shall stand forever. How truth is flowing forth this day, direct from the great Fountain Head.

> He looks! and ten thousands of angels rejoice,
> And myriads wait for his word;
> He speaks! and eternity, filled with his voice,
> Re-echoes the praise of the Lord.[5]

But there are those who will not eat though the banquet tables are heaped high with the bounties of life; there are those who will not drink though the streams of living water overflow their banks; there are those who will not believe though God himself, by his own voice, teaches and testifies. Many of them are in Jairus's synagogue this day. They murmur; they complain; they find fault. They are offended because he said, "I am the bread which came down from heaven."

Above all, they are galled and embittered over his claim of divine Sonship. This always is the chief rock of offense and the main stone of stumbling for rebellious people. "Is not this Jesus, the son of Joseph, whose father and mother we know? how is it then that he saith, I come down from heaven?"

"Jesus never met these murmurs about His supposed parentage and place of birth by revealing to the common crowds the high mystery of His earthly origin." It sufficed for them to hear the witness borne that he was the Son of the Highest; let the details of his coming be reserved for those whose spiritual stature would enable them to receive the mysteries of godliness. These murmurings, as with all those that are forthcoming from rebellious people, were met "by a stronger, fuller, clearer declaration of the very truth which they rejected." (Farrar, p. 318.) To their seething sayings Jesus responded:

Murmur not among yourselves. No man can come unto me, except he doeth the will of my Father who hath sent me. And this is the will of him who hath sent me, that ye receive the Son; for the Father beareth record of him; and he who receiveth the testimony, and doeth the will of him who sent me, I will raise up in the resurrection of the just.

Again the witness borne is plain, clear, and without ambiguity. He is the Son of God, and he so certifies, both in metaphors that their Jewish training permits them to understand, and in plain words that their Jewish disbelief will not let them misunderstand. He continues:

It is written in the prophets, And they shall be all taught of God. Every man therefore that hath heard, and hath learned of the Father, cometh unto me.

'But ye receive not my Father, and shall not be found in his kingdom, for no man can receive the Father except he first receive the Son whom the Father hath sent. And ye shall be condemned by your own prophets, for they have written of the righteous, And they shall all be taught by God. Now ye are not taught by God, neither do ye know him, nor his truths, nor his laws, for ye receive not him whom the Father hath sent into the world. Every man therefore that heareth and believeth the words of the Son shall thereby come unto the Father also, and such shall be taught by the Holy Spirit sent forth from God to bear record of the Father and the Son.'

Not that any man hath seen the Father, save he which is of God, he hath seen the Father.

'Think not because the prophets have written of the righteous, And they shall all be taught of God, that ye shall see him or be taught by him, except ye repent and believe in the Son. For no man shall see the Father except the Son and he to whom the Son shall reveal him; yea, only those who are born of God shall see the Father, for no others can enter his presence.'

Verily, verily, I say unto you, He that believeth on me hath everlasting life.

'Solemnly and soberly I say unto you, He that believeth in me as the very Son of God, and who receiveth my gospel, obeying all the laws and ordinances thereof, and who endureth in righteousness and truth unto the end, behold, he shall have everlasting life, which is exaltation in my Father's kingdom.' (*Commentary* 1:356.)

Eating His Flesh and Drinking His Blood
(John 6:48-59; JST, John 6:48-50, 54-55)

We come now to the crowning teaching of the sermon on the bread of life, which is, that men are saved by eating the flesh and drinking the blood of the Son of God. With this proclamation, Jesus pushes back the walls of the synagogue so that his words go forth to all men on all the earth in all ages. His teachings are not alone for a handful of Galileans, not alone for the few million Jews who knew the meaning of the imagery used, but for all men of all nations no matter when or where they live. Eating the flesh and drinking the blood of Him who came down from heaven to shed his blood and mar his flesh is a mystery that can only be understood by the saints as they are enlightened by the power of the Spirit.

At this point in the sermon, Jesus raises the metaphors he is using—those figures of speech which suggest a resemblance of one thing to another—raises them into a gospel similitude. Our Jewish friends of old understood fully the metaphors—"the metaphors which Jesus used had not, to an educated Jew, one-hundredth part of the strangeness which they have to us" (Farrar, p. 319)—but these same Jewish religionists rejected outright the similitude which he offered them. We, on the other hand, with a little training can understand the imagery he uses, and we must accept and apply the similitude if we are to be saved. If we may be permitted to paraphrase the words of Paul relative to the eternal nature of the gospel, we might say: "For unto us was the gospel preached, as well as unto them: but the word preached did not profit them, not being mixed with faith in them that heard it." (Heb. 4:2.) And so Jesus continues:

> *I am that bread of life. This is the bread which cometh down from heaven, that a man may eat thereof; and not die. Your fathers did eat manna in the wilderness, and are dead.*
>
> *I am the living bread which came down from heaven: if any man eat of this bread, he shall live for ever: and the bread that I will give is my flesh, which I will give for the life of the world.*

The bread of life, of life eternal, living bread, the bread which came down from heaven—such is the language he uses to describe himself; and since his body is one of flesh and blood, to eat the heavensent bread, men must eat his flesh, the flesh he "will give for the life of the world," the flesh to be broken in his infinite and eternal atoning sacrifice. Knowing what Jesus' words meant but being wholly unable to understand how they applied to salvation and to the works they must do to gain eternal life, the Jews "strove among themselves, saying, How can this man give us his flesh to eat?" Then Jesus said:

> *Verily, verily, I say unto you, Except ye eat the flesh of the Son of man, and drink his blood, ye have no life in you.*
>
> *Whoso eateth my flesh, and drinketh my blood, hath eternal life; and I will raise him up in the resurrection of the just at the last day. For my flesh is meat indeed, and my blood is drink indeed.*

"To eat the flesh and drink the blood of the Son of God is, first, to accept him in the most literal and full sense, with no reservation whatever, as the personal offspring in the flesh of the Eternal Father; and, secondly, it is to keep the commandments of the Son by accepting his gospel, joining his Church, and enduring in obedience and righteousness unto the end. Those who by this course eat his flesh and drink his blood shall have eternal life, meaning exaltation in the highest heaven of the celestial world. Speaking of ancient Israel, for instance, Paul says: *They 'did all eat the same spiritual meat; And did all drink the same spiritual drink: for they drank of that spiritual Rock that followed them: and that Rock was Christ.'* (1 Cor. 10:3-4.)

"In the waters of baptism the saints take upon themselves the name of Christ (that is, they accept him fully and completely as the Son of God and the Savior of men), and they then covenant to keep his commandments and obey his laws. (Mosiah 18:7-10.) To keep his saints in constant remembrance of their obligation to accept and obey him—or in other words, to eat his flesh and drink his blood—the Lord has given them the sacramental ordinance. This ordinance, performed in remembrance of his broken flesh and spilled blood, is the means provided for men, formally and repeatedly, to assert their belief in the divinity of

Christ, and to affirm their determination to serve him and keep his commandments; or, in other words, in this ordinance—in a spiritual, but not a literal sense—men eat his flesh and drink his blood. Hence, after instituting the sacramental ordinance among the Nephites, Jesus commanded: 'Ye shall not suffer any one knowingly to partake of my flesh and blood unworthily, when ye shall minister it; For whoso eateth and drinketh my flesh and blood unworthily eateth and drinketh damnation to his soul; therefore if ye know that a man is unworthy to eat and drink of my flesh and blood ye shall forbid him.' (3 Ne. 18:28-29.)" (*Commentary* 1:358-59.)

And then finally:

He that eateth my flesh, and drinketh my blood, dwelleth in me, and I in him.

As the living Father hath sent me, and I live by the Father: so he that eateth me, even he shall live by me.

This is the bread which came down from heaven: not as your fathers did eat manna, and are dead: he that eateth of this bread shall live for ever.

The message is now delivered to the Jews and to us. The meaning is clear; the doctrine is strong; the effects of the teaching—either belief or disbelief; obedience or disobedience; eternal life or eternal death—such are now in the hands of those who have heard the message. And that the message may live anew in our hearts, we are commanded to go to the house of prayer on the Lord's day and there partake of the sacramental emblems, offered to us in similitude of the spilt blood and broken flesh of Him whose blood we must drink and whose flesh we must eat, if we are to be his and have life with him as he has life with his Father.

Jesus Winnows the Grain
(John 6:60-71; JST, John 6:65)

"One mightier than I cometh," proclaimed the blessed Baptist. 'He comes to baptize with fire and confer the unspeakable gift of the Holy Ghost; to take away the sins of the world; to save and exalt the sons of men! He comes to preach the gospel to the poor; to proclaim liberty to the captives, and the opening of the prison doors to them that are bound! He comes to be lifted up upon the cross, and, even as he has been lifted up of men, to draw all men to him on conditions of repentance! He comes to seek that which is lost and to save all those who will believe his words and live his law.'

"One mightier than I cometh," is the divine word of our Lord's Elias. 'He comes not to condemn the world, but that the world through him might be saved. His reward is with him and his work before him. He is the Savior of all men, especially of those who believe; and all who believe in him, who feast upon his words, who keep his commandments—who eat his flesh and drink his blood—shall have eternal life.'

But he cannot save those who believe and obey without also damning those who disbelieve and disobey. If men are freed from sin and saved from eternal torment by obedience to his word, on the one hand, they are also left in the bondage of sin—bound by the chains of hell—by disobedience to his law, on the other. If they put off the natural man and become clean by the power of the Holy Ghost, they also remain carnal, sensual, and devilish if that sanctifying power never enters their souls. And so, though he came to save, with all the righteous being rewarded, the effect of his coming is that the wicked shall be damned because they are not saved.

And so: "One mightier than I cometh," saith the Baptist, "Whose fan is in his hand, and he will throughly purge his floor, and will gather the wheat into his garner; but the chaff he will burn with fire unquenchable." (Luke 3:16-17.)

The Coming One—Jesus, our Blessed Lord—has now come; and in this sermon on the bread of life, as never before in his ministry, he has taken the winnowing fan of judgment in his hand to blow the chaff from the wheat. He is sifting out the hearts of men before his judgment seat. The eternal harvest has begun and shall not cease until the threshing floor of the world is thoroughly purged, with every straw of chaff blown away, leaving only the wheat to be garnered into a heavenly granary. And the chaff he will burn with fire unquenchable! So prophesied the Baptist, and the fulfillment is a matter of record this day in Capernaum.

"The Baptist had spoken of the fan in the hand of his great successor: this discourse was the realization of the figure. Those who had hoped to find a popular political leader in Him saw their dreams melt away: those who had no true sympathy for His life and words had an excuse for leaving Him. None who were not bound to Him by sincere loyalty and devotion had any longer a motive for following Him. Fierce patriotism burning for insurrection, mean self-interest seeking worldly advantage, and vulgar curiosity craving excitement, were equally disappointed. It was the first vivid instance of 'the offence of the Cross'—henceforth to become the special stumbling-block of the nation.

"The wishes and hopes of the crowds who had called themselves disciples had proved self-deceptions. They expected from the Messiah quite other favors than the identity of spiritual nature symbolized by the eating of His flesh and drinking His blood. The bloody death implied in the metaphor was in direct contradiction to all their ideas. A lowly and suffering Messiah thus unmistakably set before them was revolting to their national pride and gross material tastes. 'We have heard out of the law,' said some, a little later, 'that the Christ abideth for ever, and how sayest thou the Son of man must be "lifted up"—that is, crucified?' 'That be far from Thee, Lord: this shall not be unto Thee,' said even Peter almost at the last, when he heard from his Master's lips of the Cross, so near at hand.

"The Messiah of popular conception would use force to establish His kingdom, but Jesus, while claiming the Messiahship, spoke only of self-sacrifice. Outward glory and material wealth were the national dream: he spoke only of inward purity. If He would not head them with Almighty power, to get Judea for the Jews, they would not have Him. Their idea of the kingdom of God was the exact opposite of His." (Geikie, p. 520.)

"There is a teaching which is, and is intended to be, not only instructive but probationary; of which the immediate purpose is not only to *teach*, but to *test*. Such had been the object of this memorable discourse. To comprehend it rightly required an effort not only of the understanding, but also of the will. It was *meant* to put an end to the merely selfish hopes of that 'rabble of obtrusive chiliasts' whose irreverent devotion was a mere cloak for worldliness; it was *meant* also to place before the Jewish authorities words which they were too full of hatred and materialism to understand. But its sifting power went deeper than this. Some even of the disciples found the saying harsh and repulsive." (Farrar, p. 321.)

"This is an hard saying; who can hear it?" said the disciples. 'Must we indeed forsake the law of Moses—which the Rabbis say is the bread which came down from heaven—and center all our hope of salvation in this One Man? Is he alone to replace all of the teachings and ordinances of our fathers? Must we forsake the whole past, feast upon his words, eat his flesh and drink his blood to gain eternal life? Is there no other way?'

Knowing "in himself that his disciples murmured" at his teachings, Jesus said: "Doth this offend you?" And offend them it did, for even they—even those who believed he was more than a man; who believed he was sent of the Father to teach truth and perform miracles; who believed that he was the One of whom Moses and the prophets had spoken—even they had not yet purged themselves of all their old Jewish notions about a temporal Messiah. Even they—receiving truth line upon line, precept upon precept, here a little and there a little, as all men must—even they were not prepared to turn away from Moses and the law and believe that salvation came in the person of the one who now invited them to eat his flesh and drink his blood.

Jesus' reaction to their unbelief—their lack of full conversion—was normal and what we have come to expect of him. He reaffirmed the truth of his sayings—there must be no wavering or doubt in any believer's mind—and spoke of even greater witnesses that were yet to come.

> *What and if ye shall see the Son of man ascend up where he was before?*

'If ye cannot believe my sayings that I am the living Bread which came down from heaven to give life to men, what will ye think when ye see me ascend up into heaven to sit on the right hand of my Father and reign with almighty power forever?'

> *It is the spirit that quickeneth; the flesh profiteth nothing: the words that I speak unto you, they are spirit, and they are life. But there are some of you that believe not.*

'All these things which I have spoken unto you are spiritual and lead to eternal life, and they can only be understood by those who are spiritually enlightened. The Spirit must quicken your understanding if you are to comprehend the things of God. No man by his own intellect and reason can understand the things of the Spirit; the wisdom of the world, standing alone, profiteth nothing in comprehending the things of God. And there are some among you who rely on your own wisdom rather than the whisperings of the Spirit, and as a consequence some of you believe not my words.' (*Commentary* 1:362.)

At this point John, in whose writings alone are all these deep and wondrous sayings preserved, says by way of explanation: "For Jesus knew from the beginning who they were that believed not, and who should betray him." Jesus continues:

> *Therefore said I unto you, that no man can come unto me, except he doeth the will of my Father who hath sent me.*

'And he said, It was for this reason that I said unto you, that no man can come unto me, except he doeth the will of my Father who hath sent me, for only those who do the will of my Father by keeping the commandments can receive the Spirit which shall bear record to them that all things which I have said about myself are true.' (*Commentary* 1:362.)

"From that time many of his disciples went back, and walked no more with him." The teaching which was intended to be not only instructive but also probationary had served its purpose. "By the simple expedient of teaching strong doctrine to the hosts who followed him, Jesus was able to separate the chaff from the wheat and choose out those who were worthy of membership in his earthly kingdom. . . . Unable to believe and accept his strong and plain assertions about eating his flesh and drinking his blood, even many classified as disciples fell away. And this process of sifting, trial, and testing was to continue with increasing intensity for the final climactic year of his mortal ministry." (*Commentary* 1:361.)

No doubt among the disciples who fell away were both believing investigators and those who had committed themselves by covenant, made in the waters of baptism, to love and serve him all their days. The test of strong doctrine is given to truth seekers both before and after they enter the Church. "This testing and sifting process has ever been part of the Lord's system. Men have been placed on earth to be tried and tested, 'to see if they will do all things whatsoever the Lord their God shall command them.' (Abr. 3:25.) After they accept the gospel and join the Church, this testing process continues, indeed, is often intensified. 'I have decreed in my heart, saith the Lord, that I will prove you in all things, whether you will abide in my covenant, even unto death, that you may be found worthy. For if ye will not abide in my covenant ye are not worthy of me.' (D&C 98:14-15.)" (*Commentary* 1:361.)[6]

"And so this was the great crisis in the History of the Christ. We have traced the gradual growth and development of the popular movement, till the murder of the Baptist stirred popular feeling to its inmost depth. With his death it seemed as if the Messianic hope, awakened by his preaching and testimony to Christ, were fading from view. It was a terrible disappointment, not easily borne. Now must it be decided, whether Jesus was really the Messiah. His Works, notwithstanding what the Pharisees said, seemed to prove it. Then let it appear; let it come, stroke upon stroke—each louder and more effective than the other—till the land rang with the shout of victory and the world itself re-echoed it. And so it seemed. That miraculous feeding—that wilderness cry of Hosanna to the Galilean King-Messiah from the thousands of Galilean voices—what were they but its beginning?

"All the greater was the disappointment: first, in the repression of the movement—so to speak, the retreat of the Messiah, His voluntary abdication, rather, His defeat; then, next day [or shortly thereafter, as we shall set forth in chapter 59], the incongruousness of a King, Whose few unlearned followers, in their ignorance and un-Jewish neglect of most sacred ordinances, outraged every Jewish feeling, and whose conduct was even vindicated by their Master in a general attack on all traditionalism, that basis of Judaism—as it might be represented, to the contempt of religion and even of common truthfulness in the denunciation of solemn vows! This was not the Messiah Whom the many—nay, Whom almost any—would own.

"Here, then, we are at the parting of the two ways; and, just because it was the hour of decision, did Christ so clearly set forth the highest truths concerning Himself, in opposition to the views which the multitude entertained about the Messiah." (Edersheim 2:35-36.)

"Then said Jesus unto the twelve, Will ye also go away? Then Simon Peter answered him, Lord, to whom shall we go? thou hast the words of eternal life. And we believe and are sure that thou art that Christ, the Son of the living God."

Peter knew; the Twelve knew (Judas only, perhaps, excepted); Mary Magdalene, who is identified by name as a traveling companion of Jesus and the Twelve, knew; many other disciples, both men and women, knew—and their knowledge came by revelation from the Holy Spirit of God. Only those who have the testimony of Jesus, which is the spirit of prophecy; only those who are in tune with the Infinite by the power of the Spirit; only those whose souls are alive with the light and truth of heaven, who hunger and thirst after righteousness, who love the Lord and keep his commandments—these only can withstand the buffetings and trials of life and drink in the strong doctrine that saves souls.

"Thou hast the words of eternal life." The words of light and truth which chart the course and mark the way—these come from Christ. These words, and these only, lead to eternal life in his Father's kingdom. Only those—having opportunity so to do—who believe the words of eternal life in this world shall gain eternal glory in the world to come.

"We believe and are sure." 'Our testimony comes by the power of the Spirit. Doubt and uncertainty are as foreign to us as the gibberish of alien tongues. The voice of the Spirit has spoken to our spirits. We are sure. There is absolute certainty in our souls.'

"Thou art that Christ, the Son of the living God." 'Whatever notions the dissembling multitude may have about a Messiah and Deliverer who wears a coat of armor and wields a sword of vengeance; whatever the hungering hosts may believe as to a Messiah who will feed us daily from heaven as our fathers were fed; however others may choose to follow the traditions of the past and adhere to the letter of a dead law, rather than believe that salvation comes by you—no matter what others say or do, to us thou art "that Christ" who of old was promised, who is "the Son of the living God."'

"Lord, to whom shall we go?" How well Peter spoke! Where else can true disciples ever go to find peace in this life and a hope of eternal life in the world to come? The truth is with the saints; the gospel saves; light and revelation are

shed forth upon the Lord's people. Where can a dissembling disciple go but to darkness and death and damnation?

"It is thus, also, that many of us, whose thoughts may have been sorely tossed, and whose foundations terribly assailed, may have found our first resting-place in the assured, unassailable spiritual experience of the past. Whither can we go for Words of Eternal Life, if not to Christ? If He fails us, then all hope of the Eternal is gone. But He *has* the Words of Eternal life—and we believed when they first came to us; nay, we know that He is the Holy One of God. And this conveys all that faith needs for further learning. The rest will He show, when He is transfigured in our sight." (Edersheim 2:36.)

Then, as a sad denouement to a sermon that had severed the sunshine disciples and the fair-weather friends from those who were steeled to withstand the storms of life, Jesus said: "Have not I chosen you twelve, and one of you is a devil?" And then our apostolic author adds: "He spake of Judas Iscariot the son of Simon: for he it was that should betray him, being one of the twelve."

From this hour our Lord's life was charted in the course leading to the cross. Heretofore the common people had heard him gladly, however much their teachers and rulers had assailed his teachings and ridiculed his miracles. Now he was sifting out the hearts of men—believers and unbelievers alike—and most were failing the test. "The greater the popular expectancy and disappointment had been, the greater the reaction and the enmity that followed. The hour of decision was past, and the hand on the dial pointed to the hour of His Death." (Edersheim 2:36.)

NOTES

1. Nephi's related statement is, "feasting upon the word of Christ," such being the bread from heaven of which all men must eat if they are to hear the heavenly voice acclaim: "Ye shall have eternal life." (2 Ne. 31:20.)

2. These words—"him hath God the Father sealed"—"which seem almost inexplicable in this connection," as Edersheim notes, "become clear when we remember that this was a well-known Jewish expression. According to the Rabbis, 'the seal of God was *Truth*.' . . . Thus the words of Christ would convey to His hearers that for the real meat, which would

endure to eternal life—for the better Messianic banquet—they must come to Him, because God had impressed upon Him His own seal of truth, and so authenticated His Teaching and Mission." (Edersheim 2:28-29.)

3. "The idea of eating, as a metaphor for receiving spiritual benefit, was familiar to Christ's hearers, and was as readily understood as our expressions of 'devouring a book,' or 'drinking in' instruction. In Isaiah 3:1, the words 'the whole stay of bread,' were explained by the Rabbis as referring to their own teaching, and they laid it down as a rule, that wherever, in Ecclesiastes, allusion was made to food or drink, it meant study of the Law, and the practice of good works. It was a saying among them—'In the time of the Messiah the Israelites will be fed by Him.' Nothing was more common in the schools and synagogues than the phrases of eating and drinking, in a metaphorical sense. 'Messiah is not likely to come to Israel,' said Hillel, 'for they have already eaten Him'—that is, greedily received His words—'in the days of Hezekiah.' A current conventionalism in the synagogues was that the just would 'eat the Shekinah.' It was peculiar to the Jews to be taught in such metaphorical language. Their Rabbis never spoke in plain words." (Geikie, p. 519.)

4. "Moses had given them manna from heaven; Jesus as yet—they hinted—had only given them barley-loaves of earth. But if He were the true Messiah, was He not, according to all the legends of their nation, to enrich and crown them, and to banquet them on pomegranates from Eden, and 'a vineyard of red wine,' and upon the flesh of Behemoth and Leviathan, and the great bird Bar Juchne?" (Farrar, p. 317.)

5. "Redeemer of Israel," *Hymns*, no. 195.

6. "In this dispensation, the promulgation of the law of plural marriage had an effect similar to the presentation of the doctrine of the Bread of Life in the meridian dispensation. Opposition from without the Church increased, while some unstable members of the kingdom itself found themselves unable to accept the fulness of the revealed program of the Lord. There were many important reasons why the Lord revealed the doctrine of plurality of wives. But if plural marriage had served no other purpose than to sift the chaff from the wheat, than to keep the unstable and semi-faithful people from the fulness of gospel blessings, it would have been more than justified." (*Commentary* 1:361-62.)

Chapter 59

THE DISCOURSE UPON CLEANLINESS

The Jews were a stiffnecked people; . . .
because of their blindness, which blindness came
by looking beyond the mark, they must needs fall.
(Jacob 4:14.)

Because of priestcrafts and iniquities,
they at Jerusalem will stiffen their necks
against him, that he be crucified.
(2 Ne. 10:5.)

Priestcrafts are that men preach
and set themselves up
for a light unto the world,
that they may get gain and praise of the world;
but they seek not the welfare of Zion.
(2 Ne. 26:29.)

"What Concord Hath Christ with Belial?"[1]

It is the hour of the third Passover—the third Passover
time during the ministry of the Mortal Messiah when all the
sons of the law are commanded to go up to Jerusalem and
appear before the Lord in his holy house.

It is the set time for all Israel to eat a paschal lamb, every family by itself apart—in remembrance of their deliverance from the bondage of Egypt; as a token that they have forsaken the world and chosen to live apart from other nations, as a people dedicated to the service of Jehovah; and in similitude of the promised sacrifice of the Lamb of God who cometh to take away the sins of the world.

It is the appointed time for the chosen people to renew their covenants with Jehovah, to pledge anew their allegiance to the God of their fathers, and to step forth in a newness of life. Out of these eight days—the days of the Feast of the Passover and of the Feast of Unleavened Bread—will come a renewed determination to honor Moses and keep his law; and with this refurbishing of the Israelite way of life will come also a reborn determination to oppose every force or person that challenges their law and threatens their traditions.

There is no indication that Jesus went from Capernaum to Jerusalem with the zealous throngs of Galilean pilgrims. Apparently he did not because it was a time when the Jews sought to kill him. Nor can we tell whether the Twelve took leave of the Master or not, whether they went to the City of the Great King to keep the not-yet-fulfilled law of Moses. But this much seems clear: After this Passover the rulers from Jerusalem—who heretofore had appointed spies and informers to dog his every footstep and overhear his every word—these priest-ridden rulers now sent new delegations to spy and to confront and to contend. Their zeal to oppose that which threatened their craft had been reborn in the emotion and worship at the Passover.

And so it is also an hour of sorrow and darkness—an hour in which the sifting process begun with the sermon on the bread of life will continue, will, indeed, rise in a mighty crescendo until, a year hence, a chorus of cries will chant "Crucify him, crucify him," and will contaminate forever the land and the people.

It is also an hour of crises, of the parting of the ways, of the division of a people. Heretofore virulence and hatred have been somewhat limited; only the rulers of the people have thirsted for his blood. Now the spirit of darkness and death is beginning to brood over whole cities and areas; whole multitudes are infected with the virus of apostasy and persecution and destruction. It is an hour when we shall see tribes and congregations, blinded by priestcrafts and looking beyond the mark, join with their rulers to oppose the Cause of truth and righteousness.

"*Looking beyond the mark!*" Such was the sin of the whole nation. Preserved from Egyptian bondage by the miracle at the Red Sea; born as a people during forty years of wilderness wanderings; entering their promised land when Joshua led them over Jordan; serving Jehovah as directed by their judges and prophets, Israel, the chosen seed, had been bathed in the light and revelation of heaven. They once knew the will of Jehovah; they once had the law of Moses in all its beauty and perfection; they once walked as pleased their Maker. But now—after the Babylonian captivity; after the long night of alien domination; after a long period without revelation; after an apostate era in which traditions and legends had become more important than the eternal word recorded in their scriptures—now, after such a period, they were looking beyond the mark. They had added to the ancient law a maze of tradition and legend. They had created ordinances and performances and rituals that had no foundation in revealed writ. They were doing more than need be done in the way of rituals and performances. Like Nadab and Abihu they were offering strange fires upon their altars. They were looking beyond the mark; salvation did not come in the way they supposed; it was not the outgrowth of their ritualistic absurdities; it came in a much easier and simpler way.

"I press toward the mark," Paul says, "for the prize of the high calling of God in Christ Jesus." (Philip. 3:14.) That too was all that the Jews needed to do; they must center their affection on the Messiah who ministered among them, not on the myriad ordinances and performances that had been added to what Moses gave them.

"Priestcrafts and iniquities!" These were at the root of their problem. Their rulers had developed an oral law that surpassed in importance the word of Jehovah given on Sinai; traditions became more important than truth; and personal righteousness faded away. It was an hour when men loved darkness rather than light because their deeds were evil. Priestcrafts and iniquities! It was an hour of persecution and rebellion, of darkness and dire days ahead.

Persecution is one of the chief weapons in the hands of false priests; they use it to preserve their false religions. Truth stands on its own; error must be defended by the sword. False ministers fear the truth because by it their crafts are in danger. They practice priestcrafts to get gain and the praise of the world, neither of which will be theirs if true religion sweeps them into a deserved oblivion. It is with them as it was with Demetrius, the silversmith, who made silver shrines for the worship of Diana. When Paul preached the gospel in Ephesus, "saying that they be no gods, which are made with hands," Demetrius responded by proclaiming that by such teaching, "not only this our craft is in danger to be set at nought; but also that the temple of the great goddess Diana should be despised, and her magnificence should be destroyed, whom all Asia and the world worshippeth." (Acts 19:21-41.) Similarly, if Jesus' new and revolutionary doctrines prevail, what would become of the priests and Levites? If publicans and fishermen become the new preachers, what of the scribes and Rabbis?

Persecutors can always justify—in their own minds— their own destructive courses. Those who raised their voices against Jesus; who testified falsely of his teachings; who sought to destroy his influence with the people—all such were doing what seemed right to them in their own minds. Nearly all propositions can be sustained to some extent or other, with arguments and reasons, when intellectuality and not spirituality is the governing standard.

With reference to Jesus the question, then, is not simply "Why was he persecuted?"—for the basic answer to that is the evil that dwelt in the hearts of the people—but, "How did they rationalize their conduct? What intellectual reasons did they give to make it seem that what they were doing was the will of him whom they supposed they worshipped?" From the Jewish standpoint, Jesus was persecuted—and finally slain—for what were, to them, three perfectly valid reasons:

1. *They said, falsely, that he was a sinner.*

This is, in fact, a perfectly valid premise, not for persecution but at least for rejection. Nothing justifies persecution; but if he were a sinner, he could not be the Messiah, the Holy One of Israel, the one sent of God to deliver his people. The Messianic prophecies foretold of a Messiah in whose mouth there would be no deceit; who would bring truth and light and gospel knowledge to his people; who would qualify as a light and a guide to all men.[2] If Jesus was a deceiver; if he was misleading the people; if his doctrine would damn rather than save—then he must be unmasked; his lies must be revealed; his iniquities must be made manifest. And it was then the duty of the Sanhedrin to bring his hidden evils and his false doctrines to light.

There is no question about the concept that the Messiah would rise above carnal things and not wallow in the mire of iniquity. The issue at hand was whether Jesus himself was a sinner or not. One day soon, facing this problem squarely, and aware of his own sinless life, he will issue the challenge, "Which of you convinceth me of sin?" (John 8:46.) At this point we need only recount why they contended he was a sinner, and the mere recitation of their reasons will suffice for us—though, in fairness, we must admit, not for them—to show the shallow and baseless nature of their reasoning.

There were some minor complaints that he was a glutton and a winebibber, because he ate and drank as others did; there was the charge that he and his disciples did not abide by the Pharisaic law of the fast; and there was considerable murmuring because he consorted with publicans and sinners, eating with them in their banquets, calling a prominent publican as one of the Twelve, and permitting a fallen woman to anoint his feet with oil. But all of this was of no great moment, and certainly would not suffice to raise a public hue and cry against him.

There were, however, two major activities that incensed and enraged the rulers of the people and the molders of public opinion. Both of these were violations of their traditions—not of any basic laws imposed by Deity, but the traditions of the elders—and both, in the eyes of the people, warranted the death penalty. One was his repeated Sabbath violations, as they supposed, and the other was the matter of eating with unwashen hands and the many formalities related thereto.

As to his Sabbath violations, and those of the disciples, we have already noted some of the traditions involved and have seen the discomfiture of his detractors when they challenged his conduct and that of his disciples. While passing through a field of corn on the Sabbath, the disciples plucked some ripened ears, rubbed them in their hands, and blew away the chaff. These acts—considered to be both reaping and threshing—were so criminally offensive and of such a magnitude in Jewish eyes as to call for the death penalty. Jesus defended his disciples by citing the case of David eating the shewbread and announcing that "the sabbath was made for man, and not man for the sabbath," and that the "Son of man is Lord even of the sabbath." (Mark 2:27-28.)

Many times Jesus himself sought occasion to perform miraculous healings on their holy day, as when, at the second Passover, he healed the impotent man at the pool of Bethesda, an act that so enraged the Jews that they sought to kill him; or, as on the occasion in the Galilean synagogue when the question was asked: "Is it lawful to heal on the sabbath days?" and he responded by asking, "Is it lawful to do good on the sabbath days, or to do evil? to save life, or to kill?" and by then saying to a man with a withered hand, "Stretch forth thine hand. And he stretched it out: and his hand was restored whole as the other." (Mark 3:2, 4-5.) And again the Pharisees sought how they might destroy him. In these and other like incidents, as we have seen, it was the violation of the Rabbi-imposed traditions relative to the Sabbath that brought down the wrath of Jewry upon the head of Jesus.

As to the matters of eating with unwashen hands and of avoiding responsibility for parental care by saying, "It is corban," we are about to see the depths to which ritualistic religion can sink. And this time we shall also see an open, almost defiant, break with the whole body of ritualistic absurdities imposed in the name of tradition.

2. *They said, falsely, that he performed his miracles by the power of Beelzebub—nay, more, that he was the Incarnation of Satan.*

"They accounted for the miracles of Christ as wrought by the power of Satan, whose special representative—almost incarnation—they declared Jesus to be. This would not only turn the evidential force of these signs into an argument against Christ, but vindicate the resistance of the Pharisees to His claims." (Edersheim 2:8.) But, as we have also seen, Satan cannot cast out Satan, for a house divided against itself will fall, and the imputation of satanic power still leaves all men with the need to decide whether the Holy Ghost or Satan spake by Jesus' mouth. That each person must determine this for himself is what life is all about; such is the very nature of this probationary estate.

3. *They said, falsely, that he was guilty of blasphemy in claiming equality with God; in testifying that he was the Son of the living God; in teaching that he was God.*

As to this crowning charge we shall have more, much more, to say hereafter. It lies at the heart and core of revealed religion. If our witness is true that he is God's Almighty Son, then salvation is in Christ and his is the only name given under heaven whereby salvation comes. If our witness—and his—is false, and thus blasphemous, then Christianity is a monstrous fraud and fallen man remains unredeemed. If our witness is false, man is still in his sins; there is no reconciliation with God; and the man sick of the palsy to whom he said, "Son, be of good cheer; thy sins be forgiven thee" (Matt. 9:2), remains as sin-stained as he ever was; and, for that matter, if our witness is false, this paralytic did not arise, take up his bed, and go to his own house.

For the present we need only observe that this "last charge against Jesus, which finally decided the action of the Council, could only be fully made at the close of His career. It might be formulated so as to meet the views of either the Pharisees or Sadducees. To the former it might be presented as a blasphemous claim to equality with God—the Very Son of the Living God. To the Sadducees it would appear as a movement on the part of a most dangerous enthusiast—if honest and self-deceived, all the more dangerous; one of those pseudo-Messiahs who led away the ignorant, superstitious, and excitable people; and which, if unchecked, would result in persecutions and terrible vengeance by the Romans, and in loss of the last remnants of their national independence." (Edersheim 2:8-9.)

And so, as we attune our ears to hear the discourse on cleanliness, we are reminded that Jesus has already begun the harvesting process. It started with the sermon on the bread of life. He is winnowing the grain, sifting the chaff from the wheat, garnering the wheat into the granaries of the Lord, and preparing the chaff for fire unquenchable. In the discourse on cleanliness he will identify the chaff, and, sorrowfully, it will consist of the generality of the people. But, joyfully, the harvested wheat, now free from husks and chaff, shall soon go on to the safety and security of the eternal granaries.

Will not Jesus on this day say to the faithful, as it were: "Be ye not unequally yoked together with unbelievers: for what fellowship hath righteousness with unrighteousness? and what communion hath light with darkness? And what concord hath Christ with Belial? or what part hath he that believeth with an infidel? And what agreement hath the temple of God with idols?" (2 Cor. 6:14-16.) The saints of the living God must come out of Babylon, separate themselves from the world, and be saints indeed. The foundations have long since been laid and it no longer suffices for believing disciples to stand with one foot on the sands of tradition and the other on the rock of revealed truth. The house of the Lord, if it is to stand forever, must be built on the rock of eternal truth and upon no other foundation.

The Ceremonial Washings of Rabbinism
(Mark 7:1-8; JST, Mark 7:4, 7; Matthew 15:1-2, 7-9; JST, Matthew 15:8)

Heretofore—with some inward revulsion—we have seen what the ritualistic robots of Rabbinism did to the Sabbath day. We have seen how they turned a day of freedom and worship and rejoicing into one of Rabbinical rules and restrictions. No longer were the Jews free to worship the Lord their God with a clear conscience on this holy day. Rather, the restrictions were so rigid, the controls so complete, the prohibitions so profuse, that it was as though man had been made for the Sabbath. Their failures on that day— for no man could keep all of the restrictions involved— created a great guilt complex over the whole nation. In some respects—for them—it was providential that the Sabbath came only one day in seven.

Now—again with some inward revulsion—we turn our attention to the ceremonial washings of Rabbinism; to the daily, almost hourly, ritualistic ablutions which alone, as they supposed, kept uncleanness from their doors. Man cannot eat with unwashen hands and be saved; judgment, mercy, and truth are as nothing compared to the Levitical lavings of the body; ceremonial washings are more important than keeping the commandments! So said the Rabbis, and such were the traditions of the elders, as we shall now see.

It is the time of the third Passover—April of A. D. 29—the time when the people are being refreshed spiritually and built up anew in religious zeal. There is not the slightest intimation that Jesus himself went to Jerusalem to appear before the Lord in his holy house, as he had done twice before during his ministry, and as he will do a year hence when he is to be sacrificed as the eternal Paschal Lamb. Whether the Twelve and the inner circle of disciples went by themselves is questionable. The Passover season was one of three festive occasions during the year when every adult male was expected to worship the Lord in the Holy City, but Jesus and his disciples are now openly breaking with the traditions of the past. It is logical to assume they chose not to face the mob spirit that would have confronted them within the hallowed walls of Herod's Temple.

That the Galileans attending the Passover gave firsthand accounts of our Lord's recent teachings and miracles we cannot doubt. His earlier teachings and miracles would have been well known. But now among all the millions of Passover pilgrims word would have soon spread of the feeding of the five thousand, the walking on the water, the healings in the land of Gennesaret, and the sermon on the bread of life. On previous occasions the chief priests and religious leaders had sent deputations to spy and harass. They must do so again. The prior assaults had been based on claims of Sabbath violations and had carried the charge that he cast out devils and performed miracles by the power of Satan. These assaults had failed. Now they would charge those of the New Order with eating when ceremonially unclean.

As to this ceremonial uncleanness, Mark says simply: "For the Pharisees, and all the Jews, except they wash their hands oft, eat not, holding the tradition of the elders. And when they come from the market, except they wash their bodies, they eat not. And many other things there be, which they have received to hold, as the washing of cups, and pots, brasen vessels, and of tables."

As with the restrictions relative to the Sabbath, so with

their ceremonial washings, volumes could be written reciting the policies, procedures, and absurdities involved. We shall, however, simply sample the source material. It will suffice for our purposes to know that failure to comply with these ceremonial washings ranked with apostasy and murder in criminality. Those so offending were deserving of death in the Rabbinical view, and to openly defy and challenge such sacred ceremonies created an impasse and raised an issue that was not subject to mediation. People either kept the traditions of the elders and retained their Jewish standing, or, failing so to do, they joined the degenerate Gentiles and traveled an irreversible course to a heathen hell.

"The law of Moses required purifications in certain cases, but the Rabbis had perverted the spirit of Leviticus in this, as in other things, for they taught that food and drink could not be taken with a good conscience when there was the possibility of ceremonial defilement. If every conceivable precaution had not been taken, the person or the vessel used might have contracted impurity, which would thus be conveyed to the food, and through the food to the body, and by it to the soul. Hence it had been long a custom, and latterly a strict law, that before every meal not only the hands but even the dishes, couches, and tables should be scrupulously washed.

"The legal washing of the hands before eating was especially sacred to the Rabbinist; not to do so was a crime as great as to eat the flesh of swine. 'He who neglects hand-washing,' says the book Sohar, 'deserves to be punished here and hereafter.' 'He is to be destroyed out of the world, for in hand-washing is contained the secret of the ten commandments.' 'He is guilty of death.' 'Three sins bring poverty after them,' says the Mishnah, 'and to slight hand-washing is one.' 'He who eats bread without hand-washing,' says Rabbi Jose, 'is as if he went in to a harlot.' The later Schulchan Aruch, enumerates twenty-six rules for this rite in the morning alone. 'It is better to go four miles to water than to incur guilt by neglecting hand-washing,' says the Talmud. 'He who does not wash his hands after eating,' it says, 'is as bad as a murderer.' The devil Schibta sits on unwashed hands and on the bread. It was a special mark of the Pharisees that 'they ate their daily bread with due purification,' and to neglect doing so was to be despised as unclean. . . .

"The Talmud maintains that 'any one living in the land of Israel, eating his daily food in purification, speaking the Hebrew of the day, and [engaging in] morning and evening praying duly with the phylacteries, is certain that he will eat bread in the kingdom of God.'

"It was laid down that the hands were first to be washed clean. The tips of the ten fingers were then joined and lifted up so that the water ran down to the elbows, then turned down so that it might run off to the ground. Fresh water was poured on them as they were lifted up, and twice again as they hung down. The washing itself was to be done by rubbing the fist of one hand in the hollow of the other. When the hands were washed before eating they must be held upwards; when after it, downwards, but so that the water should not run beyond the knuckles. The vessel used must be held first in the right, then in the left hand; the water was to be poured first on the right, then on the left hand, and at every third time the words repeated, 'Blessed art Thou who hast given us the command to wash the hands.' It was keenly disputed whether the cup of blessing or the hand-washing should come first; whether the towel used should be laid on the table or on the couch; and whether the table was to be cleared before the final washing or after it.

"This anxious trifling over the infinitely little was, however, only part of a system. If a Pharisee proposed to eat common food, it was enough that the hands were washed by water poured on them. Before eating *Terumah*—the holy tithes and the shew-bread—they must be dipped completely in the water, and before the portions of the holy offerings could be tasted, a bath must be taken. Hand-washing before prayer, or touching anything in the morning, was as rigidly observed, for evil spirits might have defiled the hands in the night. To touch the mouth, nose, ear, eyes, or the one hand with the other, before the rite, was to incur the risk of disease in the part touched. The occasions that demanded the observance were countless: it must be done even after cutting the nails, or killing a flea. The more water used, the more piety. 'He who uses abundant water for hand-washing,' says R. Chasda, 'will have abundant riches.' If one had not been out it was enough to pour water on the hands; but one coming in from without needed to plunge his hands into the water, for he knew not what uncleanness might have been near him while in the streets, and this plunging could not be done except in a spot where there were not less than sixty gallons of water.

"The same scrupulous, superstitious minuteness extended to possible defilements of all the household details of daily life. Dishes, hollow or flat, of whatever material, knives, tables, and couches, were constantly subjected to purifications, lest they should have contracted any Levitical defilement by being used by some one unclean." (Geikie, pp. 524-26.)

This digest of a portion of the rules governing ceremonial washings sets the scene and enables us to understand the significance of Mark's account of the confrontation on cleanliness. Scribes and Pharisees came to Jesus from Jerusalem. They had heard how he fed five thousand men with five barley loaves and two small fish, how the whole multitude was filled, how there were twelve baskets of fragments remaining, and how—O horrible thought!—the people had not washed their hands both before and after the miraculously supplied repast. How can this miracle be of God, they reasoned, when He who performed it did not also require the proper ceremonial washings!

And further, as these Judeans now "saw some of his disciples eat bread with defiled, that is to say, with unwashen, hands," as Mark says, "they found fault" yet again. "Why walk not thy disciples according to the tradition of the elders, but eat bread with unwashen hands?" they asked.

Here was an issue on which they were prepared to do battle. Their craft was in danger, and all men knew that ceremonial washings were essential to salvation, and that without them there was naught but sorrow and damnation!

"The traditions of the elders!" Scarcely does Satan have a more persuasive means of leading men from the glorious gospel truths set forth in the scriptures than to supplant and override these eternal verities with oral traditions. It is worthy of note that these scribes and Pharisees knew full well that their rituals and ceremonies grew out of the traditions of their fathers and were not taken from the written word given to Moses, whom they so greatly revered.

"The authority for this endless, mechanical religionism was the commands or 'traditions' of the Fathers, handed down from the days of the Great Synagogue, but ascribed with pious exaggeration to the Almighty, who, it was said, had delivered them orally to Moses on Mount Sinai. Interpretations, expositions, and discussions of all kinds were based, not only on every separate word, or on every letter, but even on every comma and semicolon, to create new laws and observances, and where these were not enough, oral traditions, said to have been delivered by God to Moses on Sinai, were invented to justify new refinements. These 'traditions' were constantly increased, and formed a New Law, which passed from mouth to mouth, and from generation to generation, till, at last, public schools rose for its study and development, of which the most famous were those of Hillel and Schammai, in the generation before Jesus, and even, perhaps, in His early childhood. In His lifetime it was still a fundamental rule that they should not be committed to writing. It was left to Rabbi Judah, the Holy, to commence the collection and formal engrossing of the almost countless fragments of which it consisted, and from his weary labour ultimately rose the huge folios of the Talmud.

"As in the case of the Brahminical theocracy of India, that of Judea attached more importance to the ceremonial precepts of its schools than to the sacred text on which they were based. Wherever Scripture and Tradition seemed opposed, the latter was treated as the higher authority. Pharisaism openly proclaimed this, and set itself, as the Gospel expresses it, in the chair of Moses, displacing the great lawgiver. 'It is a greater offence,' says the Mischnah, 'to teach anything contrary to the voice of the Rabbis, than to contradict Scripture itself. He who says [i.e. speaks] contrary to Scripture, "Is not lawful to wear the Tephillin" '—the little leather boxes containing texts of Scripture, bound, during prayer, on the forehead and on the arm—'is not to be punished as a troubler. But he who says there should be five divisions in the Totaphoth'—another name for the Tephillin, or phylacteries—'and thus teaches differently from the Rabbis, is guilty.' 'He who expounds the Scriptures in opposition to the Tradition,' says R. Eleazar, 'has no share in the world to come.' The mass of Rabbinical prescriptions—not the Scripture—was regarded as the basis of religion, 'for the Covenant of God was declared to have been made with Israel on account of the oral Law, as it is written, "After the tenor of these words I have made a covenant with thee and with Israel." [Ex. 34:27.] For God knew that, in after ages, Israel would be carried away among strange people, who would copy off the written Law, and therefore, he gave them the oral Law, that his will might be kept secret among themselves.' Those who gave themselves to the knowledge of the Traditions 'saw a great light,' for God enlightened their eyes, and showed them how they ought to act in relation to lawful and unlawful things, clean and unclean, which are not told thus fully and clearly in Scripture. It was, perhaps, good to give one's self to the reading of the Scripture, but he who reads diligently the Traditions receives a reward from God, and he who gives himself to the Commentaries on these traditions has the greatest reward of all. 'The Bible was like water, the Traditions like wine, the Commentaries on them like spiced wine.' 'My son,' says the Talmud, 'give more heed to the words of the Rabbis than to the words of the Law.' So exactly alike is Ultramontanism in every age, and in all religions!" (Geikie, pp. 526-27.)[3]

There is and can be only one answer to the charge that he and his disciples keep not "the tradition of the elders" because they "eat bread with unwashen hands." It is: 'The tradition is false; it is not of God; it leads men to destruction. I and my disciples are guiltless in this thing, but your religion is man made, and your worship is in vain. Repent or be damned.' Taking the offensive, Jesus, accordingly, says:

Well hath Esaias prophesied of you hypocrites, as it is written, This people honoureth me with their lips, but their heart is far from me.

Howbeit, in vain do they worship me, teaching the doctrines and commandments of men.

For laying aside the commandment of God, ye hold the tradition of men, as the washing of pots and cups: and many other such like things ye do.

"It Is Corban"
(Mark 7:9-13, 19; JST, Mark 7:9-13; Matthew 15:3-6; JST, Matthew 15:4-5)

Our Lord's younger brother—James, a son of Joseph and Mary; a devout Jew during Jesus' lifetime; later a converted Christian and an apostle of Him whose brother he was—this wise and good man, not many years hence, will write these words: "Pure religion and undefiled before God and the Father is this, To visit the fatherless and widows in their affliction, and to keep himself unspotted from the world." (James 1:27.)

Pure religion! It is to put into living operation all the principles of eternal truth that dwell in the heart of the Great Jehovah. As an abstract principle faith is nothing; it is of no more worth than an abstract principle of mathematics. But faith in the heart of a man—a living, vibrant faith—can raise the dead, create worlds, and save souls. Love is nothing until it operates in the lives of men. Religion has saving power only when it dwells in a human heart, when i changes a human soul. Pure religion is to operate and use the eternal truths that flow from the Author of truth.

Pure religion revolves around, centers in, and operates primarily through the family unit. The whole purpose o revealed religion is to enable men to create for themselves eternal family units patterned after the family of God the Eternal Father. This life is the time appointed during which we learn how to live in the family unit with all the love and affection that must exist in an eternal family unit. And so Je hovah says to his people: "Honour thy father and thy mother: that thy days may be long upon the land which the Lord thy God giveth thee." (Ex. 20:12.)[5] And as though this were not enough, the further decree comes: "And he that curseth [revileth] his father, or his mother, shall surely be pu to death." (Ex. 21:17; Lev. 20:9.)

How do we honor our parents? By emulating their righteous lives; by walking in the light as they are in the light; by keeping the faith and being true and steadfast as they are. And further, by caring for their temporal and physical needs in their aging years. We have no better illus tration of the operation of this principle than is shown forth by the dying words of One on a cross who said to a sorrow ing mother, "Woman, behold thy son," and to an intimate friend, "Behold thy mother," with the result that "from that hour that disciple took her unto his own home." (John 19:26-27.)

All these principles pertaining to parental honor and care were known to the Jews; all these things were written in their law; and all these things they chose, by their traditions, no to do. Pure religion was far from them; eternal principles found little good soil in the hearts of those in that day. Thus we hear Jesus say to his scribal antagonists and his Pharisaic enemies:

> *Yea, altogether ye reject the commandment of God that ye may keep your own tradition. Full well is it written of you, by the prophets whom ye have rejected. They*

testified these things of a truth, and their blood shall be upon you.

"By professing to believe in the prophets, while in practice rejecting their teachings, the Jews were in reality rejecting the prophets. Thus, those Jews were placing themselves in the same position which their fathers occupied when those fathers slew the prophets; and so the blood of the prophets would be required at the hands of the Jews and their fathers, for both rejected them. Similarly, some today, by rejecting the teachings of the ancient apostles and prophets, are classifying themselves as people who would have slain the holy men of old, and so the blood of the true martyrs of religion shall be upon them." (*Commentary* 1:368.)

Ye have kept not the ordinances of God; for Moses said, Honor thy father and thy mother; and whoso curseth father or mother, let him die the death of the transgressor, as it is written in your law; but ye keep not the law.

Ye say, If a man shall say to his father or mother, Corban, that is to say, a gift, by whatsoever thou mightest be profited by me, he is of age. And ye suffer him no more to do aught for his father or his mother; making the word of God of none effect through your tradition, which ye have delivered; and many such like things do ye.

This is the picture Jesus is painting: Parents, perhaps aged and decrepit, are hungry, naked, and homeless. They cry out for a crust of bread; they need a homespun robe to cover their nakedness; they have not where to lay their heads during the long cold nights. But they have children— children who are prosperous and well to do; whose fields are fruitful; whose granaries are full; whose flocks graze on a thousand hills. Surely there is enough for all and to spare. But no, the children say: "It is corban." That is: 'We have vowed it to sacred purposes. You, our parents, may go cold and hungry and homeless; our property is not available to help you. We have a great zeal toward the Lord, and our property is vowed to him; and we cannot break our vows.'

Or: 'It is corban; I have vowed that my property shall be as if it were dedicated to sacred purposes, and though I may continue to use it all my life, you shall have none of it because of my vow.'

Or: 'It is corban; I have vowed that "whatsoever thou mightest be profited by" cannot be used for your benefit; that is, I have vowed that my property shall not be used for your support; and it is more important that I keep my vow than that I fulfill my obligation to support my parents. The oral traditions of the elders take precedence over the divine law written by Moses.'

It seems difficult to believe that religion could sink to such depths, and that a people who professed to serve the Jehovah of their fathers could so easily clear their consciences and feel themselves free from keeping his law. Already Jesus has called them hypocrites and said their worship is in vain, and these are only the beginning of the harsh invectives he will hurl upon their sin-ridden souls.

What Defiles a Man?
(Mark 7:14-23; JST, Mark 7:15; Matthew 15:10-20; Luke 6:39)

How and in what manner are men defiled—and thus damned? According to the Rabbinic way of worship, defilement came by violating the Levitical law; by treading upon the traditions of the elders; by eating with unwashed hands; by failing to conform to the ritualistic formalisms of the day.

What must men do to remain undefiled—and thus be saved? Again the answer is found in the field of tradition and superstition. Wash all pots and vessels before eating; scrub the tables whereon food is placed; cleanse the couches on which the diners recline. Carry no burden on the Sabbath; speak the approved Hebrew. These—and such like—are the laws by obedience to which salvation comes. It is not what is in a man's heart that counts, but how well he conforms to all of the minutia and trivia of their religious formalism.

Jesus, however, is now prepared to reject and denounce

the traditions of the elders and all of the evils that grow out of them. The scribal spies from Jerusalem have raised the issue of ceremonial washings; they say that those who eat with unwashed hands—"and many other such like things"—are defiled. Jesus meets the issue squarely. He calls the multitude unto him. "Hearken unto me every one of you, and understand," he says. "Not that which goeth into the mouth defileth a man; but that which cometh out of the mouth, this defileth a man." "If any man have ears to hear, let him hear."

These cutting words, along with others of like severity, incensed and outraged the Rabbinic religionists. If these words were true, their system of worship was false. "Knowest thou that the Pharisees were offended, after they heard this saying?" the disciples said to Jesus. His answer:

Every plant, which my heavenly Father hath not planted, shall be rooted up.

Let them alone: they be blind leaders of the blind. And if the blind lead the blind, both shall fall into the ditch.

Well might these words be written in the hearts of all false ministers with a pen of steel. False religions shall be rooted up; they shall wither and die and be as the chaff of a summer threshing floor. And those blind ministers whose eyes have not been opened by the light from on high, together with all others who close their eyes to the truth, shall fall in the ditch of that evil master whom they choose to serve.

Thus Jesus declares open war upon the scribes, upon the Pharisees, and upon all who hearken to the preachments and follow the counsel of these self-appointed interpreters and dispensers of the law. The assault is not alone upon the ceremonial sin of eating with unwashed hands; it is a frontal attack upon all their rituals and performances. The scribes set aside the sayings of Moses. Their traditions make the word of God of no effect! Hillel and Shammai overrule the Lord Jehovah!

Thus Jesus "arraigned Pharisaism, the dominant orthodoxy, as a whole. The system, so famous, so arrogant, so intensely Jewish, was only an invention of man; a subversion of the law it claimed to represent, an antagonism to the prophets as well as to Moses, the spiritual ruin of the nation! . . . It was vital that the people who followed the Rabbis and priests should know what the religion and morals thus taught by them were worth. The truth could not find open ears while men's hearts were misled and prejudiced by such instructors. No one would seek inward renewal who had been taught to care only for externals, and to ignore the sin and corruption within. Pharisaism was a creed of moral cosmetics and religious masks, as all ritual systems must ever be." (Geikie, p. 530.)

Jesus and his disciples are now in a house apart from the multitude. Peter speaks: "Declare unto us this parable." Jesus responds:

Are ye also yet without understanding? Do not ye yet understand, that whatsoever entereth in at the mouth goeth into the belly, and is cast out into the draught?

But those things which proceed out of the mouth come forth from the heart; and they defile the man.

For out of the heart proceed evil thoughts, murders, adulteries, fornications, thefts, false witness, blasphemies: These are the things which defile a man: but to eat with unwashen hands defileth not a man.

Such is Matthew's account; Mark adds to the list of inner evils covetousness, wickedness, deceit, lasciviousness, an evil eye, pride, and foolishness. The meaning is clear, and Jesus has preached a sermon that no believing saint shall ever forget. Out of the abundance of the heart the mouth speaketh, and "as he thinketh in his heart, so is he." (Prov. 23:7.)

Mark also inserts in his account an inspired interpreting phrase that shows how fully and completely the sayings of this day are intended to overthrow even the true Mosaic system, to say nothing of the traditions that were added by the Rabbinists. Jesus speaks of that which "entereth . . . into the belly, and goeth out into the draught," and Mark adds that He does so "purging all meats," or in other words, as a better translation of the original manuscript has it, *"making all meats clean."*

In other words, though Moses of old had divided meats into clean and unclean—those which might be eaten and those which were forbidden—Jesus made all meats clean; all might be eaten. "It is nothing less than the plainest teaching ever given by Christ on the final abrogation of the Levitic Law," as Farrar so well says. "In the Levitic Law the distinction between clean and unclean meats was fundamental. Since the days of Ezra it had been insisted on with ever greater scrupulosity and everdeepening fanaticism.

"This, then, He said, sweeping aside Levitical ordinances as things which had no eternal validity, and 'making all meats clean.' St. Paul had to fight out to the bitter end the battle against the Judaism which attached importance to meats and drinks, and carnal ordinances which affect things which perish in the using, rather than to righteousness, temperance, justice, and the weightier matters of the Law; but Christ had already laid down the principles on which the battle was to be decided, and had uttered His fiat as to its eternal issue." (Farrar, p. 346.)

And we might add that Luke, who set forth the meaning and intent of our Lord's words here given, was also privileged to record in the Acts of the Apostles the vision of Peter affirming the same truth. Peter, as a prelude to the preaching of the gospel to the Gentiles, saw a great sheet descend from heaven whereon were "all manner of four-footed beasts of the earth, and wild beasts, and creeping things, and fowls of the air." A heavenly voice commanded: "Rise, Peter; kill, and eat." He replied: "Not so, Lord; for I have never eaten any thing that is common or unclean." Then came the divine fiat: *"What God hath cleansed, that call not thou common."* (Acts 10:9-15. Italics added.)

And so, "purging all meats," Jesus not only repealed all the Mosaic restrictions of a bygone dispensation, but also foreshadowed the carrying of the gospel to the Gentile hosts of the new dispensation.

NOTES

1. 2 Cor. 6:15.

2. See the companion volume to this work: *The Promised Messiah—The First Coming of Christ.*

3. This concept that the traditions of the elders supersede, are greater than, and take precedence over the word of God is, in my judgment, the devil's substitute for the true doctrine that the inspired utterances of living oracles are binding upon the Lord's people and have equal standing with the written word. This true doctrine is predicated upon the fact that inspired men speak as moved upon by the Holy Ghost, which, of course, is precisely and exactly what happens when prophets give forth that which we call scripture. The traditions of the elders—as is also the case with the traditions of an apostate Christendom—are wholly devoid of the least scintilla of inspiration. They are, as Jesus said, "the commandments of men."

As I have written elsewhere: "This same process of transforming truth into traditions— of changing the law of God into 'the doctrines and commandments of men,' by the interpretations and additions of uninspired teachers—is precisely what took place in the great apostasy of the Christian Era. To the pure and simple doctrines of Christ, the scribes and priests of early Christendom added such things as: selling indulgences, which freed the wicked from past sins and authorized them to commit future crimes without divine penalty; forgiving sins (supposedly) through repeated and perfunctory confessions; praying departed persons out of purgatory; burning candles for the dead; praying to Mary or other so-called saints, rather than to the Lord; worshiping of images; turning of sacramental emblems into the literal flesh and blood of Jesus (transubstantiation); laying up a reservoir of good works in heaven which the so-called Church can sell to those who need them (supererogation); sacrificing Jesus over again in the mass; forbidding priests and other church officials to marry; doing penance to gain forgiveness of sins; adorning houses of worship with costly materials; wearing of expensive robes and costumes by priests and other church officers; using elaborate ministerial titles; augmenting the Church treasury by gambling; and so forth.

"All these, and many other like traditions, are counted of more importance by some than the law of God as originally given by the Master. Indeed, the so-called Christian Church today is founded in large part on the traditions of the 'elders' rather than on the revelations of heaven." (*Commentary* 1:366-67.)

4. Isaiah's words as found in our Old Testament read: "Forasmuch as this people draw near me with their mouth, and with their lips do honour me, but have removed their heart far from me, and their fear toward me is taught by the precept of men: Therefore, behold, I will proceed to do a marvellous work among this people, even a marvellous work and a wonder." (Isa. 29:13-14.) In his confrontation on cleanliness Jesus obviously targumed a portion of Isaiah's words and applied them to the scribes and Pharisees and their followers. The intended glorious fulfillment of the words of Israel's ancient seer was, of course, reserved for the latter days when the gospel would be restored for the final time. Jesus' use of the passage here illustrates perfectly the principle that many prophetic utterances have dual or multiple instances of fulfillment. When he appeared with his Father to usher in the dispensation of the fulness of times, the Lord Jesus said to his latter-day prophet that the modern "professors" of religion—the modern scribes and Pharisees, as it were—"were all corrupt," and that "they draw near to me with their lips, but their hearts are far from me, they teach for doctrines the commandments of men, having a form of godliness, but they deny the power thereof." (JS-H 1:219.)

"There is no salvation in worship as such, even though it be directed to the true God; worship based on false principles is in vain. Men may worship Deity their whole life long, according to their traditions and rituals, and never gain true faith, forgiveness of sin, or sanctifying grace. Worship leads to salvation only when it conforms to the revealed, divine pattern, only when it is based on the rock foundation of eternal truth. 'Not every one that saith unto me, Lord, Lord, shall enter into the kingdom of heaven; but he that doeth the will of my Father which is in heaven.' (Matt. 7:21.) There is no salvation in false worship." (*Commentary* 1:368.)

5. Those who truly honor their parents, in the full gospel sense, shall in fact dwell forever upon their promised land, for the meek shall inherit the earth forever in the celestial day. (D&C 88:17.)

INDEX

Peter's mother, 37-38; of afflicted at
Capernaum, 38; of multitudes
throughout Galilee, 39-40, 43; of man
with leprosy, 45-46; of man sick of
palsy, 48-52; of paralytic on Sabbath,
65-67; on Sabbath, lawfulness of,
89-90; of man with withered hand, 90;
of Gentile centurion's servant, 181-83;
due to faith of person seeking
blessing, 289; of daughter of Jairus,
289-92; of woman with issue of blood,
294-96; of blind men, 297-98; those
blessed by, are obligated to serve God,
298; physical acts accompanying, on
many occasions, 302 n. 5; of people of
Gennesaret, 363. *See also* Jesus Christ,
miracles performed by; Miracles
eaven, laying up treasures in, 152-53
:brew targumed into Aramaic, 20
em of Jesus' garment, woman touched,
294-96
erod Antipas, 331; birthday feast of,
332-33; delivers John the Baptist's
head to Salome, 335; hallucinations
of, 337; Jesus withdrew from domain
of, 344
erod Philip, 331
erod the Great, 330-31
erodians, 91
erodias, 331
idden treasure, parable of, 263-64
oly Ghost, 122; manifests God's truths,
165; blasphemy against, 215-16,
218-20, 228 n. 2-3; gift of prophecy
bears witness of, 224; necessity of, in
understanding scriptures, 267-68;
speaking with power of, before earthly
tribunals, 318; without gift of, man's
testimony cannot remain unshaken,
361
onor: Christ received not, from men,
78-79; of men vs. that of God, 79;
afforded to parents, 406-7
osea, 15
ospitality, custom of, 199-200, 314 n. 5
umility, 168
ypocrisy, 162-63

norance, man cannot be saved in,
81 n. 7

Illustrations, parables are, rather than
revelations, 241-42
Immortality, Jesus inherited power of, 74
Isaiah: Messianic prophecies of, 15; Jesus
interprets prophecies of, 21-24
Israel: Jesus was sent specifically to, 91,
313 n. 3; shepherds of, woe be to, 305;
apostles were sent only to, 309-10;
worthy people of, 311; Jesus tested,
with miracle of loaves and fishes, 367;
apostasy of, 392; traditions of, 403-5.
See also Jews

Jairus, raising of daughter of, 289-92
James, son of Alpheus, 110
James, son of Zebedee, 33, 107
Jeremiah, 15
Jerusalem, 30; spies from, followed Jesus,
88, 391; Jesus came not to, for
Passover, 399
Jesus Christ: proclaims his divine
Sonship, 3, 70-73, 75, 375-76; Judean
ministry of, 6-7; role of, in plan of
salvation, 8, 72-73; fame of, began to
precede him, 11, 18, 39-40; preaches in
Nazarene synagogue, 20-24; Spirit of
Lord was upon, 21; applies Messianic
prophecies to himself, 23; Nazarenes
sought to murder, 27; dignity of,
27-28; dwelt in Capernaum, 31;
private prayers of, 38-39; empathy of,
41; judgment rests with, 72, 74-75;
works of, bear witness of him, 77-78;
visited spirits in prison, 80 n. 4; is
Lord of Sabbath, 88; plans laid for
destroying of, 91; prayed before
calling apostles, 104; visited Nephites
after his resurrection, 118; performing
miracles in name of, is insufficient for
salvation, 172-73; taught as one
having authority, 174, 177; teachings
of, 179-80; John the Baptist sends his
disciples to, 188-89; repentant sinner
washes feet of, 197, 200; preached the
gospel, 204, 244; disciples of,
supported him temporally, 204-5; is
accused of working miracles through
Beelzebub, 209-11, 396; family of, all
disciples may belong to, 226-27;
preaches in Galilee's cities and

villages, 304; bestowed authority on apostles, 309; whoever shall confess him shall be confessed of him before God, 321-22; promises to be with missionaries, 324-25; Herod Antipas inquires after, 336-37, 344; prepares table in wilderness, 341; preaches to and heals multitude in wilderness, 346-47; manifested his creative powers by providing loaves and fishes, 351; Jews acclaimed, as temporal Messiah, 351-52, 368 went into mountain to pray, 352; belief in, Jews were commanded to exercise, 372-73; identifies himself as bread of life, 374; eating flesh and drinking blood of, 377-80; John the Baptist prophesied of, 380-81; made clear he was not temporal deliverer, 382-83; accused by Jews of being a sinner, 394-96; provided for his mother, 406; defines defilement, 409, 410; declares open war on Pharisaism, 409-10; purged all meats, 411

miracles performed by: healing of nobleman's son, 11-12; filling of fisherman's net, 33-34; casting out of unclean spirit, 35-36, 209; healing of Peter's mother, 37-38; healing of the people of Capernaum, 38; wrought throughout Galilee, 39-40, 43; healing of leprous man, 45-46; healing of man sick of palsy, 48-52; healing of paralytic on Sabbath, 66-67; healing of man with withered hand, 90; healing of Gentile centurion's servant, 181-83; raising of dead youth in Nain, 183-86; stilling of storm, 276-77; healing of Gadarene demoniac, 279-81; raising of daughter of Jairus, 289-92; healing of woman with issue of blood, 294-96; opening of blind eyes, 297-98; feeding of five thousand, 344-48; walking on water, 359-61; healing of people of Gennesaret, 363. *See also* Healing; Miracles

relationship of, to God: did his Father's will, 21, 375; came in his Father's name, 64; made himself equal with God, 70-71, 396-97; followed his Father's example in all things, 71-72, 80 n. 2; oneness of, with God, 80 n. 3. *See also* God the Father

Jews: Sabbath observance among, 65-6 93 n. 1-2; many, will be cast out, 182-83; Jesus likens, to petty childre 194; fringes in garments of, 295; mo of dress among, 301-2 n. 2; began to acclaim Jesus as temporal Messiah, 351-52, 368; sought Jesus for temporal, not spiritual, reasons, 371 were commanded to believe in Chri 372-73; asked for a sign, 373; murmured over doctrine of divine Sonship, 375-76; disappointment of in Jesus' true mission, 386; stiffneckedness of, 390; division among, 392. *See also* Israel

John the Baptist, 60, 327-30; disciples c 62, 188-89; bore witness of Christ, 76-77; was a true prophet, 170; Jesu sent angels to, in prison, 187; heard news of Jesus, 188; sent his disciples Jesus, 188-89; disciples of, returned him, 191; many esteemed, as a prophet, 191-92; Jesus testifies of, 193-94; baptism of, many partook o 194; importance of mission of, 196 r 1; was imprisoned for denouncing Herod's incest, 331-32; Salome demands head of, 334; murder of, 335; restores Aaronic Priesthood in latter days, 338; spoke of one might than himself, 380-81

John the Beloved, 33, 107-8

Jonas, sign of, 222-24

Joseph's son, many viewed Christ as, 2 300, 376

Joshua, 357

Judas, brother of James, 110-11

Judas Iscariot, 111, 388

Judea, Jesus' ministry in, 6-7

Judgment: rests with Christ, 72; of livi and dead, 74-75; role of the Twelve 113 n. 1; righteous, 161; between go and evil, each man has power of, 17 n. 1

Keys of kingdom, bestowal of, on the Twelve, 112. *See also* Authority

King Follett sermon, 80 n. 2